THE STRUGGLE FOR A HIGHER STANDARD OF LIVING

THE STRUGGLE FOR
A HIGHER STANDARD
OF LIVING

THE PROBLEM OF THE UNDERDEVELOPED
COUNTRIES

by

W. Brand

Professor University of Leyden

THE FREE PRESS - GLENCOE, ILLINOIS

W. VAN HOEVE LTD - THE HAGUE AND BANDUNG

1958

PREFACE

This book is, in essence, a translation of a Dutch study published in October 1954 in the Netherlands. It attempts to give a comprehensive review of the many aspects of the problem of development in the economically backward countries, with which I have been concerned since I joined the Secretariat of the United Nations in 1946. Some of the material contained in the Dutch text has been rearranged in this translation and a paragraph added here and there in the light of new information which has come to my attention. I have also profited from certain observations made by friends who have read the English text. I want to express my appreciation for their suggestions.

The ideas formulated in this book are my own and not necessarily those of the Secretariat of the United Nations, with which I was associated until July 1957.

It is my hope that this book may prove a contribution to the study of the complex problems of development.

WILLEM BRAND

Contents

PART ONE

THE PROCESS OF ECONOMIC DEVELOPMENT

Chapter 1

INTRODUCTION

E conomic development or growth is a subject which, until recently, has received only scant attention from economic science. Such a lack of interest is remarkable in view of the fact that the increase of the flow of goods and services was the goal of the economic policy formulated by the earliest systematic students of economics. Mercantilism, for example, aimed at an expansion of the national economy for the greater glory of ruler and state. But both practice and theory were worked out within the framework of a static medieval concept of the economic resources of the world.[1] Adam Smith rejected the idea that economic resources were limited, and foresaw a continuously increasing prosperity for the world as a whole, as a result of the introduction of technological changes. These changes were both cause of, and condition for, an ever more productive division of labor. "It is the multiplication of the productions of all the different arts, in consequence of the division of labor, which occasions, in a well governed society, universal opulence which extends itself to the lowest rank of the people."[2]

The classical economists who followed Smith, particularly Ricardo, took a more pessimistic view, since they believed that production was limited by physical restraints (the 'niggardliness of nature'), and that the close correlation between real wages and population trends would always tend to reduce wages to the subsistence level. Later economists, however, generally accepted the idea of ever increasing national and international prosperity as the product of innovations, progressive division of labor, capital formation, increasing productivity, and growth of population. There was a tendency among theorists to go to opposite extremes in regarding economic progress as axiomatic, and therefore needing no further analysis or explanation. In some respects, the experience of the nineteenth century in western Europe and America, seemed to confirm this *a priori* character of natural growth, and economic science was hardly detained with it.

One reason for the neglect of the problem of development was the separation between economic science and policy. During the process of refinement of economics as a science, the problem of the allocation of the factors of production — the distribution of scarce means among alternative ends — became the prime subject of economic theory, while the study of the effects of quantitative and qualitative changes of the factors of production themselves tended to be neglected. Perhaps economists, studying the 'science of means not ends', also sensed that this second group of problems lay partly outside their sphere of competence, or at least required the collaboration of sociologists and historians for an adequate treatment.

In view of the complexity of the problem, and the efforts that had to be made to free economic science from the influence of special political pleaders, this dichotomy was perhaps inevitable. Indeed, the instruments developed in the course of studying economics in its narrower formulation — equilibrium analysis, the variable factor method of examining the effects of single influences, and the various techniques for measuring the results of changes over time, for example — are among our most useful tools for explaining economic phenomena on a broad basis.

In the course of our study of the obstacles encountered by the backward countries in their struggle to encourage economic growth, we will repeatedly meet political and social factors that prevent or impede economic development. Some of the reasons why economics has tended to ignore or avoid the problems that these factors raise will become apparent. In the 1930's, however, interest in the question of economic growth was reawakened. This can be explained by (1) the refinement that was taking place in the tools of economic analysis to reduce the gap between theory and reality,[3] (2) by the real or imagined stagnation in the western

European and American economies,[4] and (3) by the problems arising from the efforts of backward countries to develop their economic resources.

The phenomenon of economic progress has been rediscovered.[5] Moreover, in recent years, the investigations of Colin Clark and W. Hoffmann, among others, have significantly deepened our insight into the process of economic growth, involving such macro-economic categories as national income, national product, consumption, savings, and capital stock. It has become clear, however, that the process of economic development cannot be explained merely by the compilation of quantitative series of data over a long period of time or even by quantitative analysis alone; it also requires a qualitative interpretation. In order to indicate not only what happened but also how and why it happened, the collaboration of many social sciences is necessary. Only thus may we understand the course of events and the interplay of economic and social phenomena which together weave the pattern of economic change.

Before coming to our subject, we will have to define more clearly the concept of economic development. The term has been used to mean either the process of increasing the aggregate, or per capita, national product or income — in both cases without reference to the distribution of the additional goods and services or income so produced. Neither of these definitions require any improvement in the level of consumption of the majority of the population. We will, however, adopt as an essential condition of economic development an improvement in the material well-being for as large as possible a segment of the population. It should be kept in mind that this objective of general well-being has never been, and perhaps never will be, the sole determinant of economic behavior.

Economic growth may reflect the conscious desire of a single group within a state to stimulate it. But under favorable conditions, it can also take place spontaneously as a result of the economic activities of individuals who only follow their own economic interests. Under mercantilism it was the sovereign and a small privileged group who wished the country to be rich and powerful. The doctrine of 'the utility of poverty' ran, however, like a scarlet thread through this system. National prestige demanded a surplus of labor, since low wages tended to mean low production costs and thus encouraged the growth of export trade, bringing in greater inflows of gold and silver for the country.

For the classical economists, during the period of the so-called industrial revolution in western Europe and North America, the self-interest of the individual was the 'motive power' for economic development. The economic gains of the industrial revolution were very unevenly distributed, and only at a later stage did the masses partake more fully of the fruits of progress. The increasing participation of the populace in a continuously expanding national product occurred only when social conscience awakened, and, to a much greater extent, when the masses assumed political significance. As a manifestation of the concentration of power, first in a single person (the ruler), then in a relatively small group (the bourgeoisie), and today in the many, the state has acted as guardian of the balance between the various groups and played a significant part in the distribution and redistribution of the economic product.

This objective — providing the masses with a larger quantity of goods and services now accepted as a criterion of economic development — is indicative of the change in the balance of power in the Western countries. This new orientation has led to the obligation prescribed in the Charter of the United Nations (Article 55) for all member states "to promote social progress and better standards of life in larger freedom." Article 25 of the Universal Declaration of Human Rights, stating that everyone has a right to "a standard of living adequate for the health and well-being of himself and his family, including food, clothing, housing, medical care, and necessary social services, and the right to security in the event of unemployment, sickness, disability, widowhood, old age, or other lack of livelihood, in circumstances beyond his control," reflects the same idealism, however remote the objective in many countries.

These pronouncements are also an expression of the ever widening dissemination of the Western economic ideal or a belief in continuous economic progress. This is typically expressed in the first chapter of the first volume of the so-called Paley report:[6] "First, we share the belief of the American people in the principle of growth. Granting that we cannot find any absolute reason for this belief, we admit that, to our Western minds, it seems preferable to any opposite, which to us implies stagnation and decay. Where there may be any unbreakable upper limit to the continuing growth of our economy we do not pretend to know, but it must be part of our task to examine such apparent limits as present themselves."

This changed orientation still does not mean that the primary motive behind private production is to provide larger amounts of goods and services for the majority of the population. Production for the market is the prevalent pattern, and production is still only indirectly oriented toward consumption. In the private enterprise society, maximization of profit still is the main motivation for the economic behaviour of producers. But institutional changes and government intervention, through taxation and the expenditure pattern, are helping to bring about the social objective of an increased volume of goods and services for general consumption in the industrial countries.

In centrally planned economies, power considerations, the desire for security, and unequal pay (as a stimulus to extra effort) play a role in the investment and consumption policy of the state, as well as the professed concern about enhancing mass well-being. The present material welfare of the mass of the population can indeed be shown to be but a minor consideration in the economic planning of these countries.[7] In many of the underdeveloped countries, with their weak governmental structures, the drive for a higher standard of living is still a lesser motive in the development of economic policy, despite the revolution in expectations which has affected broad strata of the population. There are indications in several of these countries that, in spite of an increase in total income, total production, even expressed in *per capita* terms, mass poverty has not been relieved. In some cases it may even have been relatively intensified as a result of the increasing inequality in the distribution of income. In such countries, the urge toward economic expansion is still chiefly motivated by a political desire to strengthen their position vis-a-vis the more highly developed countries.

We shall concern ourselves particularly with the problems surrounding the efforts of the underdeveloped countries to encourage their economic growth.[8] We identify these as the countries with the lowest levels of living, or the lowest levels of material well-being, in comparison with the countries whose inhabitants enjoy relatively high levels of living. These countries comprise most of Latin America with a population of 173 million in 1954, Africa with a population of 208 million, Asia and the Far East with 1,307 million and southern and southeastern Europe with 90 million, which together contain more than two-thirds of the total world population.

Strictly speaking, this identification of an undeveloped or underdeveloped economy with a low level of living is improper. Countries with the lowest per capita income are not necessarily those potentially best able to utilize more land or natural resources, more capital, more labor, to provide their present population, or a larger population, with a higher level of living. The terms 'undeveloped country' or 'underdeveloped' thus does not indicate development potential *per se*, but denotes first of all, the backwardness of these countries and secondly, the stage of their economic development, resulting in their relatively low level of welfare, in comparison with those of the industrial countries of today. A better term thus would really be economically backward areas, but we shall conform to the current economic terminology and allow ourselves to use the terms undeveloped or underdeveloped countries without further qualification.

We shall begin by making a survey of quantitative differences in the levels of living. We shall then assess the difficulties which confront these countries in their effort to improve their positions on the basis of the present status of the four production factors —

land, capital, labor, and leadership plus organization. It is our aim to present a general picture, not necessarily complete. With respect to what happens in the course of economic growth, we shall rely mainly on the history of the industrial countries. For the fact that the backward countries have not yet exhibited such growth, we shall place emphasis upon noneconomic considerations. This separate treatment of the factors of production has been chosen for the sake of clarity.

The interdependence of the production factors is understood in any economy, but it is particularly striking in the backward countries, since deficiencies in one sector are reinforced by deficiencies in other sectors. The underdeveloped countries are poor because (1) the productivity of their land is low, (2) they lack capital, (3) the level of education is low, and (4) they lack leadership to initiate economic development. These conditions in turn reflect their low level of income and general economic backwardness. It is this vicious circle, or rather the existence of many vicious circles, that impedes progress. This multi-bottleneck characteristic of the economy of the backward areas, does not imply that there are no major and minor factors in the process of economic development. It will be clear throughout this book that we consider leadership and organization, whether of the private entrepreneurial type or of the state, as the cardinal point in the process of economic growth. However, leadership by itself is not enough; it needs complementary factors with which to work. Yet scarcity of land, capital and skilled labor can all be called quasi-bottlenecks, in the sense that dynamic leadership, if available, may to some extent, overcome such difficulties.

Stressing the factor of leadership, however, lifts only part of the veil covering the possible pattern of economic development. It still remains to be explained under what circumstances such leadership originates and what qualifications are required in varying internal and external circumstances. Economists are probably inclined to oversimplify, and thus omit, some essential ingredients. In our opinion, the usefulness of models, econometric or otherwise, in elucidating the problem of economic development, seems for the moment rather limited. We have, therefore, endeavored to concentrate on the various forces underlying economic growth. This task in any case is a preliminary to any theory.[9]

Land is the factor of production which, in combination with labor, primarily determines the quantity of food and raw materials produced by a country. In a country that is mainly agrarian, as most of the backward countries are, the soil feeds the 60 to 80 per cent of the population that lives on it at a subnormal level, and produces the simple raw materials required by the population for the manufacture of their clothing and housing. The low educational level of the average peasant and the lack of capital, in combination with geographical and institutional obstacles (type of soil, rainfall, temperature, forested area, transportation, tenure, etc.), are the principal causes of the low productivity of the land factor. The low level of education of the population is a deterrent to the introduction of more productive methods of cultivation. The existing forms of land tenure and the often slight possibility of expanding the arable area are additional obstacles to an expansion of agricultural production.

In this connection, consideration is given to the collectivization of agriculture in the Soviet Union, which has been cited as an example for the undeveloped countries. This reorganization was carried out, in the first place, with the object of redistributing agricultural produce in order to obtain sufficient food for that segment of the population transferred from agriculture into other sectors of production (industry, transportation, and other services). The collectivization facilitated the attainment of a greater diversity in agricultural production, the provision of a more varied assortment of raw materials for the industrial sector. It is our opinion that the conditions under which this program might serve as a basis for successful industrialization exist only in a few backward countries, apart from any consideration of the methods used in the Soviet Union in the implementation of this land reform.

The land factor is the most static one in the economic pattern of underdeveloped countries. The improvements that are possible by introduction of scientific methods of agriculture can only make themselves felt over a long period. Many of the undeveloped countries, so far as our present knowledge goes, also apparently lack adequate resources of raw materials, above all iron ore and fuels, to support the establishment of an industrial structure of any proportion. This is, of course, a moot point since natural resources in those countries have often been scarcely explored. Through the development of international trade, as many western European nations have proven, the inadequacy of domestic resources for industrial development can be compensated to a large extent, but it remains to be seen if such a pattern can be imitated by some underdeveloped countries.

Experience indicates that capital goods are also required for the expansion of agricultural production and a more intensive utilization of the available raw materials. This brings us to the second factor of production, capital. Capital formation, or an increase in the stock of capital goods, is indeed one of the major requirements in the process of economic development. One of the most striking differences between a developed and a poor country is that, in the first, an average of about 15–20 per cent of the net national product is used for capital formation, whereas in the second, only about 5–10 per cent is used for this purpose. After a general consideration of capital formation, we shall show how it is hampered in the undeveloped countries by the low level of production, the resultant high rate of consumption and low rate of savings, and the weak incentives for investment by the potential entrepreneur. We shall analyse, in some detail, the changes in the industrial structure in the more highly developed countries during the course of their growth, with an eye to the possible lessons that may lie in that experience for the poor countries. In particular, we shall consider the significance of small-scale industry for an incipient industrialization. The process of capital formation is closely connected with the pattern of savings and investment. This is treated more thoroughly in Part II, which takes up the monetary aspect of the problem of development.

Economic development postulates the training of the labor force as the third factor of production in new methods and techniques. The obstacles encountered by backward countries in the outflow of labor from the agrarian sector to the more productive industrial and service sector — the typical concomitant of industrialization — do not appear essentially different from those at a similar stage of the history of the industrial countries, but the process does seem to involve a number of new aspects. We shall also consider the rapid increase of population, which is accelerated by the new methods of disease control and which threatens to outrun the rate of economic growth.

The fourth factor of production — leadership and organization — has transformed the pattern of the other factors of production in the countries with a high standard of living and has thus created a dynamic economy. The backward countries are handicapped by the virtual absence of an entrepreneurial class. The state, which stimulated development in some industrial countries, is handicapped by the generally low educational level of the population, and above all, its domination by groups that fear the consequences of economic change, and, therefore, assume an ambivalent attitude towards economic growth.

In Part II, we shall concentrate mainly on the monetary element in economic development. It is often assumed that the monetary question is only of secondary importance, because the question of a country's ability to undertake certain economic projects is determined, in the first place, by the availability or potential availability, of labor, raw materials, and capital goods for this purpose. It is our opinion, however, that the monetary factor is, in fact, the instrument by which the real factors are moved and, therefore, must be recognized as an essential element in the process of growth.

We have divided Part II of the book, for the sake of proper analysis, into four chapters dealing with consumption, private investment, foreign trade, and the role of government, without implying any strict identification with the customary components of the national income. It will be seen that many of the same obstacles discussed earlier reappear, with the addition of the monetary factor as a second dimension. At the stage presently occupied by the undeveloped countries, consumption is primarily a derivative function. It is necessary to prevent an increase in the national product from leading directly to a proportional expansion of consumption if an increase in the future level of living is desired.

The form now assumed by private investment in most of the underdeveloped countries is, in general, not conducive to economic growth. For the same reasons the potential advantages of foreign trade are often not fully utilized. The important role of guiding investment into more 'desirable' channels by means of fiscal policy and patterns of public expenditure necessarily devolves upon government. Deficient governmental administration and the low level of living, which limits the means at the disposal of the government, are responsible for the lack of economic realism in many development plans. The characteristics of the aggregate flow of money are considered separately in a discussion of inflation, which so often appears to be inseparable from economic development in many backward countries.

Part III is devoted to a discussion of the international financial sources of aid — namely foreign loans and grants not compensated by any simultaneous or nearly simultaneous trade transactions — which are available for the development of the economically retarded part of the world. A sketch of the history of international capital movements is followed by a consideration of the present state of, and outlook for, private and public investment. We are convinced that the prospects for a revival of private foreign investment on any large scale are not particularly bright. The role of stimulating additional economic development has been largely taken over by public foreign investments, whose various forms are described. The results for the backward countries cannot yet be conclusively evaluated.

We try to show that the prospects for economic growth in the low-income countries are not particularly good in view of the inadequacy of the complementary factors of production in relation to the size of population, viz. the backwardness of agricultural technology, the scarcity of capital, the difficulty of capital formation, the surplus of labor in the agricultural sector, the continuous increase in population, and the shortage of leadership and organization. The economies of the undeveloped countries are primitive and inelastic owing to their institutional structures, which make for immobility and resistance to dynamic influences. In addition, the historic fact that their cultures, despite contact with Western technology, have failed to absorb the elements of incentive and organization essential to economic growth makes improvement especially difficult.

This generalization does not imply that all economically backward areas can be placed in the same category. The differences in the existing levels of living in the various countries already indicate some disparity in development potential. In particular areas of Latin America, southern Europe and Africa a certain growth can be observed. But it must be admitted that such development has not been widespread, nor has it diminished the gap between the levels of well-being of the developed and underdeveloped world. The relationship between population and available resources determines these differences in the first place. But the middle terms, the social and cultural structure, are more important. These, in turn, determine the suitability of labor, rate of capital formation, direction of investment, and adequacy and ability of the managerial-entrepreneurial classes. The relationship between these factors gives form to the various possible and actual patterns. We lay particular emphasis on the obstacles to the development of points of growth within the system of production factors.

Perhaps we overestimate the difficulties. Economists may be inclined to take a pessimistic view and overlook the fact that ideals and enthusiasm can accomplish things which may seem impossible. There have probably been some periods in the history of industrialized countries, too, when there seemed to be little hope for economic progress. The economist, by making frequent measurements of economic changes, may have a certain tendency to emphasize the problems of growth, expressing themselves in balance-of-payment difficulties, budget deficits, bottlenecks in the labor supply, and thus to disregard the long-term movements. As we have already stated, economics has until recently neglected the study of secular trends of growth, which is a much more difficult task than the analysis of short-term phenomena.[10]

The reader will note our conviction that the study of these phenomena is not amenable to an exclusively economic analysis. Economic science can give a detailed description and analysis of the process, but the mechanism that actuates it stems from political and social forces.[11] The magnitude and direction of these forces, within the framework of the relations between factors of production, determine the result of the process.

The ideal of a higher standard of living for the undeveloped areas is one of the typical problems to which Toynbee's image of the challenge is applicable. The challenge is posed particularly for the 'creative minority' called to leadership in the undeveloped countries. In a wider sense, it is posed for the industrial countries where consciences are uneasy about the vast disparity in levels of living. In the underdeveloped countries the conflict rages between the Zealots and Herodians, between tradition and adaptation. A parallel dispute is also seen in the more highly developed countries, where some retain the parochial view — they fear to share Western knowledge and skills with non-Western peoples — and others see this Westernization as an ineluctable corollary of the fact that we live in one world.

The struggle for a higher standard of living is thus being waged not only on the level of right, but also of might, in the sense that the groups interested in the maintenance of the *status quo* are reluctant to surrender actual or pretended privileges without a fight. Time will tell whether the unfavorable conditions of which we have spoken will allow the right 'response' to this challenge. Whether the right answer is a uniform level of well-being approximately that of the Western world, or a more equitable distribution of the national product in each country, or some other form still unknown to us, only the future will reveal.

J. M. Keynes[12] once wrote that "the economic problem may be solved within a hundred years", and that the economic question, the struggle for a livelihood, is not a permanent problem for the human race. He envisages a more generous provision of goods and services in the future, and the real, permanent problem thus becomes how man, liberated from his anxiety over economic subsistence, will spend his free time, how he will practice the art of living.

This optimistic vision will probably be viewed sceptically even in the West today. There is a growing realization that relatively large segments of the population have, at times, not been associated with the general enhancement of living standards for various reasons. Moreover, the attainment of a certain standard of comfort or riches by a people seems always to open up a multitude of new desires for which the means of fulfillment are yet insufficient. The lessening of the imbalance between material need and its satisfaction is doubtless still viewed as sheer Utopia by the undeveloped countries.

The whole struggle toward a higher standard of living, necessarily a long-term process, is related to the changes in the balance of power between nations, to the crises in society and civilization, and it is not fitting for an economist to attempt to answer all questions involved.

Historians are reproached, and according to the economist rightly so, for not paying enough attention to the economic factors in society. It may be said in their defense that they perhaps believe that our technological and organizational ability only represents the external aspect of the forces that really move the world, and in the light of history, the economic factors do not possess the significance attached to them by our materially oriented world. In our Western colored outlook, the leadership of the United States and western Europe and the technical and economic bases, on which their societies rely politically and culturally, seem unassailable unless challenged by nations which succeed in finding superior forms of techniques and organization to outproduce them. However, Toynbee[13] may well be right in envisaging that "Islam, in entering into the proletarian under-world of our latter day Western civilization, may eventually compete with India and the Far East and Russia for the price of influencing the future in ways that may pass our understanding."

The striving for a better level of living embraces many spheres that are not properly the domain of the economist. But even if economics is thus assigned a more modest role in the study of development, it must elucidate the problems that arise from the flow of goods and money in the economies of the backward parts of the world. Only in this way can economics avoid being accused of having held too parochial a view by its one-sided concentration on the problems of the already developed countries.

Chapter 2

QUANTITATIVE ANALYSIS OF THE INEQUALITY
OF INTERNATIONAL INCOME DISTRIBUTION

Total world production, or the total quantity of disposable goods and services, is very unequally distributed among the countries of the earth. Colin Clark[1] has estimated that only 10 per cent of the working population of the world enjoys a living standard of 1,000 international units ($20 per week) per capita per year (one international unit is equal to the quantity of goods and services that a dollar could buy in the United States during the 1925–34 period); 81 per cent of all workers received 500 units ($10 per week) or less. Another 9 per cent of the world's active population, in western Europe, received an average real income per head between 500 and 1,000 units. About 53 per cent of the economically active population of the world, mainly in China and India, had a real annual income of less than 200 units ($4 per week) per capita. In spite of the difficulties connected with a quantitative determination of real income in a number of countries, it may be accepted that the table compiled by Clark[2] giving the average real income per capita, expressed in international units, for the period 1925–34, in a large number of countries, did in fact, give a correct impression of the differences in level of living.

Table 1 presents per capita incomes expressed in U.S. dollars in a number of countries, for one prewar and one postwar year, showing the differences in average levels of income between various countries. These figures are based on calculations or estimates of the national income, which are now, with varying degrees of accuracy, available for most countries. The order in which the countries appear does not necessarily reflect accurately the relative status with respect to per capita output of goods and services. Certain qualifications are mentioned later on, but they are hardly significant in view of the magnitude of the differences in material well-being which are revealed. Although one cannot dispute the observation of S. H. Frankel[3] that, since aggregate income is the symbol of varying economic and social values in different societies, such a comparison of different income levels tries to do something impossible, this is not very helpful. The problem remains of evaluating and accounting for the differences in levels of living which can be observed by any objective spectator.

Table 1. PER CAPITA INCOMES OF SELECTED COUNTRIES (in U.S. dollars)

Country	(Rank)	1938	(Rank)	1954	Country	(Rank)	1938	(Rank)	1954
United States	(1)	512	(1)	1,847	El Salvador	(44)	60	(39)	(190)
Canada	(10)	340	(2)	1,264	Portugal	(30)	92	(40)	188
New Zealand	(4)	444	(3)	1,073	Nicaragua	(50)	(60)	(41)	(167)
Switzerland	(3)	475	(4)	1,036	Mexico	(45)	60	(42)	163
Sweden	(7)	386	(5)	973	Southern Rhodesia	(29)	(101)	(43)	162
Australia	(5)	397	(6)	927	Dominican Republic	(47)	53	(44)	161
Luxembourg		–	(7)	837	Ecuador	(56)	(44)	(45)	156
United Kingdom	(2)	494	(8)	807	Brazil	(53)	(46)	(46)	(152)
France	(14)	251	(9)	763	Guatemala	(51)	(48)	(47)	152
Denmark	(9)	367	(10)	762	Philippines	(65)	33	(48)	147
Norway	(8)	385	(11)	761	Yugoslavia	(43)	70	(49)	(145)
Belgium	(13)	258	(12)	704	Syria	(31)	(91)	(50)	(139)
Iceland		–	(13)	662	Honduras	(55)	(45)	(51)	127
Finland	(16)	174	(14)	549	Egypt	(48)	51	(52)	126
Germany	(6)	386	(15)	540	Costa Rica	(38)	(76)	(53)	(125)
Netherlands	(11)	311	(16)	526	Lebanon	(27)	(105)	(54)	(125)
Venezuela	(25)	114	(17)	488	Paraguay	(60)	(39)	(55)	124
Israel (Palestine)	(36)	(81)	(18)	450	Ceylon	(62)	38	(56)	109
Puerto Rico	(24)	114	(19)	430	Peru	(41)	(72)	(57)	102
Ireland	(12)	259	(20)	429	Indonesia	(68)	23	(58)	91
Argentina	(21)	150	(21)	(405)	Iran	(33)	(83)	(59)	(85)
Uruguay	(46)	(56)	(22)	(400)	Iraq	(34)	(83)	(60)	(85)
Austria	(15)	192	(23)	390	Thailand	(69)	22	(61)	75
Czechoslovakia	(22)	142	(24)	(371)	Southern Korea		–	(62)	74
Chile	(26)	106	(25)	(333)	Pakistan	(59)	(39)	(63)	67
Italy	(19)	161	(26)	321	Haiti	(49)	(50)	(64)	64
Panama	(42)	(71)	(27)	310	India	(64)	(34)	(65)	59
U.S.S.R.	(20)	(158)	(28)	(308)	Bolivia	(52)	(47)	(66)	(55)
Poland	(35)	83	(29)	(300)	Afghanistan	(57)	(39)	(67)	(50)
Cuba	(28)	101	(30)	289	Burma	(67)	24	(68)	44
Union of S.A.	(17)	169	(31)	288	Saudi Arabia	(61)	(39)	(69)	(40)

Country	(Rank)	1938	(Rank)	1954	Country	(Rank)	1938	(Rank)	1954
Spain	(23)	(126)	(32)	271	Yemen		–	(70)	(40)
Hungary	(18)	167	(33)	(269)	Ethiopia	(54)	(46)	(71)	(38)
Colombia	(34)	67	(34)	249	Liberia	(58)	(39)	(72)	(38)
Turkey	(40)	74	(35)	222	China	(66)	(29)	(73)	(27)
Surinam	(39)	75	(36)	(211)					
Greece	(32)	84	(37)	209					
Japan	(37)	77	(38)	194					

Source: 1938 and 1954 (or latest available year) estimates of per capita income are based, except for those given in parentheses, on official national income estimates, as published in United Nations: *Monthly Bulletin of Statistics* (May, 1955) and United Nations: *Statistical Papers*, Series H, No. 7 (New York: March, 1955), converted into dollars at the prevailing (official) exchange rate and divided by the mid-year population figures. The 1938 estimates placed in parentheses have been taken from a publication of the United States State Department: *Point Four, Cooperative Program for Aid in the Development of Economically Underdeveloped Areas* (Washington, D.C.: January, 1950), pp. 113–14. The 1954 estimates in parentheses are based on United Nations: *National and Per Capita Income for Seventy Countries, 1949* (New York: October, 1950), pp. 14–16, and are calculated for 1954, if possible, with the aid of national income information contained in other United Nations publications. Countries are placed in the order of their status in 1954 and the figure in parentheses before the estimate of 1938 indicates their status in 1938. A comparison between the two years for each country is not always possible in view of the different basis of calculation in certain cases.

The table shows that in 1938 the average United States citizen disposed of 64 per cent more goods and services than the average Netherlander, while the average Indian and Chinese respectively received an amount only about 6 and 5 per cent of the American income. In 1954 the American per capita income was about two and one half times as high as that of the Netherlander. The average income of an Indian and Chinese was roughly only 2 per cent and 1.5 per cent of that of the average United States inhabitant. Our comparison confirms the general impression that the inequality of the world's income distribution has actually increased since World War II.

Such close comparisons between data on national income, calculated with different degrees of reliability, are hazardous of course. Comparisons, especially between national income data of industrial and non-industrial countries, are apt to overstate differences in levels of living. In the underdeveloped countries non-monetary income, i.e., goods and services produced and consumed within the household, is usually underestimated in national income compilations. The national income in the industrialized countries includes many categories which might well be considered as costs instead of as goods and services enhancing the material welfare. A substantial portion of the transportation of raw materials and finished products, of the movement of labor to and from work, of the services of government, and banking, for example, are the result of the more complicated economic structure of the industrial countries, but represent no real addition to the material well-being. The income figures for the developed countries, on the other hand, do not reflect the shorter working week as one of the benefits of economic progress. Even when some of these qualifications are taken into account, great disparities in income levels still remain.[4]

Table 2 gives an estimate of the distribution of world income accruing to various regions. It shows how an already prosperous North America was receiving an even greater share of total income in 1954 than in 1938 (44 per cent as against 28 per cent). Europe was receiving a smaller proportion (27 per cent as against 40 per cent), while the share of the less developed areas — Asia, South and Central America, and Africa — declined from 19 to 17 per cent of the total.[5] The comparison between the income in 1938 and in 1954 in 1938 prices (through which we have tried to eliminate the inflation which has occurred during and since the war) does not bear out that the underdeveloped countries have been more subject to inflation, though this may be due to the crudeness of the conversion rates which we have used. It does bring out that, of the backward regions, only Latin America has realized a larger-than-average growth in real income.

If the national income estimates, expressed in prices of 1938, for the established regions, are divided by their populations of 1938 and 1954, and we thereby account for the different rate of

Table 2. WORLD INCOME, 1938 AND 1954 (in billions of dollars)

Regions		Income in 1938	In %	Income in 1954	In %	Income in 1954 In prices of 1938	In %	In % of 1938
North America		71.4	27.9	324.7	44.0	190.4	44.0	268
of which	United States	67.0		305.0				
	Canada	4.0		19.2				
Europe		101.6	40.0	196.5	26.6	115.5	26.9	114
of which	Austria	1.3		2.7				
	Belgium	2.2		6.2				
	Czechoslovakia	2.0		5.4				
	Denmark	1.3		3.4				
	Finland	0.6		2.1				
	France	10.7		32.9				
	Germany	32.0		26.7				
	Greece	0.6		1.7				
	Hungary	1.6		2.1[1]				
	Iceland	0.03		0.1				
	Ireland	0.8		1.2				
	Italy	6.1		15.5				
	Luxembourg	0.1		0.3				
	Netherlands	2.7		5.6				
	Norway	0.9		2.6				
	Poland	3.2		7.7[1]				
	Spain	3.1		7.8				
	Sweden	2.7		7.0				
	Switzerland	2.0		5.1				
	Turkey	1.3		4.9				
	United Kingdom	22.7		41.2				
	Yugoslavia	1.0		2.5				
U.S.S.R.		29.4	11.4	77.5[1]	10.5	45.5[1]	10.5	155
Asia		32.0	12.5	75.2	10.2	44.1	10.2	138
of which	Burma	0.4		0.8				
	China	7.7		15.5				
	India	7.6		22.3				
	Japan	6.9		16.5				
South and Central America		10.2	4.0	36.3	4.9	20.7	4.8	203
of which	Argentina	2.0		7.5				
	Bolivia	0.1[1]		0.4[1]				
	Brazil	2.0[1]		8.5				
	Chile	0.8		2.1				
	Colombia	0.6[1]		2.6				
	Cuba	0.5[1]		1.7				
	Dominican Repub.	0.1		0.4				
	Ecuador	0.1[1]		0.6				
	Jamaica	0.08		0.1				
	Mexico	1.4		4.7				
	Peru	0.6[1]		1.0				
	Venezuela	0.5		2.7				

[1] Rough estimate

Regions		Income in 1938	In %	Income in 1954	In %	Income in 1954 In prices of 1938	In %	In % of 1938
Africa		6.9	2.7	17.1	2.4	10.0	2.3	145
of which	Egypt	1.1		2.7				
	Ethiopia	0.3		0.7[1]				
	Union of South Africa	1.8		3.9				
	Southern Rhodesia	0.1		0.4				
Oceania		3.8	1.5	10.5	1.4	6.2	1.4	163
of which	Australia	3.0		8.3				
	New Zealand	0.8		2.2				
Total		255.0	100.0	737.8	100.0	432.4	100.0	170

[1] Rough estimate.

Source: See previous table. The index numbers of national income estimates in constant prices for certain countries have been published in United Nations, "Statistics of National Income and Expenditure", *Statistical Papers*, Series H, No. 7 (New York: March, 1955). These indices have been used in calculating the national incomes in prices of 1938 for the countries for which this information was available. They were subsequently extrapolated for the region on the assumption that the trend in one or more countries within the region is representative for the entire region.

Table 3. WORLD INCOME AND INCOME PER CAPITA PER REGION IN 1938 AND 1954 (expressed in 1938 U.S. dollars)

Region	Income 1938 (billions)	Population 1938 (in mill.)	Income 1954 (billions)	Population 1954 (in mill.)	Income per capita 1938	Income per capita 1954
North America	71.4	141	190.4	175	504	1,088
Europe	101.6	375	115.5	403	271	287
U.S.S.R.	29.4	192	45.5	213	153	214
Asia	32.0	1,153	44.1	1,307	28	34
South and Central America	10.2	147	20.7	173	70	120
Africa	6.9	166	10.0	208	42	48
Oceania	3.8	11	6.2	14	346	450
Total	255.0	2,185	432.4	2,493	117	150

Source: See previous table.

population growth in the areas, it becomes even clearer that the equalization in the levels of living of different parts of the world, which has been held desirable for political reasons,[6] is an ideal that is farther away than ever.

According to the figures shown in table 3, the average North American had, before World War II, an income almost twice as high as that of the average European; this difference has become almost four times as great since World War II. And yet the average European enjoys an average income that is still about eight times higher than that of the average Asian and six times higher than that of the average African. The advance in the income of the average Latin American — almost 70 per cent since pre-war — is probably due to the economic progress made in a few countries. The tragedy of increasing inequality, viewed from the standpoint of humanity, is clear to everyone. Even more tragic is the fact that this inequality has increased in spite of the conscious effort made in so many undeveloped countries to secure a higher standard of living for the population.

We do not want to imply that the above data on national income adequately express the disparities in the levels of living. They give only a general impression of the divergence in welfare and have to be supplemented by other information relevant to comparisons of well-being.[7] Generally such indices as are available on the status of illiteracy, of education, of the death rate and infantile mortality, of health, of consumption of food calories, of nutrition, show a close correlation, in almost all cases, with the level of welfare as expressed by the average national income. This connection between various economic and social phenomena and the level of living shows us that the process of economic development is closely intertwined with the economic and social pattern of the society as a whole.[8]

One of the more interesting methods for measuring the disparities in the level of living between different countries is to attempt to calculate the purchasing power of the average hourly wage in each country. This method was used in a study by the U.S. Department of Labor in 1950.[9] Figures were gathered on the average hourly wage earned in industry in the United States and nineteen other countries and the purchasing power of this wage based on prices of a representative list of foodstuffs for these countries. As will be seen from table 4, it was only in Australia that a workman had to work fewer hours than in the United States to purchase a certain quantity of food. The high real cost of food in the U.S.S.R. is particularly striking.[10]

Table 4. PURCHASING POWER OF HOURLY WAGE IN CERTAIN COUNTRIES

Country	Relative Purchasing Power of Hourly Earnings in Terms of Food	Average Hourly Earnings	Food Prices
	U.S = 100	U.S = 100	U.S = 100
Australia	107	33	31
Austria	28	13	46
Canada	78	65	83
Chile	37	25	69
Czechoslovakia[1]	46	33	72
Denmark	73	33	45
Finland	39	26	66
France	31	21	70
Germany (west)	38	21	55
Great Britain	62	27	43
Hungary	27	24	89
Ireland	46	21	45
Israel	63	56	89
Italy	24	19	79
Netherlands	38	16	43
Norway	84	29	35
Sweden	63	34	54
Switzerland	46	37	81
U.S.S.R.	14	51	364

[1] The purchasing power of the average hourly wage for Czechoslovakia would be reduced to 23 if, instead of ration prices, the free-market prices for food, with an index of 144, are used.

The marked disparities in level of living, purchasing power, and cost of living, are connected with differences in productivity of the four factors of production: land, capital, labor, and leadership, and we shall now devote our attention to some of the causes of these differences.

Chapter 3

LAND

Indications of Backwardness

The low efficiency of agriculture in which the majority of the working population of the undeveloped countries are occupied, is the fundamental cause of the poverty in other spheres of production as well. This backwardness is illustrated by many quantitative data. Compare the average yield of rice, the principal food in the major countries of the far East. In Japan, the only industrial country, the average yield in 1952 was 41.3 quintals per hectare (1 quintal = 100 kilogram). India produced 11.8 quintals per hectare, Burma 15.4 (1951), Thailand 12.9, and Indonesia 15.8 as an average.

In 1951 in Central and South America, where maize is the principal food, the yield in Mexico, Colombia, and Argentina was, respectively, 7.6, 12.0 and 15.1 quintals per hectare, against a yield of 25.4 in the United States. In Iraq, Jordan, Lebanon, and Syria the average yields of wheat in 1952 were 5.0, 8.4, 7.4, and 7.3 quintals per hectare, respectively, compared with 12.3 in the United States. In Egypt in 1952, the yield of maize was 20.8 and of wheat 18.5 quintals per hectare, which figures show that intensive cultivation and the use of relatively large amounts of labor per unit of land can produce a relatively high yield.[1] This also applies to China, where 25.3 quintals of rice per hectare were produced in 1934–38, but if we consider that the working Chinese peasant produces on the average only 1,500 kg. of grain per annum as compared to 22,000 kg. produced by the American farmer, the relative importance of the high yield per land unit becomes clear.

In eastern and southern Europe there is similarly a strikingly low yield per hectare by comparison with the more prosperous West. If the yield of seven important food products per hectare for Europe as a whole in 1931–35 is taken as 100, the yield per hectare in the Netherlands was 168.5, in Great Britain 143.2, but only 82.9 in Poland, and as low as 60.5 in Greece.[2]

The density of population per unit of cultivated land cancels out the benefits of a relatively high yield per hectare in some countries and regions, and explains how the area available to the average farmer has been gradually reduced, owing to the increase of population and the limited amount of cultivable land. The following comparison between China and the United States will be illustrative.[3] The area of China, exclusive of Manchuria, is about 860 million hectares, that of the United States is about 10 per cent less, or 770 million hectares. Topography and climate, however, limit the area of cultivable land in China to only 90 million hectares, as against 148 million hectares in the United States. The estimated prewar number of peasant families on the entire cultivated area of China was 65 millions, while only 6.5 millions lived on the greater cultivated area in the United States. The average size of the Chinese farm was 1.4 hectares, prior to the communist revolution, and that of an American farm 63.5 hectares.

The productivity of a farmer and the economic well-being of his family is necessarily a function of many variables, climate, soil, and agricultural practice. Soils of different composition, or those subjected to different climatic influences, tend to vary in productivity. For example, P. Gourou[4] considers that the tropical sun adversely affects the yield of the land, partly because of the destruction of the organic matter in the soil by termites and insects and by micro-organisms under the influence of the prevailing high temperature.

C. H. Edelman[5] has suggested, however, that there are no soils that are fertile or poor in themselves; differences in productivity are due to the effects of climate, historical use, and human intervention, consciously operating to favor, or unconsciously to lower, soil quality. Apart from the natural factor, in most underdeveloped countries the static nature of agricultural techniques is primarily responsible for low productivity. Partial or total, lack of adequate and modern agricultural equipment and implements is one aspect of this backwardness.

Beside the pattern of agricultural practices, the amount of land worked by the farmer and the mode of distributing the harvest also determine the prosperity of the farm family. W. E. Moore[6] observes that in eastern and southern Europe the Roman legal system, under which property of the deceased is equally divided in kind among the heirs, has led to an uneconomic distribution of the land into small fragmented pieces. In other backward areas similar practices prevail under different legal systems. The smallness of the average farm combined with the uncertainties surrounding agriculture is the main cause of the heavy debts with which the farmers are often burdened. This indebtedness, in turn, produces a moneylender class which may evolve into a small group of landowners for which the rest of the peasantry work as tenants or laborers. The distribution of the yield will, under such circumstances, always be at the cost of the cultivator. This is especially true in densely populated countries where there are too many farmers and not enough land. Even if it is stipulated by law that the rent has to be reasonable, it may rise to 50, 60 per cent or even more of the yield because of the land hunger. For instance, in the Philippines it proved impossible to enforce the '70–30 Cropsharing Law' of 1947, guaranteeing 70 per cent of the rice yield to the tenant and a maximum of 30 per cent for the owner.[7]

Opinions differ about the significance for economic development of the form of land tenure. It has been shown for China, by the studies of J. Lossing Buck,[8] that the yield of land is unaffected by whether it is owned or leased by the peasant working it. Also, available capital equipment seems not to differ on the owner-farm from that on the tenant-farm. He concludes that the tenure relationship between peasant and land is irrelevant to the question of development. This may be true for a certain country or a certain period, but it seems to leave the heart of the matter untouched. The relative scarcity of land is the primary cause of low productivity, but the onerous relationships between owner and lessee or agricultural laborer[9] that arise from this scarcity, and the heavy burdens placed on the cultivator in consequence, help to explain his lack of interest in increasing yield or improving methods of cultivation. In such a situation land reforms[10] help to release the peasant from a semifeudal relationship and to make him more receptive to the innovations we shall discuss. An owner is more likely to be in such a frame of mind than a lessee, though it must be admitted that no remedy for all the difficulties can be found within the agrarian sector itself.

The situation is somewhat different in most of the Latin American countries, where an archaic form of large-scale land tenure is still prevalent and the so-called latifundia are an obstacle to rational exploitation.[11] The unsuitability of this form of tenure is revealed by the fact that often a large part of the land remains uncultivated. A simple division of these latifundia, or of their uncultivated portions, as practised in Mexico,[12] is, however, not a solution. The conditions of the cultivators may even deteriorate as a result of the decline in productivity due to the lack of implements and of methods of irrigation suitable for small-scale farming.[13] Such a transition requires simultaneous support from the state, in the form of agricultural extension services, construction of irrigation facilities, and provision of cheap credit for purchase of seed and implements.

A study of the causes of low agricultural productivity in Greece, Turkey, southern Italy, and Portugal, made by the Economic Commission for Europe[14] summarize them as: low rainfall, poor soil, soil-exhausting methods of cultivation, erosion due to lack of proper drainage, intensive grazing of sheep and goats, deforestation, hillside plowing and unsuitable forms of land utilization. These show, in a nutshell, the difficulties that must be overcome before surpluses can be produced that will lead to additional purchasing power and, in turn, to additional employment.

Measures for Improvement

As noted above, Winfield has estimated the cultivable land of China (including Manchuria and other outer regions), at some 90 million hectares. He assumes this could be increased to 136 million hectares by irrigation and reclamation, reallotment of plots to eliminate boundary lines, and elimination of graves.[15] He further assumes the rational economic size of an average Chinese farm to be 5.3 hectares, which means that this amount of land would provide a satisfactory livelihood for 26 million peasant families if efficient methods of cultivation were used. But the 22 provinces of China proper already had 65 million families that depended on the land for their living.

Even if the area of cultivable land could successfully be expanded with all the difficulty it would involve, Chinese agricultural land would still be seriously overpopulated.[16] Moreover, the possibility of expanding the cultivable area in China must not be over-estimated. To bring this potential arable land under the plow would require the construction of expensive engineering works, provision of transport facilities, breaking of virgin soil, and a reorientation of the mentality of the people involved. Difficulties of this nature are encountered in Africa and Latin America as well.[17] There are no more areas left in the world that are comparable in fertility and accessibility to the virgin prairies of north America, the pampas of the Argentine, and the Australian plains, all of which were turned into plowland during the nineteenth century at relatively little cost.

R. H. Tawney,[18] comparing the situation of Europe on the threshold of its modern development and China, notes that the population of Europe was small in those days, the uncultivated areas available for colonization great, and the sea communications of exceptional quality, all factors favorable to future industrial development, while the present position of China is unfavorable for future expansion in these respects. Though the economic and technical structure of the backward countries may recall conditions in fifteenth century Europe, almost all of them, like China, are faced today with unfavorable conditions at the very outset.

The growth of the population, which is more rapid in many of the less developed countries than in the industrial countries, leads to pressure of population when (1) the quantity of new land of equal fertility does not increase at the same rate as the population, (2) cultivation of the old land does not lead to a production increase proportionate to the additional labor applied, or (3) the growth of population is not accompanied by improved methods of cultivation or increased imports.[19] In practice the fertility of new land is often lower than that of the old, and the factor of labor is as a rule already excessive in relation to the other factors of production, land and capital. In any event, increased imports can be paid for only by increased exports. Internal rigidities of the economic system, as well as external factors, operate to impede expansion of exports, so that population growth can be absorbed only by the introduction of new agricultural methods, leading to increased food production, or by siphoning off the surplus population into other fields of activity, which we shall discuss later.

G. F. Winfield[20] distinguishes biological, mechanical, and cooperative methods for increasing food production from the same cultivated area and envisages a considerable amount of government assistance in all cases. Among the biological methods, he names the improvement of natural fertilizers[21] and the use of artificial fertilizers,[22] by which, he estimates, Chinese agricultural production could be increased by 20–40 per cent. At the same time, the introduction of improved plant varieties adapted to the local climate and soil (better seed),[23] could increase the yield by 15, 20 or even perhaps as much as 30 per cent. Efficient control of pests and plant diseases[24] can prevent losses of 20–25 per cent between harvesting and consumption. Afforestation should also be undertaken to improve the quality of the fuel and building material and to prevent erosion, which every year carries off millions of tons of the humus layer to the sea. All these methods, taken together, would double Chinese production per hectare, according to Winfield, and the same conclusion probably applies to other undeveloped areas as well.

Winfield also gives methods for improving livestock — particularly of pigs, chickens, and ducks, which can be fed on available waste — which would benefit the composition of the average peasant family diet, presently low in animal protein. Among the mechanical methods, he mentions the introduction of tractors and other agricultural machinery on a cooperative basis in the dry-farming areas. He envisages no change, within the foreseeable future, in the methods of irrigated farming, since the yield per hectare is already relatively high. The irrigated areas are almost invariably characterized by land subdivision, resulting from the greater productivity of the soil, which attracts population by its capacity to carry more labor per land unit. Here, too, he foresees better methods of plowing[25] and cooperative harvesting and threshing of grain crops, which will increase the quantities available for consumption.

The government, moreover, has the important task of flood prevention and effective erosion control by building dikes and maintaining supervision over them. In his opinion the transport system will have to be significantly expanded to avoid famines and assure the efficient distribution of food grains and fertilizer.[26] Large-scale government credits are required to put the peasants in a position to utilize such improved methods.[27] The government has also to take appropriate measures to encourage standardization of the agricultural produce and construct facilities to promote more efficient storage.[28]

These suggestions apply specifically to China but, as our footnotes indicate, the agricultural situation in the other backward areas is similar to that in China. The introduction of the principles of scientific agriculture requires accompanying economic and social reforms. It also assumes a large extension program which will enlighten the peasant and make him receptive to the idea that his methods really need improvement. The process is likely to be a long-term one since that sector of the population involved is for the most part illiterate.

Governments are often not in a position to launch an effective attack on the problem because their level of efficiency is itself held down by the low educational and material level of the population. The inadequacy of the administrative machinery, partly due to the shortage of technicians, is aggravated, in some countries, by government domination by groups with little interest in new developments which may tend to undermine their own position. Large landowners, for example, are often satisfied with the present methods of extensive agriculture and have no interest in tenure or tax reforms aimed at more intensive cultivation. The government of Chile in reply to a questionnaire of the United Nations has stated frankly: "Owing to the economic and political structure of the country, land reform in Chile is difficult to carry out. Landholders who would be affected by any action of an economic, political, administrative, legal or social nature will vigourously oppose its implementation, and their political and economic influence is very powerful."[29] In a few Latin-American countries the ruling groups are also concerned with the possible threat that the native Indian population may constitute if new methods of cultivation are introduced.

The legal tradition, evolved since the beginning of the nineteenth century, which requires just compensation to the owners for every governmental action adversely affecting existing land rights, similarly handicaps agricultural reform.

In India the state governments have taken steps to abolish the 'zamindari' system (by which a long chain of intermediary collectors have acquired the right to a share of the rent apart from the arrangement between landlord and cultivator) and replace it by a 'ryotwari' form of tenure whereby the state directly settles with the peasant occupying the land, or with his village, the amount of rent to be paid. The compensation for the landowners and 'zamindari' affected and the inability of most of the tenants to pay part of the debts to be taken over by the governments, would make such heavy demands on state funds that legislation of this type can only be gradually implemented. In K. G. Sivaswamy's opinion,[30] the vigor and speed of the official agricultural program has been considerably weakened by the shortage of trained personnel, an educational system based to a large extent on urban needs, the relatively small budget appropriations for publicity and training, and by the strengthening of the land-owner group inside and outside the Congress Party.

The political, social and economic obstacles that usually combine to retard the introduction of new agricultural techniques make many people doubt the feasibility of turning the traditional family-operated farm into a more efficient unit. The suitability of the methods as sketched by Winfield and others is not questioned, but a revolutionary social development is believed necessary before it will be possible to bring the new methods to the peasants, to make them accessible to everyone, and to infuse the governments with a spirit leading to their wholehearted support and cooperation.

It may be recalled that the agricultural sectors of western Europe, though farming improvements seem to have preceded industrialization, lagged subsequently in the rise of general productivity. Only gradually by means of education, cooperation and land reform has the remuneration in primary production been elevated to the national level. This change was further partly dependent upon tariff protection in certain countries and on a relative shift from grain farming to dairy, vegetable and fruit farming. The growth of industry, urban population and incomes, provided the market for additional production under conditions which gave the farmers both the incentive and techniques required to increase and diversify their output.

Despite these developments, farmers in many European countries are still not able to compete successfully with areas where extensive agriculture is much more productive. This digression points to the fact that the agricultural sectors in the industrial countries have for a long time been, and often still are, problem children. Though the difficulties facing the undeveloped countries may well be more formidable, development in these countries has to proceed along lines similar to those in the West. Prospects for progress in the agricultural sectors in the underdeveloped countries may appear to be most unfavorable for the moment. The difficulties, however, may be successfully surmounted, given a sufficient breathing spell.

The introduction of measures to secure a higher yield from land already under cultivation is often blocked by the institutional structure, while considerable investments are necessary to bring new land into production. In many countries it does not seem possible to increase significantly the cultivated area. However, opinions are necessarily divided on this point because of the lack of surveys of actual and potential land use in many regions. K. Davis[31] draws the following conclusion for India: "The most favorable places for irrigation have already been subjected to this improvement, and the remote but cultivable corners of the sub-continent are now very few. Indeed, because of excessive deforestation, over-grazing of pastures, and water-logging from irrigation, it is probable that in the future the loss in cultivable land, or at least in its fertility, will be about as great as the gain, unless heroic conservation and expansion measures are undertaken."

Even if not applicable to India, this picture might well be true for many other countries. In the countries where new land can be brought under the plow, such expansion may leave most of the peasants on the old land unaffected because of the over-population in the agricultural sector. A high excess of births over deaths may soon reduce the cultivator on new land — even if he at first received enough acreage to grow cash crops besides food grains for himself and his family — to a bare subsistence level.

The cultivation of export products, often initiated in underdeveloped countries by foreigners, has generally had no appreciable influence on the level of remuneration in the domestic sector. The innovations brought by this foreign element have led to the cultivation of new products by the local peasants, and through the extension of irrigation, there has been an increase in the output of traditional commodities. However, these improvements seem to have been offset by the continuous population increase and the absence of native ability to carry through the dynamic features into the whole sphere of agriculture or the economy as a whole.

The Russian Example

According to the communist viewpoint, the Russian experiment indicates the future course of development in other underdeveloped countries. This example of the transformation of an economically backward country into an industrial country, with relatively little in the way of imports of foreign capital, but under the direction and control of a national economic plan, according to M. Dobb "seems likely to become the classic type for the future industrialization of the countries of Asia."[32]

By its very nature, the question lies primarily on the political level, but one is tempted to go more deeply into the economic aspect of the problem because agriculture in Czarist Russia did manifest certain features similar to the situation in many undeveloped countries today. There, too, the majority of peasants were self-sufficient, although a considerable part of their production came onto the domestic and foreign markets.[33] These products were mainly from the large and medium-sized holdings, but also from the small peasants as a result of their poverty and relatively high tax obligations.

The 1917 revolution broke up the large estates, thus making an even greater proportion of the peasants self-sufficient, and thereby reducing the production coming onto the market. For instance, in 1927–28, the amount of marketed grains fell to less than 50 per cent of the prewar total.[34] The policy of intensive industrialization, however, led to a considerable rise in the demand for food to feed the urban workers. At the same time, in spite of the shortage of food, state price-fixing created an unfavorable relationship between the prices of agrarian and industrial products for the peasant, so that he had little incentive to expand production. The state was thus confronted with the same question that faces all countries undergoing industrialization: how to satisfy this increased market demand.

In Russia, a radical method was selected. More than 20 million small family farms were combined, in the relatively short period between 1929–34, into about 200,000 collective farms, the so-called kolkhozes.[35] The state assumed rigid control over the harvest by means of a system of compulsory deliveries. The initial result, however, was that the peasants slaughtered a large part of their herds rather than accept collectivization. The number of horses fell from 33.4 millions in 1928 to 14.9 millions in 1933. The number of cattle fell from 70.4 millions to 33.7 millions and the number of sheep and goats from 145.9 to 41.8 million over the same period (p. 324). It has further been estimated (p. 553) that in the period 1931–34, there were 5.5 millions additional human deaths as a direct result of this agrarian revolution. On the basis of official statistical material, N. Jasny asserts that just before the outbreak of World War II the effect of this slaughter on production had still not been made good in spite of the increasing use of agricultural machinery.

By analyzing the official figures Jasny shows that, although the area under food grain cultivation increased from 92.2 million hectares in 1928 to 104.7 millions in 1934[36] total production was not substantially increased because the new land was often unsuitable for crops. Cereal production had fallen from 81.3 million tons in 1913 to 73.1 millions in 1927, and was estimated at 84.7 millions for the period 1937–38. The grain yield per hectare dropped, according to him, from 8.0 quintals for 1909–13 (p. 79) to 7.4 quintals in 1938 (p. 548). Russian post-revolution production figures are based on the biological yield or estimated yield when the standing crop is not yet harvested. This method, according to Jasny, may lead to an overestimation of the real yield by more than 20 per cent. For 1945–46 Jasny estimates a grain crop of not more than 57.0 million tons or about 70 per cent of the pre-World War I production, while for 1950 he considers it possible that a crop of 85 million tons was again reaped (p. 550).

A policy of rapid industrialization caused a drop in the agricultural population from 114.1 millions in 1926–28 to an estimated 91.8 or 97.1 millions in 1938–39, a fall of 12.5 to 15 per cent (p. 709). During the same period the total population increased from 148.1 to 170.5 millions. The grain harvest was distributed for the benefit of the industrial workers and to the disadvantage of the agricultural population. According to official sources, twice as much grain came onto the domestic market in 1938 as in 1913 and four times as much as in 1928 (p. 34). The share taken by government procurement rose from 11.0 million tons in 1927–28 (15.5 per cent of a total grain harvest of 71.7 million tons) to 35.0 million tons in 1939–40 (42.7 per cent of a total harvest of 82.0 million tons) (p. 794).

Before World War I the annual per capita grain consumption for the entire population was 260 kg. (p. 750). Jasny estimates the average for 1927–28 as 250 kg., and for 1932 as 209 kg. — a figure that is, he says, probably too high — and for 1938 as 245 kg. (p. 558). The prewar or precollectivization per capita levels of grain consumption had thus, according to Jasny, not yet been regained in 1938 (p. 34). He shows that the amount of grain received by the peasants organized into kolkhozes for their own consumption was relatively small (p. 686). He gives specific figures for the consumption of meat and dairy products (pp. 777–78) which show how the cities were favored over the countryside. According to him, the average income of the kolkhoz peasant fell 20 per cent between 1928–38 (pp. 702–03).

After reading Jasny's book one understands the difficulty of comparing the former and present status of Russian agriculture, since no production figures or price indices have been published since 1928–30. Also statistics have been placed at the service of propaganda. Although the picture presented by Jasny is far from complete, it does establish one thing: the method followed by the U.S.S.R. in its agrarian reform, though it has indeed led to the desired industrialization, has demanded, and is still demanding, sacrifices that can only be imposed by a dictatorial regime.

Jasny's book has, as might have been expected, received a mixed reception. One author has criticized his computation of the income of the 'kolkhozniki'.[37] Others have expressed doubts concerning his conclusions as they believe such stagnation in agricultural production to be incompatible with the achievements of the Soviet Union during the war.[38] The problem is a technical one in agricultural economics, but it is apparent from recent news items concerning the Soviet Union that all is not well in the food-grain sector, not to speak of the sector of livestock farming.[39] This seems especially due to the fact, which Jasny emphasizes, that no proper incentive or reward is offered the farmer to improve his performance.

Whether the revolution has led to increased food production or not, the measures adopted by the Soviet Union indicate that rapid industrialization can be achieved through the redistribution of grain output. In some ways, circumstances in the Soviet Union would seem to have been particularly favorable for the collectivization program. There already existed an agricultural surplus, a fund of savings with which capital goods could be purchased from abroad to put the underemployed labor from the agricultural sector to work. Abundant unused resources were available to transfer labor to more productive activities. The Soviet Union was not to any great extent dependent upon foreign countries for obtaining extra raw materials. This example has been followed in the eastern European nations[40] where, in varying degrees, land has been transferred to landless peasants and cooperative farms have been established, making it difficult for individual farmers to compete. The governments attempt to induce farmers to join the new system — the cooperative farms have more machinery, livestock and fertilizer at their disposal — and in addition use propaganda, discriminatory taxation, and force.

A report of the Economic Commission for Europe[41] estimated, on the basis of unofficial sources, that food grain production in 1952 in most of the eastern European countries had again reached prewar levels, but the retreat announced in the collectivization policy in the second half of 1953 indicated that the system had not stimulated production to the extent hoped for. One study[42] argues that the failure of the collectivization policy was due to the fact that the background of the farmers was more individualistic than that of their Russian counterparts, thus making them less amenable to direction from above.

In mainland China the government has apparently been quite successful in imposing a heavy tax load on the farmer class in order to mobilize capital for its industrialization program. As the result of the redistribution program (1948–50), 10–15 per cent of the rich peasant and landlord families saw their land confiscated and 50–55 per cent of the peasant families received some small increment of land. But the position of the others remained unchanged with respect to their land holdings.[43] As according to a census of 1934–35, the average size of crop area on a farm was only 1.05 hectares, it is clear that this reform only increased the number of small holdings.

Through the formation, under communist cadres, of mutual aid teams and producers' cooperatives in which the peasants pool their land and work it in common, but share in the returns in accordance with the size of their holding, the state apparently was able to draw off any production above a certain minimum. In 1954 it was announced that by the end of 1957, 800,000 producers' cooperatives (for all practical purposes collective farms) would have been created. There were only 14,000 of these in December, 1953, and 100,000 in September, 1954.[44] Rostow gives no details about the government's procurement policy used to mobilize the food surplus. It can be assumed, however, that considerable difficulties have been encountered as the Chinese peasant has, through the ages, developed special techniques for evading government regulations.

With less possibilities for expansion than in the U.S.S.R., the Chinese agricultural sector and its potential output constitute the weakest link in the industrialization drive, though it is evident that the minimum level of consumption will be allowed compatible with the goals set in the industrial sector. In 1953 rationing and price controls were introduced for good grains and edible oils and controls were extended to cotton goods in 1954. These facts suggest that agricultural production had failed to meet expectations.

The agricultural policy of the communist states aims to produce a sufficient agricultural surplus to feed the industrial sector. This policy is only possible because the growth of these economies is related in a different manner than in private enterprise economies to an increase and differentiation in consumption. Not the increase in private consumption does determine the rate of economic growth, but rather the targets established for investment and government consumption.

A. Baykov[45] has observed that at the root of the collectivization schemes in the Soviet Union, as elsewhere, lies a major thesis about the independent farmer who makes free decisions as to what commodities to cultivate, how much to retain for his own consumption, and how much and what to sell depending upon the price level. This farmer, according to this thesis, cannot be relied upon to deliver the quantities of foodstuffs required to feed the industrial workers and the industrial crops to keep the industrial sector going. Historically, farmers in the advanced countries seem to have responded to market incentives whether arising from domestic or foreign demand. If the agricultural sector had been left to private initiative in the Soviet Union, it would have meant that, in order to induce the farmer to produce more or make him give up a larger proportion of his crops, consumer goods would have had to be offered in exchange. The expansion of consumer goods industries was, however, excluded in the Soviet industrialization program.

Baykov's conclusion, that the fate of private farming in countries with a predominantly rural population has to be decided before the problems of concentrating and intensifying agriculture can be solved as prerequisites for central planning, applies only to countries bent on industrialization in the Soviet manner. In Western countries the reorganization of agriculture has occurred without destruction of the values embedded in family farming. Capital formation rose as a result of the increasing incomes in many or several sectors. The crucial point in the Soviet method was, however, not to allow any rise in the farmers' levels of living, but to divert a larger share of agricultural output to the industrial sector for rapidly increasing the rate of investment.

The Necessity of Expanding Agricultural Output

We have devoted special attention to the agrarian sector of the economy because such a large part of the population of the undeveloped countries derives its livelihood from it. The difficulties of introducing improvements in this branch of economic activity seem almost insuperable in the densely populated countries, largely in consequence of the relative surplus agrarian population, and in the sparsely populated countries because of the prevailing tenure pattern. We shall revert later to the labor aspect of this subject. But there are other reasons why the agricultural sector is of critical importance in any attempt at industrialization.

If agrarian under-employment exists, the transfer of this surplus labor to industrial activities need not lead to a decrease in agricultural output. But there must be, in any case, a redistribution of the food grains between the agricultural and industrial sectors, both considered as consumers. This necessarily involves an expansion of the proportion sold on the market and an additional burden on the transport system. An increase in marketable supply may be difficult to achieve in a largely self-sufficient agricultural sector. If part of the labor surplus is withdrawn there is a possibility that the remaining agricultural population will either consume more or produce less than before if no special incentive is given to deliver larger quantities for the market. The absence or inefficiency of the local transport system can also hinder the process and this may lead to the need for increasing cereal imports for the industrial workers, as has already been noted in Latin America. Since industrial workers, with their higher income, will try to consume more cereal grains and other more diversified foodstuffs, demand for food tends to rise above the level prior to their withdrawal from the agricultural sector.

There is still another important reason why an increase in the supply of primary commodities appears necessary during the growth of an economy, namely, to satisfy industry's increased demand for raw materials for processing. Either new land has to be devoted to this purpose or, if unavailable, part of the land and resources used for food production has to be shifted to fill such needs. To make sure that the required additional raw materials are forthcoming and that the quantity of food supplies does not decline, agricultural improvements are called for and the rate of investment in the primary sector has to be stepped up to accomplish this result. If certain raw materials have to be imported, additional exports have to be provided. In an economically backward country this means that other primary products must be produced in greater quantities and diverted from local consumption.

There is also a transportation problem connected with this reorientation of the flow of goods, which likewise involves an additional investment. Moreover, increased supplies of manufactured consumer goods are required to meet the additional demand of the agrarian classes if they are to be induced to produce more foodstuffs and raw materials or provide greater quantities for the domestic market.

It would thus appear necessary to increase the productivity of agriculture or primary production simultaneously with the transfer of excess labor to prevent any fall in the overall level of consumption and to provide additional raw materials to satisfy the demand of the expanding industrial sector or for export in order to make possible the import of such commodities which cannot be procured locally.

Livestock Farming, Fishing, and Forestry

The soil and the food products that it yields are obviously the foundation of an economy which is largely directed towards self-sufficiency. It is necessary to explore and exploit new material resources in order to broaden such an economy. In the primary sphere, livestock farming and fishing are generally practiced in the same inefficient manner as arable farming, and for the same reasons. Here, too, tradition and ignorance are obstacles of the first order, despite the obvious desirability of improving the protein-deficient diet of the inhabitants of the backward countries.[46] As many FAO publications show, the difficulties of overcoming these handicaps would seem to be even greater than in the field of arable farming.

Efficient cattlebreeding in industrial countries reflects an already high level of wellbeing. It is only when the need for high-energy foods, especially cereals, has already been largely met and people are able to spend more on other foods, that an economy can afford to devote part of its grain supply to the feeding of livestock. The average yield in calories of a hectare of land under wheat or rice is at least five times that of a hectare of pasture used for cattle grazing. This economic consideration is the main reason why dairy farming is so little developed in the backward countries and why the cattle which are found in these countries are mainly draft animals and beasts of burden, except for cattle kept for non-economic reasons as in Africa and India.

The dependence of a viable livestock economy upon a higher level of living does not mean that the present productivity of livestock could not be improved. Better breeding practices and the control of diseases can greatly upgrade the quality of the animals raised. Between 1947–54 the introduction of a vaccine for chicken plague (ranikket) in Singapore resulted in an increase in the number of poultry from 500,000 to 3.5 millions and an increase in egg production of 800 per cent.[47]

The application of scientific knowledge of biology, nutrition, and livestock breeding requires research based on local conditions. Underdeveloped countries cannot easily carry out such research yet. It is only in recent decades that the colonial governments, in spite of their superior resources, have gone deeply into some o the problems involved, and the poorer and less experienced independent countries may find it hard to do the necessary research with their own personnel.

This is also true of fishing with its recent improvements in equipment and its new techniques for locating and detecting fish within known resource waters, and the increased knowledge of fish biology. The views of C. J. Bottemanne[48] on fishing in tropical waters are of interest in this respect. He asserts that the seas around Java are as plentifully stocked with fish as the North Sea, but that the fish are harder to catch. The water is clearer, so that the fish see the net and the movements connected with catching them. The fish in tropical waters are faster, probably see better, and in any case react more rapidly. European methods of fishing are inapplicable, because fish of the same species do not form schools, as they so characteristically do in west European waters, and therefore the use of trawlers is not warranted. His views are probably valid for tropical waters in general, and indicate the difficulty of bringing fishing in these waters to a higher level of efficiency.

It is of interest to note that Norway, which in October, 1952, concluded a bilateral agreement for technical assistance with India, proposed as its first project the modernization of fishing in the seas off Travancore with the aid of Norwegian technicians. The native boats are to be equipped with motors to make fishing possible farther away from the coast. Cold storage warehouses are to be built and refrigerated cars introduced for the transport of fish. The question arises whether this transfer of techniques which are an integral part of the Norwegian economy is economically justified in India, namely whether these new methods will reduce the cost of fish and widen the market to which fish can be transported.

Research on Western lines is necessary to improve the methods of catching fish. A good deal of this will require investment on a scale that a low income country may find difficult to finance, and for which it lacks the qualified technicians. This reasoning is equally applicable to inland fisheries, for which, according to informed sources, the possibilities of expansion are also great.

In Haiti, fishpond culture has been introduced by a Chinese expert provided by the Food and Agriculture Organization of the United Nations. The government hoped it would eliminate the considerable import of dried fish now taking place. It will be interesting to learn whether this culture, so widely disseminated throughout Asia, can be successfully applied in other underdeveloped regions.

The forest reserves in the underdeveloped countries likewise offer unexploited possibilities. Wood is mainly used as fuel in the undeveloped countries, although coal and oil are technically more efficient fuels.[49] However, Europe, North America, and the U.S.S.R. consume 80 per cent of all wood used for construction and 90 per cent of all wood processed into paper pulp.[50] The undeveloped countries still use very little wood for other industrial purposes such as railroad ties, piles, plywood, and the production of alcohol, sugars and plastics. Of the undeveloped areas, South America has the largest per capita potentially productive forest area (4.7 hectares), Asia the lowest (0.3 hectare), while Africa is roughly halfway between these two (2.1 hectares). In the Middle East, Egypt has no forest at all, and Israel and Saudi Arabia only very small areas per capita, so that the planting of trees would also be appropriate here though unfavorable climatic and soil conditions render it difficult.

More than half of the forest in the underdeveloped areas is still inaccessible, in contrast to Europe, where practically all productive forest is accessible, thus indicating that the transport question must be surmounted before this forest can become economically productive. The value of such forests, often characterized by a very heterogeneous growth of trees, is thus for the moment only theoretical. Moreover, scientific forest exploitation exists in few undeveloped countries. Consequently both good trees and inferior trees are cut for fuel or are removed to make room for agriculture or pasture without any consideration being given to sound conservation principles.

Many areas, particularly in Asia, are threatened with serious erosion as a result of indiscriminate felling of trees. Reforestation is indicated in these cases, but this demands strong organization and supervision, and will take many years. Again the underdeveloped countries may profit from the greatly increased knowledge of the industrial countries about forest conservation. The rapid growth of certain soft woods in tropical countries and the increased price of valuable hard woods prevalent in certain areas could facilitate the introduction of modern principles of forest exploitation.

Mining

This brings us to the subsoil resources still awaiting exploitation, and in many cases exploration too, in the undeveloped countries. Those who expect large-scale industrialization of the backward countries have, to some extent, based their hopes on these resources. It should, however, be realized that only a rudimentary knowledge exists of the geological structure of many underdeveloped countries. Certain of these countries have already been subjected to more or less intensive geological surveying for the needs of industrialized Europe and later for those of the United States, but this has often been limited to certain areas. Prospecting has most often begun in regions where detectable surface signs or an outcrop of an ore showed the existence of mineral deposits. Only in such places has further exploration been undertaken in the search for new resources.

The prospects of the undeveloped world, as a whole, may not look favorable to judge by the present knowledge of reserves, but this may be due to ignorance. It should be borne in mind that the quantity of available resources is determined by the interaction of nature, man and his culture and technology. The scarcity of resources in some undeveloped countries may only be a reflection of their economic backwardness. Estimates of existing reserves are a function of the exploited resources, in the sense that the less resources are exploited the less is known about reserves. Even in the United States, which probably possesses the most advanced geological exploration service, answers about potential reserves are considered "as little better than intelligent guesses." Moreover, estimates of reserves vary not only with the extent and intensity of geological surveying, but also with changes in techniques of mining, in availability and cost of competitive raw materials. Any realistic evaluation must, nevertheless, start from the resources that are presently known. The following table, comparing the estimated reserves of coal, petroleum, hydro power, iron ore, and the amount of arable land per capita for different regions, may thus still give an indication of the disparity in resource endowment of various parts of the world.

Table 5. ESTIMATED WORLD RESERVES OF COAL, PETROLEUM, HYDRO POWER, IRON, AND ARABLE LAND PER CAPITA (1953 or latest estimate)

Region	Population (millions)	Coal (metric tons)	Petroleum (metric tons)	Hydro power (kilowatts)	Iron ore (tons)	Arable land (hectares)
World	2,599.1	1,348	7.1	0.16	33	0.51
America	331.7	4,258	18.1	0.33	102	0.97
North America	174.6	7,971	24.2	0.32	78	1.33
Centr. America and Caribbean Islands	55.1	59	4.3	0.22	10	0.43
South America	102.1	170	15.2	0.43	194	0.65
Europe	401.5	1,057	—	0.13	41	0.37
Northwest Europe	199.4	1,370	0.5	0.15	75	0.27
Southern Europe	111.2	79	—	0.12	10	0.36
Eastern Europe	90.7	1,568	0.7	0.09	5	0.51
U.S.S.R.	207.0	5,990	6.5	0.28	15	0.66
Africa	211.3	363	0.1	0.43	19	1.25
North and Northeast Africa	71.7	2	0.3	0.09	4	0.62
Tropical Africa	122.6	21	—	0.67	10	1.14
Southern Africa	17.0	4,355	—	0.02	153	0.58
Asia	1,434.1	231	7.7	0.07	18	0.24
Western Asia	69.1	51	153.9	0.03	6	0.65
Southern Asia	476.1	131	—	0.06	44	0.34
Southeast Asia	178.0	9	1.9	0.11	—	0.23
Far-eastern Asia	711.0	371	—	0.07	6	0.14
Oceania	13.7	1,231	0.9	0.37	73	1.53

Sources: United Nations, *Peaceful Uses of Atomic Energy, Proceedings of the International United Nations Conference in Geneva, August 1955*, Vol I (New York: 1956), pp. 96–101; United Nations, *Survey of World Iron Ore Resources* (New York: 1955), pp. 20–34, and *1953 Yearbook, Food and Agriculture Organization*.

Restricting ourselves to the underdeveloped areas, for the time being only eastern Europe seems to be well endowed with coal. Petroleum reserves are plentiful only in western Asia (Middle East) and South America. Hydro power is more uniformly distributed, but eastern Europe, North and Northeast Africa, western Asia, southern Asia (mainly India and Pakistan) and far-eastern Asia (mainly China and Japan) seem to be deficient. For iron ore, Central America, southern and eastern Europe, North and Northeast Africa, western Asia, Southeast Asia and fareastern Asia are apparently below average world endowment. The figures on arable land bring into focus some of our foregoing analysis on agriculture. Especially southern Europe and Asia, in particular Southeast Asia and fareastern Asia, show the overcrowding on land now under cultivation.

We say above 'for the time being', because the developmental power of technology must not be underestimated, although it may be assumed that the most accessible deposits are already being exploited. With our present equipment we are already able to dig and bore deeper than before, but the costs of exploration at greater depths are higher. Greater investments and an ever-expanding theoretical and practical knowledge are required to adapt new methods to the exploitation of natural resources.

It must be allowed that advancing technology may develop important uses for new raw materials which are abundant in certain backward countries but for which, as yet, no application has been found. It is likewise conceivable that new forms of energy, such as atomic or solar energy, may make it feasible to industrialize regions that now lack conventional energy resources — a typical feature of many backward countries. In the case of atomic energy one gains the impression, though it may still be somewhat early to judge the prospects, that the high capital cost of installation of nuclear power plants and the economies of size resulting therefrom favor the industrial countries and not the underdeveloped countries. Energy is indeed a crucial element in development as has been pointed out by E. C. Olson.[51] He found that the amount of energy used is more closely correlated with the level of national income than it is with certain other indices (e.g., active population, head of cattle, or cultivated area).

However uncertain the future development of technology may be today, it seems already apparent that in almost all respects the ability of the industrialized countries to utilize new raw materials and new techniques will remain superior for a long time. They possess better basic research facilities for developing new technology, and their margin of capital formation is greater, so that the savings necessary to start out on new lines of production are more readily available to them. The view of E. Wagemann[52] and others that the disparities in natural resources between one country and another, or between one region and another, are tending to diminish progressively as technology advances, fails to give proper weight to historic reality. Differences in resource endowment have been important in the past and are likely to remain so in the future. Present deficiencies will count more heavily in the underdeveloped world than the advantage that its resources are largely unexplored.

The technological knowledge and capital wealth of the industrial countries will keep them for the foreseeable future in a favorable position to alleviate critical shortages through foreign trade or the development of substitutes. Reference might also be made here to an article by F. Tabah.[53] He has made an estimate of the world's need for energy, steel, copper, aluminium, and potash if the underdeveloped countries were to attain the average consumption level of the now industrialized countries. Surprisingly enough, it shows that the world output of these products would only have to be increased between 200 and 250 per cent to reach such a consumption level. However, Tabah points out that it is not likely that this will happen as this implies that consumption by the developed countries would remain static, whereas it is far more realistic to assume that the industrial countries will take a larger, even if diminishing share of the potential increase of production, although it implies lessening the possibilities for the backward regions to improve their relative status.

Chapter 4

CAPITAL

Definition and Composition of Capital

Though the classical economists recognized the importance of the capital factor in the process of production, it was only later that as a result of the accelerated introduction of power, tools and machinery, hand in hand with the development of science and technology and the improvement in the economic organization as a whole that capital became as essential as it now is to efficient production. Yet Clark's investigations[1] have shown the absence of any simple, direct relationship between the increase in capital and the rise of real income, because of the influence on productivity exerted by such factors as changes in the quality of labor and in the quantity of natural resources available to a country, whether domestic or imported, and by changes in the quality of capital itself. A close relationship between the amount of capital employed and the resultant real hourly income per worker may be inferred. Clark[2] offers a graphic representation of such data in a large number of countries. However, he emphasizes that the relationship should not be taken as causal as there are other variables acting in the same direction on both capital and income.

We define capital in the usual way as the collective term for those goods that are the fruits of the past cooperation of land and labor and that possess indirect utility to the extent that their services, combined with the original factors of land and labor, yield a greater quantity of final product than would be obtained without such services. This formulation is, of course, somewhat arbitrary. It takes account only of reproducible material capital, and ignores the investments in education, training, and health services, sometimes also termed 'human capital', that are of primary importance for economic development. The report of the five United Nations experts,[3] which we shall discuss later, contains the following reference to this aspect: "In our opinion, most underdeveloped countries are in the situation that investment in people is likely to prove as productive, in the purely material sense, as any investment in material resources, and in many cases investment in people would lead to a greater increase in the flow of goods and services than would follow upon any comparable investment in material capital."

Resources in the form of land, minerals, etc. — which are called non-reproducible capital by some authors — are also neglected by the above definition, although in economic history the export of this non-reproducible capital was often the beginning of the process of economic growth. Such exports paid for imports of machinery and raw materials — to complement domestic factors of production. In the present context, however, we shall adhere to the more limited definition of capital, partly because the experience of industrialization in advanced countries has shown that growth of national income has always been associated with an increase in reproducible capital.

Capital in this sense consists of a great diversity of goods, as has been vividly shown in those countries where a capital inventory has been taken. It includes private and public buildings, dwellings, ships, public utilities, machinery, stocks of materials and other goods, cattle and other agricultural assets, furniture and other durable personal property, together with similar holdings abroad. For the United States it has been estimated that of the total capital stock in 1938 ($253 billion), 56 per cent ($141 billion) consisted of buildings and housing, 33 per cent ($85 billion) of machinery and means of transport, and 11 per cent ($27 billion) of inventories.[4]

These different categories of capital do not contribute equally to the increase in production,[5] though they are complementary. We cannot conceive of the use of machinery without a stock of raw materials, a factory building and government buildings as a manifestation of the services provided by the state for the orderly conduct of production and trade. However, for a clearer under-standing of the different income productivity of the various forms of capital it is useful to distinguish between economic directly productive capital (factory and farm buildings, machinery, in-ventories, etc.), economic 'overhead' capital (transport and com-munication facilities, power stations, irrigation works, etc.) and social 'overhead' capital (housing, schools, hospitals, etc.). Eco-nomic directly productive capital is of more immediate signifi-cance for the growth of the national product. The role of 'over-head' capital, as the term implies, is to provide an adequate technological and social environment that results indirectly in raising the productivity of investment of the direct type. A first-rate transport and education system in itself does not lead to an increase in production except in so far as it encourages the growth of investment in agriculture and industry.

The need for the first category of capital goods is directly deter-mined by the structure of additional consumption resulting from a rise in incomes. For this reason, investments in this category of projects in a country with an industrial climate will be attractive to private entrepreneurs. The requirements for investments of the 'overhead' type are not so easy to determine in a growing economy. Although it is clear that they rise with an expansion and diversification of output, it is not easy to state in quantitative terms how much investment (e.g., in transportation, electric power and education) is required for a balanced economic growth. As the income productivity of such 'overhead' capital is hard to foresee and large outlays are involved in its construction, governments have, to an increasing degree, assumed responsibili-ty for the erection of this form of capital.

C. Clark[6] has noted that countries with a relatively low level of living tend to have a greater amount of capital stock in relation to their income level than those countries with a higher level of well-being. He presents a table showing that in a country with an average product of 0.10 'international units' per man-hour, an average ratio of income to capital of 0.22:1 exists. From this it can be calculated that an investment rate of 4 per cent of the national income is necessary to achieve a 1 per cent increase in production. By contrast, in a country with an average product of 1.0 'international units' per man-hour, since according to Clark the ratio between income and capital is 0.28:1, an investment rate of only 1.6 per cent would suffice to obtain a 1 per cent increase in national product.

From this he deduces that the former type of country requires a greater investment rate to produce an identical increase in national income. This conclusion does not seem to be justified, because it disregards differences in income-generating effect of various types of capital goods. These observations could, indeed, be taken to show that a relatively larger percentage of the stock of capital in undeveloped countries is of an inert nature. It is quite possible that a given investment of special income-generating capital goods in a backward country might produce a greater yield than a corresponding investment in an industrial country.

It is not the average or overall ratio between existing capital and income (which is, in any case, based on the application of techniques and organization forms of the past) that is important for economic development, but rather the marginal productivity of new investment, i.e., the increase in income created by an additional unit of new capital. This relation of the value of capital to the value of output may indeed be relatively low as there is a large gap in technical skills between undeveloped and industrial countries. In backward countries there may also be a considerable 'productivity reserve' in the capital stock in existence. This implies that the capital-income ratio would be lower if equipment were better utilized. Through better maintenance of machinery and training of workers and managers, income could be substantially increased without the addition of new capital. On the other hand, such general observations on the capital-income ratio tend to overlook the fact that widely different capital-revenue ratios exist for the various sectors of the economy. In certain countries, relatively little investment may be required for a significant increase in agricultural and industrial output. However, in many countries, continuous growth may require large investments in irrigation, transport, and electric power that generally have a very high capital-income ratio. Because the initial utilization of such investments will be below their maximum use level, additional investments in agriculture and industry are needed to make outlays for transport, electrical power, etc., really productive. Deficiencies in managerial and technical skills cause inefficient productive use of capital. They make it imperative to devote substantial outlays to education and training whose effect upon income-generation may be measurable only in the long run.

In fairness, it should be stated that Clark indicated at the World Population Conference (Rome, August 31–September 10, 1954) that he had changed his mind on the subject. There, he warned against the conventional attempt to analyze the problem of capital formation simply in terms of income and capital per head. In this connection he suggested the breakdown of capital requirements into three components: housing, other construction, and equipment. The c.i.f. cost of equipment is not very much greater for poorer countries than for industrial countries, but the cost of housing, adequate by conventional standards, and other forms of construction is probably far cheaper in the former than in the latter countries. The amount of capital necessary to achieve a given rise in output, therefore, may be much lower than is often believed. To the extent that a smaller rate of capital formation is required to generate a given rate of income growth, the prospects for development of the backward countries are brighter. For the Latin American economy as a whole, it has been estimated that to obtain an increase in income of 1 per cent, about 2.3 per cent of income had to be devoted to net capital investment.[7] This confirms the idea that the capital-output ratio for underdeveloped countries is much lower than Clark had earlier assumed.

It has been definitely established that the changes in the quality and quantity of the capital stock has been of primary importance in the economic rise of all industrial countries. But the manner in which the various types of capital goods make their respective contributions to economic growth and material improvement remains to be studied. We shall, therefore, discuss the problem of capital formation in more detail.

The Process of Capital Formation

In most of the undeveloped countries there is still an important, and for the most part self-sufficient, sphere of agriculture and handicraft, within which a division of labor characteristic of the industrial countries has not as yet taken place. In this sphere no division between the factors engaged in the production of consumption goods and those engaged in the maintenance and replacement of existing machinery, and the production of new machinery, exists. The farmer and the artisan themselves repair and replace their simple implements, houses, and furniture. Sometimes they have the help of their village neighbors, to whom in return they render similar services. The introduction of improvements into such a predominantly nonmonetary economy is feasible up to a point. But, historically, more radical improvements have always been linked to the growth of a money economy, i.e., to commercialization, that facilitated the exchange of surpluses between the various households and thus resulted in a more extensive division of labor.

In all underdeveloped countries a monetary sector, mainly concentrated in the cities, exists side by side with this more self-sufficient sphere. This sector has been created by three factors: the activity of government that collects cash for its share of the national product for financing various functions, the initiative of foreigners concerned particular with foreign trade, and the native traders and entrepreneurs who meet local and national requirements not supplied by the subsistence sector. The monetary sector provides evidence that the construction of public buildings, public utilities, and industries has been financed in the past from savings or surpluses. The greater capital intensity of this sector helps also to explain its higher productivity. There is in reality no clear-cut demarcation between these two sectors; through taxation, trade and migration the monetary sector is tied with the subsistence sector. The smallness of this "capitalistic sector embedded in an otherwise precapitalist world" (Schumpeter) and the weakness of the impulses to its expansion make it so important for undeveloped countries to devise ways and means of increasing surplus production, so that the capital stock can be expanded to provide a more plentiful future supply of goods and services.

In a static economy, a greater concentration of the factors of production on the production of capital goods can take place only through a diversion of those factors engaged in the production of consumption goods, thus involving a decline in the level of consumption. We shall see later that in various undeveloped countries increased capital formation does sometimes take place in this way. The economic system contains so many economic and social rigidities, with the low per capita income leaving practically no margin for voluntary saving that it is only by creating new money supplies, and thus forcing up the price level and shrinking the volume of consumption, that the state is able to procure the means for initiating new capital construction. In this connection it is advisable to examine the extent to which unutilized resources in the undeveloped countries are available for capital construction and new activities in general. J. Schumpeter[8] has tried to prove that, historically, the significance of new resources has been unimportant in the sense that "as a rule the new combinations must draw the necessary means of production from some old combinations", so that "the carrying out of new combinations means. . . simply the different employment of the economic system's existing supplies of productive means." The problem thus seems to be too narrowly stated. In countries like the United States, Australia, and Canada, it is evident that the acquisition of new resources by the economic system has contributed to economic growth. It can be argued that the emergence of the factor of leadership as innovator by introducing a new product or an improved technique means in any case an addition of a previously unused factor to the economic system.

When referring to the potential resources in the poorer countries, one has in mind particularly the labor surplus in the agrarian sector.[9] A United Nations expert estimated for the Philippines that the active agricultural population of about 3.5 millions was occupied economically for only 120 days per year, so that more than 600 million man-days [(300–120) × 3.5] were available each year for other activities. If the result of such activities, based on unutilized or underutilized resources, leads to an increase in the quantity of goods and services available for consumption in the immediate future, the level of consumption need not fall when capital formation is increased.[10] However, this may require a major reorganization of production.

It is clear that an expansion of production depends not only on the use of previously underemployed labor but also on the availability of additional raw materials and capital goods. Moreover, transport and market conditions must be suitable for such a reorientation. A. R. Prest[11] has pointed out, as one of the lessons learned from World War II, how difficult it was to increase production in the Middle East and India due to the impossibility of importing complementary raw materials and machinery. A similar situation obtained in Latin America. Whether a country is in a position to increase its capital stock without lowering its level of consumption also depends on whether its surplus labor is mobile enough for transfer to more productive activities.

R. Nurkse,[12] in particular, has called attention to the fact that concealed unemployment in agriculture in undeveloped countries constitutes an unutilized savings fund which could be used, if provision were made to have food that these workers consume in the agrarian sector available to feed them while they are producing capital goods. The argument is theoretically unassailable. But it passes too lightly over the difficulties connected with the imposition of such a load on the food-growing sector, the resettlement of labor, and the need for mobilizing other factors of production. Such a formula cannot be employed without qualification. Almost every successful industrialization effort is *ex post facto* proof of Nurkse's proposition. Yet this sheds no light on how the necessary redistribution of the factors of production can best be brought about in practice. In other words, how to develop a surplus to feed the industrial sector during the interim period before the increased productivity resulting from the additional use of capital has yielded an increased flow of consumer goods remains one of the great problems in the process of capital accumulation. This is not dependent upon the existence of some sort of a fixed savings fund, but rather requires drawing underutilized resources into the production process. The employment of these resources for capital construction is imperative for a future increase in the flow of goods. Only a sustained utilization of resources in this manner can ultimately raise the standard of living. If such elasticity in the supply of production factors exists or can be generated, an expansion of investment can be accomplished without a decline in the consumption level, and the increased rate of savings can be created out of the resulting higher incomes.

Undeveloped countries are more likely to be able to produce a surplus in the primary sector than in the secondary industrial sector. Expansion of agriculture or mining, however, involves difficulties in most undeveloped areas. During the nineteenth and the beginning of the twentieth centuries the inflow of foreign capital, attracted by a favorable combination of soil and climate, led to an expansion of the primary sector in a large number of undeveloped countries. Additional capital formation was made possible by the resultant increment in income, even allowing for the outflow of a part of the surplus thus created for the service of the foreign capital and the remuneration for foreign management. The impetus was often damped, however, by increased consumption of a small group or by the needs of an increasing population.

As will be shown later, many underdeveloped countries have a larger annual population increase than the now developed countries had at the beginning of their industrial revolution. If the growth of additional employment and output lags behind population growth, every increase of population tends to raise the proportion of the national product devoted to consumption. A population increase has a favorable effect only in a dynamic economy where the expected increase in demand due to increasing population leads to additional investment and production.

It has been pointed out that the foreign investment inspired by anticipated profits from agricultural and mineral exports did not always encourage industrialization or other forms of economic development. In Latin America, for instance, railroad construction by foreign investors from the production sites of their agricultural and mining activities to the ocean ports often resulted in lines of different gauges even inside the boundaries of a single country.[13] This made national or regional economic integration difficult, sometimes down to the 1950's. This criticism is not unfounded, but it fails to account for the lack of new capital construction that the surplus produced by foreign activity should have rendered possible.

In the private sector where the profit motive is the regulator of capital formation, the limited size of the national market and the low real purchasing power of the majority of the population are the basic causes for the feebleness of the incentive for capital formation. In the present industrial countries the undeveloped transport system and low purchasing power also probably checked the growth of the industrial sector in the beginning. But here too it was foreign trade, made possible by an initial surplus in the primary sector, that provided the original impetus to capital accumulation.

The low average income of the undeveloped countries leaves room, understandably enough, for only a low rate of saving and investment. Whether increased capital formation does take place, or surpluses are lost to constructive purposes as a result of temporarily or permanently increased consumption by a small group, or are cancelled out by population increases, is largely determined by the existence of an entrepreneurial class and the presence of social and cultural conditions conducive to the emergence of a spirit of innovation in a society. At the same time, the low level of saving makes it difficult for the government to accelerate the rate of capital formation or to channel savings into more desirable directions by means of fiscal and investment policies. Such public investments as those for improved transport facilities or power plants, require large amounts of capital and yield a return over a long period of time. This makes it particularly difficult for the undeveloped countries to undertake such investments out of their own resources.[14] Their potential benefit lies in the fact that such investments create 'external economies' that facilitate the future establishment of industries. The efficient operation of such 'overhead' facilities is of course a *sine qua non* for their being a potential force for continuous growth. Poorly maintained transport or power systems, as they often are in undeveloped countries, may constitute a bottleneck rather than a point of growth within the economic system.

Even if 'overhead' facilities are properly functioning, the risk and cost of industrial pioneering may still be judged too high by private investors, due also to the absence of nuclei of other enterprises from which economic and technological benefits accrue to a new undertaking. Such a divergence between private profitability and social productivity of those projects which are necessary to stimulate economic development, is typical of a pre-industrial society and explains why public investment in many fields is required to initiate the process of growth.

Historical Development of Capital Formation

Although the initial period of economic growth in the industrial countries of today was obviously important for the subsequent stages of industrialization, we have little precise data on the events of that period. Thus we cannot obtain full insight into the historical process of their development. There is a need for studies to trace, country by country, the trend of the magnitudes important in economic development and a theoretical treatment of the nature of the economic problems arising in the course of industrialization and the means by which they were solved.

In an unpublished study entitled "The Study of Patterns of Industrialization", presented in 1948 to the United Nations Sub-Commission for Economic Development, S. Kuznets endeavoured to show the importance, for the problems of the contemporary backward countries, of a wider and more systematic knowledge of the various facets of industrialization in the diversity of its historical accomplishment. Some of the data he listed for study in this connection were: (1) growth and differentiation of the national product, (2) patterns of population growth, (3) changes in the quantity and utilization of natural resources, (4) utilization of labor power, (5) volume and composition of reproducible capital, (6) distribution of income and property, (7) organizational structure of the productive system, (8) changes in the consumption pattern, (9) sources and channels of savings, (10) growth and composition of foreign trade, (11) foreign investment, (12) the balance of payments, (13) changes in attitudes and thinking that result from industrialization. He suggested that by following the changes in these categories during the period of industrialization in a number of developed countries, one might learn general trends and directives of use for the guidance of the underdeveloped countries. The subcommission, however, failed to adopt his suggestion.

It has, for some time, been a matter of controversy whether agrarian improvement should precede industrial development or whether industrialization necessarily results in a corresponding evolution of agriculture. The problem seems insoluble, although it would now seem to be generally accepted that a development program should try to expand production in both sectors in a co-ordinated manner so that the output of food and industrial raw materials rises *pari passu* with industrial output. However, one can imagine development with primary emphasis on industrialization provided an export market for manufactured products can be created to pay for the import of additional food and raw materials. Conversely, growth can also result from an expansion of agricultural output of which the excess is exported in exchange for manufactured products. An outline of the events in England and Japan may give us a certain insight into the manner in which capital formation and development took place in those two countries.

As a result of the introduction of crop rotation, deeper plowing, improvement in livestock, row planting, and better equipment, English agriculture had made fairly rapid progress in the century preceding the industrial revolution. P. Mantoux[15] asserts that it was only the agrarian reforms in the eighteenth century, associated with a change in certain areas from an intensive arable farming to more extensive livestock farming, that released agricultural laborers for work in the growing industrial sector and created the conditions for the development of manufacturing. The increase in livestock farming, and above all in sheep raising, was inspired by favorable opportunities for the export of raw wool, and later woolen products. The wool trade and the wool processing industries, however, ultimately fell behind in comparison with the cotton and metal industries, which, in fact, ushered in the industrial revolution. The inventions and technical improvements that led to the expansion of industrial production were preceded, and to a considerable extent determined, by the commercial expansion. In speaking of the significance of foreign trade for British economic growth during this stage, Mantoux used the apt metaphor: "Only a negligible quantity of ferment is needed to effect a radical change in a considerable volume of matter."[16] The rise in capital formation reflects both a more productive rearrangement of the factors in the primary sphere, and the opportunities for export, the incentive being provided by the then current price relationships, from which a leading commercial and industrial class profited.

In England the commercial expansion, although fostered and preceded by a reorganization in the primary sphere, would seem to have been responsible in the first place for the accumulation of savings from which equipment for the industrial revolution was constructed in a later phase. The repercussion of the commercial and subsequently industrial transformation on food farming in later stages is difficult to trace for lack of statistical data. The practically continuous fall in the prices of food grains after the Napoleonic wars would seem to indicate that the increasing demand for food from the growing urban centers was more than met by an improving efficiency of agricultural production. Food imports were relatively unimportant in the first half of the nineteenth century. Consolidation of scattered tracts of arable land and the reclamation of waste land continued. The introduction of better plows, harrows, threshing machines, drainage methods, and artificial fertilizers were also factors in the expansion of marketable output. Generally the average farm holding tended to grow because the declining price for grains was detrimental to the smaller farmer, who for economic and social reasons was less adept or inclined to transfer to other crops or dairy farming. The railway revolution (1820–50), bringing the products of new areas within the reach of consumers' centers, also worked especially to the disadvantage of the small cultivator for the same reasons. Gradually a shift occurred from food farming to dairy farming and horticulture. This trend was reinforced by the growing significance of cheaper imported food grains. For wheat, e.g., in 1852–59 the proportion of imports to total consumption was 26.5 per cent. It had risen to over 48 per cent for 1868–70 and to nearly 70 per cent in the late 1870's where it stayed until recently.[17]

In Japan which began its industrialization so much later, and where the government participated actively in the development, the industrial transformation went hand in hand with a rapid increase in agricultural production due to the introduction of more productive varieties of rice and the use of artificial fertilizers. The index of production of the six principal agricultural products rose from 100 to 177 between 1881–90 and 1911–20, while the population increased 44 per cent from around 1885 to 1915. The cultivated area increased only about 20 per cent, but the yield per hectare rose by almost 50 per cent.[18] This increased yield was obtained with only slight additions to fixed capital, but new working capital was made available by granting the peasants

credits to purchase new varieties of seed rice and artificial fertilizers.

There was practically no improvement in the peasant level of
living, however, as a change in taxation led to an increasing indebtedness of the farmer. Through a new land tax, instituted in
1873, farmers had henceforth to pay a fixed charge based on the
value of their land; it constituted in that year an estimated 25 per
cent of the value of the crop. This levy, which did not vary with
the annual yield or the price of the crop, was partly responsible,
given the small plot of land per farmer and the vagaries of weather
and prices, for the gradual replacement of the owner-cultivator
by the tenant farmer. The heavy burden on the tenant farmer
can be surmised from the fact that the land rent, which remained
fixed in kind, amounted to about 68 per cent of the yield in 1873.
Thus, the landowners and the government were the only ones to
profit from the increased agricultural productivity.

Since the increase in food production more than kept pace with
the population growth, however, it was possible to feed the increasing number of industrial workers. The land tax provided
the state with the necessary means to finance industrial ventures
and the large landowners with the funds to initiate such local
industries as were feasible. At the inception of Japan's industrialization silk culture was also encouraged. An export surplus was
brought into being — two-thirds of total exports in 1868 consisted of silk — in exchange for which raw materials and machinery were imported to supplement the internal formation of
capital.[19] Other sectors of the textile industry were established
on the basis of imported raw materials, first cotton goods, then
woolen fabrics and artificial silks as well. Since its production
was largely for export, it assisted in the financing of imports of
raw materials (and of foodstuffs after World War I) and of
machinery for further capital accumulation. The process of
growth depended only partly on increasing domestic purchasing
power. For several branches of industry foreign markets were of
decisive influence. The elasticity of the combined domestic and
foreign demands and the profitability of industry serving these

demands provided the incentive for investment of surpluses, initially often small, in new activities. Subsequently, investment of larger surpluses in an increasing number of sectors helped to bring about profound structural changes in the economic organization.

We have intentionally selected two countries in which the relationship between population and land area was not particularly favorable. In countries such as the United States, Canada, and Australia, the expansion of the area under cultivation, leading to the export of cotton, wool, and food grains, provided the surplus that enabled the rate of industrialization to be increased. From 1865 to 1884 exports of farm products still averaged 75 to 80 per cent of total U.S. exports. Here too, foreign trade facilitated industrialization, with the receipts from an expanding volume of exports paying for the imports of raw materials and capital goods.

The process of industrialization is ordinarily studied within the framework of a single country, but this procedure may obscure the fact that changes in the state of technology and economic leadership in one country may affect the 'independent variables' of the whole world. Various countries not endowed with large agricultural or mineral resources have been able to attain high levels of material welfare by developing an export trade — in specialized manufactured goods, for example — and by the provision of services such as shipping, banking and insurance. W. Hoffmann[20] shows that in England the industries oriented towards export (pig iron, iron products, coal, cotton yarn, and cloth) over the period 1813–1913 experienced a larger annual rate of growth than those industries producing for the internal market (sugar, bread and pastry, flour, and leather).

The integration of the economies of the colonial areas with those of metropolitan countries has likewise been a factor whose influence in improving the level of living in the more developed country has not been sufficiently investigated. A study by J.B.D. Derksen and J. Tinbergen[21] estimates that in 1938 Indonesia was responsible for 14 per cent of the national income of the Netherlands. But they point out quite rightly that this figure only imperfectly illustrates the stimulus which Indonesia gave to the Dutch economy. The pattern of world trade that developed during the nineteenth century — in which the more developed countries sold their industrial products and services against the raw materials of the undeveloped areas — has also been an important factor in the process of growth of the industrial countries. It is only now, when this trade pattern, with its underlying multilateral orientation and free trade philosophy, is in a state of transition, that its significance for the past development of western Europe, for example, is more clearly appreciated.

A small or medium-sized country with a limited array of resources seems to be particularly dependent on a favorable external climate for its economic development. The smaller western European countries with domestic markets too limited for large-scale industrialization were privileged in being surrounded by larger highly developed countries. The smaller countries were able to specialize in providing goods and services which larger countries did not produce themselves. At present the whole world is drawn into the process of development, and each country tries to set up its own industries, means of international transport and communications, and commercial services including banking, insurance, etc. The countries which are less affected by foreign influences, such as the United States and the Soviet Union, are in a more favorable position, but so far the smaller industrial countries, which have geared their economies to a world economy, have apparently not suffered from this new trend.

Clark has compiled an interesting table from the available material on the composition of the capital of various countries over a series of years. The table gives a schematic picture of the way in which continued accumulation takes place.

The accumulation of agricultural capital constitutes the first phase in capital formation, but this sector soon receives only a modest part of the further additions to capital stock. Adam Smith[22] had really a preindustrial society in mind when he observed: "According to the natural course of things, therefore, the greater part of the capital of every growing society, is first directed

TABLE 6. CAPITAL INVESTMENT PER WORKER IN VARIOUS COUNTRIES, BRANCHES AND PERIODS

Total capital investment in international units per capita of working population	Farm capital	Railways	Buildings	Industrial and commercial capital
About 500 (Japan, 1913, Sweden, Hungary, 1880)	100	50	100–200	100–300
1,000–2,000 (Great Britain, 1865–75; Ireland, Austria, Denmark, 1880; Hungary, Italy, Spain, 1913)	100–300	200–300	200–600	300–800
About 3,000 (Great Britain, 1885–1913; Germany, France, Sweden, 1913)	300–400	200–500	900–1,300	1,200–1,600
4,000–5,000 (United States, Canada, Australia, Argentina, 1913)	300–500	400–700	1,400–2,400	1,600–2,000

Source: C. Clark, *The Conditions of Economic Progress* (First edition, London: 1940), p. 417.

to agriculture, afterwards to manufacture, and last of all to foreign commerce." And "though this natural order of things must have taken place in some degree in every such society, it has, in all the modern states of Europe, been. . . entirely inverted. The foreign commerce of some of their cities has introduced all their finer manufactures. . . and manufactures and foreign commerce together have given birth to the principal improvements of agriculture." Railroad construction absorbed an important but not a preponderant share of capital during the second phase, but later took only a small portion of the total. In the 3,000 group, in the phase around 1913 in western Europe, the growth of industrial and commercial capital began to falter, and the flow of investment capital into buildings, particularly into housing, took first place.

In a study by the Netherlands Central Bureau of Statistics,[23] it has been shown that for six industrial countries over the period 1870–1910 the capital stock in industry showed the largest average annual growth. This was followed by railways in France, Sweden, and the United States, while in Germany, England and the Netherlands, the merchant marine took second place in rate of growth. In practically all these countries the annual population increase was larger than the increase in livestock or housing. The predominance of industrial capital is characteristic of the third phase of Clark. The historical data thus tend to suggest that in the past the investment in housing, particularly in the developed countries, lagged behind the investment in economic directly productive capital and economic 'overhead' capital.

This is probably due to the political weakness of the broad masses in the initial phases of development. It seems also to indicate that the provision of more adequate housing has, to a large extent, been a function of a higher consumption level. Investment in housing has apparently not been given a high priority because it did not augment national output in a visible and direct manner. For the United States, it has been ascertained that capital invested in agriculture, industry, and commerce fell from around three-fifths of total capital in 1850 and 1890 to around two-fifths in 1939 and 1948.[24] This also gives an impression of the significance of the increase in residential construction and durable consumer goods as categories of capital stock in a relative late stage of development.

Probably the underdeveloped countries will have to show a similar restraint in the construction of social 'overhead' capital, despite the "pressure of rising expectations" and the increase in political influence of the masses, if they are bent on maximizing investment leading to a higher rate of increase in output. In Mexico in the period 1939–50, investment in construction of all varieties represented 18 per cent of all investment, while in England in the latter part of the nineteenth century housing alone absorbed 22 per cent of gross domestic investment.[24] This rationing of social capital in total capital formation has also been hinted at for India. It has been estimated[25] for that country that a minimum standard of housing for the 41.4 per cent increase in urban population during the period 1941–51 (compared with an increase in total population of 13.4 per cent) would have required an investment of approximately one year's net national income. The impossibility of providing for such large investments is one of the reasons why the Indian Government in its Second Five-Year Plan will try to locate industry in smaller and medium-sized towns where the requirements for additional housing and public health facilities can more easily be met.

It would be inaccurate to infer from the above considerations that the growth of capital stock as a whole has been a continuous process in the history of the industrial countries. For England, Hoffmann[26] has calculated that between 1781 and 1931 the average annual rate of growth of industrial production was 2.8. From 1700 to 1781 it was only 0.9. From 1782 to 1792 it was between 3.0 and 4.0. Then a retardation appeared, probably due to the Napoleonic wars that lasted until 1817. From 1818 to 1855 the rate of growth was again between 3.0 and 4.0. From 1856 to 1876 it was only between 2.0 and 3.0; and from 1877 to 1933 it was about 2.0 (1923 to 1933, 1.2).

Hoffmann[27] also ventures an opinion about the causes of stagnation he observed in forty-two of the forty-five branches of production considered. Eighteen showed an absolute decline in production. He argues that the process of growth of an individual industry is a function of the 'developmental possibilities' of each industry and is independent of the time factor. Technical and financial factors plus external and internal competitive relations are, in his opinion, responsible for retardation or retrogression. That his inductions have any general validity remains doubtful. But it is probably true that most industrial sectors do not have an indefinite growth, and that such a growth is dependent on the elasticity or inelasticity of the demand for their products or services in a changing economy.

J. Schumpeter[28] has expressed his general ideas on the subject as follows: ". . . why is it that economic development. . . does not proceed evenly as a tree but grows but as it were jerkily. . . The answer cannot be short and precise enough, exclusively, because the new combinations (of factors of production) are not, as one would expect according to general principles of probability, evenly distributed through time. . . but appear, if at all, discontinuously in groups or swarms." The idea seems to be neither profound nor clear in the sense that it gives no clue as to why the growth of industry is uneven or taking place in clusters, but it shows how little is yet known about the growth process. It still remains to be shown how free play of market forces, resulting in changes in the price system and in the price-cost relationship in the private enterprise economies, continued to provide the incentive for investment for entrepreneurs in economic directly productive and 'overhead' capital. These changes have been ultimately responsible for the present status of the developed countries.

The Pattern of Industrial Growth

W. Hoffmann[29] has made a special study of diversification in the industrial structure during the process of industrialization. The first stage has been marked by the growth of consumer goods industries and the second by vigorous development of capital goods industries. In the third stage a certain equilibrium between the two types of industries is established, with the capital goods group tending to dominate. He has found, for a number of industrial countries, that at first the ratio between the net production of these two groups has been of the order of $5 \pm 1 : 1$, falling in the second stage to $2 \pm \frac{1}{2} : 1$, and to $1 \pm \frac{1}{2} : 1$ in the last stage.

In the United States[30] between 1850 and 1927, the share of consumer goods in total industrial production fell from 43.5 to 32.4 per cent, while the share of capital goods rose from 18.2 to 39.9 per cent. In Great Britain[31] between 1812 and 1924 this ratio declined from 6.5:1 to 1.5:1. In the Soviet Union,[32] which Hoffmann does not mention, the share of consumer goods is said to have fallen from 66.7 to 37.8 per cent during the relatively short time between 1913 and 1942, while the share of capital goods showed a corresponding increase from 33.2 to 62.2 per cent.[33]

As in the case of all aggregate analysis, such figures are not entirely free from objections, so that only a judgment on the general trend appears warranted. The process of industrialization has usually begun in the sphere of the consumer goods industries, more specifically those producing textiles and foodstuffs. These industries generally originate close to their sources of raw materials and labor — areas where the agricultural raw materials are cultivated, and labor, already skilled in arts and handicrafts is ripe for factory employment. Other reasons for the prior development of these industries are that their final products are already well-known, and the demand for them is extremely elastic following an increase of real income at the initial stage of development.

Heavy industry — iron and steel, metal ware, chemicals, machinery, and implements — has tended to develop in a subsequent phase, stimulated by the markets opened up by the consumer goods industries after the latter have reached a certain level of maturity.[34] The profits or surpluses from these light industries often provide the capital for the establishment of the heavy industries. When the demand of light industries will give rise to the erection of capital goods industries, it is hard to say as the changes in the structure of demand with rising real income are complex. For certain light industries there may be rather soon a relative stagnation due to the limited capacity of the human stomach and in general to the inelasticity of demand for basic necessities of life (food, clothing, etc.) after it has been satisfied to a reasonable extent. For example, in Great Britain the per capita consumption of cotton goods showed practically no increase between 1860 and 1913, in spite of the rise in real income.[35] However, consumer goods industries long remained predominant due to the high elasticity of foreign demand for the products of light industry. In other industrial countries, heavy industry came to the foreground much earlier. This, in some cases, can be explained by their possession of raw materials for the establishment of capital goods industries and in others by the nonexistence of handicrafts or cottage industries organized by middlemen.

More generally, the conditions under which agriculture or mining are practiced may form a stimulant for the domestic production of capital goods, such as machinery, chemicals, and railroad material. If real income keeps rising, new wants appear and durable consumer goods will become a substantial portion of consumers' expenditure, increasing the potential demand for capital goods. The development of capital goods industries may also be reinforced by the greater intensification of transport and communications as a result of industrial development. The growth in consumer goods and capital goods industries, and any variation in the rate of growth between and within these groups, is determined in any country by the elasticities of domestic and foreign demand and the changes brought about by rising incomes, factor endowment, etc.

The tempo of this development depends on both the material resources available to a country and the strength of the generating factor — leadership and organization — that brings about the strategic changes in the other factors of production. The United States, Canada, and Australia owe their rapid growth and high level of living primarily to the rather sudden influx of European immigrants. Already familiar with the Western pattern of society and means of production, they were confronted with a great abundance of virgin soil and other natural resources.

Representatives of the Soviet Union often assert that initial emphasis on heavy industry results in a more rapid transformation of the economy. This view, as expressed in the economic organs of the United Nations, may be motivated in part by propaganda purposes, but it is presumably also based on actual experience in the Soviet Union and in other centrally-planned economies. M. Dobb[36] has elaborated the argument that more capital-intensive methods of production are indicated for underdeveloped areas, as the higher productivity of such methods will lead more quickly to an increase in consumption. His model indicates that the volume of consumer goods will be larger once the more roundabout method of production has terminated its gestation period, but that initially the consumption level will remain lower than by using capital-extensive factor combinations. Theoretically, this reasoning has a certain validity, though it has naturally its limitation in view of the fact that capital is the factor in short supply in underdeveloped countries. One wonders too on what products such capital-intensive industries should concentrate and where they would find their markets.

In an annex to a study[37] by the Economic Commission for Europe, it is pointed out that steel industries in underdeveloped countries may show a tendency, arising from the technical and economic necessity of establishing plants of at least a certain minimum capacity, to increase their production more rapidly than the domestic market can absorb it. Export outlets have thus to be found for this surplus. Such outside markets may be difficult to locate as the production costs of such new ventures are generally higher than those of similar enterprises in older industrial countries.

Another difficulty is the relative amount of capital and the relative number of trained personnel required to manufacture more complex machinery and implements. Historically, it was precisely in the consumer goods industries of the now advanced countries that this additional capital was formed, and skilled labor trained, for future use in the capital goods industries. Dobb merely states that if the increase in capital-intensive industry is limited by the lack of qualified labor, this only proves that the training of a larger number of qualified workers is imperative for a development program. He does admit that the expansion of capital-intensive industries might remain limited unless there existed a cluster of complementary industries to provide the products and services essential to the operation of heavy industry. These practical difficulties are precisely the crux of the matter and show why it is so difficult for underdeveloped countries to apply the principle.

The ability of the Soviet Union and other centrally planned countries to make expansion of the capital goods sector their primary objective is connected with the already mentioned fact that in such economies demand and cost-price relations and private consumption are less important as determinants of economic growth than they are in private enterprise economies. By giving less attention to these considerations the planning authority can decide first what capital goods are to be produced and then the volume of private consumption allowable on the basis of this degree of capital formation. The Soviet Union was to some degree favorably placed for reorientating investment and labor toward the expansion of heavy industry. It had inherited from prerevolutionary Russia a sizeable industrial capital stock, an already highly literate labor force,[38] and a relatively extensive railroad network.[39] Yet the cost to the consumer was very high, apart from the sacrifice in human values which was and still is involved in its particular brand of planning. The example of the Soviet Union has certainly not proven that concentration on capital-intensive production methods leads to a higher rate of increase in mass consumption.

The above reasoning does not imply that underdeveloped countries can rely on the price mechanism and the resulting changes from present development for guiding their investment priorities. It is now admitted that governments in those countries, with their lack of external facilities and industrial environment, will have to start providing basic services — power stations, transport, etc. The capacity of these services may be beyond immediate requirements. Industrial plants, which at first have to be high-cost producers, may also have to be established to create conditions under which economic growth may be fostered. Such efforts may lead in the end to a higher rate of increase of mass consumption, provided they give rise to complementary investment and an increased capability to manage industrial undertakings. This method of initiating development is circumscribed by the amount of state revenue available for such purposes unless the government does increase its income by depressing the present consumption level, as so drastically occurred in the Soviet Union.

Hoffmann,[40] in particular, has pointed out the inequality of development or differential rate of growth among the various British industries and the sudden spurts of growth that especially characterized new industries. Among the consumer goods industries, the average annual percentage rate of growth between 1781 and 1913 was 4.0 for the cotton yarn industry, 3.7 for the paper industry, and 2.1 for the sugar industry. In the capital goods sector, the iron, steel, machinery, and building industries showed the greatest growth over this period. In the period 1855–1913 the high rate of growth of the aluminium, zinc, and rubber goods industries was striking. The rapid expansion of the electrical goods and automobile industries in the period 1922–35 was equally impressive. Hoffmann[41] points out, however, that the consumption of flour, beer, and spirits did not increase greatly from 1855 to 1913, implying that the rates of growth of these industries roughly correspond to the growth of population.

New industries meeting new demand or replacing the products of older industries by virtue of technological and cost factors, for instance the artificial silk industry, exhibited a relatively rapid growth. It is clear that in a private enterprise economy factors both inside and outside of industry make it necessary for the industrial leadership to keep adjusting to changing circumstances, whether of domestic or foreign origin. It may well be that an economy like that of the Soviet Union has to make fewer of these 'wasteful' adjustments. It should be stressed, however, that this implies the sacrifice, to some extent, of consumer sovereignty and individual freedom of economic decision, which are important elements in human welfare.

The theoretical problem as it was stated above is still oversimplified. Assuming the government to have sole responsibility for investment decisions, it will in any case have to undertake many projects at the same time. Given the relative scarcity of capital and surplus of labor the government will decide where capital-intensive and where labor-intensive methods of production are indicated. To bring new cultivable land into production tractors might be used and subsequently mechanized agriculture might be practiced. To improve irrigation in overpopulated rural regions labor-intensive means may be called for. Besides productivity, which is Dobb's only yardstick, the cost factor has to be considered and especially the effect of any investment on the employment level in the underdeveloped countries. It does not make sense to introduce mechanized rice cultivation in the main rice growing areas of China, India, or Indonesia unless jobs are available for the labor thus displaced. Such methods would also most probably decrease the yield per unit of land and thus place the government under an obligation either to import more food or to increase the acreage in other areas. These alternatives, as we have already seen, are not easily achieved in backward countries.

Although the relative abundance of labor and the paucity of capital place a premium upon the introduction of capital-extensive forms of production, the criterion for their application still remains the marginal social productivity of each factor. In other words, before each project investment is undertaken, it should be asked whether some other investment of a capital unit would not produce greater socio-economic advantages.[42]

It is not merely present marginal productivity that is involved, but that of the future as well. An investment that will lead to greater future growth in the economic structure as a whole is usually preferable to an investment that will yield a greater short-term increase of national product but will not stimulate additional activities. Unemployment of labor, whose cost of subsistence constitutes a fixed social charge, makes it desirable to attempt to employ it for capital formation, even if some other form of investment, using less labor, would yield a higher return. The technology to be applied should be up-to-date, that is, the combination of factors of production should be technologically and economically the best possible.[43] This implies, in general, that priority in an industrialization scheme should be given to those industries in which wages constitute a large part of the operating cost, and in which the share of domestic raw materials is relatively great.

Recently several efforts have been made to define more precisely than hitherto what has to be considered in choosing between investment alternatives. H. B. Chenery[44] has developed criteria covering capital intensity, effect on the balance of payments, and social benefit, which he has applied to the distribution of investment funds for the period 1949–50 in Greece, Turkey, Portugal, and Southern Italy. All three factors have to be weighed in conjunction in assessing the contribution of a particular investment. In agriculture and branches of industry processing domestic materials, an investment with low capital intensity is often associated with a high value of the balance-of-payments effect, an increase in exports, or a decrease in imports. In such cases the priority of the investment is rather easy to establish. Concentrating on investments with the highest rate of turnover on the capital invested, or with a low capital intensity, in other sectors, may lead to a slower increase in social product. Some of the natural resources remaining to be exploited (water, improvable land, chemical raw materials) require large capital outlays for their inclusion in the economic system. And labor-intensive industries in several sectors need substantial imports of raw materials, thus having an adverse effect on the future balance of payments. The social benefit concept he considers a necessary correction to the result obtained by using the two other criteria in order to rule out uneconomic employment of scarce resources. In applying his theoretical tools, he suggests that the capital turnover concept is most often neglected and the direct balance-of-payments effects frequently overemphasized, while the indirect effects are usually ignored and the concept of social benefit only recognized in the case of labor. In general, the governments tend to favor large projects over groups of small ones and to follow the line of development of older industrial countries, rather than a pattern suitable to their own resources. Chenery's analysis is rather involved, but the practical rules which he deduces seem obvious.

An interesting analysis of the industrial pattern of sixty-two different countries has recently been carried out by K. A. Bohr[45], using three indicators, capital, skilled labor, and plant size. He comes to the conclusion that new industries with the least need for capital and skill, and those which can most easily be organized in multiple small units, are most appropriate for most of the less developed countries.

It is open to debate whether applying input-output analysis to underdeveloped countries will give a more precise, quantitative indication of what industries to establish.[46] Through this method, precise knowledge is to be obtained on the requirements for capital, labor, and raw materials of each industry and sector relevant in the development program of a particular country, given its endowment with such resources, possibly through additional imports, to aim at a certain growth rate of the economy. The construction of such a growth model is necessarily complicated. It involves among other things, a selection between various methods of factor apportionment among alternative uses and rather detailed statistical and technical information of the economy in question. A useful purpose may be served by trying to procure more economic data as a tool for guiding investment decisions, but it seems possible that studies based on comparative cost, market, and family budget analysis could give a quicker and better result than the rather intricate input-output method.

At the present state of our knowledge, it seems appropriate for the economist to display a certain modesty in formulating investment directives. New industries or activities, not meeting the qualifications laid down by a rule-of-thumb method or a more refined analysis, can produce an unforeseen 'snowball effect'. This can stimulate national energy to such an extent as to more than compensate, by the advantages accruing to subsidiary and associated industries, for the initial irrationality or for the social cost. Investment implying the mobilization of resources over a period of time will always involve an evaluation of future development. Any external economies accompanying alternative types of investment can under any circumstances be compared only roughly. An estimate of the balance-of-payments effect remains beset by the uncertainties about the future development of export markets or of prices of imports.

The 'Handicap of an Early Start'

The Dutch historian, J. Romein,[47] has posed the paradoxical thesis that undeveloped countries, backward as they are in technology and organization, would have an advantage for precisely that reason when a new beginning is made. A similar argument can be found in the writings of other historians and economists,[48] but, as far as I know, only Romein has explicitly elaborated this line of thought. The technological examples cited by him are not convincing to the economist. He does not go deeply into the reasons why gas lighting still persisted in the City of London in 1924, while the streets of Amsterdam were at that time already lighted by electricity. He assumes, without further examination, that the initial forwardness of England, in this case of London, acted as a brake on the introduction of new developments in the field of illumination. He gives figures for coal production per man-shift in several countries[49] and believes that the differences can be explained by the fact that, as coal mining started later in the countries with a higher production, the seams were worked by better methods. No account is taken, in this reasoning, of differences in natural conditions of the coal regions or of the depth and thickness of the seams which are important in explaining any differential productivity, even aside from variations in coal quality and in capital investment per man-shift. These, and other technical conditions, are in fact responsible for the great differences in labor productivity between the various coal mining areas of the earth. They likewise determine the extent of mechanization possible.

This is not to deny that there is a kennel of truth hidden in Romein's trend of thought. We know in the case of Germany, for instance, that it skipped in its industrial evolution certain processes in iron and steel manufacturing still in use in Great Britain at the time and thus attained a higher productivity in this branch of industry. For Japan, too, similar examples have been reported for the textile industry, specifically in cotton spinning. In a United Nations report on the productivity of the textile industry in Latin America,[50] it is stated that one weaving mill in Brazil is using a shuttleless loom and that one spinning mill is employing a spinning jenny fed directly from the card lever, both processes still in the experimental stage in the United States. Such observations, however, are exceptional and probably have little significance for the condition of industry in the backward countries or for the industrializing country as a whole.

Japan and the Soviet Union are obviously, for Romein, typical examples of countries that were not bound to traditional forms of organization. They were, therefore, able to pass over the phase of the private entrepreneur in the process of industrialization and directly set up a form of organization more appropriate, according to Romein, to the economic and political configuration of the times. A more thorough study of the economic history of Japan and Russia teaches us that there was, in fact, nothing like 'skipping' in this evolution. The methods followed by Japan had been tried and tested in other countries in earlier times when they had no native entrepreneurial class. Russia, having already reached a certain stage of development, abolished the private entrepreneur on ideological grounds and succeeded in carrying out an accelerated industrialization without, however, proving in any way that state directed production is a superior type of organization. The real per capita income in the Soviet Union is still substantially lower than in western Europe, not to speak of the United States. Aside from this aspect, it should be observed that the Russians are pioneering too, and probably making costly mistakes that other countries may later be able to avoid. The sweeping statement of Romein:[51] "In Russia they were successful in breaking through the limits of capitalist society, not in spite of the socio-economic backwardness of the country, but precisely because of it, by virtue of the law I claim to have discovered, and which I have named the law of the 'handicap of an early start', or what amounts to the same thing, seen from the other side, the law of the 'premium on backwardness'", seems to be entirely unfounded.

Experience teaches that the relative backwardness of the economically undeveloped countries makes it especially hard for them, in their struggle for improvement, to break through the strong vicious circles in which they are caught. Though it may be admitted theoretically that a country which starts afresh with a clean economic slate, if there is such a thing, is potentially able to adopt the most modern methods of production, this is difficult to realize in practice. In this connection, it might be pointed out again that there is no single technique which is most suitable in all cases and that the introduction of machinery is related to the whole pattern of available production factors and their cost relationships within a country or area. In an area rich in coal, the use of coal burning steam locomotives may be economical, while diesel electrics may be more economical in other areas, irrespective of physical efficiency.

In underdeveloped countries with their usual labor surplus and a scarcity of capital, and the resulting relative cheapness of the labor factor, labor-intensive combinations of production factors are likely to be most appropriate, even though more capital-intensive combinations may be more productive per unit of capital. The idea that agriculture in undeveloped countries, for instance, would necessarily be more economical if primitive methods of cultivation were replaced by agricultural machinery has been refuted by Lossing Buck.[52] He calculated that the cost of tractor plowing in 1930 in China would have amounted to 10.43 Chinese dollars per hectare, while plowing with a team of water buffaloes cost only 4 dollars per hectare. The introduction of tractors does yield a considerable saving in time, but its use becomes economical only if the tractor can be used continuously for an adequate period throughout the year and the time thus saved usefully employed for other purposes. The low level of living, the paucity of capital equipment, and the small volume of savings tend to limit the quantity of production factors available for investment purposes, while the scarcity of trained workers and of qualified leadership often prevents the introduction of more complex and refined techniques.

F. R. Jervis[53] has most effectively indicated that Britain's early start is still an advantage. He admits that no country with an original lead in the process of industrialization is likely to maintain such a lead in all fields. Countries that have already accumulated a substantial capital stock, however, do possess a source of capital formation by way of earnings and normal depreciation for the construction of new industries or the modernization of old ones. The canals of Great Britain, for instance, however inefficient they became in a subsequent phase as a result of insufficient length and gauge, provided a surplus that helped finance the construction of the railroads. This argument also shows the false reasoning of T. Veblen,[54] who suggested that Germany was able to play so important a role in the world economy during the second half of the nineteenth century as the other more advanced countries were held back by the large amounts of capital in their old pioneer industries, which he regarded as a collection of technologically useless ballast. Another point in Veblen's argument, that the appearance of a rentier class may have slowed down progress in the originally advanced countries, has a certain validity. The initial lead can engender a certain conservatism and complacency among the leading group,[55] blinding them to new possibilities. This 'idealistic' interpretation of stagnation, however, is entirely different from the automatic, historical-materialistic vision postulated by Romein.

In Japan and the Soviet Union, leading classes had the opportunity to exploit favorable internal and external conditions to build up a great industrial structure. The explanation differs for these countries, as we shall show later, but this trend of thought, though less spectacular than Romein's, appears to be more in accordance with the truth. The countries now considered underdeveloped have technological and social rigidities of their own. These make it difficult to introduce the latest innovations and forms of organization and thus to skip unsuccessful and already obsolete techniques of the advanced countries. Incidental examples may be cited for the argument of Romein, but there are no countries whose experience confirms this thesis *in toto*. On the contrary, the general picture of their industrial structure is one of backwardness. H. W. Spiegel[56] shows that according to a 1939 census probably three-quarters of the industrial machinery operating in the state of São Paulo, Brazil, was more than ten years old or antiquated.[57]

The United Nations study on the textile industry in Latin America (referred to above) makes an interesting attempt to determine the causes of the low labor productivity of industry in Brazil,

Chile, Ecuador, Mexico, and Peru. Two groups of deficiencies are distinguished: the first related to the quality of the machinery, and the second to leadership and organization. The study bore out that the two groups of causes have about equal importance. The influence of equipment, mainly the use of old instead of modern equipment, causes the use of the labor factor to be 33 per cent higher than a calculated standard labor use (a theoretical index of labor consumption per kilogram of fabric of a factory with modern equipment, of an adequate size and with good management) in the spinning mills and even up to 164 per cent above this standard level in the weaving mills. These old machines operate below their optimum capacity, not only because of their technical obsolescence, but, equally important, because of inadequate maintenance. Frequently the machinery is also badly installed, the control of humidity in the mills is deficient or nonexistent, the mills are not well cleaned, and the quality of the yarn is not uniform.

In the enterprises equipped with modern machinery, the average number of workers is 54 per cent above the normal or standard organization, as defined above. This is mainly attributed to the lack of trained workers, although the quality of the yarn, lack of humidity control, defects in warp preparation and in the twisting and winding of the filling are also contributory factors. The backwardness of the textile industry, as far as equipment is concerned, is attributed primarily to the fact that since the development of the industry at the beginning of the twentieth century, the owners have had little incentive to modernize. The relatively low wage level does not always make it economical to replace labor by machinery, and the high tariff walls for textiles assure sales in the domestic market without danger of severe foreign competition.

We have quoted rather extensively from this report because we believe that the picture it gives is representative of the industrial problems found in several underdeveloped regions. This does not contradict the statement that, indeed, one of the most favorable factors for the undeveloped countries is that they do not necessarily have to go through all the economic and technological stages which the industrial countries followed. The underdeveloped countries have the potential advantage of being able to borrow the latest technical and organizational experience of the developed countries. The adaptation of such techniques and methods is not a mechanical transfer, however, but is, in fact, a human problem. The technical and economic capabilities of the industrial leaders and the entire socio-political milieu determine whether such a transfer of technology can successfully be accomplished.

The Significance of Small Industry in Industrialization

The considerations thus far presented have not taken into account the fact that, in Europe, the modern factory system had its inception in a decentralized, small-scale industry or cottage industry that was united and organized by tradesmen, who advanced materials and credit and bought the final product. The earlier handicraft enterprises, an integral part of a self-sufficient agrarian economy, were absorbed into a wide nexus of economic relationships. The manual worker did not have the temperament or disposition to perform the new functions now required of him, so these tended to fall into the hands of the middleman.

J. Schumpeter[58] cites Clapham to prove that in 1800 the ratio of workers to employers in industry and commerce in London was still lower than 2:1. Even at the time of the 1851 census of England and Wales, this ratio was only 8.3:1. In its more recent industrial development, Japan has shown a similar pattern. In the middle of the eighteenth century, the growing textile industry was concentrated in the villages, and iron and steel, plows, shovels, weapons, and ornaments were made for the most part in small workshops. Industrial development from the time of the Meiji Restoration (1867) did not replace this old structure, but it was intimately connected with it. In 1930, industrial workers totalled about 4.5 millions, and the proportion in small enterprises (employing less than five workers) has been estimated at about 53 per cent.[59]

In many undeveloped countries industrial activity is still mainly concentrated in handicraft and cottage industry.[60] The basis of this small-scale industry has already been substantially impaired by contact with the world economy.[61] In spite of the difficulty of building up a viable small industry, there are numerous advantages to beginning industrialization by the establishment of small-scale industries. The following table, worked out by P. S. Lokanathan,[62] for the textile industry, illustrates the possible significance of small industries in a developing industrial structure.

TABLE 7. CAPITAL AND LABOR INTENSITY AND PRODUCTIVITY IN THE INDIAN TEXTILE INDUSTRY

Mode of Production	Capital Investment per Worker (Rupees)	Production per Worker (Rupees)	Ratio of Capital to Production	Amount of Labor Employed Per Unit of Capital
1. Large-Scale Industry (Modern)	1,200	650	1.9	1
2. Small Industry (Power Loom)	300	200	1.5	4
3. Cottage Industry (Automatic Loom)	90	80	1.1	13
4. Cottage Industry (Hand Loom)	35	45	0.8	34

Small industry, according to this table, employs four times as many workers per unit of capital as large-scale industry. Its production per unit of capital is 23 per cent higher than in large-scale industry, though the yield per worker is 69 per cent lower. This table does not give an insight into the viability of small-scale industry, but in a more recent report by the Government of India,[63] it has been estimated that for 1948–49 the average productivity of a worker in a cottage industry was less than one-third that of a factory worker. Although his average wage was not much more than half that of the mill worker, the unit cost of production was substantially higher.

What is suggested by the above table for Indian textile industries at various levels of capitalization, applies *mutatis mutandis* to other branches of industry. Although the small establishments are in general less productive than the large ones, they require only a small outlay for buildings and much of their equipment can often be made from locally available materials. Since they provide more workers with employment, they are more effective than capital-intensive factories in drawing off the surplus labor from agriculture.

H. Belshaw[64] is a special proponent of the small decentralized industry approach to industrialization. He mentions as advantages: (1) no extensive transportation is necessary to establish them; (2) they do not assume the same mobility of the labor factor necessary for large-scale industry; (3) they can utilize seasonal labor; (4) less technical skill is required for small units; (5) technical leadership can be found more easily for small enterprises; (6) the distribution system is simpler as they serve a smaller market; (7) the tools and implements can often be produced locally; (8) local financing is more easily possible in view of the smaller capital required; (9) this form of investment may perhaps more readily wean the local capitalist away from his partiality towards land and buildings; (10) the sociological changes that accompany the establishment of large industries, such as urbanization, impersonal relationships, housing shortages, are less marked.

In connection with point (7), a hand-operated mechanical loom, improved in 1926 by the Textile Institute at Bandung, Java, is a good example. While in 1930, 500 of these looms were in operation, their number had risen to 50,000 in 1951. The productivity of the hand weaver increased five times. These looms could be made almost entirely from domestic resources, with the exception of a few imported inexpensive components, mainly from Japan.[65] Earlier industrialization efforts in Indonesia, incidentally, at the beginning of the twentieth century and in the 1920's, had failed because the market for the large industries then set up was too small, partly on account of the relatively high domestic transportation cost, so that the competition from abroad could not be faced. It must be added that the Netherlands Indies Government at the time did not apply protectionist measures for fear of impairing the market for Indonesian primary products in the industrial countries.

It is, however, no simple matter to put small industry on a basis that is economically sound, and above all, that meets social requirements. It is not primarily a technical problem, but a complicated socio-economic one. In the history of the advanced countries — and the pattern still fits many undeveloped countries of today — small-scale industry was organized by the middleman. He took all risks connected with the provision of raw materials, the granting of credit, and the marketing of the final products. The middleman could charge a high price for his services due to his quasi-monopolistic position while the poverty of the workers and the excess supply of labor kept the wage level down.

The long working hours and the primitive provisions for health and safety were notorious in these small-scale industries. Similar conditions now prevail in many of these industries in the undeveloped countries. However, governments finding these conditions incompatible with the spirit of the times, are presently attempting to guide the development of cottage industries along more socially accepted lines. The government has, therefore, to assume the same functions as the middleman and improve on them. The state must assure a regular flow of raw materials and make better tools and equipment available, if a standardized marketable final product is to result. Credits made available for this purpose involve the same difficulty that attends agricultural credit under such circumstances, namely that additional money will be used for consumption instead of productive investment. All this adds up to no easy task for the state with its weak and untrained administrative organization.

In programs of this kind the establishment of cooperatives is often recommended to foster initiative among the villagers and enable them to organize some of the above mentioned functions. It is thought by some authors[66] that cooperatives can be encouraged by appealing to the communal spirit that once existed or may still linger in the agricultural village society in many undeveloped countries. But they tend to forget that economic cooperation is a form of organization, developed in a society in which individualistic tendencies already exist and the people seek mutual ties to protect their own interests against the forces that threaten the individual. Technical abilities and commercially oriented attitudes have to be developed, especially among the leaders. Even then, there will be little chance of the old social bonds being able to protect handicraft workers in the agrarian village sphere against the economically superior power of factory manufacturers unless the government makes special provisions.

Small industry in the past, has always declined during periods of industrialization. Thus, in Germany between 1882 and 1925, the proportion of enterprises with one to five workers fell from 55.1 to 22.3 per cent of the total, while the proportion of enterprises employing over fifty workers rose from 26.3 to 54.9 per cent.[67] The improvement of transportation and the introduction of new machinery and equipment whose use is more economical in larger industrial units made possible by the extension of the market appear to have been mainly responsible for this development.

Japan has been held an exception to this trend. Apart from the lower wage costs and longer working hours in the small industries, it was argued that, with Japan's later industrialization, the provision of cheap electricity and the appearance of the electric motor and internal combustion engine placed it in a position to compete successfully with factory industry. Smaller enterprises also made possible a higher degree of specialization[68] and an easier transfer to new lines of production, especially in textiles, to meet changes in consumers' demand. The smaller industries, often located in the countryside and using seasonal workers, were also said to be in a better position to absorb the shock of a decline in domestic and foreign demand. The majority of the small industries were, however, really subsidiaries of larger enterprises; they were often either operated directly by these larger firms or subject to their control of prices and markets. The government had, moreover, assumed the control of output, price, and quality of a large number of products through the formation of associations of small industrialists.

Uyeda[69] claimed that the small decline between 1920–30 in the number of persons employed in enterprises with less than five workers from 55.6 to 52.9 per cent of all employees, showed the economic viability of these industries and the success attained by a conscious policy of supporting this form of organization. E. Reubens[70] has indicated that Uyeda's figures must have been incorrect. More recent information showed that in 1939 only 23.5 per cent of the industrial workers (out of a total of about 5 million) were employed in enterprises with from one to four workers. But 52.6 per cent of the industrial labor was concentrated in enterprises with from five to forty-nine workers. Although Reubens suggested that the postwar prospects for small industry were more favorable since many large industrial plants were badly damaged, capital was relatively scarce, and labor was more abundant, actual developments did not bear out this prediction. In 1951, 12.5 per cent of all employees in manufacturing were engaged in establishments with less than five employees and only 48.4 per cent in enterprises with five to ninety-nine employees.[71] Other reported figures indicate, in accordance with the experience in other industrial countries, that the downward trend in employment and output in small- and medium-scale factories in Japan was accompanied by a relative increase in employment and output of larger establishments. Despite the active postwar support again given by the government to small industry, because of its labor intensity, its influence seems to be waning. However, the importance of home and small industries is still a striking feature of Japan's industrial structure.[72]

Both cottage and small industries still appear to deserve prominent attention in any program of industrialization. In this way, labor and management are trained and the use of the scarce factor capital spread to offer maximum employment to labor which is in excess supply in many underdeveloped countries. This path is slow, strewn with economic, technical, and social obstacles, and may not initially give rise to impressive quantities of manufactured products. However, Burma, India, and Pakistan, for instance, have placed great emphasis on the development of small industries.[73] This approach seems now more difficult to follow as economic conditions, even in underdeveloped countries, often favor the expansion or establishment of large-scale production as far as the limited capital resources permit.

At the beginning of western European industrialization, the machinery was rather simple and inexpensive, and small industry employing it did not face any serious competition. Gradually, more productive and more costly machinery was invented, and the accelerated accumulation of capital led to the erection of larger factories using less labor per unit of capital. Small industry was in certain sectors displaced, but the general increase in wants and purchasing power made the absorption of surplus labor in new activities possible. In other branches of production, openings for new small-scale establishments arose due to the diversification in the demand structure and changes in price-cost relationships between small and large-scale industries.

In the underdeveloped countries, demand for manufactured products is largely directed to processed foods and textiles. The experience gained in the production of these articles in advanced countries has already become known in undeveloped countries. Thus, those trying to stimulate the growth of small industry, in those branches suitable to their wants, have to reckon with the fact that the gap in productivity between small and large-scale industries is continuously widening. Information on this point is scanty, but the protectionist measures, apparently necessary to promote small industry in undeveloped countries, seem to indicate that 'the penalty of being late' has risen and a greater effort is required from the start in any attempt to catch up with the advanced countries.

The underdeveloped countries are also handicapped because they cannot borrow for the improvement of small industries from the techniques and methods developed and now used in industrial countries. In the latter, the type of new machinery that is introduced is determined by the fact that capital resources are relatively abundant and labor relatively scarce, while opposite conditions prevail in the underdeveloped countries. This places on the governments of these countries the responsibility for initiating the necessary research on the technological and organizational level to raise the efficiency in small-scale industries and thereby reduce the gap in cost between those and large-scale manufacturing.

The difficulties of sustaining a small industry program have been frankly stated for India.[74] Handloom production declined from its prewar annual peak of 1,920 million yards to only 750 million yards in 1950–51. Although its share is now only one-fifth of India's cloth output, cottage weaving units still employ about four-fifths of Indian cloth workers. Though cottage industry, as we have already seen, is not competitive with factory industry, the employment aspect forced the government in 1950 to establish quotas for both the mills and handlooms. When the mills went beyond their target in 1953, a special tax was levied on the cloth produced by specific types of mills, and a system of penalties was introduced for excess production. These revenues were earmarked for assisting and developing the hand loom and the khadi (hand spinning, hand weaving) industries. The partial success of the scheme can be seen from the fact that output of handloom cloth increased to 1,400 million yards in 1954; production of mill made cloth was, however, 5,046 million yards in the same year. Similarly, the Indian Planning Commission has recommended that large-scale industry be confined to nonedible oils, that edible oils be processed at the village level, and that the huller type of rice mill be replaced as far as possible by traditional hand pounding. Such a reversal is not conducive to a maximum rate of economic growth, but it is socially necessary to prevent the too rapid dissolution of the traditional village organization with resultant unemployment. The future course would seem to be: (1) to modernize cottage industries or small-scale industry in general in order to raise their productivity and minimize the cost of keeping uneconomical, but socially advantageous, forms of production alive; (2) to expand more productive industrial and other activities outside the primary sphere in order to open up additional employment opportunities. Gradually, both types of industries may be complementary and competitive in the industrial structure.

In the Second Five-Year Plan (1956–61), small industries in India are apparently being given an even more crucial role.[75] Household and hand industries are assumed to be the only ones in a position to absorb a major portion of an additional 11 million workers (i.e., about 1.8 million per annum because of the normal growth of population and 0.4 million per annum of the unemployed workers over the plan period). They are to be given, therefore, the task of producing a substantial share of the additional consumer goods required to meet the increase in demand resulting from the investment expenditure of 56 billion rupees envisaged in this plan. An increase of 25 per cent in the output of consumer goods is planned. This entails a 20 per cent rise in factory-made consumer goods and a 33 per cent rise in non-factory consumer goods. A sum of 2 billion rupees is to be allocated to the small industry sector for this purpose, but it is admitted that rather little is known of the expansion potential of this sector. Besides the organizational problem of increasing the output of small-scale industries, it is realized that an intricate system of excise taxes and subsidies like those for cotton weaving will be required to make it possible for small-scale industry to face the competition of factory production.

Chapter 5

Labor

Population Increase and Economic Growth

The relation between population growth and economic development is complex and cannot be fruitfully discussed apart from other economic and social phenomena. The fallacy of Malthus' reasoning was that he assumed a simple relationship; an improvement in the level of living would lead to a faster increase in population than in food production so that the larger population would soon be brought back to its original, or even a lower, scale of living. Thus the world was considered doomed to support a maximum population at a minimum standard. This train of thought overlooked technological changes, among which the transport revolution made possible the opening up of new, more distant lands. It permitted simultaneously a rapid population growth in western Europe and a rising level of living.

Apart from the two variables — population and land (including other resources) — there are a large number of other factors influencing the situation. Moreover, population is not, as Malthus thought, exclusively a biological variable; it is intimately connected with a wide range of economic and social factors. The degree of economic development, for example, has had profound repercussions on birth and death rates and migration in various countries. It may be due partly to a realization of the complexity of population growth and its significance for economic development that the population factor has received so little attention from economic science in later years. Another explanation for this neglect may be that technological progress and the accumulation of capital in the industrialized countries has apparently been largely independent of population trends. However, it is possible that certain countries, for example, the Netherlands,[1] might have shown a greater improvement in the average level of living if they had had a lower rate of increment in population.

For a more realistic discussion of the relation between population size and resources, the concept of productivity is a useful means of allowing for some of the other production factors — capital and leadership, for example — that affect the relationship. By itself, however, this innovation does not advance theory much beyond the idea that an optimum population is that population which, given certain quantities of other factors of production (land, other natural resources, status of technique, capital, and organization) will give a maximum output.

Economic development is probably never directly influenced by population growth, nor has population increase alone determined the rate of economic progress. Viewed historically, economic development seems always to have been the result of many forces, either encouraged or checked by the growth of population, mainly through its effect upon the rate of capital formation. One can imagine a primitive agricultural society in which population growth is accompanied by a parallel extension of the area under cultivation. The addition to the labor force, usually about 35 to 40 per cent of the population increase, proportionally increases the capacity to produce more food and other goods to maintain the existing per capita level of consumption and the required level of investment to provide implements, housing, etc. However, as soon as land and other resources become scarcer in relation to population, the effects of diminishing returns set in as a consequence of the more intensive application of labor. With a continuous population increase and unchanging resources and techniques, the marginal productivity of labor will gradually decline and may lead to a situation in which the last unit of labor working on the land will fail to produce its own sustenance. The term 'underemployment', used to describe such a situation, implies that the withdrawal of part of such labor will not affect output.

The above description fits, more or less accurately, the economies of a number of underdeveloped countries. In some of them absolute overpopulation may exist, in the sense that output per capita would be greater if the population were less. Given the manner in which resources are currently utilized, capital scarcity and deficiency in organization, the spurt in population growth experienced by most of the undeveloped countries in recent years, places some of the more densely populated ones in a serious position.

The development problem of the backward areas has led to a revived interest in the Malthusian aspects of the population question. In these areas the average death rates are already equal to those prevailing at the beginning of the twentieth century in the industrial countries while their average birth rates are still at a height encountered in the developed countries in the eighteenth century. Such a spread between birth and death rates implies that economic development in the undeveloped countries generally must proceed at a much faster rate than occurred in western Europe. The question of whether the much greater reservoir of technology and organization from which the underdeveloped countries can borrow will more than compensate for the more rapid population growth is unanswerable for the moment. We can only reiterate that the larger amounts of goods and services needed by an increasing population require an acceleration in the rate of capital formation and technological progress. As indicated earlier, the rate of capital accumulation depends first upon the availability of resources, in the form of productive land, minerals, sources of energy, and so on, and secondly upon the volume of savings that can be generated. The latter may require a reorganization of production, so that a larger proportion of resources can be devoted to capital formation. It is evident, however, that the ability to increase capital formation is also related to the quality, age structure, and rate of increment of the population.

As a result of undernourishment, lack of training, and illiteracy, the population in underdeveloped countries is less effective as a labor force than it might be. To raise efficiency, the food situation has to be improved and expenditure for education increased. Many of these countries are also handicapped in their development efforts by a heavy 'youth dependency'. The proportion of children under 15 years of age is generally 40 per cent or more of the total population in backward countries compared with 22–30 per cent in industrial countries. This age structure causes an unfavorable distribution between producers and consumers and partly explains the high ratio of consumption to output and the small margin of savings in their economies. Since this age structure is usually the result of a high birth rate and a relatively high death rate among children, it also entails a considerable waste of economic strength, which a poor country can ill afford.

About India, D. Ghosh[2] has written: "First we nurse, feed, clothe, house, and train every batch of newly born population to lose 45 per cent of them before they reach the age of sixteen at which they can make any contribution to national income." His statement is still applicable to most underdeveloped countries although the recent decline in death rates, which is due to improvements in public health, has diminished this waste to some extent. However, the accelerated population growth that results from a drop in the death rate will have no substantial effect on the proportion of economically active workers in the total population. It will only tend to increase absolutely the number of active workers and — in so far as sickness is reduced — their ability to work. To translate such an increase in potential labor force into productive power requires a concomitant increase in resources and capital.

The acquisition of additional resources and an increased rate of capital formation are circumscribed by the fact that, as a result of past population growth, the density of population in several underdeveloped countries is already much larger than in some industrial countries in their corresponding phase of development. The following table bears out his point.

Though such density figures should be interpreted with care since they are averages and, in any case neglect potential trade

TABLE 8. DENSITY OF POPULATION PER KM²

Industrial countries — Eighteenth century		Underdeveloped countries — 1953	
Belgium	93	Egypt (inhabited area only)	630
Netherlands	61	Puerto Rico	253
Italy	56	Ceylon	124
United Kingdom	54	Haiti	116
France.	48	India	113
Germany	44	Philippines	70
Switzerland	33	Indonesia	54
		China	48

Source: A. Sauvy, "Théorie Générale de la Population" (Paris: 1954), p. 221; United Nations, *Demographic Yearbook 1954.*

and industrial development, they give some indication of the problem that faces certain countries. A further population increase is especially burdensome for these densely populated countries because 60 to 80 per cent of their population is occupied in agriculture, and it is in this sector that a higher density of population usually results in diminishing returns per laborer. Colin Clark[3] has reached an optimistic conclusion about the world's capacity to feed an increasing population on the assumption that the present annual increase in world population as a whole is only 1 per cent, while, as a result of technological progress in agriculture, the annual rise in world food output amounts to 1.5 per cent.

The United Nations Population Division[4] now estimates that world population increases at a rate of 1.7 per cent per annum, but even if Clark's assumption were correct, his generalization overlooks the fact that in some of the countries threatened with a higher than average rate of population growth no increase, or only a slight increase, in food production is at present being realized. It is usually the industrial countries with their lower rate of population growth that have shown a higher than average improvement in agricultural productivity. His thesis, if correct, could thus be used to emphasize the accentuation of inequality in the distribution of world income.[5]

Even before World War II, the death rates in many undeveloped countries were already lower than in industrial countries in the middle of the nineteenth century; the 'natural checks' —

epidemics, famines, floods, etc.— to population growth had already been reduced by the introduction of public health measures, evolved in industrial countries. Recent advances in medicine have substantially increased the possibility of lowering death rates in backward countries, irrespective of major improvements in standards of living. In Ceylon, for example, the average death rate stood at 20.3 per 1,000 in 1946, or about the same level as in the preceding fifteen years; but by 1953 it had fallen to 10.9 per 1,000, largely as a result of an antimalaria campaign using insecticides such as DDT. Similar instances and figures can be found in other undeveloped countries. There is a real danger that intensified contact with western technology — so necessary to stimulate economic growth — will reduce the death rate still more before economic forces are sufficiently developed to allow a corresponding expansion of productive capacity. This is one of the liveliest issues among social scientists.[6] A League of Nations publication[7] referred in this connection to the risk of a false start — meaning that new impulses from modern knowledge and technology threaten to increase the population as fast or even faster than the national product. On the other hand, it is difficult to see how such a possibility can be arrested. It is hardly feasible to hold up the introduction of death-reducing methods in underdeveloped countries. The subtle distinction that is sometimes made between sanitary measures beneficial only to health — which would contribute only to a higher productivity of labor — and measures affecting mortality directly, appears impossible to make in practice. Furthermore, it would seem that no government can afford to ignore the comparatively inexpensive means of death reduction. The activity of the World Health Organization, which continually spreads medical knowledge to backward areas to combat epidemic and debilitating diseases, is helping to make methods of lowering death rates more generally accessible.

In western Europe during the industrial transformation the spurt in population increase due to the fall in the death rate gave no cause for anxiety because of the space still available within the region, the 'safety valve' afforded by the opportunity of emigration to north America and elsewhere, and the industrial development which absorbed the increase in manpower. In addition, the expansion of agricultural imports from these new areas facilitated the feeding of the growing population. After a time lag, the birth rate also began to drop, at first because of the later age of marrying, which often reflected longer periods of education, and later because of the control of sex life (conscious limitation of births).

In Great Britain the fall in the birth rate did not begin until a century after the decline in mortality had begun. In Japan, however, a fall in natality set in about sixty years after 1860, when Japan commenced its modern development. In certain European countries that started their industrialization considerably later than England there was a shorter span between the beginning of a decline in mortality and the beginning of a decline in fertility.[8] G. F. Winfield[9] has based an optimistic prognosis of future development in China on the possible shortening of the period between the drop in death rates and the drop in birth rates. Although no country has yet attempted to check its population growth while industrializing, he believes that, because countries with a later start can draw on a far greater amount of available technological knowledge, they may be able to bring the birth rate under control earlier. In the case of China, he believed that if all existing checks on population growth remained intact and no additional public health measures were introduced before popular information on methods of birth control had been disseminated, then almost the entire population increment could be absorbed by industry, trade, transport, and other services during a program of rapid industrialization.[10] Though aware of the difficulties involved in modifying individual, family, and community morals in this respect, Winfield thought that there was promise of success on the basis of an experiment carried out by a clinic at Tinghsien (Hopei) before World War II.

Until recently there were no signs that the government of mainland China had taken any of the recommendations of Winfield and others to heart. On the contrary, public health facilities were expanded to the extent that it was reported[11] that China's population increase had risen to 2 per cent per annum. There were some individual expressions of apprehension about the present rate of growth. For instance, Shao Li-tzu, one of the deputies of the National People's Congress, referred to the necessity of setting a limit to population growth "in an environment beset with difficulties" and called for a campaign to spread medical theories and provide practical guidance on birth control.[12] The official view apparently remained that economic organization must ensure that any increase in population is more than compensated by a rise in production. However, since 1955 the burdens of bearing and rearing children to future mothers and the country have been realized. A legal basis was prepared to permit not only contraception but also abortion and sterilization. In August 1956 an intensive campaign was launched to extend knowledge to reduce natality.

In India, D. Ghosh[13] has urged a new sexual morality for his country — a morality sanctioning birth control by contraceptive means. And the government of India[14] is now making a conscious attempt to check population growth in order to ease the task of improving individual welfare. The government has pledged itself to help disseminate information on family limitation and has already instituted research on inexpensive and effective methods of birth control for all classes of the population. In spite of this development in India, and a similar awareness in Egypt, for instance, of the danger of population growth, it will probably take several generations before the effect of any measures that may be taken, will be felt. K. Davis,[15] who was familiar with the prevailing ideas in India on the subject, closed his chapter on fertility in his book as follows: "All told, the observer inevitably reaches the melancholy conclusion that an early and substantial decline of fertility in India seems unlikely unless rapid changes not now known or envisaged are made in Indian life."

So far only Japan, already industrialized, has succeeded in deliberately reducing fertility rates. The crude death rate, which in 1920–24 and 1935–39 averaged 23.0 and 17.4 per 1,000, respectively, was only 8.9 in 1953. This decline was largely the result of improvements in public health instigated by the occupation authorities. On the other hand, the birth rate soared from 23.2 per 1,000 in 1945 to 34.3 per 1,000 in 1947 as a result of the return of emigrants and soldiers. The fall in the death rate occurred in spite of the general decline in the scale of living compared with the 1930's. The "Council for the Population Problem", established in April, 1949, drafted the Eugenic Protection Law which was adopted by the Diet in June, 1949. It provides for clinics to disseminate birth control information and authorizes sterilization for hereditary reasons and abortions for economic reasons. The number of abortions performed under this law is estimated to have been around 1 million in 1953, a fact which was largely responsible for the drop in the birth rate to 21.5 per 1,000 in that year. This method of birth control is deplored in Japan as elsewhere, but reports concerning the slow spread of contraceptive methods indicate that even in a literate country educating peasant women in this respect is a long-term process.

The foregoing analysis applies particularly to countries that are poorly endowed with resources in relation to the size of their populations. It is evident that, in countries with a favorable population-resource ratio, a stagnant or only slowly rising population and labor force may be a disadvantage as far as economic development is concerned. In view of the lack of information regarding the resource potential of the underdeveloped world, it is difficult to place any particular country in one or the other of these categories. Even if it could be ascertained that a country belonged to the densely populated group and another in the sparsely populated category, a high rate of population increment in the latter country might impede progress more than in the former country because of a varying capacity to acculturate technological innovations in the economic system.

In any event, the development of the economically backward countries will not be influenced immediately by the potential population growth; probably a higher rate of population increment will be accompanied by greater efforts or exhortations to that effect. Even those countries, where there exists no fundamental religious or ideological objection to measures to bring down natality, would like foremost to see a vigorous attack made on those forces which inhibit economic development, since enhanced capital formation will in any case equip them better to provide for a growing population. Moreover, they can point out that economic development is a prerequisite for the strengthening of those social factors that are most likely to lead to a future decline in the birth rate. Since a drop in the birth rate would decrease the growth rate of consumption and increase the proportion of active workers to total population, it would thus become easier to obtain the volume of investment required for a quicker rise in output. Given the general desire for advancing consumption levels, the successful introduction of methods to spread knowledge of birth control would no doubt facilitate economic development in certain areas.

Such a two-pronged approach is made more necessary by the fact that the possibility of emigration from those underdeveloped countries that are afflicted with excessive populations seems at present to be extremely limited. Though a demographer from India[16] has proposed that north America, south America, and Australia should be opened for emigration from China and India, he must have been aware of the numerous political and social obstacles to such a movement at the present time. Even with a more appropriate political climate the cost of movement on the scale necessary to relieve the population pressure in those countries would probably be prohibitive. A more modest outflow would have an insignificant effect on the future population. Hence, if rising levels of living are desired, progressive economic development policies must be pursued.

Whatever the possibilities for the expansion of agriculture, it seems certain that the transfer of both population increment and surplus labor from the agricultural sector to other economic activities should be one of the primary objectives of economic policy.

Changes in the Occupational Structure During Industrialization

Opportunities for emigration have been substantially reduced, since the world has no more virgin areas that can be placed under the plow without great capital expenditures. There is also a greater awareness of the difficulties involved in the economic and social integration of newcomers in a receiving country, and the governments of those countries that still have room are anxious to control the inflow of immigrants.[17] Thus, except for free land that may still be available and agricultural productivity that can be raised, only industrialization, in the broadest sense, remains as a possible means of raising the level of living.

Generally speaking, the percentage of active workers in backward countries tends to be somewhat lower than in more developed countries, partly because of differences in age composition of the populations. To give an example: in 1950 economically active persons numbered 39.1 per cent of the total population in India, compared with 46.2 per cent in the United Kingdom. In India in 1951, 38.3 per cent of the population was under 15 years of age compared with 22.5 per cent in the United Kingdom. The important difference between the economically active population in the undeveloped countries and in the industrial ones is, however, that in the former a preponderant proportion is occupied in agriculture. Colin Clark has shown in chapters IX and X of his work, *Conditions of Economic Progress*, that the most significant phenomenon accompanying economic growth has been the transfer of the working population from agriculture to industry and from industry to commerce and services.

In all countries with a relatively high level of living, a comparatively small fraction of the population is occupied in the so-called primary sphere of production, namely agriculture, animal husbandry, fishing, forestry, and hunting. In the United States this percentage fell between 1820 and 1920 from 72.3 to 27.6 per cent and in 1950 to 11.7 per cent.[18] As a result of development there is an increase in the percentage of the population employed in secondary branches of production — mining, manufacturing, building, construction, public works, gas, and electricity supply. After a certain growth this percentage has remained fairly constant in some countries or has even shown a tendency to decline. In the United States the proportion of workers in this sector rose from 12.1 per cent in 1820 to 30.3 in 1920 and to 36.0 per cent in 1950. The fact that the increase in this group is tending to level off is due to the increasing dependence on complementary services — transport and distribution — of this sector of activity and to the relatively growing inelasticity of demand for its products in a highly developed economy.

There may be considerable variations in this respect among advanced countries, but Clark[19] has pointed out that the demand for manufactured goods, which comprise the bulk of the production of this branch of activity, tends to reach a maximum level at about 20–25 per cent of the national income. On the other hand, countries with a high level of material well-being are supposed to exhibit a long-term increase in the tertiary production sector, which includes all other economic activities — commerce and finance, transport and distribution, government administration, professional services, domestic and personal services, and the like. In the United States, this group made up 15.3 per cent of the economically active population in 1820, 39.5 per cent in 1920, and 51.8 per cent in 1950. The great elasticity of demand for the services of this sector during an increase in national income is partly attributed to the fact that such services must be performed by local workers and cannot be imported.

The explanation for these changes thus lies on the side of demand as well as on the side of supply. When the average real income increases, the proportion of it devoted to products from the agricultural sector declines largely because of an inelastic income-demand for food — considering the natural limitation of the human stomach and the limited range of products from agriculture as compared with those from the secondary and tertiary sectors — although the absolute expenditure for such goods may well continue to rise. It has been found[20] for the United States that the per capita demand for agricultural produce increased

22 per cent between 1870 and 1930, while the demand for industrial products increased by 450 per cent during the same
period. However, recent investigations have shown, even for
developed countries, the inaccuracy of the general proposition
that the income-elasticity of demand for food is less than unity,
or that demand for food does not rise proportionally with a rise in
real income. For certain commodities, — beans, flour, potatoes,
— this ratio may be low, but the demand for meat, vegetables,
and fruit is more elastic. The fact that food expenditures in backward countries, absorbs 60–80 per cent of family income, given
the low nutritional level, means that every increase in income is
first translated into an increased demand for cheap food. We
shall return to this aspect of the situation in our discussion of the
consumption pattern.

Since the products of industry normally have a greater income-
elasticity of demand, these branches of activity tend to offer labor
a higher remuneration when the general income level is rising.
This encourages the outflow of workers from agriculture. Technological improvements in agriculture have made it possible to
produce the same amount of food, or even more, with less labor,
but this outward flow has, even in many industrial countries,
been too slow to prevent periods of agricultural depression.

The attraction of the higher reward in the other sectors of the
economy naturally exists in the undeveloped countries as well,
but up till now the outward movement has not assumed any progressive momentum, since the economy as a whole does not exhibit
a dynamic character. V. K. R. V. Rao[21] estimates that in 1931–32
the average annual income of the workers in agriculture in India
was 86 rupees, in industry and mining 192 rupees, and in commerce and transport 305 rupees. For other countries similar data
are available,[22] but it is difficult to decide whether the difference
in nominal or money income also implies a difference in real
income. The cost of living is higher in the urban centers where
industry and commerce usually are located, but it may be assumed
that the relatively higher wages offered by industry and commerce form an indication that the training and schooling required

in these branches command a premium above labor in agriculture. The margin for unskilled labor cannot be very great
because of the relatively limited demand for industrial labor in
the undeveloped countries and the fact that the overpopulation
in the agricultural sector exerts a downward pressure on any
earnings deviating from the subsistence level.

It should be pointed out here that more important than the
financial and economic factors, which exercise an attraction to
workers to transfer to more productive occupations, are the social
forces. In the end social considerations play a significant part in
determining whether the worker prefers to remain in the countryside or to move to the city. Not only unfavorable conditions in
the rural sector, such as the decreasing size of family holdings,
soil exhaustion, but also the loosening of family and village ties
and of the bond with the land, influence the decision to make the
change. For many underdeveloped countries, descriptions can be
found of the psychological obstacles to the transition to new and,
in pecuniary terms, more rewarding occupations.[23] However, it
is not the lack of mobility and lack of response of the workers to
new employment opportunities which are the main causes for the
slight diversification in their occupational structure which the
backward countries show. Rather it is the want of technological
change and the deficiency in indigenous entrepreneurial and
organizational talent, able to bring about an improvement in
traditional methods of production, which is primarily responsible
for the slowness of industrial growth. This lack in dynamic forces
explains why, in India, where between 1910–51 the population
increased from 235.5 million to 356.9 million, — a growth of 52
per cent — in 1910, 71 per cent of the active population was
occupied in agriculture, husbandry, forestry, and fishing and in
1951 this proportion was still 68.1 per cent. Also, in other undeveloped countries, despite a certain amount of industrialization, the overwhelming weight of the rural population has tended
to obscure whatever change the economy may have undergone.
In Egypt the percentage of working population in the primary
sector declined from 1919–49 only from 69 to 66, in Mexico over

the same period from 64 to 61, and Turkey even had an increase from 82 to 85 over the period 1938–49.

Moreover, not every relative increase in the secondary and tertiary sectors is necessarily sound economic growth. An increase in the working population in commerce, banking, etc., in spite of the higher productivity of this sector in current money terms, may reflect a less productive investment pattern brought about by a process of inflation rather than a change to be greeted with jubilation. A large portion of public employees may be a sign of a deficient government administration or a lack of alternative employment possibilities. A relatively high percentage of workers in tertiary economic activities in underdeveloped countries is also often an indication of an unequal income distribution resulting in a relatively large quantity of personal services which the wealthy class can afford. This points to the fact that one should be careful in using the modification in the tertiary sector as a measurement for economic progress. P. T. Bauer and B. S. Yamey[24] have argued, on the basis of conditions in West Africa, that linking relative increases in tertiary employment with economic development is untenable, largely because the distinction between tertiary and other activities in underdeveloped economies is almost meaningless. Many farmers, or some members of their families, spend part or most of their time in transport or trade, and such intricacies are often not registered. The objection does not seem entirely valid, since the fact that those different activities are not specialized or defined as separate occupations is itself a sign of underdevelopment.

An underdeveloped economy is precisely an economy characterized by a limited division of labor, which implies that many persons perform a great variety of functions which fall to some extent in all three categories of employment. It must be admitted, however, that the tertiary group consists of a collection of heterogeneous activities which are often poorly circumscribed in underdeveloped economies, or are included in this category because of its character as an assembly of nonagricultural and nonindustrial workers. Perhaps if some refined distinction is made between services (1) directly bought by consumers (professional, personal, domestic services, and recreation), (2) facilitating the movement of goods through space and time (trade, transport, and finance), and (3) performed by the government (administration, education, social welfare, police, and postal services), and international standards established for this purpose, certain comparisons may become more illuminating.[25] Such comparisons should naturally be weighed in the light of other information on the changes in the structure of the economy.

The trend in the classified occupations may be very different in various countries, depending upon their status of development, factor endowment, and income distribution. It is perhaps indicative of the difficulty of keeping the tertiary sector separate from other activities, that Colin Clark,[26] when stating that the demand for services in the most advanced countries may rise to 70 per cent or more of the national income, includes also in this group building, handicrafts, and the products of small-scale manufacturing, which actually belong to the secondary sector.

It is customary to regard Adam Smith's distinction between productive and unproductive labor[27] and between capital and revenue — so defined that capital maintains productive workers and revenue unproductive workers — as antiquated. Yet his arguments appear remarkably up-to-date for the economies of the backward countries. There the accumulation of capital is a particularly slow process, partly because, among the minority able to save, a substantial part of their revenue is dissipated in the consumption of articles and services which do not contribute to economic development.

Considering as productive all work that contributes to the production of commodities and services that satisfy human wants is, perhaps, a conception that should be revised. On a physical or biological level, groups of needs can be classified according to their degree of urgency, therefore it might be appropriate to regard work directed toward the satisfaction of the primary needs of life as more 'productive' than work involved in the production of luxuries. The price system, as a reflection of the marginal utility attached by society to the priority of the needs filled by particular commodities and services, is often an indicator of a direction of resources not conducive to economic growth. Such an interpretation of the price mechanism introduces a value judgment which might become less and less tenable as the scale of living rises. For a poor country, however, this interpretation would justify conscious intervention to have the remuneration awarded to different kinds of work more clearly indicate their significance for a better allocation of resources.

The Training of Labor

There are no inherent differences of quality between the labor factor in undeveloped countries and in industrial ones. "The denunciations of the 'luxury, pride, and sloth' of the English wage earners of the seventeenth and eighteenth centuries are, indeed, almost exactly identical with those directed against African natives today. It is complained that, compared with the Dutch, they [the English workers] are self-indulgent and idle; that they want no more than a bare subsistence and will cease to work the moment they obtain it; that, the higher their wages, the more — 'so licentious are they' — they spend upon drink; that high prices, therefore, are not a misfortune, but a blessing, since they compel the wage earner to be more industrious, and that high wages are not a blessing, but a misfortune, since they conduce merely to 'weekly debauches'."[28]

This train of thought — that workers in backward countries are characterized by a certain lack of wants — is found also in mercantilist theory, which held that an increase in wages would lead to a decrease in the amount of work performed and that a decrease in wages would serve to encourage acceptance of longer working hours. For workers at a low income level who have no alternative employment, this inverse elasticity of supply does have a certain validity. However, once the laborers have reached a higher level — the definition of high and low obviously depending on many factors — this tendency ceases. "It appears there-fore, that between Eastern and Western mentality, so far as it represents the typical attitude of the workers in the pre-capitalist epoch, there is no fundamental difference. In both cases. . . it is the subsistence motive which determines the relation to work. The aversion to any unnecessary exertion. . . and the readiness to while away the greater portion of the day in idleness and torpor. . . is an expression of the same difference of values as that which divid-ed the mediaeval world from that of the twentieth century."[29]

The worker in the undeveloped countries is, for the most part, untrained and unschooled. But experience has shown that he can even master relatively complicated techniques. Compare, for instance, the description by American J. L. Keenan[30] of the training of workers in the iron and steel industry at Jamshedpur in India. An industrial engineer of the Lever soap factory at Jakarta reported to a United Nations economic mission that the average efficiency of the Indonesian worker was not much differ-ent from that of the European working in a European plant. For some operations, such as hand packing, the accomplishment was even higher, but for heavy work it was lower, as a result of phys-iological differences and the need for longer rest periods on account of the climate. The fact that the mental activity and intelligence of the Indonesian workers appeared to be lower than that of the European, was probably due to the lack of schooling. As a result, the organization of the work makes greater demands on the supervisory staff. Therefore, the selection and training of foremen was considered a greater problem in the Indonesian factory than in a similar European enterprise.

Scarcity of trained labor imposes a severe limitation on any development program. In most underdeveloped countries it is aggravated by the low educational level of the population as a whole.[31] For this reason, the fight against illiteracy through mass instruction is usually emphasized as an important part in any development program.[32] It might be recalled here that the older industrial countries — France and Great Britain,[33] for example — still had a large number of illiterates, even after considerable progress in industrialization. On the other hand, the quick transformation of Germany and Japan has sometimes been ascribed to the provision for general education for the masses of the people.[34] The two types of experiences are not necessarily incompatible. On the contrary, they point to the conclusion that education should be in step with economic development.

In many underdeveloped countries worsening conditions in the countryside have already led to a blind drive toward the cities. This is also one of the results of the attraction of the cities as places where the paraphernalia of a more sophisticated culture are on display. Although in the industrial countries such a movement seems to have been accompanied by new economic opportunities, migration to urban areas in the backward countries often precedes economic growth. Therefore, in addition to a modest program of general education it seems most important to emphasize vocational and on-the-job training in factory and office. This program might stimulate, and be stimulated by, the introduction of technological innovations. It would require enthusiastic leadership to take the initiative in such a reorientation. The difficulties to be overcome are much the same as those faced in the West during the rise of capitalism. They include the transformation of a rural subsistence population into an efficient group of industrial workers, involving, among other things, the introduction of regular working hours and labor discipline.

A study by the International Labour Office,[35] reported that the turnover of Iranian workers at the Anglo-Iranian Oil Company in 1948 amounted to 20 per cent of the labor force. This cannot be considered particularly high if the following considerations are kept in mind: that industrial work at Abadan and other oil installations is still largely considered temporary, that the laborer plans eventually to return to his tribe in the hills, that the climate in the oil region is unfavorable, and that the worker, after training, can often command a higher wage in other industries.

The regularly published figures on absence from work in India[36] (in the form of a ratio of manshifts lost due to absence to total man-shifts scheduled to work) show a range from 10–20 per cent, depending on the branch of industry and the state. The causes for absence are given as sickness, leave for social and religious reasons, and other personal reasons. Introduction of a bonus for regular attendance is often recommended to combat such absenteeism, but in some countries, an especially large turnover occurred at the payment of the bonus. The large turnover and the high absenteeism are signs that the worker still has his roots in a traditional economic and social organization and has not yet experienced a sense of belonging in his new environment.

The government evidently has a heavy responsibility for the transformation and reeducation of the labor force. The disruptive tendencies and maladjustments that are likely to appear because of the need for a different social behavior appropriate to factory production have to be countered by a reorientation of the value system. The development of new loyalties and the provision of security and advancement for those able and willing to undertake new obligations must be consciously fostered to compensate for the human values lost in the transition. The small margin between national income and total consumption and the need for greater capital formation in undeveloped countries make it desirable that underemployed labor should be engaged, if only for increasing the capital stock. Roads, railways, irrigation, and flood-control works can, for example, be built at relatively slight expense by enlisting underutilized labor either on a voluntary basis or in return for a small wage.

It has been calculated for the United States, where the high wage level encourages mechanization, that the cost of machinery amounts to only 15 per cent of the total cost of road building and to only 12 per cent for construction in general.[37] The ratio between capital cost and total cost may not be the same in underdeveloped countries, in view of the lower wage level and the higher price of capital prevailing there. But it may be assumed that projects of this nature are eminently suitable for public work programs, especially since they can often be coordinated with seasonal variations in the supply of agricultural labor.

In certain countries the army, especially the engineering corps, has been used for constructing such facilities. It has been re-commended for India that a "national labor force" be organized under the Second Five-Year Plan. The force would withdraw a significant number of workers, unemployed and underemployed, from the distressed areas of the country and mobilize them to undertake certain projects under the Plan. This labor force apparently is viewed as a revolving organization for which new recruits would be called up as required. Such a youth conscription, undertaken to enhance capital formation, may also help to depress the birth rate by delaying the time of marriage for part of the male population.

There is at least one important difference between the working class in undeveloped countries today and their counterpart in the Western world a century and a half ago. The aspirations of the former rapidly turn toward the living standards that characterize the wealthier countries. Through modern means of communication they see and hear of the multitude of material gadgets inseparable from the scale of living in the developed countries. In countries that have not yet evolved an industrial structure the real cost of such amenities is extremely high, and the desire for them can only be satisfied piecemeal to the extent that national output expands. The trade unions in poor countries stand in the forefront of this movement. Their demands and expectations remind one of the revolutionary spirit of the workers' organizations of the mid-nineteenth century in western Europe.[38] Such demands do sometimes seem out of keeping with the situation of their societies, however. Because of the unionists' action, and also because of a more developed social conscience, working time has been regulated in practically all underdeveloped countries and numerous social provisions — prohibition of child labor, limitations on women's work, and insurance against accidents, disability, sickness, unemployment — have imitated corresponding legislation in industrial countries.

Nevertheless, in many of the less advanced countries, because of inadequate inspection and enforcement, conditions in shops and factories still leave much to be desired. The United Nations

Mission to Bolivia reached the following conclusion: "It may be doubted whether all this legislation has resulted in any real improvement in the worker's standard of living, whether it has contributed to the formation of an efficient labor force, and whether it has brought about any increase in the productivity of the country's industries." This may also be applicable to other backward countries. These measures, regardless of their implementation, are an expression of the state's intensified sense of responsibility. However, by increasing operational costs, they tend to narrow the margin of profit from which further industrialization might be financed.

One of the steel factories in India has reported that the action of the trade unions is responsible for low productivity because it compels the enterprise to engage 60 per cent more labor than is technically warranted.[39] Similarly, it is stated that the trade unions in the Latin-American textile industry[40] often resist improvement in the organization of enterprises, in so far as it involves any reduction in personnel. These attitudes are explained by the limited opportunities for alternative industrial employment in these countries. Moreover, some of the laws in these countries tend to encourage restrictive tendencies. A Mexican law of 1912, for example, prescribed that a textile worker should not tend more than eight cards, although the introduction of a few technical changes made it possible for one person to tend forty machines. If the mill owner makes the required technical modification, he is obliged to pay the card-tender five times his previous wage, and indemnify the four discharged workers. The report of the International Bank for Reconstruction and Development on Cuba[41] gives several striking examples of the adoption of standards common in more advanced countries without regard to the state of the economy in which they are to be enforced. Workers may be protected by this type of legislation, but only at the cost of holding back technological progress.

The productivity of labor is not determined exclusively by the performance of the workers; the degree of mechanization and the efficiency of organization are at least as important. The last mentioned factors are conditioned by the existence of an entre-preneurial class imbued with a spirit to do things differently. The complaint has also been voiced in Western society that the attitude of the workers sometimes puts a brake upon the intro-duction of innovations that may be harmful to labor in the short run. But it is clear that a similar behavior on the part of labor can be less afforded by underdeveloped countries in which a new technological climate has still to emerge.

It is impossible to weigh, in quantitative terms, the influence of Western patterns on the attitude of labor. Higher aspirations are a condition for economic progress. On the other hand, if demands are set too high they may defeat their purpose. Foreign enterprises in backward countries are often particularly susceptible targets of labor infected with Western ideas. Although they usually pay more than the local wage, they are reproached because wages in their country of origin are still higher. They are criti-cized for not giving enough opportunities for the advancement of native workers — sometimes rightly, but sometimes regardless of the capabilities of the labor force. Even if promotion possibilities are offered, the speed at which such openings are made, is scoffed at. Laborers in foreign-owned companies, because of their higher level of living, their concentration, their closer association with thoughts emanating from the outside world, are often the most articulate spokesmen of nationalism. Their claims thus tend to transcend a simple conflict between employer and employ-ees. They become a demonstration of a country's awakening to the fact that part of the profits from exploitation of its natural resources are accruing to foreigners.

It is interesting to note that conflicts between management and labor were given as the reason for the action taken by the govern-ments of Mexico and Bolivia in expropriating certain foreign enterprises.[42] Regardless of the justice of their demands, irre-sponsibility of laborers in foreign companies tends to deter other foreign capital, which might play an important role in training workers in modern industrial techniques, from entering certain undeveloped countries.

Chapter 6

LEADERSHIP AND ORGANIZATION

Leadership and Environment

L eadership is only a more specialized form of labor, but owing to its exceptional importance in the development process it deserves separate discussion. In this chapter it is grouped with organization, since the factor of leadership expresses itself in part in the creation of new, and the transformation of old institutions — in industry as well as in government.

In popular discussion, the higher levels of living found in industrial countries are often attributed to the intelligence, energy, enterprise, and perseverance manifested by a relatively small group of leaders. Economists may have contributed towards this oversimplification of an essentially complex problem, since factors such as population (size, age, occupational composition, geographical distribution), natural resources (quantity, quality, geographical distribution), and institutional structure (form of government, legislation, technology, status of science, and education) are usually taken as data, while economic leadership often is regarded as the generating force which introduces change and progress into the process of economic growth. Leadership, however, is to a large extent a product of environment and the social and other mores that are subject to change in the process of growth, but which also exert their own independent influence upon this process. Mainly on the basis of a comparison of Great Britain and the United States, G. C. Allen[1] has come to the conclusion "that while material progress is affected by numerous circumstances, it is fertility in resource and imaginative enterprise which lie at its root. I suggest, therefore, that the capitalization

of industry is a function of enterprise, and that the higher productivity which the extensive use of capital makes possible,
depends ultimately on the supply of entrepreneurs." This is
typical of the economist's viewpoint.

This question should be approached historically. How did
economic life in a small number of countries become so much
more dynamic than in the rest of the world? We know that at a
certain stage in the private enterprise countries it was mainly the
profit motive and the expectation of profit that led many of those
with initiative to develop their exceptional gifts. But what
favorable conditions were present and what unfavorable conditions absent, to place entrepreneurs, "the individuals whose
function it is to carry out 'new combinations of means of production' "[2] in a position where they could find full scope for their
abilities? Very little systematic research has as yet been done on
the social conditions that rendered possible the development of
such individual initiative. There is abundant information on the
characteristics of the entrepreneurs and the talents with which
they were endowed, but this gives only half the picture. It is
difficult to imagine that similar qualities were not present in other
cultures as well. What is needed is an explanation of how the
peculiar social and economic environment in the Western world
enabled those particular traits of character to assert themselves.

This is a field for the economic historian, but a few economists
have set forth their ideas on the problem. A. Marshall[3] attributed the dynamic development of western Europe to such factors
as (1) temperate climate, which stimulated a greater physical
and mental effort than the tropical climate in which many of the
primary necessities of life are more readily available, (2) the
technical conditions that existed during the breakdown of the
feudal system, (3) the breaking through the crust of custom during
the Renaissance, and (4) the Reformation's emphasis on the
personal responsibility of the individual. He also mentions the
widening of the mental horizon aided by the discovery of the sea
routes to America and India; the labor discipline, which was
already implicit in the feudal system; the medieval and later

urbanization, which brought new classes into the foreground; the conflicts involving Spain, Portugal, France, Holland, and England for economic resources and other advantages. All these elements helped to shape the pattern of development.

In England, where the industrial revolution had its first triumphs, there were other factors that helped to create a different economy. The custom of primogeniture, which denied younger sons rights to landed estates and forced them to seek their own fortunes; the early introduction of money rent in agriculture; the inflow of immigrants, mostly French and Flemish; the very advantageous maritime trade, which brought the 'undertaker' to the fore as organizer of the production of manufactures; the invention of steam power and machinery that made possible the factory system, and the gradual abolition of restrictive regulations in the fields of trade and guild organization are some of the factors enumerated by Marshall. The relatively flat surface of England, which facilitated the solution of the transport problem, the discovery of coal and iron, and a far flung colonial market, in which industrialization was at first repressed for the benefit of industry in the mother country, must also be considered as factors in this development. At the same time, England's isolated position encouraged an undisturbed industrialization at a time when many parts of western Europe lacked political stability.

For Germany, Schumpeter,[4] *inter alia*, has shown that the state had to take the initiative in the first attempts at industrialization. His explanation is that the Thirty Year's War (1618–48) had exhausted the country to such an extent that private initiative could not mobilize the material or intellectual strength to get the process started. In effect, the development had its roots in the social strata that provided the personnel for the public administration. "Those entrepreneurs were public servants and acted by virtue of official appointment, but both in type and behavior entirely conform to the idea of a 'captain of industry'."[5]

Japan showed a similar pattern.[6] Once the goal of industrialization had been set in order to keep pace with the West, the limited capability of the existing mercantile and industrial class and the general shortage of capital forced the state itself to assume the role of entrepreneur. New enterprises were established and placed under state supervision until they could safely be turned over to private entrepreneurs.[7] The leading classes took a prominent part in this process; the samurai and nobility placed their energies and talents at the disposition of state and industry. Prince Shimizu, the Lord of Satsuma, was the pioneer in the cotton industry. He bought shuttles in Great Britain and built his mill in 1867. In 1865, Mampei Kashima, president of the guild of cotton goods wholesalers, established a cotton mill at the order of the Tokugawa shogunate, and it commenced production in 1872.[8] Among the 'Zaibatsu', Mitsui, Mitsubishi, Sumitomo, and Yasuda were commercial houses that had originated in feudal times.[9]

The genius for adapting Occidental technology to a feudal society, the rapid acquisition of knowledge, and the reorientation of attitudes involved were the most striking features of this development. We know too, that Japanese industrial development was stimulated by the Russo-Japanese War, and by the disappearance of effective competition from the other industrial countries in Asian markets during World War I. Later its imperialistic foreign policy brought the additional foodstuffs and raw materials necessary for continued industrial growth into the sphere of influence of the mother economy. The aggressive sales policy of the Japanese contributed at the same time toward the conquest of markets that had previously seemed reserved for the older industrial countries.[10]

In this respect the pattern followed by Russia[11] seems to have been far more gradual. As early as the time of Peter the Great (1689–1725) a number of large-scale state industries had been established, some of which were purchased by private interests at a later stage. This development was followed by the establishment of industries on the estates of nobles throughout the eighteenth century. From those 'estate' factories, household workshops originated. There, persons trained in the factories taught

their acquired skills to members of their families. With the eman-
cipation of the serfs (1861–65), of which the avowed purpose was
to make every peasant a landowner, a large number of the 'estate'
factories disintegrated, though some were sold to private entrepreneurs. The household workshops, however, expanded and
many industrial workers formerly engaged in 'estate' factories
organized themselves under the leadership of a headman in
associations that undertook temporary work in cities or places
where the headman had concluded contracts for specific projects.

The industrial revolution came to Russia in the latter half of
the nineteenth century when, aided by a high tariff, new factories
arose and railways were built, thus stimulating the export of
grains. It has been estimated that at the beginning of the twentieth century between seven and eight million industrial workers
were engaged in home industries compared with three to four
million in factories. Though the stimulant to this development
came from the influx of foreign capital and skills, a substantial
group of native entrepreneurs was responsible for the spurt in
growth until 1914. The 1917 Revolution probably resulted in less
cleavage and change than is commonly imagined. Dobb[12] states
that in 1914, 53 per cent of all Russian factory workers were
employed in plants with over 500 workers, while in the United
States this percentage was only 31 at that time. What was new
in the subsequent state-directed planning was the concentration
on industrial growth regardless of social obstacles.

We have already referred to the policy of controlling the output
of the agricultural sector and obtaining surpluses for the industrial
program. Similar methods were pursued in bringing the material
resources of the still underdeveloped regions of the Soviet Union
within the orbit of the new Soviet economy. W. Wilhelm's[13]
description of the extension of cotton cultivation in Soviet Central
Asia, which was undertaken in order to reduce dependence on
imports, shows that such "elements of culture as religion, family
organization, economic arrangements were fitted on the Pro-
crustean bed of the Soviet state". The increase in cotton output
paid, according to Wilhelm's estimate, for all imports the region

required to carry out its development, so that net capital assistance from the outside was probably zero. This example helps to explain Soviet insistence that capital formation can be increased rapidly without foreign aid through the reorganization of production. But as M. Holdsworth[14] has observed, writing about the same area, "the Central Asian republics [though]. . . successfully developed as part of a greater whole. . . have not been the arbiters of this development or of the price they had to pay."

Leadership in the Underdeveloped Countries

There can be no doubt that another disadvantage that undeveloped countries face is the lack of a class of dynamic leaders, that is, a true creative minority, to use Toynbee's terminology, which supplies the stimulus and impulse to the process of development. It is hard to lay one's finger upon the precise differences between the economic spirit (*Wirtschaftsgesinnung*) of the Occident during its industrial rise and that which prevails in the economically backward countries.[15] Differences in the pattern of utilizing resources — in the West, e.g., industrial pioneers made use of newly formed capital to expand production still further, while in the East the capital so acquired serves to expand personal consumption — is to some extent more effect than cause.[16] In a primarily agrarian society, where large landowners set the social pattern, there is strong opposition to changes whose repercussions on vested interests cannot be gauged.

A remark made by K. Davis[17] about India is also applicable to other countries: "Many would like to see India a wealthier nation, but not at the expense of their own relative wealth. Many would like to see India an educated nation, but not if it includes the lower castes. . . Many would like to enjoy the privileges of climbing socially, but not at the extension of that privilege to persons beneath themselves." This fear of change is, in part, realistic since the forces conjured up will undoubtedly tend to dissolve or weaken existing family and village relationships and will thereby undermine the foundations of traditional society.

The underdeveloped countries of today remind us of the earlier times of the industrial countries, when exponents of the ideas that ushered in the Industrial Revolution were forced to make their way against the stubborn opposition of an agrarian and feudal society. The opposing groups continued for a long time to live in different philosophical worlds. On the one hand, the court and landed aristocracy "remained more or less frivolous and licentious, but the middle class and some part of the working classes adopted a severe view of life. . . and had a high standard as to those material comforts which could be obtained only by unremitting, hard work."[18] The peculiarity of this middle class was not its status as capital owners or as risk bearers, for those functions are also borne by traders in underdeveloped countries. But it was the role of the middle class as managers and coordinators of new activities that constituted the decisive break with the past. These people were uniquely the practical executors and adaptors of the technological innovations, and their cultural norms coincided with their economic inclinations.

In some undeveloped countries, the literary culture that is still dominant is perhaps the foremost obstacle to incorporating the fruits of Western technology into their societies. Not long ago it could be said that "China is a country in which literary scholarship has enjoyed for many centuries exceptional prestige. . . The belief that to write words on paper is to perform an act seems to be almost ineradicable. The result is that policies too often end where they should begin, with the assertion of intentions."[19] Though mainland China now shows a particular eagerness to adopt Western techniques, the statement still has a certain validity for other countries. In several undeveloped countries also, a feeling of superiority on the part of the intellectuals, who could develop talents for organizing technical and commercial enterprises, impedes the introduction of modern methods. These intellectuals often seem to view such innovations as the products of an exclusively technological spirit, something like "the products of automatons, that are able to turn out huge quantities of uniform products", as one of my Latin-American friends has put it. They do not possess adequate understanding of the cultural source from which this technical civilization flows. They contrast the character of their cultures, which, they say, is based on humanity, justice, and morality, with that of an industrial civilization, which they term scientific, utilitarian, and materialistic. By thus labeling the spirit of industrial cultures they prevent themselves from realizing the value of rational thinking, of the mastery of nature, and of the 'divine discontent' with things as they are that are embedded in such cultures.

It is this attitude that makes many of the brightest intellects choose the study of law, the liberal arts, or at best medicine, when from an economic point of view, it would be more beneficial to their countries if they became engineers or technicians. Even in the industrial field this behavior lingers on. In China and India, foreign technicians have repeatedly observed how academically trained personnel refuse to perform manual labor, and thus prevent the knowledge they have acquired from being transmitted to others. In certain countries there is also a preference noticeable among the intellectuals for occupations holding out prospects of government employment. Such an 'obsession with security' is usually an indication that the spirit of enterprise has not been highly developed. In some societies the economic aspects of life, the desire for bettering material conditions, the amassing of wealth, have often had a low place in the hierarchy of values.

None of the traits mentioned above have remained untouched by recent political changes and the much closer association between nations in the postwar world. Everybody coming in contact, for example, with inhabitants of undeveloped countries that were formerly under colonial rule, will be struck by the difference in behavior today. Less inhibition about expressing desires and ambitions, more enthusiasm, initiative, and energy can be noted. Though it is still too early to appraise the ultimate significance of such modifications for the development of these countries, they are signs of the latent human resources which have hitherto remained unutilized.

In the Western countries, many are inclined to think, because of their history, that a greater scope for individual freedom is an essential condition for economic growth, or that economic development, with its corollary of wider educational opportunities, will lead to forms of government similar to those evolved in the West. But Japan and Russia have shown that Western technology can also be grafted on other cultural patterns. The attraction of the examples of Japan and the Soviet Union to the intelligentsia in some parts of the underdeveloped world, in which the value of the individual personality tends to be subordinated to that of the state or the group, lies perhaps in the fact that these countries were able to take over the technical features of the West and create forms of organization particularly their own. With the disintegration of old values already occurring in many countries, and the adaptation required to integrate new techniques and organization methods, it is hard to predict in some cases what pattern of government will ultimately emerge.

The Significance of Foreigners

Reading the economic history of industrial countries, one is invariably struck by the influence of foreigners on the acceleration of the economic process of growth. They have usually brought fresh ideas into the country, which in many cases was characterized by a relatively immobile structure. Thanks to the prestige that surrounded them as foreigners, they were often able to realize goals that native technicians could not attain on their own account.

Marshall[20] points out how, under the patronage of the court, immigrants in the fourteenth and fifteenth centuries taught the English population how to weave (the cloth was still being sent to the Netherlands, many years afterwards, for processing!), how to cure herring, reel silk, and make lace, glass, and paper. On the other hand, in the period 1750–80, Englishmen (or Frenchmen who had come to England for study) helped to introduce factory spinning and weaving of cotton into France.[21] In Russia, the cotton industry was modernized by a German (Ludwig Knoop) who went there in 1839 to buy yarn for an English firm, and instead built cotton-spinning and weaving mills with the aid of English carders, spinners, weavers, foremen, and assistants, whom he imported. The railroads in Russia were constructed almost entirely out of foreign material, mostly from France, until in 1871, an Englishman (John Hughes) was granted special privileges for the construction of iron foundries. After the English came the Norwegians, and later the French and Belgians, who contributed greatly to the industrial development of Russia.[22]

Japan followed a somewhat similar method of attracting foreign technicians. In addition, it sent its promising young people abroad with specific instructions to learn technical practices in the types of industries that it desired to encourage in Japan.

We have already pointed out that the United States, Australia, and Canada owe their high material welfare partly to the fact that immigrants, imbued with Western economic ideas and techniques, found themselves confronted with undeveloped natural resources. The environment, too, less bound in the 'cake of custom', afforded opportunity for the freest possible development of these resources. Europe probably still presents more institutional obstacles (survivals of outmoded social structures) to economic development than do these new countries. It manifests more conservatism, both with respect to labor and in the sphere of ideas. And there is not the same preoccupation with a continuously rising level of living that animates state, entrepreneur, and worker in the United States, for example.

In the foregoing, we have merely touched on the process through which various economies were energized in the nineteenth century and earlier by an ever-extending international movement of goods, persons, and capital. The aid from foreigners usually meant the transfer not merely of technical knowledge, but of foreign capital at the same time. This knowledge and capital were not made available with the development of the recipient countries in mind. Both technician and capitalist were attracted primarily by a compensation greater than they could command in their native land.

Historically speaking, this transfer of more highly qualified labor led to an enormous increase in labor productivity that would have been unattainable by the unaided power of the countries involved. The self-interest of the owner of capital, in whose wake the technician usually journeyed, was the dominant factor. This caused leadership and capital very naturally to attempt to create conditions as favorable as possible to their objective — profit — in the country of their activity. They exacted special privileges, for instance, extraterritoriality in China or were able to put through institutional changes, such as the conversion of communal lands into individual property. It was this tendency that was responsible for the establishment of colonies and the growth of the phenomenon known as imperialism.

It would, of course, be an oversimplification to attribute the whole process to this cause. It must be pointed out that in many of the highly developed countries of today, foreign leadership and capital did not have to demand special advantages but were instead offered inducements to settle and establish new industries. In the course of time native groups, spurred by the example of foreigners, developed their own talents and then sometimes opposed further concessions to outsiders.

In industrial countries foreign elements have often identified themselves with the country to which they migrated, partly because the spiritual climate they helped to create made them forget their earlier environment. It was especially in those countries which have remained underdeveloped that foreign technicians and capital often had to force their entrance. The reasons why quick adaptation in the backward countries was not forthcoming are rooted much more in indigenous psychological factors than in the conservatism of the foreigners, though they are always likely to defend privileged positions they may have obtained. In these countries, Western enterprises remained enclaves and gave rise to the origin of a dualistic economy, a modernized sector separated by a wide gulf from the traditional methods of production. In this connection it may be observed that in several undeveloped regions new activities have *mirabile dictu* been undertaken by citizens of other backward countries who have retained their original characteristics and are only partly assimilated in their countries of settlement. The enterprises established by Chinese in south-east Asia, by Lebanese and Syrians in Brazil, Colombia, etc. are examples in point.

The time now appears to have passed when highly developed countries shared their technical knowledge and capital with the less developed exclusively through private investment and the search for profit. The underdeveloped countries, conscious now more than ever, of their backwardness, desire to receive 'unattached' technical assistance and capital in order to direct the development of their country according to their own views. This aspiration, prompted by an intensified national consciousness, reflects the contemporary ideal of equality — transposed into the international sphere — implying that every country should have the same opportunity for full development of its resources and should receive adequate compensation for its contributions to the world economy regardless of present differences in economic well-being. Recognition of the justice of this aspiration, plus the interest of the advanced countries in an expanding world economy, with the broad masses of the population in backward regions exercising a greater purchasing power, constitute the foundation of technical aid programs that have been developed in the postwar period. Many of these programs, set up either by bilateral arrangements or under United Nations auspices, are still in *statu nascendi*, or are in such an early stage of execution that little can yet be said about their long-range results.

These programs take the form of: (1) the dispatch of experts to advise governments on specific technical problems, (2) visits by personnel from underdeveloped countries to the advanced countries to learn how organization and efficiency in specific fields can be improved in their own countries, (3) the establishment of regional schools or courses where nationals of neighboring countries are taught how specific administrative, economic, and financial problems can be tackled, and (4) the provision of equipment for the establishment of pilot plants or projects in order to show by actual example how new techniques can be integrated into the underdeveloped economies.

One of the unavoidable drawbacks of these technical assistance programs is that aid is given only on the basis of formal application from the needy countries. In many cases, such countries are only dimly aware of their own needs. Moreover, the government concerned is naturally free to decide whether to carry out or to lay aside recommendations made by visiting experts. The archives of the governments of the backward countries are already bursting with experts' reports on plans that were considered urgent at one time or another. The inactivity of government amid this *embarras du choix* can have many reasons, but one of them usually is that it is either politically or administratively powerless to execute such plans in a competent manner.

Now that colonial rule is outmoded and private foreign investment less important, there is another possibility, namely, that an organization such as the United Nations places internationally recruited civil servants at the disposal of governments to help them carry out development programs. The United Nations' report of the mission to Bolivia remarked, in this context: "Whatever the priority today, governmental weakness and economic debility form the two segments of a single vicious circle; each supports and contains the other."[23] The mission then proposed that the United Nations "assist the Bolivian Government in obtaining the services of a number of experienced and competent administrative officials of unquestioned integrity drawn from a variety of countries, and that the Bolivian Government appoint these officials on a temporary basis to positions of influence and authority as integral members of the Bolivian civil service."[24]

This form of technical aid, which placed foreigners as officials in executive positions in the government, was rendered by the United Nations in 1952 upon the request of the Bolivian government, but it is still too early to express a judgment on the ultimate results of this step. However, it would seem to be one of the most promising forms of technical assistance. It might lead to the establishment of a permanent corps of international civil servants, who, given the power of world opinion behind them, might be able to give valuable guidance to governments.

The future will tell whether this idea is feasible. For the moment the amount of money involved in these bilateral or international aid agreements is so small that only limited benefits can be counted upon. Another weakness is that the technical assistance programs of the United Nations and its specialized agencies are not associated with means for capital financing. Therefore, plans drawn up with the aid of foreign technicians are not necessarily backed up by the financial resources required for their realization. This drawback applies with less force to the aid programs of the United States government, to the Colombo plan or to the International Bank for Reconstruction and Development whose activity is often a mixture of technical assistance and the furnishing of funds. They will be further discussed in chapter 16.

The Significance of Government

Government is, in a certain sense, the instrument through which the leading classes in a country exercise power. The aggregate of social values and objectives, the strength or weakness of those strongly interested in development and those that are indifferent or even hostile to it, the changes in spiritual orientation and motivation of these groups, are all reflected in the policies adopted by the government.[25] This political factor is another aspect of the industrialization process that economists tend to neglect.

In its evolution as a centralized instrument of power, government has had a significance that is difficult to overestimate in the history of the industrial countries. It has accomplished political unification, reduced regionalism and localism, standardized systems of weights, measures, and currency, provided mass education, built roads, ports, etc. and has thereby created the conditions under which potential economic development can become a reality. The most important contribution of the state has perhaps been its creation and maintenance of a stable political, social, and administrative framework, within which economic development could take place. The government has also been a source of encouragement — in the roles of financier and guide for the transfer of resources to the most desirable goals — functions that have varied according to time and place in accordance with the political tradition and social mores of the society.

In England, the concern of the state made itself felt at an early stage, above all by the encouragement of maritime trade. As a result, the process of industrialization was left to private initiative. "The explanation (for the absence of government activity in industry) lay in the fact that England was an international world power while the other countries were working out a national economy which England had outgrown."[26]

An important instrument in the process of industrialization by which many countries have found their places in the economic sun was the tariff system — the manipulation of import and export duties. "In the United States an almost prohibitive tariff, put on during the Civil War and reinforced at intervals in the 'eighties and nineties' helped that country to attract capital and utilize its immense resources."[27]

The state was not merely an instrument of power, for it also constituted a rallying point for the enthusiasm and energy that accompanied successful industrialization. Marshall[28] realized this clearly in discussing the rapid industrial rise of Japan, when he wrote: "Their quick rise to power supports the suggestion made by the history of past times that some touch of idealism, religious, patriotic or artistic, can generally be detected at the root of any great outburst of practical energy."

Native authors in the underdeveloped countries appear to feel the necessary connection that exists between politics and economy. The following quotation[29] is a good illustration of the spirit that imbues the Herodians among them: "We must become the first industrial country of South America. . . [This] principle points the true path of future destiny. A country without its own

industries is destined to end up as a colony of countries more industrialized than herself. It is manufacturing industry that gives
the tone of progress. To possess natural riches, whether agricultural or mineral, amounts to nothing if the country cannot or
does not know how to transform them. The mere wealth of
materials without an industrious and intelligent population is
rather a danger than an advantage. A people which is not
capable of producing its own machinery, motors, tools and arma-
ments, has no right to call itself independent."

The development of an awareness of backwardness among broad
strata of the population, an awakening of national pride, and the
will to change seem indispensable to economic progress.[30] But
they are naturally insufficient by themselves. Illustrative of this
is a description by L. H. Hughes[31] of the work of the missions in
Mexico in the field of health services, agriculture, housing, art,
and literacy, inspired by the revolution of the 1920's. The goal
was set too high, the means remained primitive and naive, and
the results were poor, reflecting, *inter alia*, the insufficient education and training of the mission personnel and the stubborn traditions of the Indians. Economic development remains a long-
term process, hence there arises the necessity of sustaining the
motivation for positive action. An idealistic spirit is not enough.
The teachers involved, as found in Mexico, may all too soon be
attracted by other, more lucrative, activities.

The absence of an entrepreneurial class must itself cause the
government to take a hand in the beginning of industrialization.
The government has to assume the role of educator in industrial
activities, not only by setting up schools, but also by attracting
foreign experts and by sending suitable nationals abroad for
training. And where the climate for private investment in industry does not attract the individual entrepreneur, the government
may find it necessary to provide the funds and management for
new industries to be established. The time factor — the need to
catch up and keep up with the economies of the advanced countries — may also compel state intervention especially where accelerated population growth, due to falling mortality in the face

of a high birth rate, demands a higher rate of production increase even to maintain existing scales of living. The call for public control from many quarters is sometimes also the consequence of a desire to avoid domination by foreign elements or a reflection of the communal bonds that still exist in underdeveloped countries and of patterns of thought associated with such ties.

It has been remarked, in this connection, that the economically backward countries may be consciously skipping the phase of private enterprise production, passing over into an economy that is largely controlled by the government. But the atomistic economy of many industrial countries was also preceded by a mercantilistic phase in which governments played the leading economic role. When there are almost no private entrepreneurs, the state must take the initiative in economic activity. What Bonné[32] has noted for Turkey may apply equally to many other countries: "Turkish étatism is no rigorous conception. It is neither anti-capitalistic nor xenophobe nor tied dogmatically to any particular doctrine. The activity of the State consists just as much in exercising a constructive and effective policy as in encouraging private enterprises and in controlling and regulating their execution."

The capability of the government to lead in those economic and social tasks is circumscribed by the strength of the forces within each country ready to accept change and by the quality and quantity of personnel available to make blueprints and carry out the policies appropriate to the natural and human resource patterns. If the need for a positive role of the government in promoting development is not sufficiently recognized, plans are apt to be halfhearted and their implementation ineffective. The second factor usually weighs heavier since the government machinery is necessarily a function of the economic and social level of its citizens. The number of qualified technicians and administrators is unequal to the task laid upon the government. Programs initiated by this small group often remain below expectation because of the deficiency of intermediate personnel and, even more important, the lack of inspiration and motivation of those who are part of the governmental machinery.

Much has been said for the possibility of balanced, harmonious development, provided the government steers the economic process instead of leaving it to private initiative.[33] The argument generally runs to the effect that the backward countries, with their relatively scanty resources, cannot allow themselves any waste, and therefore cannot apply the method of trial and error, which appears to be unavoidable whenever growth is not planned but is left to the spontaneous operation of the profit motive. It does, indeed, seem desirable to encourage industry without, for instance, neglecting the interests of the agrarian sector or of labor. In this respect it should be observed that the terms 'balanced' and 'integrated' development contain certain contradictions within themselves. They reflect the interpendence of the various elements in the process of growth, but also of the basic truth that before continuous development is achieved successive bottlenecks may have to be overcome.

Historically, the fact that economic growth has by-passed certain geographic areas has been due to (1) their resource pattern, (2) to their failure to connect with the developing centers, or (3) to the inadequacy of the impulses received. Development seems generally to have been unbalanced, as can be seen from the economic and social disparities between different areas in all industrial countries. The demand for balanced development is now very strong in the advanced countries and is met, to a degree, owing to the intervention of the governments of those countries. The readaptation of the government apparatus from the traditional task of administering laws and regulations to that of initiating measures to direct economic life is still in progress in those societies being governed in a democratic manner.

From the experience and the difficulties encountered in those advanced countries, one can envisage the extent of the problem in underdeveloped countries. Deficiency of data and lack of competence on the part of technical and administrative personnel often prevent a careful balancing of interests prior to the execution of a project. Action can hardly be expected if all advantages and disadvantages have first to be assessed accurately. A more important obstacle to effective direction of economic life in many countries is perhaps the weakness of the government itself.[34]

In many underdeveloped countries public opinion is not really aware of the importance of reducing institutional obstacles which impede economic growth. A subtle balance in economic and political power often exists between those who want to introduce changes and those who have a vested interest in the traditional forms of production and trade. This precludes any sweeping innovations, but also creates a lack of determination on the part of the administration in executing gradual measures, which, moreover, tend to be circumvented by those whose positions are threatened.

The lack of vigor also imparts itself to the provincial and local governments which have to carry out the policies laid down by the center. The decentralization of decision so necessary for a purposeful direction of the economy is thus thwarted by the same or similar vacillating forces underlying the workings of the central government. One of my friends described in the following way the operation of the government of the country where he was stationed: "The first thing to understand about the government is that it does not govern. Thousands of laws, emergency laws, decrees, and ministerial decisions are issued but few are earnestly implemented. A loose federation of politicians, civil servants, army and navy officers, established families, wealthy newcomers, and the clergy (who are also newcomers) is usually able to arrange matters for their mutual benefit. The details of the pattern change only too frequently, the cut of the cloth never." This seemingly harsh statement is applicable to the governments of several undeveloped countries. The pre-conditions for economic planning — a willingness to abide by the regulations promulgated and a devoted civil service — do not exist in such countries.

An efficient and honest administration is a relatively recent phenomenon in the history of mankind. In some of the advanced countries economic progress seems to have occurred in spite of a corrupt and inefficient public administration.[35] Various forms of corruption were in vogue at some periods, but such countries were fortunate in having an entrepreneurial class and an associated labor force which set the pace for economic growth. Probably this entrepreneurial group partly manipulated the administration through bribes, but remained itself unaffected by the consumption pattern of the official class. Corruption must still have been responsible for the diversion of resources to consumption which otherwise might have been available for capital formation.

The deficiency of the governmental system in underdeveloped countries is a more serious problem since they generally do not possess a powerful entrepreneurial group. Corruption, though benefiting officials whose remuneration often is out of line with that in private business, will lead to the squandering of resources and thus reduce the productive action of the government. These officials, moreover, as a rule will follow the same pattern of investment and consumption as the well-to-do classes and their increased incomes are not likely to contribute to sound economic development.

The tendency for the level of consumption to rise at the cost of investment is strengthened in the underdeveloped countries by the 'demonstration effect' of the consumption habits of the industrial countries, above all of the United States. The governmental élite allow themselves to be guided in their consumption pattern by the prevailing level of living in the developed countries. In this connection, Nurkse[36] has pointed out that, to a certain degree, countries such as Japan and the Soviet Union owed their rapid industrialization to the fact that they held their population isolated from the rest of the world, thereby facilitating the task of keeping the scale of living of the average person low and making a high degree of saving and capital formation possible. It is difficult to determine the precise significance of this factor, but it is certain that the imitation of the consumption patterns of rich countries before the undeveloped countries can afford them, constitutes an additional obstacle to the economic progress of the underdeveloped parts of the world.

In spite of the widespread weakness of the governmental machinery the Herodians demand that government provide direction for economic advancement. At the same time the awakened social conscience, as well as economic and political world conditions, tend to drive the governments along this path. This aggregate of forces is responsible for the industrialization goals professed by virtually all statesmen, and for the drawing up of elaborate development plans in the economically backward countries. For the time being, many of these countries are incapable of giving effect to these programs. It is not that the leaders lack the necessary ability, but the administrative apparatus is so inadequate, the social and political obstacles so great, that it is in most cases beyond their power to implement their ideas.[37] It might be added that the changes planned, given the natural resource pattern and the quality of leadership, often seem too grandiose for the grafting of foreign concepts and methods onto native cultures. However, even plans that are too ambitious may fulfill a useful role in economic education if the reasons for the disparity between targets and achievements are scrutinized and the results of such analysis heeded in future programming.

PART TWO

DOMESTIC FINANCIAL RESOURCES

Chapter 7

INTRODUCTION

In this chapter, we analyze more closely the problems that arise in connection with the domestic financing of economic development. Parallel to the stream of goods and services originating from domestic production, i.e., the national product, and imports, there flows the stream of money representing both the income of individuals and government and expenditures for consumer and capital goods. This monetary complement to the flow of goods — the national income or expenditure — can be divided into: (1) private expenditures for home produced and imported goods and services for consumption, (2) private investments in buildings, machinery, commodity stocks, imported raw materials and equipment, and the like, (3) governmental expenditures, both for consumption and for investment, and (4) expenditures resulting from the income from exported goods and services.

The following figures illustrate this picture:

Income		*Expenditures*	
National product	4,000	Private expenditures for consumption	3,000
Imports of goods and services	1,000	Governmental expenditures for goods and services	500
		Private investment	200
		Public investment	100
		Exports of goods and services	1,200
Total	5,000	Total	5,000

The figures used also give an idea of the relative order of magnitude of the various components in an undeveloped country.[1] The wages, rents, dividends, interest, etc., paid out during the production process are spent on the current supply of goods — except for that portion of private savings, reserves for depreciation, and the undistributed profits of enterprises, not used for capital formation. Funds that are withdrawn from the stream of money by taxation are paid out again by the government to individuals in such form as salaries, benefits under social legislation, and interest on the public debt. Gross private income is thus equal to the sum of private expenditure for consumer goods and services, gross private investment, the export surplus, and the budget deficit of the government.

In the present context, it is not the equilibrium between the commodity flow and the money stream that concerns us, but rather how an increase in the national product takes place as a result of changes on the money side. In the backward countries, a relatively large proportion of commodity production takes place outside the money economy. The organization of the factors of production in this non-monetary sector — directed primarily toward food production — remains practically uninfluenced by financial motives. Where the other, more dynamic sector is based on private enterprise, the utilization of the factors of production is determined largely by price level and income distribution. This, in turn, is influenced by the compensation accruing to land, capital, labor, and leadership in alternative types of employment.

In these circumstances the entrepreneurs, motivated by expectations of profit, are largely responsible for the dispositions of the factors. During the nineteenth century, the growth of the economies in western Europe and North America was largely the result of the micro-economic plans of individual businessmen. The search for profit led these entrepreneurs to efforts which brought about an increase in the supply of productive resources as well as a rise in the productivity of existing resources through better allocation and combination. The result was a greater national product. The government, by its taxation policy and supplementary investments, among other things, created an institutional framework within which the entrepreneurs could function.

In the centrally planned economies, the redistributive functions of money are somewhat different since few opportunities for private gain in money terms exist. Targets that are set in terms of the quantities of goods and services to be produced — based in turn upon the production factors available or to be made available — are the main determinant of the allocation of raw materials, manpower, and capital. The management of the money stream through taxation and public expenditure is part of the framework of planned prices and incomes. It is another instrument for achieving the desired distribution of resources. Here, as in the private enterprise economy, the function of money is not purely a neutral one. The quantity and distribution of the stream of incomes and savings, and their reaction upon the production and allocation of goods and services, are the essential elements of the financial problem of economic development in both types of economic systems.

Given the low level of living in the undeveloped countries, the current pattern of consumption is the principal determinant of the allocation of the factors of production. A low income level leaves little room for savings or for investment. However, a different pattern of spending and consumption — in which, e.g., the proportion spent for ceremonial and family obligations was lower — would probably contribute to a more rational employment of resources, in so far as it benefited over all productivity and released funds for capital accumulation. This applies, *a fortiori*, to the wealthier classes, who in many underdeveloped countries display a tendency towards luxury consumption which reflects both their feudal style of life and the demonstration effect of the standard of living in western Europe and the United States. Continued growth of the national income can occur only through a reallocation of the factors of production that will enhance capital formation, and thus make a greater supply of consumer goods available in the future.

Additional savings are a prerequisite for increased capital accumulation. Such savings may result from a more productive arrangement of the factors of production. During the production process itself, the degree of saving is enhanced if the capital stock is augmented through money created by bank credit or additional note circulation or if a greater part of the income accruing from the additional products and services appearing on the market is used for further investment. However, it is not merely the amount of existing savings, but rather the existence of suitable investment opportunities for private enterpreneurs and public agencies that ultimately determines the volume of total savings.[2] The entrepreneur or government employing these savings or additional funds is not interested primarily in sums of money but in the control over labor and other resources that disposition of money gives. More specifically, such money may be used to put otherwise unemployed factors of production to work, or to transfer production factors already in use from projects of low efficiency to the production of goods and services of higher utility. In these circumstances, entrepreneur and state alike are led to invest by expectation of an increase in the demand for goods and services in a subsequent phase.

The private investor may pay attention only to the relatively short-term profits to be gained from such disposition of funds. The government can usually afford to make investments that will become fruitful over a much longer period. The volume of investment is not, in any given economy, predetermined but depends upon the quantity of unutilized or transferable production factors, the social and political framework of the society, and the technical ability and imagination of entrepreneurs and government to see the possibilities in creating potentially productive capacity. The quantity of unutilized or underutilized production factors is also a variable. It is subject, for example, to modification as a result of new methods of combinations made possible by new techniques or institutional changes.

Assuming this potentiality for growth in an economy, the absolute level of consumption is bound to rise since increasing incomes are necessary both as a reward for the more productive utilization of resources and as an incentive for continued investment. Every increase in consumption while the national income is expanding signifies, nevertheless, a reduction of the margin available for new investment; thus in a developing economy a substantial portion of the expansion in income has to be mobilized for sustained capital accumulation. In view of the fact that investments are paid out partly in wages, investment itself contributes also to an increase of consumption expenditure. An exception is the theoretical example already mentioned, in which the underutilized labor transferred from the agrarian sector to the capital goods sector maintains the same consumption level and receives as previously, its food supply from the farming community to which it was formerly attached. As a rule, however, the workers must receive a higher compensation than previously earned to make their transfer attractive. The demand for additional raw materials and machinery required for new capital construction leads, in turn, to an increase of the wage payments in other branches of industry. This growth in consumption is particularly threatening in undeveloped countries as a result of people experiencing what has been termed the "pressure of rising expectations." The government, which is usually the most important dynamic influence at the inception of development in backward countries, must therefore, strive to restrain any rise in the proportion of consumption in the increased national income so that a larger proportion is available for increasing savings and investment.[3]

The government must take measures to siphon off some of the extra purchasing power created through additional investment by appropriate taxation. The ratio between money incomes and quantity of goods available for consumption must not be suddenly increased, in order to assure real savings to finance the newly produced capital goods. During a period of economic development there are always certain groups or classes that receive a higher reward than before. It requires a subtle tax policy and careful planning of government investment to allow as many groups as possible to benefit from greater consumption and yet not reduce the stimulus to continuous accumulation of capital. Naturally, it is not only the volume of investment that is important, but also the quality. If the government utilizes the additional savings to construct public works that merely enhance its prestige, or to maintain a larger army, it is clear that such investments generally will not lead to an expanded stream of goods and services. Projects of a rather unproductive nature may have a place in a government program, if stagnation is solely the result of underconsumption, but in undeveloped economies this will hardly be the case. Investments that bring about improvements in the transport system or electric supply are more likely to result in a rising stream of incomes. This makes it attractive for private investors to use their savings to establish enterprises that may be expected to profit by the increasing demand for goods and services.

It cannot be emphasized strongly enough that the trend toward new methods of production or 'innovations' that has been responsible for rising productivity of capital, leading to a steady stream of new investments out of additional savings, has been among the main causes of improvements in Western levels of living. The price mechanism through which the preference of consumers and the reaction of producers were expressed has formed the principal instrument for the balanced growth of the different categories of capital. This is particularly true for private investment that flowed, subject to the pull of demand and profit, into the construction of directly productive capital and 'overhead' capital. It should not be forgotten, however, that in all developing economies collective savings have been used by the state for the construction of economic and social 'overhead' capital for which no remunerative price could be set. The latter investments, motivated by overall economic or social considerations, therefore, may not have been less important in achieving economic growth.

When discussing consumption and investment patterns in underdeveloped countries, one should beware of value judgments. The concept of more productive consumption or investment tends to involve the values of an industrial society. This implies, in the private enterprise economies of today, the provision of more consumer goods, or in the centrally planned economies, a relatively greater increase in the capital stock, which might lead to a rise in material welfare in the future. For an economist, it is immaterial whether a society devotes a substantial part of its resources to ceremonial consumption, to putting more gold leaves on its religious images, or to ostentatious public buildings. He can only point out that if a country wants to develop an economic structure similar to that of the West, it also has to adopt the appropriate scale of values.

The Keynesian dictum that a high rate of investment is the secret of a dynamic economy is particularly relevant to undeveloped countries. Because of the lack of motivation, however, those in backward countries who are in a position to invest prefer instead to retain their savings in liquid form, or to use them to acquire precious metals or jewels, stocks of commodities, land, cattle, or houses. This investment pattern is related, on the one hand, to the lack of political and economic insecurity often prevailing in undeveloped countries, which accentuates the desire for liquidity, and on the other hand, to the relatively high profit rate often obtainable from real estate transactions and trade and the high interest paid on loans for consumption purposes. Such transactions add no new production factors to the economy. They usually involve merely the transfer of existing assets from one owner to another.

We have already pointed out that the smallness of the local market in conjunction with the level of technology and the institutional framework, which determine the viewpoint of the privileged classes, is partly responsible for this disinclination to invest in industrial activities. Foreign trade, which at a corresponding stage of development in the industrial countries formed the stimulus for a growing economy, does not play the same role in the backward regions of today. Their expanding exports consist mostly of raw materials whose production has often been developed by foreigners. They have not resulted, given the existing pattern of consumption and investment, in new industrial ventures that would have diversified the economies. Industrial growth, so far as it is stimulated by the increase in incomes, has remained limited since the conquest of foreign markets for industrial products is hampered by the competition of the more efficient industries of the advanced countries. Thus their existing export structure tends to be perpetuated.

These factors also limit the opportunities of the government to improve the investment climate by appropriate measures or to undertake investment itself. The low level of real income of the mass of the people limits taxable capacity and social and political considerations often prevent due taxation of the small well-to-do classes. Government efforts to provide dynamic impulses for the economy, in the face of the limited volume of individual and collective savings, tend to lead to an expansion of the money supply by means of credit or additional note circulation. If there are idle or underutilized resources that can be put to productive use, the creation of additional money can be justified. However, we have already concluded that in spite of an over-supply of labor in some countries other factors such as raw materials, capital, and leadership often have an inelastic supply schedule in the under-developed countries.[4]

The tendency to create a larger supply of money than corresponds to the quantity of unutilized factors of production then arises. This extra money will exert an upward pressure on the prices of the factors of production already employed. The competition of this additional purchasing power implies that those who do not see their incomes rise will find themselves compelled to restrict the satisfaction of their needs, to the extent that certain goods and services are now acquired by the newly created purchasing power. Those with fixed incomes are thus penalized or forced to restrict their physical consumption, or to save on account of the application of available resources to new uses due to the increase in money supply. It is probable that in the history of the industrial countries economic progress was stimulated because of a similar forced saving on the part of those whose incomes stagnated in the process of growth. "Would the railways or the electric plant of the world ever have been built if we had been a-fraid of a little forced saving? Is it not rising prices that empty the workhouses and the employment exchange registers and fill the factories and the shipyards?"[5] It seems, however, that inflation in the underdeveloped countries does not exert such a catalyzing influence on economic growth for the time being.

The prevailing consumption and investment pattern, and the obstacles to giving the economy a more dynamic character by expanding the domestic money supply, induce the undeveloped countries to ask for external capital in order to make increased imports of goods and services possible, and thus obtain a pump-priming effect to stimulate the growth of their economies. This will be the subject of Part III.

Chapter 8

THE CONSUMPTION PATTERN

An increase of consumption, especially of the masses, is now generally considered to be the ultimate objective of economic development. We have seen, however, that increased investment must precede any rise in the level of consumption, and that capital formation constitutes the energizing power that helps to bring about an enlarged stream of goods. The continuing expansion of consumption consequently, gives an impetus to progressive capital formation.

It is often argued, particularly in the undeveloped countries themselves, that a low average income level leaves no margin for saving, thus making it difficult to employ additional production factors for capital formation.

It is, indeed, true that the real income of the poorer groups is often barely sufficient to assure even a subsistence minimum. On the other hand, while more than half of the income is often spent for food,[1] in many countries a disproportionate share of income tends to be spent for ceremonial and religious purposes.

A study of a Bolivian village[2] reports the average annual expenditures per family on food as 4,318 bolivianos, while 1,250 bolivianos, about 30 per cent of the expenditures for food, were spent for alcoholic beverages, consumed mostly at fiestas. In other Latin-American countries, a similarly high consumption of alcohol has been noted. It is significant that in Mexico the index for the volume of beer production stood at 380 as an average during the first ten months of 1953 (1939=100), while for the textile industry the index was only 145 and for the food industry 216 in the same period.[3]

Observers of the Asian countries have often drawn attention to the extraordinary expenditures for family affairs (births, deaths and marriages). Lossing Buck[4] reports that, according to a survey conducted in several provinces in China during the 1920's, the cost of a wedding amounted to four times, and the cost of a funeral three times the average monthly farm family income. In the same category may be placed the keeping of cattle in Africa and India and other investment or consumption habits which, regardless of their ratio in the past, are now out of date.

We know of no community that does not allow itself, in some way or another, an organized, ceremonial waste of goods that first had to be produced and accumulated. Any distinction between what can be termed 'rational' consumption and extravagance involves an arbitrary and subjective evaluation. This is colored by the scale of values of the society involved, but it is clear that an underdeveloped country can afford relatively less of such waste. To obtain an increase in the level of living the structure of wants must also be adapted to a more rational distribution of the factors of production. Since underdeveloped countries are attempting to achieve higher levels of living, there is some justification for assuming that the Western scale of values is an appropriate measuring rod in the economic sphere of life.

The proposition that there is no possibility of saving in underdeveloped countries, on account of the low level of living, is too broad a generalization; it neglects the unequal income distribution. This inequality is often greater in undeveloped than in developed countries. S. Kuznets[5] reports that the share of total income accruing to the top quintile (before direct taxes and excluding free benefits from government), was 55 per cent in India (1949–50), 50 per cent in Ceylon (1950), and 56 per cent in Puerto Rico (1948), in comparison with 44 per cent in the United States and 45 per cent in the United Kingdom. The figures of Colin Clark,[6] based on the Pareto coefficient, also show that inequality of income distribution is greater in undeveloped than in industrial countries. H. W. Spiegel[7] has calculated that the Gini index of concentration in the federal district of Brazil rose from 0.453 in 1934 to 0.488 in 1938 and 0.556 in 1942, showing thus a constant rise in the inequality of income distribution.

There are several reasons why such a phenomenon may also be occurring in other underdeveloped economies. The poverty of the lowest income groups tends to lead to an increasing inequality in an economy whose development does not raise the status of these groups. Their inability to accumulate savings tends to force them to draw on other people's capital to meet their needs for food and other essential consumer goods whenever the precarious balance between production or income and consumption is upset. The fact that the larger part of the active population is engaged in agriculture — whose yield is often unfavorably affected by the weather and other circumstances — strengthens this borrowing tendency. In this connection, it should be recalled that the working classes in western Europe in the nineteenth century also often showed little foresight in distributing their incomes between present and future needs. The demand for credit in underdeveloped areas is further increased by the traditional expenditures for ceremonial purposes, as indicated above, that are sometimes out of proportion to the normal earning capacity of the borrowers.

Before World War II a budget study,[8] covering various labor groups on some eighteen plantations and in factories on Java (Indonesia) and carried out at three month intervals, disclosed that the expenditures of the lowest income groups exceeded their incomes. Consequently, debts outstanding at the end of the period under study were higher than at the beginning. This pattern is probably characteristic of other countries as well. The chronic credit needs of the masses lead to the ever-increasing poverty of this group, while those in a position to save enrich themselves. The effective and potential demand for money, given the relatively scanty and quasi-monopolistic supply of it, gives rise to interest rates which are many times higher than in the industrial countries. The high rates are also related to the smallness of the amounts involved and the risks attending such loans for consumption. The only security which the potential borrower can provide is his land, often already overburdened with debt.

Legislation to check the usury that thus arises has little influence because of the magnitude of the problem. In some cases the law is evaded by compelling the borrower to sign a note for a certain amount while he actually receives a far smaller sum. Thus, interest on the effective principal of the loan is partly paid in advance.

Another reason for the continued increase in inequality of incomes may lie in the process of development itself. Clark[9] and others have demonstrated (on the basis of household budgets for various income groups in a large number of countries) that, as incomes rise, an increasing proportion of the purchasing power is spent on manufactures. This increase in effective demand should make it attractive for those able to save to invest in industrial ventures. However, such a development is not automatic. In countries with large low-income groups, a rising income may well result initially in a larger per capita demand for high energy foods, particularly cereals, and meat and dairy products in a subsequent phase. Hence, in the absence of a simultaneous and substantial increase in appropriate agricultural supplies, an increase in the flow of money income may lead to a sharper rise of food prices than of other prices. This will tend to decrease the margin for other purchases. The resulting decline in the real income of industrial workers may not be offset by a proportional increase in the purchasing power of agricultural producers. This is at least true when the weak bargaining power of the small food producer causes the rise in the price of agricultural produce to accrue to a large extent to middlemen. Thus, the expected diversification of consumption may not materialize and the unequal income distribution may not be lessened. The tendency just described can be observed in several Latin-American countries. It proves that industrial growth does not necessarily induce growth in consumers' demand.

This is but one aspect of a larger problem that has received little attention in development economics, namely, the consequences of the fact that income generated by investment expenditures is not necessarily directed towards the products and services resulting from the investment. As supply does not increase and change its composition automatically with the expansion and in sympathy with the composition of demand, a disequilibrium may arise. This may be rectified by differential price changes, as for example, a disproportionate price increase for food (as mentioned above), or by an expansion of imports. If exports do not increase proportionally with the demand for imports, balance-of-payments difficulties are likely to ensue. It must be assumed that the divergent trends between the price of food and the price of manufactures did not occur in industrial countries, either because agricultural productivity rose simultaneously with industrialization and the rise in real income, or because at an appropriate time food grains at relatively low prices became available from overseas areas. The high elasticity of foreign demand for manufactured goods, despite a temporary decline in domestic demand due to price changes, may have been an important contributing factor to the continuous growth of the economy in certain countries.

It is generally admitted that the savings of the more prosperous elements — resulting in some cases from the initially more unequal income distribution — of the now advanced countries brought about increased capital formation, and thus contributed substantially to the industrialization of those countries. W. A. Lewis[10] has stressed the point that the key to economic development lies in altering the distribution of income in favor of the saving class. The mere withholding of purchasing power, however, does not lead to capital formation. It results — assuming the supply of goods and services to remain constant and the absence of any secondary effect — in a decline in effective demand and hence a price fall. What is required, as Lewis implies, is that the increasing savings or profits will be invested in productive capacity so that capital formation will increase more rapidly than national income. As Lewis rightly points out, however, the growth of a capitalist class is no simple matter. He emphasizes only economic factors, such as "the emergence of new opportunities especially something that widens the market, associated with some new technique which greatly increases the productivity of labor if labor and capital are used together."[11]

From our previous discussion it will be clear that in many countries the problem lies mainly in the socio-political sphere; it is there that the reasons must be found why the backward countries have lagged in developing a capitalist class. In any case, it is evident that the well-to-do classes in today's underdeveloped countries are potentially in a position to make substantial savings. However they often tend to follow a consumption pattern that does not encourage economic development, using a high proportion of the export proceeds to pay for imports of luxury consumer goods. An illustrative example would seem to be the postwar imports of certain types of goods from the United States by Latin America, as shown in the following table:

Table 9. U.S. EXPORTS OF SELECTED COMMODITIES TO LATIN AMERICAN REPUBLICS (values in millions of dollars, unless otherwise stated)

	1938	1947	1955
Cotton Cloth, Duck, and Tire Fabric	12.5	102.7	47.6
1,000 sq. yd.	(136,129)	(264,355)	(168,502)
Piece Goods of Synthetic Textiles	2.7	49.2	27.8
1,000 sq. yd.	(10,871)	(66,768)	n.a.
Hosiery	1.3	7.5	5.6
1,000 doz. pr.	(348)	(1,304)	(1,332)
Refrigerators, Electric, Household	2.9	19.6	14.6
1,000	(36)	(134)	(93)
Passenger Cars (new)	25.7	122.0	144.7
1,000	(41)	(94)	(78)
Medicinal and Pharmaceutical Preparations	6.9	81.6	106.5
Radio Receiving Sets: Home and Automobile	4.4	32.4	5.4
1,000	(191)	(960)	(245)

n.a. Not available

Source: International Economic Analysis Division, Bureau of Foreign Commerce, U.S. Department of Commerce.

The increase in exports of more refined cotton cloth, synthetic textiles, passenger cars, and consumer durables between 1938 and 1947 gives some impression of the propensity to consume, especially of the upper income groups, even if we take into account the 'pent-up' demand as a result of the interruption of exports of such articles during the war and the increase in the price level. Compare, for example, the exports of agricultural machinery which amounted to $82 million in 1947 as against $22 million in 1938. Though increasing incomes will usually lead to increasing imports of quality goods, the order of magnitude of the rise in imports for certain goods would seem to be incompatible with sound development aims. The decline of most of these exports by 1955 reflects in part the rising industrialization in Latin America, particularly the serving of this market by branch factories established by U.S. firms in certain countries, as well as a more stringent import control policy followed by some countries. It may be observed that such a large increase in luxury imports as occurred between 1938 and 1947 due to accumulated reserves may also be related to the uneven flow of export earnings. Large fluctuations in export income are not conducive to long-term development planning. This aspect is illustrated in the World Economic Report 1950–51,[12] where it is calculated that while export earnings of the primary producing countries rose by about 30 per cent between the first half of 1950 and of 1951, less than a tenth of this increase was devoted to imports of machinery, metals and manufactures, and trucks. Imports of passenger cars into Latin America and certain countries of Asia and the Middle East on the other hand went up by 100 per cent or more.

Returning once more to the behavior of the well-to-do classes in western Europe at the beginning of its industrialization, it is generally supposed that the formation of capital was encouraged by an inflationary process, such as is now found in some underdeveloped countries. J. M. Keynes[13] agreeing with many economic historians has linked the influx of precious metals into western Europe in the last quarter of the sixteenth century with this increased capital formation. There was a marked rise in prices and the discrepancy between prices and costs stimulated the expectation of profits, and thereby the motivation to invest.

"A relatively low level of real wages is necessarily a characteristic of a period of profit inflation, because it is partly at the expense of current consumption that the abnormal growth of capital

wealth which accompanies a profit inflation is derived . . . Thus
a profit inflation is almost certain to bring about a more unequal
distribution of wealth — unless its effects are balanced by the
direct taxation of the rich of the kind which characterizes modern
England but no other place or period. . . Thus, if we consider a
long period of time, the working class may benefit far more in the
long run from the forced abstinence which a profit inflation imposes on them than they lose in the first instance in the shape of
diminished consumption. Moreover, the amount of the diminu-
tion in their current consumption corresponding to a given increment of capital wealth is no greater if it comes about in this
way than if it is due to voluntary saving, and, *so long as wealth and
its fruits are not consumed by the nominal owner but are accumulated*, the
evils may not be so great as they appear."[14]

In the above quotation we have italicized the condition necessary for that type of inflation to result in development: that recipients of additional income do not consume their gains but use
them for productive investment. Compare this with Salvador de
Madariaga[15] on the effect of the overseas production of precious
metals on the Spanish economy in the sixteenth and seventeenth
centuries. He demonstrates that the increase in the flow of money
likewise led to accentuated inequality in income distribution, but
that the augmented profits, instead of leading to new industrial
activity, stimulated the consumption of luxuries by the rich. This
meant an enlarged market for the manufactured products of the
rest of Europe and for spices, silks, and other imports from Asia.
According to De Madariaga, stagnation in the Spanish economy,
added to the financial demands made by the navy and army, was
the cause of Spain's downfall. However, he does admit that the lack
of data makes it difficult to follow the thread through the maze of
economic and financial determinants.[16] The inflation, with the
resulting increase of mass poverty, contributed to the disintegration of the Spanish empire, accentuating the inclination toward
idleness and the contempt for technology which he mentions as
traits of the Spanish character.[17]

The pattern to be found in many underdeveloped countries

shows a certain similarity to that of Spain of that period, although naturally with a number of differences. Increasing inequality in the distribution of income leads merely to increased consumption by a small class. It also has a tendency to reduce the domestic market for manufactured goods, which would increase as income rose if income were more uniformly distributed. This situation dissuades the potential investor from using his savings to initiate new productive activities.

Chapter 9

Private Investment

W e have noted that those in a position to make substantial savings in undeveloped countries, though constituting only a small group, do in many respects differ from the early European and American entrepreneurs who reinvested most of their profits into further expansion of their commercial and industrial activities.[1] A disproportionate share of the income of the prosperous group in many undeveloped countries is spent on luxuries, especially in the form of imported goods. In western Europe, too, the landed aristocracy probably continued to live in a corresponding style during the period of early industrial development. Consider the following quotation from Adam Smith:[2] "What is annually saved is as regularly consumed as what is annually spent, and nearly in the same time too; but it is consumed by a different set of people. That portion of his revenue which a rich man annually spends is in most cases consumed by idle guests and menial servants, who leave nothing behind them in return for their consumption." The merchant or industrialist, in contrast, acts differently. "That portion which he annually saves, as for the sake of the profit it is immediately employed as a capital, is consumed in the same manner, and nearly in the same time too, but by a different set of people, by labourers, manufacturers and artificers, who reproduce with a profit the value of their annual consumption." The moral indignation of Smith at the former type of consumption is evident.

In addition, in the undeveloped countries, a substantial portion of savings is kept in liquid form. Gold coins or bars, jewels, and foreign currency are typical forms of investment in the undeveloped regions. We have calculated, for example, that from 1900 to 1931, the average annual import of gold coin and bullion into India was 170 million rupees. Only part of this was used for monetary purposes; most of it was hoarded in order to satisfy the desire for liquidity.[3] B. Datta[4] assumes that India has a 'hoard' of $4 billion in gold and silver that would be available for capital formation if a method could be found of mobilizing it. The size of this hoard may not seem significant in comparison with total national wealth, but considering it as a leak of unproductive investment over time, one can imagine that if applied to the building up of capital stock, it could have helped to expand national output at a considerable rate.

It is generally difficult to obtain exact data on the savings held in foreign currency. The International Bank in its report on Cuba[5] estimates that in 1949, out of 219 million pesos of savings (about 12 per cent of the gross national product), about 40 million, or almost 20 per cent, flowed abroad. This gives an indication of the capital flight. This same tendency may be observed from the dollar holdings held by business and individuals of certain undeveloped countries in the United States. These often seem excessive in relation to national income and size of foreign trade, and they frequently vary inversely with the gold and foreign exchange held by governments and central banks. When the latter decline, private holdings rise, indicating an increasing lack of confidence in the stability of the national currency. In many Latin-American countries, and perhaps elsewhere, the U.S. dollar circulates alongside the national currency notes, and the deviation between its price and the official exchange rate reflects its attractiveness to potential savers.

Other preferred forms of investment are land and livestock, whose possession carries a traditional prestige, and various types of housing. In this connection, A. Marshall[6] has remarked: "Land, houses and livestock are the three forms of wealth which have been in the first rank of importance always and everywhere. But land differs from other things in this, that an increase in its value is often chiefly due to an increase in its scarcity, and it is therefore a measure rather of growing wants than of growing means of meeting wants." The investment in land sometimes tends to reduce the holdings of the small peasant whose marginal position has already been noted above, and it accentuates the unequal income distribution. In the economic literature on Latin America, one sometimes finds expressed the ideas that the feudal style of living is in decline and that the landed aristocracy is living beyond its means, the high mortgage debts on latifundia being offered as proof. It is difficult to determine the extent to which this is so, but there is as yet no sign that this class, as was the case in England in a comparable stage of development,[7] is transferring part of its interests to commerce and industry.

Investors in real estate or in mortgages on real estate usually prefer housing built for the high-income groups. Housing for the poorer groups — drawn to the cities by the industrial development there and in some instances the relative overpopulation of the rural areas — may not be a profitable investment, where wages are low and the percentage available for rent relatively small. This particular use of savings, likewise, does not contribute to sound economic growth.

These forms of hoarding and investment, so common in backward regions, were also customary in western Europe during the precapitalistic era, and they may still persist there in certain spheres. In some respects they reflect the greater political and economic instability that prevails in the undeveloped countries in comparison with the industrial countries. Adam Smith[8] had an underdeveloped economy in mind when he said: "Upon equal, or nearly equal profits, most men will choose to employ their capitals rather in the improvement and cultivation of land than either in manufactures or in foreign trade. The man who employs his capital in land has it more under his view and command, and his fortune is much less liable to accidents than that of the trader, who is obliged frequently to commit it, not only to the winds and waves, but to the more uncertain elements of human folly and injustice, by giving great credits in distant countries to men with whose character and situation he can seldom be thoroughly acquainted."

Further, the high interest rate to be obtained from loans for consumption may also tend to keep investible funds away from productive enterprises. A desire for liquidity often explains the lender's preference for commercial borrowers. Commercial transactions are frequently interwoven with loans for consumption purposes — for example, loans granted to agricultural producers in exchange for a share of the harvest at a later date. The pledging of land as security for loans is often a consequence of the need for consumer credit, which thus exerts an influence on land tenure.

In addition to the liquidity of commercial investments in the underdeveloped countries, there is the high margin of profit they sometimes yield.[9] The International Bank's report on Turkey[10] notes with respect to the pattern of private investment: "Turkish private enterprise has a distinct trading complex. . . A high return on investment and quick return of capital are expected as a matter of course, with the result that industrial investment is relatively unattractive. Such investment as does take place in industry is often speculative. The desire for a quick turnover and high profits and the fear of inflation have blocked long-term investment commitments."

It is often pointed out that backward countries need to develop an efficient system of banking and credit to collect savings. However, the quantitative importance of personal savings should not be overemphasized. In India, where institutional facilities exist (postal savings, credit unions, etc.), personal savings have never accounted for more than 0.5 per cent of the national income.

The banking system can perform a useful function in economic development, especially since it has the power of creating credit and thus of making funds available for productive investment in excess of the amount deposited. But the banking system cannot create an effective demand for capital for expanding the means of production or using more effectively the existing factors. In the light of the existing investment pattern, it is not surprising that in many countries private banking tends to serve domestic and foreign trade rather than the financing of industrial development.

In many underdeveloped countries, the most important source of industrial development is profit retained in existing enterprises, as rates of operating profits in these countries are frequently higher than in the industrial countries,[11] a sign of the paucity of capital and of the greater risk connected with investment. It would seem, therefore, that these profits could constitute an important and continuous source for industrial financing. Though there may be few industrialists who can do such reinvesting, and the limited size of the national market may circumscribe the amount of potential productive investment, the disinclination toward financing an expanding industrial sector can often be ascribed to other, deeper causes. It is evident that in a low-income economy investment has to start in a small way, but in any country there are opportunities to fill needs better, cheaper, and to expand output with existing means. The lack of spirit to introduce innovations, a deficiency in its turn related to the nonindustrial cultural pattern, the absence of external economies, etc., may be more important than the limitation of the market or the scarcity of savings in explaining the status of the economy in certain backward countries.

In this connection, it may also be observed that most enterprises in underdeveloped countries — aside from foreign concerns — are family undertakings whose capital is closely held and for whose financing no support from outsiders is sought. This is in principle no drawback for an expanding economy. The same situation prevailed in most industrial countries in an analogous stage of development. The rudimentary character of the capital market is a normal concomitant of being undeveloped.[12] That, in spite of the obstacles mentioned, some private investment in industry occurs, is the result of special encouragement offered by the government in the form of subsidies, tax concessions, protective tariffs, guaranteed prices or markets, etc.

Lack of reliable statistical data in the undeveloped countries makes it difficult to give a quantitative picture of the manner in which aggregate savings are utilized. According to an estimate for Brazil,[13] total savings in 1947 were 12 billion cruzeiros, of which 5 billion were made by individuals, 5 billion by enterprises, and the remaining 2 billion by way of social insurance institutes and private insurance companies. More than 60 per cent of these savings appear to have been used for construction. This amount can be broken down as follows:

Type of Construction	Millions of Cruzeiros
Factory construction	500–750
Housing for lower-income groups	2,000
Office buildings and housing for higher-income groups	4,500–5,000
Total	7,500

Such an investment pattern is hardly conducive to rapid economic development, but it seems to reflect the situation in other Latin-American countries too. A report of an International Monetary Fund Mission to Chile[14] gives a calculation made by the "Corporacion de Fomento", according to which over the years 1947–49, 27 per cent of gross domestic investment was in luxury residential building. Likewise, the International Bank's Mission to Cuba[15] estimates that in that country "in recent years between one-quarter and one-half of gross private capital formation and well over one-half of net real investment have gone into the building of new homes and commercial premises."

In the Philippines, also, a United States Economic Survey Mission[16] has found that, in the postwar period from 1945 to 1949, a disproportionate share of investment was in the form of luxury residential housing. The estimated distribution of investment was as follows:

Type of Investment	Million pesos	In %
Agriculture, Fishery, and Forestry	990	25
Industry, Transport, and Public Utilities	909	23
Commerce	1,255	32
Public Works	250	7
Housing	503	13
Total	3,907	100

With American aid, agriculture and industry were almost restored to their prewar levels by 1950, but the Mission's report notes that the investment in commerce and housing — even after allowing for the depletion of inventories after the war and for the war damage to buildings and dwellings — was lavish, and that income distribution had become even more unequal than before the war.

The report of the International Bank's Mission to Ceylon[17] notes the strong preference for investment in land, partly for traditional reasons, since the price of land often has little or no relation to its yield. It points out that if they do not buy land, capitalists import goods or speculate in rice and other commodities that offer more attractive returns than industry. The investment pattern for Costa Rica has been summarized as follows: "Most people in Costa Rica use their savings to build houses, to purchase automobiles and other consumers' durable goods, to buy land, to buy urban commercial property, to build up bank balances in the United States, or to hoard Costa Rican or United States currency."[18]

It is not surprising that various authors, after an analysis of the economies of the undeveloped countries, reach the same conclusion as M. W. Thornburg[19] does for Turkey: "There is little doubt that any present apparent scarcity of capital for the development of private industry does not arise from lack of accumulation but from reluctance to use it for this purpose." Likewise, G. Wythe,[20] referring to the economies of Latin America says: "Capital is not the major problem in connection with most types of manufacture... The expansion of industry along sound lines is now conditioned more by human and socio-economic factors than by financial limitations."

Although a substantial portion of investment in several underdeveloped countries is not conducive to economic development, it would not seem justified to compare it with the pattern of capital accumulation of the advanced countries discussed in Chapter 4. In industrializing countries there is bound to be a certain amount of unproductive investment since some groups are still immersed in a preindustrial climate, and a growing inequality in income distribution may lead to conspicuous consumption. Such excesses are no longer evident when the countries have reached a state of maturity, or they are then insignificant in relation to the direction of total investment. The aberrations in backward countries reflect, to a degree, the growing pains of a developing economy. The irrationality of this pattern is fully recognized in some of the countries concerned.[21]

Although one sometimes reads that the leading groups, able to make substantial savings in the backward countries, are not particularly distinguished by the thrift, love of work, and soberness so characteristic of the entrepreneurs during the rise of western capitalism, such statements should also be considered with a certain reserve. It should be granted that, from the individual's point of view, the investment pattern chosen is to some extent highly rational. In the absence of an industrial climate, external economies, and political stability, the private investor selects those channels of investment that offer him maximum returns. Because those investments often do not contribute to a sound economic growth, governments in underdeveloped countries have to shoulder the responsibility of creating an environment more conducive to increasing the level of material welfare for the population. Some of the investment in economic and social 'overhead' capital necessary for this purpose does not attract private capital even in the more favorable circumstances prevailing in the industrial countries. To this subject we shall return in our chapter on the government sector.

Chapter 10

FOREIGN TRADE

The Theory of International Trade

The growth of international trade[1] since the beginning of the nineteenth century to its present volume and worldwide scope was stimulated by the development of industrial centers in western Europe and, later, in North America. The countries on the periphery of the industrial centers, in some degree, owe their incorporation into the world economy to the flow of capital and leadership to a majority of these areas. In nontropical peripheral regions there was the additional consideration of immigration of labor, particularly in the half-century preceding World War I, from these centers. As a result of the movement of these factors of production, the outlying areas became providers of raw materials and outlets for the manufactured products of the industrial countries, which in turn experienced further growth from this stimulus.

Classical economists explained the recent growth in world trade as an application of the principle of the international division of labor. This principle held that each country, given its geographic and economic resources, would apply itself to those activities in which it was relatively more efficient than other countries. Since the pattern of production depends on the prices and quantities of the available production factors, each country would tend to specialize in those processes requiring the maximum amount of those factors relatively cheap in that particular country. This process illustrates the principle of comparative costs, according to which, each country tends to export those goods for which there is a foreign demand and imports those goods that can be obtained more cheaply from foreign countries than be produced domestically. It is through foreign trade that the relative disadvantages of a geographically and historically determined distribution of the factors of production are mitigated.[2]

K. E. Hansson[3] tested this theory against the prewar trade pattern.[4] He found that the movement of trade, capital, and people between the United States, the 'Great Plains' (Canada, Argentina, Uruguay, South Africa, Australia, and New Zealand), Continental Europe, and the tropical regions of Latin America and Asia was to a large extent based on the relative abundance or scarcity of the production factors — land, labor, and capital — of these regions. The United States, with ample land and capital resources, and a scarce labor supply tended to be an exporter of raw materials and capital and an importer of labor-intensive products and labor. The 'Great Plain' countries, with ample land, scarce capital and labor supplies, were principally exporters of raw materials and importers of labor-intensive manufactures, capital, and labor. Continental Europe, possessor of ample capital and labor resources and a scarce land supply, was an exporter of capital, labor, and labor-intensive manufactures, and an importer of land-extensive materials. The tropics, with an ample labor, and scarce capital supply, were exporters of labor-intensive products requiring a tropical climate and importers of capital-intensive manufactures and capital. Despite some frictions and variations, which Hansson notes, the given resource patterns tended to pull the world economy into a 'natural' multilateral exchange system.

J. H. Williams,[5] however, has pointed out that this theory assumes a substantial immobility of the quanta of employed productive factors. It, therefore, throws no light on the dynamic relationship between international trade and the development of new natural resources and productive forces. This interrelationship is basic in seeking an explanation for the differences in wealth between the industrial and backward countries.

Apart from other objections which may be raised against some of its static implications, the undeveloped countries automatically oppose the principles of this theory — upon which the idea of free trade and a liberal trade policy were based — since the acceptance of their validity would also imply that the present division of labor is the most efficient. They object to this theory because it pays no attention to the fact that the prices of primary products, on which the export earnings of undeveloped countries depend, fluctuate more than the prices of manufactured articles, which they import. These fluctuations in price trends tend towards instability in their economies.[6] The frequent precipitous reductions in export receipts disrupt their long run development plans, as such fluctuations imply an uneven flow of foreign exchange resources to finance their development. This situation has been among the main motivations for the underdeveloped countries to attempt a diversification of their economies in order to expand the domestic market. This would mitigate the effect of the changes in demand and vicissitudes in the prices of their export commodities.

The second objection involves the validity of the 'given' quantities of existing and utilized factors of production that, according to the theory, determine the pattern and volume of international trade between the various countries. The critics say that this pattern is based on the assumption of full employment of the production factors in the trading areas. But in underdeveloped countries the problem is often one of underemployment of human and natural resources; substantial surpluses of labor may be found side by side with unexploited natural resources. This situation strengthens the demand for intervention in foreign trade to make up for the lag in capital formation and technological knowledge.

Countries such as the United States, Canada, and Australia can boast of a high level of industrialization, in part made possible, it may be pointed out, by the erection of high tariff walls for manufactured goods that effectively encouraged domestic industrial activity. The rapid industrialization in those countries reflected the interrelationship between the diversification of the economy and the expansion of domestic purchasing power. The tariff, however, stimulated indigenous entrepreneurs to initiate domestic production of articles formerly imported. Foreign capital and leadership were attracted by the same conditions. Previously unused raw materials were thus exploited and capital flowed toward these new activities. Protected from foreign competition by import duties, they provided expectations of ample rewards to investors. A strong demand for industrial workers arose, in turn, leading to a relatively higher wage level in the new industries. The depressing effect on real wages in the agricultural sector, as a result of the initial price rise of manufactured goods, imposed by the tariff, accelerated the outflow of labor from agriculture to industry. The productivity of the factors added to the national economy determines whether the protective tariff policy increases or decreases the efficiency of the economy.[7] The harm caused to the country whose export industries are hurt by the tariff depends upon the capacity of finding other markets or of shifting resources to other uses. A certain lowering of the productivity of the world economy is probably always induced at first by the imposition of import duties, but what is significant is the ultimate effect on the future regrouping of the factors of production.

Some writers[8] believe that if a poor country benefits by a protectionist policy, and the only losers are richer countries, this indicates an improvement in the international distribution of income, even though it does result in a reduction in world income. This conclusion cannot be accepted without reservation. In several undeveloped countries it can be shown that the growth of industry, materially aided by the protection of high tariff walls, has merely operated to create an inefficient industrial sector beneficial to national prestige and a small elite, leaving the local consumer indefinitely impoverished.

The domestic effect of an import duty may be likened to an imposition of a tax on one part of the population simultaneously with a subsidy to another part. This redistribution of wealth seems warranted if the protective tariff may be expected to produce an increase in social productivity outweighing the loss in welfare by the consumers affected. It is naturally difficult to weigh these alternatives against each other in a particular situation; only time can tell whether the initial sacrifice outweighs the expansion of the national economy that may result from the imposition of an import duty. No studies have as yet been made analyzing in quantitative terms the cost of industrialization fostered by various undeveloped countries. However, data on certain Latin-American countries give an idea of the initial burden laid upon the consumer by a high tariff policy.

For Chile, S. G. Hanson[9] has calculated that import duties and taxes on various textiles brought the landed cost to 100–400 per cent above the c.i.f. (cost, insurance, freight) price. This gives an indication of the amount of protection required to make domestic industry competitive with foreign producers. G. Wythe[10] states that in Ecuador extensive smuggling existed as a result of the spread between the domestic and foreign price levels. For Brazil, G. Wythe[11] gives the prices for a number of consumer goods produced locally, showing that the average price level was 50 per cent above that of the United States. In certain cases, subsidiaries of United States corporations have been forced by the government to raise their prices so that domestic producers can continue to compete with them. A United Nation mission to Mexico[12] estimated that the average 1950 prices in Mexico of the principal iron and steel products were almost twice those in western Europe. In an unpublished report by a United Nations expert on the textile industry in El Salvador, it was stated that, though the wage rate in the United States was six to eight times higher than in El Salvador, the unit cost of cloth in the latter country was at least twice as much as in the former, though the domestically grown cotton was of excellent quality.

Apparently in India and Egypt[13] the initial handicaps in starting certain industries were, to a degree, overcome so that tariffs for a number of industries could be withdrawn. The underdeveloped countries have a valid argument for the use of custom tariffs to protect industries. Because of their deficiency in managerial and technological skills and lack of external economies, they cannot be expected to establish new industries able to compete immediately with those of the more advanced countries. This argument applies *a fortiori* to those countries burdened with substantial underemployed manpower in the rural regions. The social cost of this waste in the labor force makes it highly desirable to find productive employment. Import duties on articles that can be produced domestically seem justified, as the higher initial cost to the consumer is offset by the more productive deployment of the labor force. Theoretically, the underdeveloped countries, when they gain industrial experience, should be in a position to establish a viable industrial sector because of the relatively low labor cost compared with the industrial countries. The organizational backwardness of the industrial structure in many countries, however, would seem to be responsible for the fact that existing industries force the consumer to pay much higher prices for manufactures than he might well pay under a free trade system.

The high cost of domestically produced manufactures in several underdeveloped countries is also caused by the fact that apart from the rational reasons for industrialization, emulation of the industrial countries and the desire for political power and economic self-sufficiency, also play a role in the efforts made toward economic diversification. Ellsworth[14] quotes a Chilean author, who writes: "Protection by tariffs or import licenses should be established *a priori* and as an immovable economic doctrine whenever a national industry needing protection is involved, since whatever production replaces an import is and will always represent an increase in national wealth, independently of its apparent cost in money values." Such attitudes can be found in other backward countries. No country can, of course, afford to follow such a policy *ad libitum*. Available manpower and the capacity to earn foreign exchange to pay for the required imports set a limit to what can be done. To the extent that such motivations influence official policy, they lead to a stimulation of uneconomic industries, for which the national market is not sufficiently large and for which the natural and human resources are not available. It may be pointed out, again, that in a particular case it may be difficult to distinguish between the rational and irrational reasons for such development. The effect of an industry on the future deployment of the productive pattern of a country can only be assessed in an approximate manner. Depending upon the degree that such a policy is adopted, it eliminates the gains that normally flow from trade relations based on the benefits that arise from geographic specialization.

Export Sector and Domestic Sector

The economies of many of the poor countries are characterized by a dynamic export sector, often developed under the influence of foreign technicians and capital. In contrast to its influence in the industrial countries, it has had only a weak secondary effect on the growth of national income and opportunities for employment in other sectors of the underdeveloped countries.[15] On the other hand, the productivity of this export sector is often higher than that of the domestic sector, and it frequently accounts for a relatively high percentage of the national product. Large countries, such as China and India with a high population density and a consequent labor-intensive agriculture, have a relatively small per capita foreign trade, but the latter accounts for a relatively high percentage of the national product in many small and middle-sized undeveloped countries. As the rest of the economy is often relatively static, the export sector tends to provide the main stimulus for growth. Imports tend to increase disproportionally following a rise in domestic demand because of the supply inelasticity of agriculture and local industry. In spite of its relative marginal character, foreign trade thus acquires a significance in the economically backward countries analogous to that of investment in the industrial countries.[16]

This can be most easily demonstrated by a description of what actually happens when export yields fall and the government attempts to support the domestic economy by expenditures for public works. Such a policy leads to increased imports and to a loss of foreign exchange that few countries can long afford. If the government attempts to check the increase in imports and the loss of gold and foreign exchange by imposing import controls, a rise in the price level, especially of consumer goods, will tend to occur. The supply inelasticity of additional factors of production hampers any substantial expansion of domestic production in the short run. On the other hand, the rise in the money stream as a result of additional government expenditure, will increase effective demand for food and essential manufactures, in view of the relatively high proportion of such items in the limited budgets of the general population or the high marginal consumption propensity. The tendency of the price level to rise will lead to a demand for higher wages in certain branches and in general increase production cost of exports in local currency. Thus, the profitability of exports will further decline, and there will be a strengthening of the forces clamoring for currency devaluation already induced by the initial fall in export proceeds. Any attempt to counteract a fall in exports by an active government policy, whether or not assisted by import restrictions, thus tends to lead to inflation and ultimate depreciation of the national currency.

The fact that their economies are thus dependent on the stimuli of foreign trade is looked upon with misgiving by the governments of undeveloped countries. They try to alter this passivity, both by diversification of export production, which distributes the risk of possible price declines or changes in the requirements of the world market, and by industrialization so as to enlarge the domestic sector of their economy and reduce their dependence on imports.

This disquiet is naturally connected with the fact that the strength or weakness of their economies is, to a large extent, determined by the changes in demand for raw materials from the industrial countries. This dependence applies to any country in a world economy, but because of the limitations in underdeveloped countries to counteract any decline in export proceeds by domestic measures, they feel that they are forced into a passive position in the present world trade constellation by the superior economic power of the advanced countries. F. Perroux[17] shows how this phenomenon is connected with every collision between unequal partners, and how this domination effect, particularly in international trade, puts the more highly developed countries in a position to lay down the rules of the game for the weaker side.

The diversification in the composition of the exports of most backward countries often has in the past originated from the activities of foreigners. This was the case in the former colonial areas in Asia. It is apparently also true of many Latin-American countries. H. W. Spiegel [18] notes that in Brazil most of the coffee and cotton export business is handled by foreign firms. Foreign investors and technicians coming in their wake saw the possibilities for expansion of the export potential for certain raw materials in response to an expected increase in world demand. They either, themselves, initiated the cultivation or exploitation of new products, or induced domestic growers or producers to augment their activities for their benefit.

The call for industrialization became stronger in the depression of the 1930's when the prices of raw materials and foodgrains fell to unprecedentedly low levels.[19] It has not diminished in vigor since that time, due to the general concern with the improvement in living standards. In many undeveloped countries the opinion is widespread that only through further industrialization can the wage levels in agriculture and existing industry be raised.

The argument seems too simple. In Australia, Canada, and New Zealand economic development was spearheaded by the expansion of agriculture. The elasticity of foreign demand for their farming products, plus technological progress making it possible to attain larger agricultural outputs with less labor, determined the farmers' increasing prosperity. Argentina and Uruguay have also followed this pattern with some success. The rise in living standards resulted in a more than proportionate growth of expenditure beyond the basic needs of food, clothing, and shelter, and it formed the stimulant to the establishment of domestic industries and the extension of services. Some of the early secondary industries set up in these countries were, however, ancillary to farm production. Only in more recent years did other large industries spring up as a result of the high level of internal demand and an active government policy of encouraging local industry.

In these countries primary production is practiced on a land extensive basis that cannot be imitated in densely populated countries. In the latter countries, industrialization may also be required because improvements in the agricultural sector will tend to save labor rather than create work for additional hands.[20] In some of the more sparsely populated countries in Latin America, the extension of the cultivated area also faces such formidable institutional and natural obstacles that industrialization may be considered the only alternative gradually to overcome them and to create the surplus with which to finance the expansion of agriculture.

In a United Nations study,[21] it is argued that industrialization is required for undeveloped countries as world demand for exported raw materials does not grow in proportion to the domestic demand for industrial goods and services. It has been calculated that a one per cent increase in per capita income in the United States tends to invoke a 0.7 per cent increase in imports of primary products. The same per capita increase in Latin-American income induces an increase in demand of 1.6 per cent for industrial goods and services. There is thus a tendency toward a disequilibrium between the demand for industrial imports and primary exports and the general need for each country to try to set its own rate of growth of per capita income in conformity with the increase in the number of active workers. In view of this, industrialization (especially the development of import substituting industries) is considered necessary to bring the level of imports in line with that of exports. Sound industrialization, warranting protection and import restrictions, is considered in this study to be determined by the growth rate of exports. The smaller the proportion of the increase in active population required for the rise in exports, as induced by the increase in income of the advanced countries, the greater should be the extent of industrialization.

Also, in this case, one factor seems to have been arbitrarily selected as influencing industrialization without regard to other factors. Not only the income elasticity of demand of the industrial countries for additional exports of underdeveloped countries and the diversification of demand in the latter upon a rise in incomes, but also the price elasticity of such foreign demand, the relative significance of export proceeds in the economic structure, the need for imported raw materials for new activities, and in fact, the whole resources pattern of a country, have to be considered in guiding investment decisions between the export and the 'internal' sector. It might be reiterated that more important than any external influences in an acceleration of development in poorer countries will be their potential to introduce modern production techniques. This applies to agriculture as well as to other branches of the economy.

The Pattern of International Trade

In order to understand the importance of stimuli produced by foreign trade, we must review in more detail the character of international trade. The industrial production of the world increased sevenfold between 1876–80 and 1936–38, the trade in raw materials fourfold, and the trade in manufactures by a factor between two and one-fourth to three. In 1870, Great Britain accounted for 31.8 per cent of the industrial production of the world; the United States, 23.2 per cent; Germany, 13.2 per cent; France, 10.3 per cent; Russia, 3.7 per cent; and the rest of the world, the remaining 17.8 per cent. In the 1936–38 period, the share of the United States had risen to 32.2 per cent, that of Germany had fallen to 10.7 per cent, while Great Britain had only 9.2 per cent, France only 4.5 per cent, Russia 18.5 per cent, Japan 3.5 per cent, and the remaining countries 21.4 per cent. It is worthy of note that, except for the rapid industrial growth of the Soviet Union, the somewhat slower expansion of the United States and Japan, and the modest growth of some other industrial countries (Italy and Canada), there was not a single undeveloped country in which the increase of industrial production influenced the distribution of world industrial capacity. It was entirely the unequal rate of growth within the group of industrial countries themselves which modified the total.[22]

For the year 1935, this League of Nations[23] study calculated that two-thirds of the exports of twelve industrial countries (not including the USSR, since its foreign trade was of subordinate importance) to the rest of the world were manufactured goods. These twelve countries imported four-fifths of the raw materials exported by the rest of the world. It showed at the same time[24] that, although the imports of manufactures in 1935 by the industrial countries were only about 35 per cent of the world total, their per capita consumption of imported manufactures was twice as large as that of the rest of the world.

This phenomenon springs chiefly from the increasing demand for manufactures accompanying an increase in wealth. It is plain that the smaller a country, the smaller *ceteris paribus* is its raw material base and the less its ability to produce efficiently a large variety of manufactures, the sooner its economy will demand the import of manufactures as it grows. The conclusion of this study is that, except for the depression of the 1930's when the normal trade pattern was disturbed, increasing industrialization tends to expand the import of manufactures.[25] The advancing industrialization of the world would thus produce a more varied demand in more countries, opening up the way for the import of higher grade manufactures. The effect of this structural change on the more advanced countries would depend on the extent and manner of the reorientation of their industrial system to meet this shifting demand.[26]

We have already mentioned that the diversification in consumers' demand, tending to result from industrialization, may be frustrated if population increases faster than production or if agricultural supply does not keep pace with the increase in purchasing power, with the result that prices for foodstuffs are forced up in relation to those of manufactures. The government may also deliberately adopt a policy of depressing consumption levels that might necessitate the export of manufactures by industrializing countries. S. H. Frankel[27] had this factor in mind when he recommended that any postwar aid program for the underdeveloped world be combined with the introduction of measures designed to improve the wellbeing of the population, so that greater markets would be opened up for foreign products and the pressure for exports by new domestic industries might be reduced.

Apart from these considerations, the study of Dominguez tries also to show that the facts on the world trade structure do not bear out the conclusion that industrialization would necessarily lead to an increase in the volume of world trade in manufactured goods. He calculates from the world trade figures for the period 1880–1951, after deflation by a wholesale price index, that the volume of world trade increased from 100 to 405.[28] The exports of the main industrial countries - responsible for about two-third of world trade during this period (United States, United Kingdom, Germany, France, Belgium, Japan, Italy, Netherlands, and Sweden until 1928, and these countries plus Czechoslovakia and Switzerland thereafter) - rose in terms of volume from 100 to 340, while those of the rest of the world increased from 100 to 549.

Dominguez calculates, and this is the most important point in his argument, that the trade among the industrial countries, or the so-called reciprocal exports, remained practically constant in volume throughout the period 1900–50.[29] The proportion of these reciprocal exports to their total exports fell from 58 per cent in 1900 to 37 per cent in 1950, and its share in total world trade from 36 per cent in 1900 to 19 per cent in 1950. It thus appears that almost the entire rise in the exports of the industrial countries is to be ascribed to the increasing trade between them and the raw materials producing countries, which embraces most of the undeveloped world. This trade accounted in 1951 for 65 per cent of the total world trade.

The above mentioned industrial countries show an increasing proportion of manufactures in the composition of their exports (1901–05, 54 per cent; 1936–38, 65 per cent; 1951, 69 per cent), while the exports from the rest of the world consisted of 85 per cent raw materials in 1936–38 and 83 per cent in 1951. The increase in world trade from the 1880's was thus principally caused by the expansion of exchange between manufactures of industrial countries and raw materials of the rest of the world. It should be observed that the 'rest of the world' includes several countries that cannot be considered underdeveloped. Australia, Canada, New Zealand, and the Union of South Africa, for example, appear among them. Their inclusion would seem to indicate that a preponderance of primary materials in the export pattern is, in any case, no hindrance to economic growth. The inclusion of those countries among the 'rest of the world' would also seem to be the explanation why the reciprocal exports of the raw materials-producing countries have risen even faster than their exports to the industrial nations.[30]

The world trade structure would seem, nevertheless, to have been geared to the need of the industrial countries for additional raw materials and the need of the not yet industrialized countries for higher quality consumer goods and additional capital goods. Once all countries are industrialized, Dominguez seems to imply, only the exchange of raw materials against raw materials, based on the different physical natural resources pattern of the trading partners, would have a bright future. All countries would then be able to satisfy their own demands for manufactures to a large extent. This situation may still be far off, but as the backward regions are now eager to withdraw from the role of being only a source of primary materials for the industrial countries and to promote rapid industrialization, the long-run prospects for an expanding world trade in manufactures do not seem to be particularly favorable.

On the other hand, it should be observed that the inelasticity of the exchange of manufactures against manufactures, which Dominguez has stressed, is also related to a nationalistically minded world. Theoretically, there seems no reason why the trade of manufactures against manufactures should not also have a high elasticity, as the diversification of the economic structure of more countries increases the disparities in the comparative costs of producing finished articles. The desire of the countries in western Europe to integrate their economies, in order to widen their markets and allow each country to concentrate on those activities for which it is more particularly suited on the basis of acquired skills and natural circumstances, is perhaps a sign that the industrial countries are combatting the static character of the exchange of manufactures between industrial countries.[31]

In the G.A.T.T. study, *International Trade 1954*, certain compilations were made about the postwar trade structure, as compared with a prewar year, that seem to show that Dominguez' analysis might have been oversimplified or new tendencies have appeared that he has not taken into account. In this study,[32] it is pointed out that between 1937 and 1954 the share of exports from industrial areas to nonindustrial areas and of exports from the latter to the former countries declined from 58.0 to 53.5 per cent of total world exports. This is ascribed to the rapid growth of trade among the industrial countries, especially in western Europe. In turn, it is related to the much larger increase in output of food and industrial raw materials in the industrial (especially North America) than in the nonindustrial regions. Agricultural production (food and raw materials) rose by 38 per cent between prewar and 1952 in industrial regions, whereas, in the nonindustrial regions, food production rose by only 16 per cent and agricultural raw materials production by 25 per cent over the same period. Mining production in the industrial world was 150 in 1952 (1938=100) and 205 in the nonindustrial areas, mainly on account of the rise in petroleum production.[33] As a result of this divergence in growth from 1938 to 1952 the exports of foodstuffs from industrial (again primarily the United States) to nonindustrial areas have more than doubled, while similar exports in the opposite direction rose only about 30 per cent. The trade in other raw materials (agricultural and mineral) between those two regions showed a decline by nearly 10 per cent between 1938 and 1952.[34]

The decrease in exchange between the industrial and nonindustrial areas is also attributed to the growth in trade in sheltered channels, i.e., within adjoining industrial areas and between those and the parts of the nonindustrial world with which they are associated through political and monetary ties or a common commercial policy.[35] The tendency for the input of raw materials to increase at a lower rate than the output of manufactured goods is given as the second reason for the decrease in trade between industrial and nonindustrial areas. It is shown that while the volume of world agricultural production (foodstuffs and raw materials) was only 29 per cent higher in 1952 than in 1934–38, and the output of world mining had risen by about 62 per cent, the volume of world manufacturing production had increased by 88 per cent.[36] These figures indicate that advancing industrialization does not involve a proportionate increase in the need for raw materials. Many industries process the semimanufactures or final products of other industries.

The improvement of technology also increases the amount of final product that can be obtained from a unit of raw material and, in certain cases, the amount of raw material that can be reclaimed from the final product after its utilization. It is probably true that there is a marked increase in raw material consumption at the beginning of industrialization but a leveling off during the later stages. For the industrial countries, it is demonstrated that the ratio between the consumption of raw materials and energy and the value added by manufacturing was roughly 33.5 per cent in 1938, but decreased to 24 per cent in 1952. On the contrary the ratio of input to value added by manufacturing was 87 per cent in 1938 and 83 per cent in 1952 in the nonindustrial areas.[37]

The tentative conclusion of the G.A.T.T. study is that this trend is likely to continue. Any increase in the price level of raw materials would encourage the further development of synthetic substitutes, as well as intensify efforts at lowering the ratio of input to value added by manufacturing.[38] However, as there are obvious limits to the relative decrease in input, most studies on future estimates of requirements for raw materials, as for example the Paley Report, foresee a substantial increase in world demand for foodstuffs, agricultural industrial crops and metals.

Industrial Europe imports 3.5 times as much raw materials per unit of value added by manufacturing[39] than the United States. However, the latter country is also becoming increasingly dependent upon imports of commodities critical to further growth. It seems natural that industrial countries that have been depleting at an accelerated rate their domestic resources will increasingly, in the long run, have to turn for additonal raw materials to underdeveloped countries whose resources are not yet exploited.

As a final observation, it is noted in the G.A.T.T. study that the fall in trade between the industrial and nonindustrial world cannot be understood without recognizing the protection offered to agricultural production by price support measures in the industrial countries and the protection given to industry in the nonindustrial world, with a subsequent tendency in some cases to neglect primary production.[40] The erection of tariffs and quantitative trade restrictions that this protection entails, result in a relatively high price for foodstuffs in the industrial countries and for manufactures in nonindustrial areas. They also have had an adverse effect on the exchange between industrial and nonindustrial regions.

No attempt is made in this study to weigh the importance of these different tendencies on the future pattern of world trade. But there appears to be a need to modify Dominguez' conclusion that the only expansive factor in world trade is, and has been, the exchange between manufactures from the industrial countries and raw materials from the nonindustrial countries.

The Significance of Foreign Trade for Economic Growth

Any expansion in the production of a commodity takes place in anticipation of increased demand. We have already noted that the production of essential consumer goods at the beginning of industrial development is usually first undertaken with the high elasticity of the demand for these articles in view. The limited extent of the domestic market makes this expansion difficult. Historically the opportunity for exporting to unindustrialized regions constituted a strong stimulus for the expansion of these industries[41] in some of the more advanced countries. This gain of export markets has often been at the cost of domestic handicrafts and cottage industries in undeveloped regions that could not compete in price with the imported factory products. At the beginning of industrialization, there are probably, in most cases, unutilized domestic natural resources sufficient for the initial expansion. The tendency to export is sometimes more important than the need to import.

In this connection, Keynes[42] has more or less justified mercantilism as an economic system within its contemporary framework. He pointed out that one of the objectives of attaining an export surplus was to stimulate domestic industry, since the additional funds thereby acquired depressed the interest rate and encouraged investment. It can probably be postulated more broadly that international trade was initially almost the only dynamic factor in several now industrialized countries, and that only gradually, through the capital accumulation occurring in this sector, were the other branches of the national economy affected. From this it should not be deduced that the growth of foreign trade of the western European countries prior to the industrial transformation automatically provided the capital for the next phase. The experience of many of the underdeveloped countries shows that different aspirations and attitudes reign in the sphere of commerce from those in the sphere of industry. But it can be assumed that the channels created by the commercial expansion facilitated, at a later stage, the export of a larger amount of manufactured goods.

We stated above that the propensity to export was initially stronger than the need for imports. This somewhat simplified assumption was based on the possible disproportion between the output of the industrial sector and internal demand, so that exports were necessary to widen the market. The necessity to export is, in a great many cases, inspired by the need to import capital equipment and foreign skills to foster development. However, it can readily be understood that after a time lag — depending on the extensiveness and variety of resources a country possesses — there arises the need for complementary raw materials to continue the process of growth.[43] Every expansion of the supply of one commodity involves an increase in the demand for other goods, and an industry can only keep expanding continuously if other industries also increase their outputs in a certain balanced proportion in response to rising demand. This proportion is determined in part by technical considerations and in part by the consumption structure of the country in question. This latter factor is, in its turn, related to the income level, the income distribution, and the relative magnitude of the various branches of production, dependent upon the pattern of resources.

The rate of growth depends, on the one hand, on the elasticity of demand for the goods whose production is being increased, and on the other hand, on the possibility of attracting additional factors of production. Evidently, the process of growth will be facilitated if the supply elasticity of the various required natural resources is great, particularly for the production of commodities with a high income-elasticity of demand. When the domestic supply of raw materials is becoming inelastic, the need for imports becomes imperative. Any country, given its available natural resources, will now try to fit the quantity and structure of its imports to the demands of the process of growth. In the beginning, it will still import manufactures that it can get more cheaply abroad than it can produce them at home. However, as continued growth requires additional raw materials, which industrial trade partners are likely to use more and more themselves, the foreign trade of the industrializing country will, perforce, turn to nonindustrial countries for primary commodities.[44] As new sources of raw materials appear, the conditions for economically producing more manufactures will improve. The country will thus try to diversify its industrial production to be able to offer as broad as possible a series of manufactures in exchange for the raw materials required. The trade with the countries producing primary commodities broadens the raw materials base for the industrializing countries. For countries endowed with a modest assortment of natural resources, income tends to become a dependent variable, while imports tend to become an independent variable in the process of growth. This is the conclusion reached by Dominguez,[45] whose reasoning we have followed in the above paragraphs.

The Dominguez scheme seems logically correct, but it places a one-sided emphasis on the significance of imports of raw materials in the process of growth. Even on the import side, imports of capital goods and foreign experience may be, as already noted, more critical in the development process than the increasing needs for foodstuffs and raw materials. The influence of industrialization upon the course of imports is a more complex matter.

In the League of Nations' study, *Industrialization and Foreign Trade*, it is assumed that the initial reduction in imports of the type of goods produced by new industries is — under a free trade system — bound to be offset over time by increased imports of capital goods and higher quality consumer goods, due to the rise in wealth. However, in the United Nations' study[46] already referred to, it is shown that the import patterns of Argentina, Australia, Brazil, Mexico, and the Union of South Africa — all countries that have experienced a substantial industrialization in recent years — have differed in a number of ways. Quantitative and qualitative import restrictions also make it difficult to generalize about the relationship between industrial growth and changes in the composition of imports.

In Argentina, for example, the per capita imports declined by more than half between 1910–14 and 1945–48. The same holds true for Brazil — when comparing per capita level of imports in the period 1945–49 with 1910–14. This decrease in per capita imports or in the volume of imports is explained in this study by the rather vague concept of "capacity to import" that is related to the growth potential of the export sector and the development of the terms of trade.

It seems self-evident that the country's power to import is circumscribed by the foreign exchange obtained through exports. What requires explanation is why a particular pattern of industrialization that affects export capacity and import structure is adopted. Unfavorable terms of trade for traditional export products do not necessarily affect economic growth unfavorably. They may, among other things, lead to a transfer of resources to more productive combinations and thus to new impulses for economic development. How such adaptations influence the volume and structure of exports and imports is the question which requires to be investigated.

In all the countries mentioned, however, a rise in the value of total imports has accompanied the process of industrialization, though in varying degree. Relative expenditure on capital goods, raw and semi-finished materials, and fuel (especially petroleum) has increased, while relative expenditure on manufactured consumer goods (especially foodstuffs and ordinary types of textiles) has declined. The need to import additional natural resources for continued growth, which Dominguez emphasizes, may well have been overriding, but it does not seem feasible to consider it more important than the need for the import of capital goods in an industrializing country.[47] The fact that the demand function determines the supply of raw materials and that price changes have little effect on the quantities offered, as W. A. Lewis[48] has demonstrated, would seem to prove that this demand is largely of a physical character. But this still would not warrant placing it in a class apart.

It can be argued with better reason that it is not the import factor that formed the most important link in the chain of growth in many countries, but the increasing need to stimulate exports in order to maintain a continued development. Generally, it is more difficult to find specific purchasers over and over again for additional raw materials and especially for more specialized manufactures, than it is to obtain such goods as a buyer. It is significant that Cordell Hull, the father of the more liberal United States tariff policy, should have based his defense on America's compelling need to export its surplus production.[49] This need for export prevails, particularly in the case of the United States, in the sphere of primary production (wheat, cotton, and tobacco). This illustrates again that industrialization may well be accompanied by a continuing effort to export raw materials.

A distinction should be made between sparsely populated and densely populated countries. The first group could theoretically maintain growth by continually exporting additional primary commodities. The second group would seem eventually to be dependent on the export of manufactures to pay for its needs for additional raw materials and foodstuffs. This would imply that the sparsely populated countries could build up an industrial structure largely in conformity with the changes in internal demand, resulting from the increase in incomes. It is clear that their industrial growth might be accelerated in so far as they could export manufactures of those industries for which economic and technical considerations favor a larger output than can be absorbed by the internal market.

In this connection, it is interesting to note that a substantial degree of industrialization has caused no major change in the composition of exports in Australia and Brazil.[50] They thus seem to have met their growth requirements by exporting more of their traditional raw and semimanufactured materials and foodstuffs. On the other hand, Mexico and the Union of South Africa[51] show a considerable increase in exports of manufactures, as percentages of total exports. The fact that in the first two countries the relative share of manufactures in total exports has remained the same implies, of course, that exports of manufactures have expanded *pari passu* with total exports. A more thorough analysis would be required to reach any conclusion on the relationship of capturing export markets for manufactures to the growth pattern of the countries in question — all of which would seem to fall into the sparsely populated country class.

A distinction ought probably also to be made between

manufactures whose value consists largely of raw materials that the country produces in abundance and manufactures largely incorporating labor and managerial skills. The first type of manufactures might give no clue to the efficiency of the country as an industrial producer. The second type, if not subsidized, needs to match the standards of the older industrial countries.[52]

Whether a country would need to export manufactures or raw materials to sustain its economic growth might not be easy to decide in each individual case. The relation between population size and resources is an elastic one, as we said before. The extent and quality of a particular resource and the elasticity of world demand for it may be more important in the long run for economic growth than the diversity of the resource pattern, in view of the importance of obtaining foreign exchange for the import of supplementary capital goods. In any case, the raw materials basis of most underdeveloped countries would seem to be rather limited. Relatively soon they will have to call on imports to supplement their requirements. G. Wythe[53] estimated for a prewar year that in Brazil and Mexico 20 to 25 per cent, and in Colombia even 50 per cent of the raw materials used in the industrial sector had to be imported. It would be interesting to know the dependence of other undeveloped countries in this respect.

The undeveloped countries, whatever their trade needs for economic development, may face a difficult situation if they require external markets for industrial products to achieve a balanced growth. The general backwardness of their industrial sector usually does not enable them to meet the competition in quality and price of the older industrial countries in third markets. Their internal price level for manufactures, held up by high tariffs, is often considerably higher than the world level. In the immediate postwar period, Brazil and Mexico, for example, built up a sizeable export of cotton fabrics, due to the general scarcity and a relatively high price level for such goods. Subsequently these exports declined to a negligible quantity.[54]

India's cotton textile industry, on the other hand, seems to have become highly competitive. Its postwar export of cotton piece goods was substantially larger than its prewar export. Although it has been tapering off since 1950, India is now the second largest exporter of cotton goods.[55] Though a more thorough investigation would be required, it seems from a superficial study of postwar Indian trade figures that Indian cotton goods have kept their ground in underdeveloped countries in the British Commonwealth, but that they lost ground due to Japanese competition and import restrictions in territories outside this bloc. India has, at the same time, increased its export of 'greys' to the United Kingdom where they are further processed. It is, of course, too early to predict whether this export of factory made cotton goods will be affected by the emphasis placed in India's Second Five-Year Plan on the expansion of cottage industries and restriction of the increase in factory production of essential consumer goods.

An additional obstacle in gaining foreign markets is that the manufactures that the undeveloped countries might offer for export are just the ones that other countries desiring to industrialize will strive to produce themselves. The changing composition of world trade in manufactured goods, as analyzed by T. Tyszynski,[56] bears out this tendency. He has shown that textiles, apparel, and other consumer goods (simple metal manufactures, drinks, tobacco, and miscellaneous) comprised 40 and 16 per cent of total trade in manufactures respectively in 1899, but only 20 and 10 per cent respectively in 1950. Motor vehicles, industrial equipment, electrical goods, and agricultural machinery, on the other hand, show a substantial percentage rise over the same period. These are just the products on which the older industrial countries will concentrate as they are trying to shift their resources from the declining to the expanding groups of articles in world trade. The undeveloped countries will thus initially have to enter an export market for goods that show a downward trend.[57] So, the countries potentially able to expand their production of raw materials for exports would seem to be in a better position to further the process of growth.[58]

According to R. Nurkse,[59] the underdeveloped countries are now reluctant to expand their primary production. The demand for primary products today no longer shows the secular rate of expansion it did in the nineteenth century — as a result of the declining rate of population growth in the industrial countries and the efforts of those countries to reduce their dependence on imported raw materials by developing substitutes. In our opinion, the problem is more complicated than Nurkse indicates. Historically, the undeveloped countries have played a more or less passive role in the world economy; the potentiality for the expansion of their raw materials base has generally been made effective through the inflow of foreign capital, leadership, and, sometimes, immigrant labor. These countries desire now to apply part of these resources to their own industrialization. Increasing the export of surplus resources, in their eyes, would tend to reinforce their dependence on the markets of the older industrial countries. The relatively large price fluctuations make them hesitant to expand raw materials output for this purpose, as well as the often implied necessity of admitting foreign capital for their exploitation.

A United Nations study[60] has proposed that the countries endowed with adequate iron ores — but lacking suitable metallurgical coal supplies — attempt to procure such coal in exchange for their surplus iron ore. The establishment of an iron and steel industry is recommended for these countries, in spite of the limited market, because of the general effect it would have on the expansion of the industrial sector. Since coal and iron are raw materials that lose a large proportion of their weight during production, the iron and steel industry is 'raw-material-oriented' rather than 'market-oriented'.[61] Because coal loses relatively more weight than iron ore (on the average it takes a ton of coke to smelt a ton of good iron ore, but two or more tons of coke to convert this pig iron into steel products), the iron and steel industry is attracted towards coal deposits. This customary reasoning has lost much of its force with the improvement of transportation and of techniques of smelting. In the United States, an effectively organized system of transporting iron ore to coal mining regions and coal to iron ore regions has allowed these industries to spring up both in coal and iron ore regions. The above recommendation for backward countries possessing iron ore is based on this experience. Before such an exchange is warranted, however, a great number of other economic and technological factors have to be considered besides the desire of the underdeveloped countries to establish iron and steel industries.

The 'Terms of Trade' and Economic Development

As we have seen, the pattern of foreign trade in recent decades has been shaped by the needs and potentialities of the industrial countries. International trade was a means for fostering their economic growth. The ingenuity and perseverance of their entrepreneurs were developed and sharpened in the continuous adjustment of their economies in the struggle for foreign markets.

The undeveloped countries are well aware of the connection between trade and development. This is shown by the following remark by the Argentinian economist R. Prebisch: "The solution (for developing Latin America) does not lie in growing at the expense of foreign trade, but in knowing how to extract from a yet greater trade the dynamic elements necessary to its economic development".[62]

He argues[63] that history has shown that technical progress has been greater in industry than in agriculture and mining. If, owing to higher productivity, the prices of industrial products had fallen in comparison with those of raw materials, the "ratio of exchange" would have shown a consistent trend in favor of the raw materials producing countries. But, he reasons, in the period of upswing — the cyclical process is considered characteristic of the development of the capitalist economy[64] — the wage level rises in the industrial countries as a result of trade union pressure. The decline in the prices of manufactures, therefore, does not take place which means that the advantages of increasing productivity accrue exclusively to the industrial countries. In the downswing period — whose typical characteristic is a relative oversupply of consumer goods with respect to effective demand — the entrepreneurs and workers are able through their organization to achieve a relative stability of the profit and wage levels in the industrial countries. Thus a large part of the burden of the reduction in profits and wages is thrust onto the undeveloped countries, so that the prices of their primary products exported by the latter fall off more sharply than those of imported manufactures. The solution, according to Prebisch,[65] is for the Latin-American countries to industrialize. Then the wage and price levels will rise in the agrarian sector as well, and the countries producing primary commodities will ultimately pluck the fruits of technical progress, which they would have enjoyed if the prices of manufactures had fallen in relation to the prices of raw materials.

The idea of Prebisch that the undeveloped countries have not profited from the increased productivity in the industrial countries seems at variance with historic reality. W. Schlote[66] has calculated that the terms of trade, i.e., the ratio between the average price of export goods and the average price of import goods for a country, moved unfavorably for England over a long series of years during its industrial development. On the basis of a price index for 109 imported raw materials (including foodstuffs) and 56 export commodities, he shows that, taking the year 1694 as 100, the index for import goods stood at 169 in the period 1854–60, while it was 43 for export goods in the same period.

Elsewhere,[67] he demonstrates how the ratio between the index of export prices for manufactured goods and the index of average import prices between 1814 and 1854 — and the ratio between the former and the index of imported raw materials between 1854 and 1933 — continued to deteriorate until the last decade of the nineteenth century. Taking 1913 as the base year, the terms of trade were 129 in 1814, 93 in 1854, and 107 in 1894. The terms of trade kept fluctuating around 100 from 1871 to 1918, and it was only after 1918 that the index suddenly, by jumps, became favorable to Great Britain and stood in 1933 at 175.

These data tend to show that the countries that sold raw materials to Great Britain received a continuously increasing yield, measured in British export products, up to about 1880. This conclusion is exactly contrary to Prebisch's reasoning.[68] These countries, therefore, would seem to have really benefited from the increasing productivity of British industry, manifesting itself in a relative decline of the export prices of British manufactures up to 1870.

After 1870, various new tendencies appeared. The increased export of foodstuffs and industrial raw materials from previously virgin regions (the United States, Canada, Argentina, and Australia) depressed prices of primary products. But this phenomenon expressed itself only gradually in a shift of the terms of trade in favor of the industrial countries, probably owing to the partial counterbalancing of this trend by the continuous price decline of manufactures. It is generally assumed that this drop in the price of raw materials from the beginning of the 1870's to the end of the 1890's resulted from the improvement of the transportation system, which was stimulated by the flow of private foreign investment and immigration from the industrial countries to these new regions.[69] It seems quite likely that the unfavorable shift in terms of trade for the primary producing countries was the consequence of a differential increase in the productivity of the world's primary production, which improved more rapidly than that of manufacturing activities.

The often cited quotation from a United Nations study[70] — that the terms of trade for the countries producing raw materials deteriorated so much between the last quarter of the nineteenth century and the outbreak of World War II, that, on the average, a certain quantity of primary products at the end of this period would purchase only 60 per cent of the amount of manufactures it had bought at its beginning — would thus find a logical explanation. The terms of trade turned more favorable for the industrial countries in the 1920's, and even more in the 1930's. As a result of the relative inelasticity of the production and consumption of cereals and raw materials, by 1933 the price level of food products had fallen 33 per cent below the 1919 level, that of raw materials 41 per cent, but that of manufactures only 18 per cent. However, if we consider that this was also a period in which most of the industrial countries were afflicted with chronic unemployment, it seems hard to maintain that this development operated exclusively to the disadvantage of the countries producing raw materials.[71]

Since the publication of Prebisch's analysis and of the United Nations study mentioned above, a considerable literature has appeared on the importance of the terms of trade for economic development.[72] It has been pointed out that price trends without reference to volume have little practical value. Instead of a commodity terms-of-trade index (i.e., the ratio of export to import value), an income terms-of-trade index, using the total value of exports divided by an index of import prices, has been recommended to indicate the changes in the volume of imports purchased through export trade. As imports are usually valued c.i.f. (i.e., inclusive of transport charges), and exports f.o.b. (i.e., exclusive of freight), long-term changes in transport cost can also give a distorted picture of advantages or disadvantages resulting from a change in the price relation between exports and imports.

As terms-of-trade indices over a long period exist only for now industrialized countries, their trend is generally used for drawing conclusions of the effect on underdeveloped countries. A favorable movement in the terms of trade for the industrial country may, however, coincide with a favorable trend for the undeveloped trading partner. The price decline of exports for the underdeveloped country can be more than offset by a fall in the freight rates for imports, so that the c.i.f. price of imports drops relatively more than export earnings.[73] Even if such refinements are taken into account, the terms of trade will give no clue to the changes in productivity in the production of export goods, of the influence of increasing or decreasing exports on the mobilization of domestic labor and capital for other activities, and, similarly, of the effect of imports on the general welfare of the country.

H. Myint[74] has observed that the distribution of income should also be considered. In underdeveloped countries, an improvement in the terms of trade may actually be accompanied by a fall in the proportion accruing to the domestic population, and only lead to an increase in the amounts of profits being remitted by foreign capital overseas. A more fundamental objection is that over a period, considerable modifications usually occur in the composition of exports and imports, which create distortions in the comparisons of price indices based on certain weights in the structure of exports and imports in one particular year. Also, an index can never reckon with quality improvements that generally affect manufactured goods more than primary commodities. Thus they should be an important factor in weighing the gains from foreign trade for an undeveloped country, which is usually an exporter of raw materials and an importer of manufactures.

In the postwar period the terms of trade have, in general, been more favorable than before the war for the countries producing raw materials.[75] Colin Clark has connected this tendency toward a favorable price relation between the exchange of raw materials and manufactures with the fact that the production of raw materials takes place principally under the law of diminishing returns.[76] Due to the relative inelasticity of the land factor and the fact that more mineral resources can be obtained only at greater cost, prices of raw materials would tend to rise faster than prices of industrial commodities, whose production generally occurs under the law of increasing returns. Clark does not explain why this tendency happens to manifest itself at this particular period of world history. In earlier periods, the possible effect of this tendency has been pointed out, but it apparently was offset, from the 1880's till the depression of the 1930's, by the extension of the cultivated area in new regions, technological improvements in food productions and the discovery of new and not necessarily costlier mineral resources. Clark has also advanced another reason for the relative greater rise of prices of primary products compared with manufactures in the future. Due to the general growth in world income and the relative inelasticity of demand for the products of primary activities in comparison with the demand for the products of secundary and tertiary industries, an accelerated outflow of labor from the primary sector would occur, tending to an increase in production cost in primary production.[77] However, this tendency seems unlikely. The relative inflexibility of demand for raw materials accompanying a rise in world income might have a depressing influence on the prices of raw materials, while a movement of labor out of primary production could be compensated by a greater application of capital or technological improvements, so that the relative cost of primary production would not necessarily rise.

In a G.A.T.T. study,[78] the improved ratio between the prices of raw materials and manufactured products in the postwar period is attributed to the relatively larger advance in manufacturing productivity. It will be noted that this argument is similar to that expressed before. This cause might well have been the basic reason for the unfavorable trend in the terms of trade for the industrial countries, as shown for the United Kingdom, which could be observed in the eighteenth century and until about 1880. This tendency would then have reasserted itself again in recent years, after having been inoperative from around 1880 or later until the 1930's.

It would seem too early to decide whether any particular law underlies the fact that the postwar prices of primary products have been more favorable in relation to those of manufactures. The pent-up demand and the requirements for foodstuffs and raw materials for postwar reconstruction, the increase in consumption of foodstuffs and raw materials in many potential export areas due to an accelerated rate of population growth, the retention of a larger share of primary commodities due to the efforts towards industrialization, and political changes (e.g., the elimination of eastern Europe as a raw material export area), may be more plausible reasons for the explanation of this tendency for the time being. It should also be observed that the price support programs for primary commodities instituted in certain countries has had an effect on the price levels of some products appearing in world trade.

Most authors would now seem to agree[79] that the price ratio between raw materials and manufactures is likely to remain more favorable in the foreseeable future than in the 1930's for the primary producing countries, though for different reasons. This does not exclude the possibility that price movements of foodstuffs and other raw materials, and of the various commodities included in each group, might exhibit different tendencies. Price and income elasticities of demand and supply differ during different stages of development.[80] Independently, or as a result of divergent price trends, technological innovations may favor the substitution of one article for another in industrial processing. This would affect again the pattern of world trade.

The favorable price trend for raw materials versus manufactures will perhaps also contribute to a better understanding of the limited usefulness of the terms-of-trade concept for long-term development analysis. In every industrializing country a relative low level of remuneration in agriculture seems to have gone hand in hand with a relatively higher level in industry. This differential in remuneration is usually explained by a difference in productivity. However, it can also arise from conscious action, through the fixing of a relatively low purchase price for agricultural products (e.g., in the Soviet Union) or by raising the price level for manufactures by tariff walls.

It would seem hard to discern a similar trend for the world economy in which prices for raw materials and manufactures appearing in world trade are formed, as a rule, free from the influence of a single supplier or buyer. However, the higher productivity of labor in industry than in agriculture makes an unfavorable secular shift in the terms of trade for industrial countries seem a normal situation. Experience has shown that such a tendency is not detrimental to an industrializing country, provided the increasing productivity of its export industries and the expanded volume of its exports more than offset this effect. The favorable terms of trade for manufactures between 1880 and the 1930's, of course, may well have been responsible for the substantial rise in levels of living of the general population in some of the western European countries during that period.[81] However, it did not prevent the growth of some of those new countries, whose resources came into effective use due to the improvement of the transport system and the stream of foreign capital and immigrant labor. The export price of their products was still well above domestic cost, which happened to be lower for the commodities in question than in older supply areas.

Private entrepreneurs are not likely to be greatly influenced by movements in the terms of trade. As far as they are dependent on foreign prices, their decision whether to undertake an activity or not is based on the anticipated export price of their commodities as compared with the domestic cost, or by the import price of competitive products compared with the anticipated domestic selling price. Any unfavorable development in the terms of trade will naturally affect the economic structure of a dynamic economy. If import prices of manufactures rise relatively, the establishment of new industries will be encouraged. If export prices decline relatively, a transfer of resources to more productive activities will be attempted or an effort made to improve the efficiency in old industries to restore former profit levels.

It must readily be admitted that in underdeveloped countries such a readaptation is more difficult to achieve. A relative price rise of imported goods may not be a spur to the setting up of import-replacing industries, due to the lack of industrial skills and in general the absence of an industrial climate. For the same reasons, a price fall of export commodities, *a fortiori* because they are products of a sector in which relatively large fixed and small variable cost are normal, may not stimulate efforts to increase productivity or a shift to other activities.[82]

It would seem that the largely static character of the economies of the undeveloped countries, with its resultant inflexibility of resource allocation and slow pace of technological change, is largely responsible for the emphasis they place on a shift of the terms of trade in their favor. A favorable trend, signifying the possibility of procuring a larger amount of import goods for a given amount of export articles, however, will lead to economic growth only if entrepreneurs, or governments, or both are encouraged — by the domestic disposition of the factors of production and a suitable institutional framework — to utilize the additional proceeds for the import of complementary raw materials and capital goods for this purpose. In an underdeveloped economy, the relative increase in export prices may lead to a further expansion of primary production or, more often, to a larger consumption of imported consumer goods. The domestic private investment pattern and the absence of an industrial environment would seem ultimately the reasons why underdeveloped countries have so far not reaped the benefits of the impulses provided by foreign trade, whether the terms of trade have been favorable or not.

The Future of International Trade

It is hazardous to predict the future role of international trade in economic development. The present pattern differs from the prewar pattern, as a result of the efforts toward industrialization as well as the political changes. The world trade structure before World War II, particularly before 1928, was assumed to tend toward a specialization based on the comparative scarcity of the factors in various countries. Now there is a growing awareness, especially in the undeveloped countries, that these differences were largely manmade. The organizational and managerial talents in the advanced countries are mainly responsible for their relative capital abundance. These same characteristics determine their domestic resources utilization (for example, their ability to take advantage of the economies of scale) and their dependence on outside supply resources. Because the backward countries are trying to develop similar skills, it is difficult to foresee in what direction the future trade pattern will evolve.

The underdeveloped countries will still need an export surplus of primary products to finance the import of additional foodstuffs, raw materials, capital goods, and the services of foreign technicians and capital, which, considering the general scarcity of more highly qualified labor and of capital, will continue to be necessary. Over the long term, these countries can themselves develop the factors to take over the functions of foreign labor and capital and diversify their industrial production in such a way to supply a larger fraction of the domestic market. By training native workers, dependence on foreign technicians can be diminished. By agricultural improvements and industrialization (the processing of raw materials for export, for example) the composition of exports can be modified. And more emphasis can be placed on imports of capital goods and complementary raw materials for capital formation than on imports of luxury consumer goods for a small well-to-do group.

A country richly endowed with natural resources and a potentially great domestic market, such as the Soviet Union, may be more or less independent of foreign trade. But, as we have shown, there seem to be few countries that can follow such a policy. W. A. Lewis[83] has emphasized that there may be more countries that need to export manufactures in order to achieve economic growth than many people think. He obviously has in mind the densely populated regions where the pressure on natural resources is usually greatest. He mentions China, Java, India, and Egypt. In his view, they would have to become exporters of simple consumer goods with a large labor content, since their limited domestic market does not allow large-scale industrialization. Only through exports of processed goods could they purchase the additional foodstuffs, raw materials, and capital goods for their continued development.

Lewis, however, fails to indicate how these countries — in spite of the advantage of a relatively low wage level — can acquire the experience and can construct the complementary capital goods to enable them to compete with the industrial countries. Although a few countries in this category are exporting manufactures at present, the magnitude of such exports remains small in relation to their total foreign commerce. In Lewis' study on the British West Indies,[84] he makes similar proposals for these islands, which are also afflicted with "too many farmers and too little land" and practically no other resources except an abundance of labor. In this case, he had in mind the example of Puerto Rico, where indeed considerable progress has been made[85] by a purposeful industrialization policy. Unfortunately, it does not seem that this policy can easily be duplicated elsewhere, as Puerto Rico belongs to the American economic orbit. United States private capital was easier to attract by special measures (low taxation, free factory buildings, etc.), as well as the low wage level. Also, substantial gifts from the United States government and the repayment of excise taxes on Puerto Rican rum sold in the United States made possible the expansion (through public investment) of the necessary 'overhead' capital. The process has, moreover, been eased considerably by the unrestricted flow of Puerto Ricans to the mainland, thus reducing population pressure on the island.

If, and when, such densely populated countries are in a position to increase their industrial productivity to such an extent as to become potential exporters of simple consumer goods or manufactures in general, they may still face the prospect of entering markets for goods that show a declining trend in the composition of world trade, and which are high on the priority list for other countries bent on industrialization. It would, therefore, seem logical for such countries to concentrate on the export of manufactures, preferably with a large labor content, based on some natural resources with which they are well endowed. India seems to have followed this path by now exporting jute manufactures (burlap, hessian, and bags) instead of raw jute. She may in the future become an exporter of iron and steel products due to the possession of ore with a high iron content and large coal deposits.

Limitation of the local market, which is an obstacle to industrialization, may be lessened by the formation of custom unions among undeveloped countries. A custom union provides for the free flow of commodities among member territories and the establishment of a uniform tariff on imports from nonmembers. It is feasible chiefly among neighboring countries, and these often have similar resources. Although such unions generally do not expand the supply of factors for industrialization, the increased demand for manufactures may provide opportunities for erecting one industry in one country serving the market of all partners and another industry in another country, fulfilling the same role, thereby contributing to a more effective utilization of resources within the union area. The political obstacles to be overcome for a smooth functioning of such a union should not be underestimated. The prerogatives of sovereignty are no less anxiously guarded in underdeveloped countries than in industrial ones.

Despite the industrialization efforts of the underdeveloped countries, their development is likely to depend for a long time on the export of primary commodities, of which they can produce a surplus under favorable conditions. However, changes in the structure of demand of their trading partners are not necessarily conducive to their growth. Whether their export articles encounter a low income-elasticity of demand in a growing world economy may be partly beyond their control, but they are interested in a more stable price level for primary products.

This desire is motivated by the larger past fluctuations of prices of raw materials than of manufactures, to which we have already referred, and by the fear of a relative decline in raw material requirements — especially of the industrial countries because of technological changes. A significant manifestation of this anxiety was the unanimous support by undeveloped countries of a resolution proposed by the representative of Argentina in the Economic Committee of the General Assembly of the United Nations. It called for the establishment of parity between world prices for primary commodities and finished articles and urged the governments "to refrain, unless unavoidably required by national security. . . from encouraging the production of any synthetic or substitute materials that unnecessarily affect the international demand for natural primary products."[86] Although no base year was indicated in which the price relationship between raw materials and manufactures was considered as being normal, one can imagine a price support scheme similar to the schemes now instituted in many industrial countries to strengthen the position of primary producers. Not unaware of the political implications of any such schemes, they claim protection of their interest on the same social grounds, especially in view of their economic backwardness and the dependence of their economies on the proceeds of one or a few export commodites in external markets. The above resolution was toned down under the influence of the industrial countries, but this subject is likely to be a recurring one in the organs of the United Nations.

Most writers on the subject of future world trade are in agreement that the growth of such trade can be expected to lag behind the growth of industrial production. This is partly because an increase in industrial activity, and in national income in general, implies a relatively greater rise in the utilization of domestic raw materials, capital, and labor than in the need for imports of complementary factors of production. This inequality between the increase of industrial production and the increase of international trade has again been confirmed by the recent G.A.T.T. study.[87] The share of total production traded internationally dropped from 28 per cent in 1925–32 to 20 per cent in the postwar period. Primary production exchanged in foreign trade fell from 30 per cent in 1927 to 26 per cent in 1951. The proportion of manufacturing output traded internationally declined from 26 to 16 per cent over the same period. This tendency does not necessarily imply a continuing relative decline in world trade, as is apparent from the figures on the expansion of international trade already given.

D. H. Robertson[88] contends that the volume of foreign trade will diminish, as the comparative advantages between "granaries and workshops" in the conditions of production become smaller. Viner has expressed his doubts about this view: "Even leaving 'backward' peoples out of account, I am not convinced that there is more levelling of industrial knowledge and skills today in the textile industry or in manufacture at large than there was a century ago."[89] The industrializing countries — and at present the whole world is involved in the process — will modify the structure of their imports. They will tend to import those manufactures for which the comparative productivity of national and foreign production differs most sharply and additional raw materials to complement their own resource basis. This remains true, in spite of the fact that such countries are usually prepared to support certain 'key industries' at home, irrespective of comparative cost.

It is difficult to evaluate the effect of this tendency upon the future size and structure of international trade. Besides differences in resources patterns, the influence of government intervention on import and export patterns would have to be weighed. Such changes have, however, been in progress for a long period, and the older industrial countries have had to meet the challenge by timely shifting of capital and labor into industries producing goods for which an increasing external demand could be expected.[90] Though certain branches in the latter countries have been affected, the following statement of a League of Nations study would still seem to be true of their overall industrial position: "Up to 1913 there was nothing to indicate that the gradual spread of industry tended to upset the balance of the older industrial countries so as to hinder their economic growth; on the contrary, there are strong indications that these countries more than held their own."[91]

The rise in the relative importance of private foreign investment in the expansion of raw materials resources may tend to increase the future supply of primary commodities in world trade. But this tendency may be offset to some extent by the diminishing needs of the older industrial countries. The need for international trade will persist as long as climates and natural resources patterns differ from one region to another, and the great differences in the availability of complementary factors of production, capital, and leadership continue. The more industrialized countries will have a continuous interest in the traditional exchange of raw materials against manufactures.

The overriding goal of the undeveloped countries, especially of those that are densely populated, is to provide full employment for their labor forces. To achieve this aim, they must create additional employment opportunities for their fast growing populations. World needs for primary commodities of which they have a surplus may not grow at a sufficient rate. Internal supply limitations may prevent the expansion of production of raw materials for which world demand is highly elastic. In either event, the requirements for the continued economic growth of those underdeveloped countries will not be met. The size of the industrial sector has then to be increased over and above the establishment of such industries that have become economically warranted because of the rising level of living. Such 'infant industries' may have to be protected against competition from abroad by tariffs or subsidies. Despite the initial loss in consumer welfare due to the difference in price of national and imported products, this might lead to a better utilization of local resources, especially if the raw materials for such industries can be found locally. Such industries may hasten the diversification of their economies. Protection, on the other hand, may give rise to an uneconomic industrial sector, especially if the country lacks managerial and technical abilities. Such a development would not yield an efficient international division of labor as might result from free trade. However, as already explained, free trade does not assure underdeveloped countries the full employment of their resources.

The basic conflict between the already industrialized countries and the underdeveloped countries was apparent in the discussion on the Charter for an International Trade Organization, which received its definitive form in 1948 in Havana.[92] This Charter did not come into effect, mainly because the United States, in spite of its protectionist past, opposed the freedom of action demanded by the undeveloped world to institute import quotas, import licensing, and tariff discrimination to foster their own industrial growth. This Charter might have provided a set of basic principles governing international trade and a measure of control over the actions of industrializing nations. The member countries could have judged the validity of the claims put forward for protection against the prescribed circumstances laid down in the Charter allowing a raising of duties or other trade restrictions.

The functions of the Charter for the regulation of international trade have to some extent been filled by the General Agreement on Tariffs and Trade, signed October 30, 1947, by some twenty countries. Thirty-four countries have since become members. The Charter dealt with the whole gamut of commercial policy (tariffs, quantitative restrictions, subsidies, state trading, customs formalities, the prevention of restrictive business practices, standards and procedures limiting the negotiation of international commodity agreements, and rights and obligations of governments in the treatment of foreign investments within their borders). The G.A.T.T. is more limited than the I.T.O. would have been, being in essence an arrangement by which governments agree to grant tariff concessions to each other and to observe certain procedures when establishing trade barriers.

Under Article XVIII of the G.A.T.T., underdeveloped countries have practically unlimited rights to introduce or increase restrictions and tariffs on the basis of the infant industry argument. However, the Agreement provides a forum of regular consultation, and thus it contributes to instilling in its members a sense of international responsibility by requiring valid reasons for any deviation of the previously negotiated tariff patterns. It is to be hoped that the legislatures of the industrial countries will approve the Organization for Trade Cooperation (O.T.C.), to be established as the body to administer the G.A.T.T., as it and the G.A.T.T. seem likely to incorporate for the foreseeable future the only international code of behavior in world trade now acceptable to most countries.

Chapter 11

THE GOVERNMENT SECTOR

The Role of the State

A small national per capita production suggests that only a relatively small margin of the national income is likely to be available for capital formation. In some cases, this margin is still further reduced by the utilization of part of the income by the wealthy strata for the consumption of luxuries. Also the orientation of much of the private investment that does occur is not conducive to economic growth that might lead to an improvement of the level of living of all elements of the population. Moreover, in some countries the structure of foreign trade has not encouraged economic diversification that might have accelerated the increase of capital stock and eventually the increase in mass consumption.

In many underdeveloped countries, the responsibility of stimulating the process of economic growth and of guiding investment into more desirable channels tends to fall on the government. This is in spite of the handicap of an inefficient administrative organization as well as an inadequate fiscal and monetary machinery from which many of them suffer. The fact that, in many of the undeveloped countries, a large proportion of the economy is only partly monetized makes it difficult for the government to procure resources adequate for financing the desired development. However, this did not prevent the levying of a heavy land tax at the beginning of Japan's industrialization — a tax that yielded more than 85 per cent of that government's income in 1875–76.[1]

It has already been noted that the primary objective of the

collectivization of agriculture in the U.S.S.R. was also to tax the primary sector for the benefit of industrialization. In mainland China,[2] too, a land tax collected in kind accounted for 41.4 per cent of the total estimated state revenue in 1950. In Japan, the raising of additional tax revenue was accompanied by a substantial increase in agricultural output, so that the low living standard of the average peasant was not further reduced. Collectivization in the Soviet Union and mainland China, despite its professed aim, seems so far only to have resulted in keeping the farmers' standard of living at the barest minimum. Such a policy seems out of keeping with the political climate of most underdeveloped countries; they strive especially to raise the status of the primary sector in which most of their human capital is embodied.

Remarkably enough, there is an extensive literature on the manner by which the governments of the undeveloped countries could increase their share of the flow of money. That represents the income side of the question, but relatively little attention has yet been given to the expenditure side: the question of how capital formation can be encouraged by public expenditure and other means. Theoretically, the principle upon which such an expenditure policy should be based can be stated rather simply. During a given period of time, the four money streams (arising from consumption, private investment, exports, and government expenditure) compete for the available factors of production. It is necessary to aim at a distribution that will maximize the rate of growth of the national product, or according to marginal analysis, assure that each of the last units of income of every sector shall make a similar contribution to the national product. In practice such a distribution is arbitrarily determined, and the principle thus provides only a very rough guide for the expenditure and investment policy of a government.

Relative ignorance of the effect of government expenditures on development may be attributed to the circumstance that, while the revenue of the state has been a subject of study since antiquity, the significance of the public spending policy, especially for the diversification of the production structure, has hardly been investigated. The former problem also lends itself more readily to analysis. No precise line of demarcation, however, can be drawn between these two sides of the question, since the fiscal and lending policy of the government also exerts a direct influence on the allocation of resources, the volume of private expenditure for consumption and investment being automatically limited by the taxes levied. Thus the extent to which private consumption and investment may reasonably be reduced by the tax system should be determined by the social utility of the pattern of government expenditure. That is to say, maximization of public revenue should not be the goal, but rather the maximization of desirable investments and of the well-being of the people.

In principle state expenditures are not essentially different from private expenditures. In many undeveloped countries they are devoted mainly to consumption purposes, the pay of officials charged with what Adam Smith calls the first and second functions of the state, the defense and judicial functions, in the broad sense. These expenditures, however indispensable they may be for the creation of an environment in which the economy can develop, do not themselves directly contribute to economic development. It is the outlay for Adam Smith's third function of the state — "that of erecting and maintaining those public institutions and those public works, which, though they may be in the highest degree advantageous to a great society, are, however, of such a nature that the profit could never repay the expense to any individual or small number of individuals, and which it therefore cannot be expected that any individual or small number of individuals should erect or maintain"[3] — that contributes to real capital formation. Expressed in more modern terminology, the government has the power, through its so-called autonomous investment, i.e. investment not induced by prior or expected short-term changes in income, to create conditions which may facilitate economic growth.

The preponderance of consumption expenditure over investment can be illustrated for several countries. In Iran, it is estimated that 80 per cent of the 1949–50 budget was paid out in wages and salaries. The expenditures for salaries alone comprised 60 per cent of Chile's 1947 budget. In Cuba, the International Bank[4] reports that salaries and pensions made up more than 90 per cent of government expenditure, and concludes that the government exercises little direct influence on the investment pattern. But this argument needs to be qualified, as part of wages and salaries might have been paid for construction that would help to increase the capital stock. A large number of civil servants, according to the Bank's report, perform no useful function (as has been noted for other under-developed countries). They owe their position to political influence, which, in itself, is an indication of concealed unemployment and the lack of alternative employ- ment. Similarly, it is deplorable that such a large share of state expenditures in many economically backward countries consists of outlays for defense. Often this is a sign of internal political weakness in such countries, where the army, in addition to being responsible for maintaining internal security, tends to dominate national politics.

Investment expenditures also consist partly of wages and sala- ries, but they differ from consumption expenditures in that they help to enlarge the capital stock and hence future productive power.[5] Such expenditures may, among other things, be used for education and public health, for public works (irrigation, open- ing up of new land, construction of roads and canals), and for the establishment of public utilities. Such autonomous investment, not geared specifically to market demand or commercial profit- ability, can create the framework or the external economies within which private investment is subsequently encouraged to undertake new industrial activities, or induced investment. In this way, the process of growth initiated by the state is continued. More- over, in view of the lack of incentive or managerial and technical ability on the part of private investors, the state, in addition to its task of providing the economic and social 'overhead' capital, has often to initiate and finance new industrial ventures. Besides this direct concern with economic activity, the state can indirectly

assist development by granting subsidies to new private undertakings, increasing import duties on certain manufactures, offering special tariff concessions on imported equipment, or freedom
from taxes for certain enterprises for a definite period, to encourage the founding of pioneer industries.

The Pattern of Government Income and Expenditure

In the past, the most important claim of public finance was
military expenditure. Land taxes yielded most of the income received from feudal lords granted fiefs for services to the ruler.
A. Bonné[6] states that it was only as a result of western influence
in the Middle East after World War I that income, inheritance,
and turnover taxes were introduced in the area. Widening of the
tax base made it necessary to centralize administrative power,
and this process of establishing and strengthening a central administration is still in progress in various countries. Where the
government lacks an efficient body of officials to assure the implementation of tax laws they remain dead letters.

With the integration of undeveloped countries into the world
economy the difficulties connected with the assessment and collection of land revenue tax tended to make governments turn to
an ever increasing extent to import and export duties to pay for
state activities. In India, for example, the land tax that comprised 53 per cent of state revenue in 1883–84 comprised only 21
per cent in 1923–24. Import and export duties, which accounted
for only 3 per cent in the former year, accounted for 24 per cent
in the latter year.[7]

The depression of the 1930's, which was accompanied by a
sharp decline in foreign trade and in the yield of import and
export duties in many countries, reinforced an already noticeable
shift from revenue to protective tariffs. The subsequent expansion
of the domestic economy caused substantial changes in the revenue structure. In Argentina, Colombia, and Mexico, the proportion of the import and export duties fell from 48, 62 and 37

per cent, respectively, of the total state revenue in 1923 to 39, 44 and 30 per cent, respectively, in 1937. This decline gives an exaggerated impression as other forms of taxation derived from foreign trade, such as consular fees, excise taxes on articles of foreign origin, port charges, and income from foreign exchange control, increased. H. C. Wallich[8] considers this decline still to be characteristic of the modified tax structure in Latin America.

But any taxation policy necessarily remains a function of the economic and social structure of a country. In Iran, an American mission under the direction of Dr. A. C. Millspaugh attempted to introduce a number of sweeping reforms in the tax system from 1943 to 1945. A commercial accounting system was proposed for all government enterprises and monopolies, but there were not enough qualified personnel to keep accounts. The new income tax, reaching a maximum of 80 per cent for the highest brackets, aroused the opposition of parliament and senior public officials. The tax of 50 per cent on all income derived from land could not be implemented in view of the dispersal of many tracts, the lack of data on income levels, and the absence of any system of property registration. As a result, the receipts remained far below estimates. In 1946, after the departure of the mission, the former system was restored with its 30 per cent maximum tax rate on income and its exemption of income from landed property, which remained subject only to a land tax. While in 1938–39, import duties and fiscal monopolies contributed 38 and 32 per cent of budget revenues, respectively, these percentages in 1949–50 were 31 and 37, respectively. Income tax yielded 13 per cent of state revenue in 1938–39 and 16 per cent in 1949–50.

Although in most industrial countries the demand for social justice has made direct and progressive taxation of income the major source of state revenue, the consistent application of such a tax is not yet practicable in the undeveloped countries. Only a relatively small group rises above the prevailing modest level of living, so that the opportunities for direct taxation are relatively slender. Exact assessment of income is usually a matter of difficulty. In many cases, higher income recipients exercise an important influence on government policy and, to protect their own position, they tend to resist the introduction of a progressive tax system. As a result of the inadequacy of the fiscal and administrative apparatus of the state in many backward countries, it is less the citizen's ability to pay than the government's capability to collect that constitutes the principal criterion for the tax policy.

A study by the United Nations[9] shows that the level of income tax-exempted in many underdeveloped countries was many times the average estimated national per capita income, and that these two levels were much closer together in the industrial countries. In India in 1953, for instance, a married man with a wife and three children was liable for income tax only when his income reached seventeen times the estimated national per capita income. In Great Britain and the United States in 1950 this obligation would have begun when the income exceeded about twice the national per capita income.[10] It should also be borne in mind that redistribution of the national income by means of a progressive system of taxation tends to increase the rate of consumption. Since taxation in itself does not lead to an increase of the national product, such a reorientation may contribute to a strengthening of inflationary forces.

As was the case during the development of the industrial countries, indirect taxes still provide the major part of state revenue. In Asia, indirect taxes range from 61 per cent of state revenue in India to 95 per cent in Thailand.[11] The cumulative effect of these levies on consumer goods increases the price level, thus tending to limit the possibility of absorbing additional consumer goods. Similar patterns prevailed in the now industrial countries. Ursula Hicks[12] states that over 70 per cent of the state revenue in England in 1828 consisted of import duties and excise taxes. More than one-fourth of this came from duties on foodstuffs and nonalcoholic drinks, and a substantial part of the rest came from excise taxes on bricks, glass, hides, and other articles appearing directly or indirectly in the consumption budget of the average working man. These taxes had the effect of reducing real wages and thus caused involuntary saving, which encouraged capital formation at the expense of immediate consumption.

A. H. Hansen[13] reports that, in the United States, the yield of import duties and excise taxes in 1902 made up about half of all tax revenue, and in 1913 about 40 per cent. The personal property tax was almost entirely responsible for the rest of the receipts, and insofar as it affected rental buildings in the cities, this tax was passed on to the public. Hansen thus concludes that, up to 1914 when the Federal income tax was introduced, the tax system in the United States was highly regressive and imposed a heavy burden on the lowest income groups. In the Soviet Union, too (where in 1940, 70 per cent of the state revenue consisted of 'excise' taxes) there is still an extremely regressive tax system. Perhaps these levies on consumer goods, however, are not quite the same as in the private enterprise economies, since the relative compensation of the various factors of production is included in the planned price and wage level.[14]

It may be noted that indirect taxes are not necessarily of a regressive nature. Tariffs and excises imposed primarily on luxury goods (liquor, automobiles, radios, gasoline, and public entertainment) may even be progressive. But in view of the relatively slight importance of such articles and services in the economy of undeveloped countries, the government usually has to have recourse to excise and turnover taxes on such simple consumer goods as sugar, salt, matches, and kerosene.[15] It is interesting that, in order to increase the receipts of the Indian government, which in relation to national income have remained rather static in postwar years, it has been recommended that Article 286 (3) of the Indian Constitution be amended to remove the present exemption of articles "essential to the life of the community" from the scope of sales taxation.[16]

Among the indirect levies, duties on export commodities continue to be particularly attractive because of the ease of collection. This is so above all in the countries where export production is mainly in the hands of foreign enterprises. Such a tax is particularly important when world price levels are high in relation to domestic cost and when the price elasticity of demand is low for the export articles in question — that is, when an increase in price causes only a relatively small change in demand.[17] Following the practices developed in Germany during the depression of the 1930's, various countries have also combined their tariff policy with their foreign exchange policy. Differential export exchange rates are set up so that a smaller equivalent in national currency is paid for the so-called strong products (articles for which a strong world demand exists at a relatively high price), while a larger quantity of such currency is paid for weaker products (articles for which world demand only exists at a relatively low price).

E. R. Schlesinger[18] shows how a variable exchange rate for different types of import goods can influence the volume and the pattern of consumption and investment. Similarly, multiple exchange rates for export products can stimulate the export of certain commodities. But Schlesinger shows that this method may be ineffective in underdeveloped countries as a subsidy alone is not necessarily sufficient to increase production. Setting a low conversion rate for the proceeds from a strong export product appears to be a suitable way of obtaining foreign exchange at low cost expressed in local currency, but if such a measure is combined with unfavorable exchange rates for imports then the incentive for expanding production may be lost. If foreign capital is affected by such measures, it may attempt to liquidate its possessions, for example, by neglecting its existing installations or refusing to import new machinery. This practice may also be followed by national producers.[19]

By establishing a government monopoly or controlling the marketing of the principal export products, a few countries have succeeded in obtaining substantial funds for their public investment programs from the difference between the world market price and the domestic price. E. Reiche[20] reports that in Argentina the Institute for Promoting Foreign Trade made a profit in 1947 of 1.2 billion pesos on a turnover of 5 billion pesos. This profit was about equal to the estimated annual investment during the First Five Year Plan (1947–51). In Burma, the State

Agricultural Marketing Board was responsible for about 40 per cent of the total state income in 1949–50 and 1950–51; of the profits of this Board, about 50 per cent was used for public investment.

Such a form of taxation is likely to give rise to dissatisfaction among the producers of the commodities responsible for the profits. In Argentina, taxes on farmers have led to a substantial decline in agricultural production but in Burma, the peasant seems to be less conscious of state interference, since the spread between domestic and foreign price in the years mentioned seems about equal to the share formerly retained by middlemen for their services. Fiscal experts have often pointed out that an adequate income tax would be more equitable than export duties, whether or not supplemented by foreign exchange discrimination. But collection of direct tax is more costly and presents many administrative difficulties.[21]

The land tax prevailing in many undeveloped countries is archaic. It rarely takes account of differences in productivity, but usually involves a single uniform rate per unit of land. A modification of the land tax to assure maximum cultivation of potentially arable land, by the imposition of additional taxes on uncultivated arable land, seems to have been adopted by very few countries. It has often been proposed that investments benefiting agriculture, such as irrigation schemes leading to higher yields, should be combined with a land betterment levy to recoup part of the cost, but this, too, has seldom been practiced.

The increment in land prices resulting from the pressure of increasing population on a relatively fixed area of arable land is also often taxed relatively lightly, thus encouraging investment in such land. The income from buildings also remains undertaxed. Their value is often determined as of the time of construction or of some past date and does not take into account the increment due to increased prices.

Another proposal of experts is that profits on real estate transactions should be taxed more heavily so as to make investment in buildings less attractive. Such a measure would require a system of registration for land and buildings, and the government is often held back from establishing such a system by the groups that have an interest in continuing this weakness in the tax structure. It is reported,[22] for example, that new buildings in Turkey are exempted from the buildings tax for three to ten years. Moreover, tax is relatively low on income from rentals and on capital appreciation of houses and buildings. According to the International Bank: "With the exemption and special treatment described above, housing, particularly of the luxury type in the major cities, has undoubtedly attracted an excessive amount of investment and one result has been to limit. . . investment funds required by industry."[23]

Income tax, although in effect today in most countries, still encounters the traditional objections.[24] In many parts of Latin America, for example, different categories of income are taxed at different proportional rates, and there is also a progressive tax on total income. The system is complicated by the many preferential schedules and by the exemptions received by certain groups. In many countries, the tax authorities depend on the filing of returns by the groups subject to income tax. Since there is inadequate control and many potential taxpayers keep unsatisfactory account of their income, receipts remain below estimates. Government workers and employees whose tax is deducted from wages and salaries by employers pay their full tax. Commerce, agriculture, self-employed workers, and the liberal professions, tend to remain undertaxed. We often find that foreign concerns, which frequently are the largest and most important companies in the country, pay more scrupulously than small native enterprises. Some types of shareholders also tend to escape taxation. For example, the fact that bearer shares are mostly unregistered makes it impossible to trace the recipients of dividends, except as this tax is collected at the source.[25]

To stimulate productive investment, new industrial undertakings are often exempted from income tax for a number of years, and accelerated depreciation is allowed on buildings, plant, and machinery. Reinvested profits are sometimes taxed at preferential rates for the same purpose. Such losses to government revenue are justified if the new private investment leads to desired economic development.

A progressive inheritance tax is now common in most developed countries. It is argued that a substantial part of any fortune should revert to society through the state on the grounds that the environment — society — made possible the accumulation of such wealth. Progressive inheritance taxes are seldom used in most backward countries.

The careful balancing of higher rates and preferential treatment for certain types of developmental activity require both sound administration and skillful manipulation of the tax structure. Few countries pursue a redistributive fiscal policy, and punctilious compliance with tax legislation is still a rare virtue in many countries; nevertheless, one can note that governments in several countries have succeeded in tapping new sources of income in recent years.[26] This can be ascribed partly to the awakening of a sense of social justice in such countries and partly to a gradual modernization of the tax system as a result of outside expert advice. Such changes in the tax structure usually take time since they also involve social changes which may be resisted.

One of the weakest points of the tax system in many underdeveloped countries remains the unorganized nature and lack of clarity of the revenue structure of the government. A case in point, reported by an expert of the United Nations, concerns the duties on foreign trade imposed by Ecuador in 1950.[27] Superimposed on the ordinary tariff, all imports were subject to an additional impost of 1.5 per cent ad valorem for the water system in the capital, Quito, and the port, Guayaquil, 4 per cent for the water systems in other provinces, 1 per cent for tuberculosis control, 1.5 per cent for dredging the Guavas river, 1 per cent for public works and hygienic measures in Quito, and 0.5 per cent for the maintenance of the Palace of Justice and university buildings. All exports were subjected to an ad valorem tax of 1 per cent for tuberculosis control and 0.75 per cent for an Ecuadorian cultural center. A 5 per cent tax was levied on cocoa exports for the Chambers of Commerce, and 0.20 sucres per quintal of rice for the youth movement in Guayaquil. One sucre per dollar had to be paid on all import licenses for the benefit of a number of public and semi-public institutions, 4 per cent of the total value for general purposes, and finally a 10 per cent surcharge for a number of other specified institutions. The purpose of such practices is to safeguard revenues for specific purposes against the risk of parliamentary opportunism. Such an unwieldy tax structure, apart from its administrative complexity, places also a strain on the accounting system of the private enterprises involved as many of these taxes have to be paid separately.

Obtaining an insight into the budgetary situation in many undeveloped countries is difficult indeed. The anticipated receipts are sometimes only roughly estimated, since no basis for a more exact approximation exists. Often, moreover, the budget is not scrupulously followed. Transfers from one section to another may be made, or extraordinary expenditures voted by the legislature or undertaken by the executive branch without specifying the means by which they are to be covered. The budgets of the governments of undeveloped countries often lack unity and universality. That is, some public revenues and expenditures remain outside the regular budget. Ideally, the budget should be consolidated, that is, should include all revenues and expenditures of the state. Under such a budget, all departments and state enterprises receive only funds from appropriations annually authorized. The absence of unity tends to encourage extravagant expenditures — apart from the complex administrative machinery that must be maintained by the finance ministry and the central bank through which the funds for the special institutions usually pass.

The desirability of introducing a distinction between current and capital budgets has often been emphasized in reports of visiting experts on the tax structure of underdeveloped countries. Such a distinction may serve several purposes. On the revenue side it may be desirable to list, as receipts in the capital budget, yields of the inheritance tax, of other capital levies, and of mining enterprises which signify the dissipation of a production factor and for which renewable capital should be created by the government. Such taxes could not then be used for current, but only for capital expenditure by the state.

The separation of current and capital accounts is generally considered to be even more important in order to determine the different nature of government expenditure, particularly how much of government funds is used for investment. Most of the wages and salaries of civil servants, the purchases of goods and services for the daily government administration and the armed forces, would be accounted for in the current budget. The capital account would show the government's contribution to real asset formation, preferably distinguishing further between revenue producing and nonrevenue producing capital. Indirect investment by the government, i.e., loans and advances to individuals which may lead to capital formation in the private sector, should also be listed separately. Through the use of appropriate capital accounts, the measurement over the years of the government's development program becomes possible. The keeping of a certain balance between projects that will soon yield a return and those that will mature only in the more distant future may be facilitated. It is claimed that such distinctions will serve to provide guidance with regard to tax and government lending policy, though it is admitted that other factors must also be considered, in particular the general inflationary tendency of capital expenditures.

However desirable such a budgetary distinction and its ramifications may be, as a means of gaining an insight into the significance of government activity for the national economy and as a deterrent to any tendency toward extravagant expenditures and borrowing, the adoption of such a distinction is too exacting for the fiscal machinery of most governments in undeveloped countries. The idea that the state budget need not be balanced, and that an increasing state debt merely involves a shift of funds from one group of citizens to another, is only too readily accepted by these governments. This is despite the fact that a deficit policy tends to be particularly inflationary because of the rigidity of many elements in their economies, and the high propensity for consumption when per capita income is low.

It is sometimes pointed out that a rising national debt, if it stems from borrowing from individuals, may lead to the growth of a *rentier* class at the expense of a producer class. It may thus diminish the small industrial sector, which is precisely where the entrepreneurial element should be strengthened. This objection is rather theoretical for an underdeveloped country in view of the low level of productive investment by private capitalists. Moreover, the increase in national debt often stems from an expansion of bank credit or of the currency issue. Thus it does not represent real savings, i.e., a foregoing of private consumption or investment. If the additional government expenditure does not lead to an increase in the production of consumer goods but forces up the price level instead, the required reduction in consumption usually comes about involuntarily for those groups whose remuneration lags. Such a development will not necessarily affect the savings capacity of the small group of entrepreneurs. As a result of the increasing price level, they will see their profits and the monetary value of their capital assets rise. The justification of a rising national debt depends on the wisdom of the investments undertaken by the state.

It is easy to reproach experts who make unrealistic suggestions for improving the tax structure, but such recommendations may satisfy a deeply felt need of those in charge of economic development in backward countries. The same tendency may also be observed in their interest in analysis of national income, social accounts and the input-output structure. In view of the relative importance of government direction of economic development, information on the working of the economy, on consumers' expenditure, private investment, government revenue and expenditure, and on the possible sources of savings to finance additional investment is especially desirable. Unless the relative importance of the various economic variables and their interrelationship is known, sound policy can hardly be formulated. However, the idea that the scarcity of data on the economies of the undeveloped countries is a handicap for an effective policy has often been over-stressed by economists of developed countries. In reality, their economies are often relatively simple, and the weight of the forces making up the national product easy to establish, at least roughly. An undue concentration on purely economic analysis, further-more, may lead to a neglect of the institutional factors hampering development.

The ineffectiveness of the tax system and continually increasing government expenditures (as a result of the economic and social tasks that the state feels compelled to undertake) have resulted in chronic budget deficits in several backward countries. Due to the still rudimentary money and capital market, the government usually has only limited possibilities of borrowing. Among the reasons for this situation are inadequate saving by the public at large, political and monetary instability that leads to lack of con-fidence in the government on the part of those able to save, and relatively low rates of interest on government bonds in comparison with alternative fields of investment.[28]

In Latin America, government bonds are often marketed by giving them to contractors in payment for public works, and by prescribing that they be purchased in specified amounts or pro-portions by social security and other institutes. The social secu-rity system, which in many countries is financed from withholdings of wages and salaries of workers, tends to reduce the volume of consumption and stimulate capital formation. As long as receipts exceed payments, the government possesses an instrument for the transfer of funds from the private sector to more productive public investment. In Brazil, the social insurance institutes have contributed to industrialization by subscribing to bond issues for semipublic corporations in the fields of iron and steel, electric power, machinery, and the development of the basins of various rivers.[29]

The most convenient way for the governments to borrow is directly from the central bank.[30] The government can fix the interest rate payable to the bank, and since it also shares in the bank's profits, it can pay part of the interest out of these profits.

Also, the central bank often pioneers by placing certificates of participation in government bonds with the commercial banks. Since this involves short-term paper, and the credit of the central bank is often better than that of the government, the certificates can often be more easily placed.

A somewhat different method of finance has been followed in Latin America in the setting up of development corporations ('Institutos de Fomento') to diversify the economy by providing more flexible and generous credit facilities than are granted by commercial banks. In some countries, these corporations have established research agencies that perform market analyses for new industries. They usually study the technique, structure, and location of applicant firms before making a decision to invest. Surveys of natural resources, establishment of pilot plants, laboratories, and experimental stations, and the training of qualified labor are also undertaken under the auspices of some of these institutes. New industries may be established or the long-term credit needs provided for suitable private enterprises within the industrialization program. Development corporations and industrial banks are financed in ways that vary with the economic and political climate of the country, but a large proportion of the capital is usually subscribed by the government.

In India, for example, an Industrial Finance Corporation[31] was established in 1947 with an initial capital of 50 million rupees. The state and central bank each subscribed a fifth of its capital. Trading and insurance companies, investment trusts, and similar institutions were responsible for the balance, on which the government guaranteed a fixed rate of interest. The corporation has the right to guarantee loans raised by industrial enterprises on the private market, it may itself subscribe for shares or bonds, and it may issue its own bonds to an amount equal to four times its original capital. The corporation is exempt from income tax and excess profit tax. In March, 1955, outstanding loans had reached 128 million rupees. An International Bank report on Ceylon[32] proposes the establishment of a development agency to be financed through the issue of a 'suitable range of government securities'.

In this way, private savings now used to purchase tea and rubber plantations from foreign owners, for speculation or held as bank deposits would be used for new productive purposes.

Because of the complexity and heterogeneity of the public sector, it is not possible to discuss all the ramifications of the problem within the short space available here. Moreover, the importance of the government sector in the economy differs from country to country. In India, for example, in 1948–49 the government's share of national expenditure was 9.2 per cent,[33] while in Turkey, government expenditure is said to have been between 26 and 28 per cent of the national income.[34] According to the ECAFE Survey for 1949,[35] the proportion of investment in the state budget in India rose from 13 per cent in 1947 to 44 per cent in 1949, but the share of government revenue in national income remained at about 7 per cent. This was also the average proportion of the state budget to national income in Thailand, Malaya, and the Philippines, compared with 14 per cent in Burma and Ceylon. The fact that public development expenditure in the countries of south and southeast Asia increased by 27 per cent from 1952–53 to 1953–54 and by 31 per cent between 1953–54 and 1954–55 shows that to an increasing extent, the state is assuming responsibility for capital formation.[36]

Published reports contain little quantitative information on the extent to which government activity has contributed to economic diversification and a change in industrial climate in undeveloped countries.[37] However, one does sometimes find criticism of the organization of public corporations or of government industrial activity in general. There are often allegations that projects have been initiated for which the economy is not yet ripe and for which the necessary managerial ability is lacking.

The report of the International Bank on Turkey[38] shows that the organization of the Sümer Bank, concentrating on industrial investments, and the Eti Bank, dealing with mining and electric power, does not encourage the efficiency of established industries. The same report[39] also draws attention to a number of unwise investments made by the Turkish government: an airplane engine factory and a rayon factory, requiring both highly qualified labor and expensive equipment, but not producing essential goods. It also mentions the example of the establishment of a woolen textile industry, although the wool produced locally was too coarse to be spun into cloth for garments. Thornburg[40] notes the errors committed in setting up a steel industry in Karabük reflecting lack of industrial experience. Wythe says of Brazil's plan for setting up its own merchant marine: ". . . the possibility of developing a big international merchant fleet, on a sound and economic basis, is limited in a country with large undeveloped internal resources, a shortage of manpower and capital, and limited metallurgical industries and skills. Certainly improvement of the internal transportation problem should come first."[41] Writers on the economic problems of backward countries often refrain from going into details on such mistakes. A similar reluctance to dwell on institutional obstacles to economic growth, or to criticize the public investment pattern, can be observed in reports of international agencies dealing with underdeveloped countries.

Despite the inefficiency of the revenue collecting system and errors in the expenditure pattern, the state's share of the national income is tending to increase in most underdeveloped countries. This seems a healthy tendency in the early stages of development, especially when private investors have a predilection for land, commodity stocks, and luxury residential building. Whether the government's increased command over resources has led to the improvement of the well-being of the citizens might be hard to prove in any particular case, though the international attention devoted to economic development and the pressure of the masses may encourage the state to invest in projects for the enhancement of the level of living.

Data for Mexico[42] throw some light on what a purposeful policy can accomplish in an underdeveloped economy. Between 1939 and 1950 public investment rose from 38 to 45 per cent of total investment.[43] Investment in the transport sector (mainly roads and railroads) was greatest, followed by investments in agriculture and irrigation, electric power and the petroleum industry, and construction.[44] As a result, the length of the road system increased, the railroads transported a considerably larger tonnage, agricultural production rose, more electric power was generated and consumed, and oil production showed considerable improvement.[45] The structure of private investment seems not to have been greatly affected by the public investment. Only private investment in agriculture, mainly consisting of investment in agricultural machinery, increased from 11 per cent in 1939 to 18 per cent in 1950 of total private investment.[46] However, the resulting increase in income and effective demand, added to the reduction of imports and the elimination of foreign competition as a result of the war, stimulated the textile industry, the iron and steel industry, cement production, the pulp and paper industry, and the chemical industry.[47]

Total per capita consumption and food consumption rose considerably,[48] although it is pointed out in the report that the material welfare of both peasants in the old agricultural areas and industrial workers as a whole failed to show any improvement. It implies that the benefits accrued mainly to agriculturists who migrated to the newly developed regions and to those workers who moved from lower paid to higher paid occupations.[49] In Mexico expansion was accompanied by severe inflation. As a result, the share of wages in the national product declined from 30.5 in 1939 to 23.8 per cent in 1950, while the share of profits rose from 26.2 to 41.4 per cent. Whether this change in income distribution led to substantially larger private investments in equipment — unfortunately the private investment pattern is the least thoroughly treated in the Bank study — is to be doubted. Other observers[50] have remarked that the new income distribution has contributed to a narrowing of the market for manufactured goods, in accordance with the tendency noted earlier, and has resulted in an increased channeling of savings into inventories, luxury building, and deposits held in the United States. From the slowing down of the rate of expansion after 1950, it is evident that previous government activity has not yet ushered in an era of autonomous and accelerated growth.

Due to the absence of sound private investment and shortcomings in the industrial climate, the government will have to participate more actively in economic development in underdeveloped countries for a much longer period than in many industrial countries. The collection of increased revenue through higher taxation, which such a role implies, is handicapped by the low level of living of the mass of the population and by the need to maintain incentives in a private enterprise economy. It is even more exacting in existing conditions, as it is now claimed, in the name of social justice, that a fair and equitable burden should be imposed on the different classes of society. Such an inequality of income distribution should be allowed that will maximize investment and individual initiative. Any transfer from high to low incomes resulting in an increase in aggregate consumption should, at the same time, be a stimulant for increased investment in industries providing for such an expansion of effective demand. But such a balanced policy is hard to carry out in practice.

Perhaps we take too gloomy a view of the difficulties of the governments of undeveloped countries in supplementing and modifying the private investment pattern. An historical perspective would no doubt reveal similar obstacles in the development of the industrial countries of today, where, in any case, public investment, financed by public borrowing,[51] also played an important role in the process of growth.[52] In the United States, the improvements in the transport system, above all the construction of roads, canals and railroads, was financed by state expenditures. It was only in the second half of the nineteenth century that the growth of private fortunes caused government credit to decline in relative importance in the development process.

What really matters is whether public investment does, in fact, help to create conditions suitable for continuous economic growth. Since a large part of the economic and social investment undertaken by the state leads to an increase in the quantity of money, and while such expenditures by their very nature will help to expand the flow of goods only in the relatively distant future, it must be one of the major tasks of the government to mop up that portion of the increased income to which no new consumer goods and services correspond. It is especially in this respect that governments of many undeveloped countries show a notable weakness, as will appear in the following chapter on inflation, in which the economic and social variants already discussed will reappear in a somewhat different light.

Chapter 12

INFLATION

Inflation: Definition and Causes

The four components of the national income which have been discussed — consumption, private investment, exports, and government outlays — reflect and correspond to the allocation of the factors of production available to the economy during the period in question. The expenditures, or total demand, arising from these components determine the aggregate flow of goods and services in the monetary sector. The prices of the factors of production and of the available goods and services help to determine, and are in turn determined by, the actual distribution. People can consume no more than the current quantity of domestically produced and imported goods and services. But to the extent that income is also generated by private investment, by an excess of exports over imports (export surplus), and by an excess of government expenditure over revenue (budget deficit), prices are higher than they would be if total income were derived only from the production of goods and services available for consumption. The excess in the income flow not derived from the production of currently available goods for consumption constitutes the savings of the economy and is equal to the volume of investment. If the increase in income through a rise in private investment, an increase in export surplus, or in budget deficit is not compensated by new savings, the volume of monetary expenditure (or effective demand) will increase without a corresponding increase in the supply of goods and services. Such a disproportion between effective demand and the supply of goods and services is indicated by the term inflation and expresses itself in a rise in the price level.[1]

In view of the relevance of this phenomenon to the course of economic development, it deserves discussion. No inflationary pressure will arise when an expansion of income coincides with an increase in the supply of consumer goods as a result of previous investments. The inflationary pressure will remain small when unutilized or idle resources are absorbed into the production system by investment expenditure and the corresponding counter-flow of disposable consumer goods soon increases. Schumpeter[2] has shown how in various industrial countries reckless banking was responsible for increasing the productivity of existing and new factors of production.

However, it has already been pointed out that, in spite of disguised unemployment in the labor force in many underdeveloped countries, the factor supply schedule is generally inelastic. If the additional expenditures described above take place at a time when all production factors are already employed, some of the resources that were previously used in the production of consumer goods will be transferred to the production of investment goods. The new flow of money so created will compete with existing expenditures for goods and services for the diminished quantity of consumer goods and will force up the prices of such commodities.

This price rise tends to lead to a modification in income distribution; in particular, the ratio of profits to wages tends to increase. Since usually a smaller proportion of profits than of wages is consumed, a point in the price rise will ultimately be reached where the demand for consumer goods again equals the reduced supply of these goods. A new equilibrium is thus attained. Corresponding to the reduction of consumption, there is an increase in savings, incorporated in the newly constructed capital goods. In a private enterprise economy these savings originate primarily from increased profits, while in the centrally planned economy they are derived mainly from additional state revenue. It has already been noted that such a process of reducing consumption may be called forced saving implying an involuntary increase in savings, brought about by a rise in the prices of consumer goods and a change in income distribution.

It is evident from the foregoing that the quality of the investment, the time lag between the additional investment expenditure and the appearance of an additional flow of consumer goods, and the duration of the 'excess expenditure' largely determine whether the price rice will be short lived, continuous over a period, or followed by a drop in prices. It will also be clear that many development projects tend to create inflationary pressures. Some, for example, involve the transfer of workers from primary to non-agricultural occupations where incomes will increase the demand for foodstuffs and essential manufactures. If such a shift is not accompanied by a proportional increase in food supplies released from the countryside, food prices will tend to go up. To avoid such a development requires imports or simultaneous investment in agriculture in order to assure that agricultural output and marketable supplies rise *pari passu* with the increase in demand. While increased food imports may alleviate such a situation, they tend to have the disadvantage of diminishing the funds available for the purchase abroad of raw materials and equipment that may be required for the new activities. This disadvantage could be offset to the extent that the new industries produced commodities which were formerly imported or which will be exported. Nevertheless, our brief analysis may suffice to show the need for coordinated development if inflationary tendencies and pressures on the balance of payments are to be avoided.

The pattern of investment in underdeveloped countries with many rigidities in their economic and institutional structures makes it difficult to avoid the inflationary tendencies evoked by the development process. In many underdeveloped countries little private investment tends to occur spontaneously; more comes in the wake of inflationary trends already in progress. This may account for the fact that a substantial part of private investment in many countries takes the form of investment in land, luxury building, and commodity stocks for which a continuous price rise is expected.

In many of the economically backward countries, export surpluses have been responsible for pressure on the domestic price level, especially during World War II in those countries whose products were in great demand. If the increased income resulting from an expanding export surplus accrues mainly to the more well-to-do group whose needs for locally produced consumer goods have already been satisfied, pressure on the price level will remain slight. But if the increased export surplus means a rise in income for a relatively large segment of the population, or if the addition to exports is at the expense of the domestic supply of consumer goods, the additional income will exert the same effect on the price level as described above.

Some governments were able to tax part of the resultant expansion of income. A number of countries used the savings thus acquired to take over certain private foreign investments or to reduce public foreign debt, thereby relieving the future balance of payments. However, since the inflation ensuing from the increase in the supply of money was seldom effectively curbed by price controls or rationing of scarce essential goods, it led to a proportionately larger increase in profits (and savings) of the well-to-do classes. These liquid assets were largely responsible for the pent-up demand for foreign durable consumer goods that led to the substantial imports of such goods in the early postwar period in spite of import controls. Thus the public and private savings, on which several governments had fixed their hopes for financing industrialization, were quickly dissipated.

Increasing budgetary deficits constitute the most important cause of constant upward pressure on the price level, especially in many Latin-American countries. Since a large part of state expenditure often represents outlays for consumption, an increase in the deficit may tend to raise the share of consumption in the national income. These deficits — whether financed indirectly by placing government bonds with the central bank or directly by issuing bank notes — increase the quantity of money and claims on goods and services, and are responsible for the expectation of higher profits in the private sector. The assistance of the banking system may be invoked to bridge the possible gap between the volume of investments planned and the volume of existing savings.

Through the expansion of bank credit, expenditures are increased and upward pressure on the price level renewed. Those whose incomes do not rise proportionally have to restrict their consumption, and the profits of the business class ultimately finance the increased volume of investment.

An additional cause for inflation in the process of development is the increase in the proportion of income that tends to be consumed as a result of rising expectations. This may also reflect inflation in progress leading to an increasing dishoarding. People may save less, and the increase in consumption expenditure may also lead to inflation, namely a rise in prices and a relative shift to profits in the distribution of income. In a particular country, a combination of inflationary forces may be at work, so that even when one factor abates, inflationary pressure may not lessen as it is reinforced by the other causes.[3]

Inflation and the Investment Pattern

In several undeveloped countries, the view is held that with a stable price level, the volume of voluntary savings is inadequate to sustain a desired rate of increase in output and that inflation, by redistributing income, will increase savings and thereby the rate of investment. After continuous inflation,[4] such as some Latin-American countries have experienced, however, it is doubtful whether the process of forced capital formation through inflation, as above described, actually results in a greater volume of investment than would be obtained through voluntary savings with a more normal growth.

Inflation, as R. H. Tawney puts it, "at once a stimulant to feverish enterprise and an acid dissolving all customary relationships"[5] has the tendency, if it becomes a regularly recurring phenomenon, to awaken a general distrust in the future value of the monetary unit. This undermines all tendency to voluntary saving. Though impossible to measure, it is thus possible that normal voluntary savings decline as much as, or even more than, savings created by inflation increase. In a country where inflation is of a continuous character, the groups that see their real income diminished seek compensation by demanding higher wages or higher prices for their products or services. During the initial stage of an inflation, this reaction tends to lag behind the price rise, but as more and more groups become conscious of the continuous upward trend of the price level, the rise in the income of the various groups follows that of the general price level more rapidly. We have already pointed out that, up to a certain degree, workers in undeveloped countries often tend to make their demands regarding wages and working conditions on the basis of those in the industrial countries. In some areas, they seem to be aware that inflation threatens to impair their level of living.

The social tensions caused thereby compel governments to intervene by ordering compulsory mass pay increases, for example, without distinction between efficient and inefficient workers and enterprises. These compulsory wage boosts in turn play an important part in the spiral development of price and cost relationships. H. W. Spiegel[6] gives indices for the cost of living and wage level in São Paulo, Brazil, from 1914 to 1938. Despite all reservations about the manner in which these indices were compiled, they show that, except for the depression years, the movement was of the same order for both indices (1914=100, 1938 cost of living 318, and wage level 315). It should be borne in mind that these wage statistics probably cover only the more skilled workers, and thus are not representative of all wage earners.

Once inflation becomes an established pattern, every group will try to maintain its share in the national income. Thus only small variations in the income distribution may result. The major effect then remains in the ever-renewing rise in prices and incomes. Another consequence of continuous inflation is the distortion in the investment structure. In their endeavor to maximize profits, entrepreneurs seek to invest in activities expected to benefit most from inflation. It has already been noted that the traditional investment pattern — with its preference for investment in land, luxury residential building, and inventories of commodities expected to share in the price rise — is strengthened. Those investments related to the most pressing needs of the community and to those of the groups whose incomes are likely to rise in an inflationary situation, assure a profit in the short run.

The results of investments in industrial ventures may be highly uncertain. Unless wages rise proportionately, a rising price level will tend to induce wage earners to expend a larger percentage of their reduced real income on food, and this would have an adverse effect on the demand for other essential goods. In the World Economic Report of 1951–52,[7] it is reported that in various Latin-American countries for that period, the inventories of textiles increased as a result of the decline in effective demand because of the continuous inflation. In an inflationary situation, moreover, everyone strives to be a debtor, so that investment in commodities and paper acceptable as collateral for bank loans forms an additional attraction. Mortgageable construction also falls into this category.

The disproportionate increase in the volume of money in relation to the quantity of goods and services also tends to distort the money market. Though this market has often a rudimentary character in underdeveloped countries, the rise in the price level will tend to make medium and long-term borrowing, either by the government or by private investors, virtually impossible. This lack of credit will increase the pressure on the government to create additional money with the consequences described above.

This inflationary development is also the cause of the flight from the national currency, and it is one of the reasons for the dollar deposits maintained by citizens of underdeveloped countries in the United States. The continuous price rise also has the tendency to discourage the inflow of foreign capital because of the fear of potential investors of devaluation or the imposition of exchange controls. The danger of devaluation occurs as soon as the rise in the internal price level forces up the prices of export goods to such an extent that exports at world market prices are no longer profitable, or conversely, the pressure of lower prices of import goods threatens domestic industrial activity.

Continuous inflation also has the tendency to further impair government administration, since the salaries of officials tend to lag behind the general prices rise. The danger of corruption may be increased. Of Brazil, Spiegel reports: "In public and private employment low salaries have caused gratifications (luvas) to be freely accepted and this custom is tolerated by employers. It is in effect encouraged by legal provisions allowing the public officials to participate in the fines which they are authorized to levy."[8]

The government has the power to dispel the danger of inflation by increasing taxation and thus increasing savings and restoring the equilibrium between the money supply and the flow of commodities and services. Only taxes at the expense of consumption are really anti-inflationary, but taxes that prevent savings from being used for purposes which might generate inflationary tendencies may produce a similar effect. It has been pointed out by some that it is not an increase in overall taxation that is required, but rather a higher taxation of the additional income generated by the expansion of the money supply. This reasoning is obviously correct, but it tends to overlook the fact that transferring resources to new activities usually implies the payment of higher remunerations than paid previously. And these rewards cannot be easily taxed without reducing the incentive for the movement of such resources.

Sometimes governments try to encourage private savings in special institutions by fixing higher interest rates, but because the real income of the masses remains low, such a measure is not likely to yield substantial results. In a number of undeveloped countries various social insurance schemes, to which the participating workers contribute by wage deductions, have been established partly with the objective of drawing off part of the money flow. One of the measures often recommended to sterilize money in an inflationary situation is to increase the deposits that the commercial banks must maintain with the central bank. However, such attempts are often thwarted by spokesmen for business, who exercise a significant influence on the conduct of government and can easily prove that their need for working capital increases as prices rise. The government is often too quickly persuaded that any curtailment of credit will lead to a liquidation crisis and the development of deflationary tendencies resulting in the non-collectibility of many loans and a rise in unemployment.

The government can curtail its own activity and build up a budget surplus, but this is contrary to the inclination to expand government expenditure in fulfilling the state's role in the process of development. If government expenditure were to contribute to the creation of productive capital, leading to rapid expansion of the flow of commodities, some of the inflationary forces might be selfneutralizing. However, the greater proportion of public investment is often directed toward the establishment of overhead capital, which needs complementary investment before giving rise to a larger volume of consumer goods. Such public expenditure may generate a demand for such industrial products as cement and steel and lead to a consequent increase in domestic capacity of facilities to meet such a demand. Stagnation of food production and misallocation of private investment, resulting from rising prices for foodstuffs and the tendency for profits to increase at the expense of labor income, may check the expansion of demand for other consumer goods and thus any rise in scales of living of the masses.

The fact that inflationary tendencies coincide with economic development in many backward countries may be proof that development without inflation is not possible under the circumstances in which those particular countries find themselves. In so far as productive capital investment is financed in this manner, it will increase the equipment for growth of an economy and, in time, governments may be able to regulate and control some of the contrary forces hindering continuous development.

Inflation in the Centrally Planned Economies

It is of interest to inquire how inflationary tendencies have been warded off in the Soviet Union during the process of forced industrialization. Since wages are fixed in advance on the basis of a consumption and investment plan, no inflationary pressure can result from a general wage increase, as it is always accompanied by a corresponding rise in the volume of consumer goods. Neither does a price rise in export goods create inflationary tendencies in a planned economy, since foreign trade is a state monopoly and increased export proceeds only swell the revenue of government. In the Soviet economy, the worker has the free disposition of his income on the consumer goods market. Since some workers are engaged in the production of capital goods, the stability of the market for consumer goods is threatened unless that part of the money flow originating in the capital goods sector is absorbed by taxes, savings, or loans.

Dobb[9] has discussed a simplified idea of how the state, in the Soviet Union, brings about equilibrium between the flows of money and consumer goods. He first assumes that the whole amount of wages is expended on the purchase of consumer goods. Accordingly, no saving, dishoarding, or taxation takes place. Further, he assumes that all production is directed toward the manufacture of consumer goods, implying no capital formation. If then the average wage level be w, and the number of workers x, the product wx will represent the total cost of production and, at the same time, the total income of workers. However, if capital goods are produced, in which part of the labor force $1/y$ is engaged, the expenditure of the workers for this period will still remain wx, but the costs of the consumer goods so produced will fall by wx/y, i.e., $wx - wx(1 - 1/y)$. This difference between total consumer expenditures and the cost of production of the consumer goods represents the proportion of investment, and this difference can be offset by raising the prices of the consumer goods by wx/y.

The turnover tax in the U.S.S.R. has precisely this function.[10] This state revenue can be called state saving. It is, in essence, similar to the savings of individual enterprises in capitalist economies. Dobb's scheme best fits the situation in the period 1927–38, when the labor force expanded in industrial activities, and there was a large increase in the amount of money in circulation. Since the amount of consumer goods remained more or less constant, prices of essential consumer goods had to be increased to about seven times their previous level.[11]

In a private enterprise economy, too, the selling prices of all goods, not merely those of consumer goods, are higher than their cost prices. From this difference, *idealiter*, a surplus for new investment is obtained, although from this margin rewards to stockholders (the providers of capital) and bonuses to leadership are also paid. In an economy based on private initiative, this surplus comes about as a result of the pursuit of profit by entrepreneurs, while in the Soviet Union such relations are planned.

Dobb's system seems extremely simple, but it should also be observed that there may be disturbing factors that could upset the equilibrium in the planned economy. First, it should be noted that a free sector exists in which production and prices are not controlled. Presumably, because of its limited size, its effect can be measured rather accurately in advance. This might not be true, however, of the expenditure pattern of cash reserves held by enterprises and private persons from previous periods. Also, the wage bill may be greater than originally planned because plant managers may try to attract additional labor by offering higher than the fixed wage rates. This practice was apparently quite common in the 1930's when enterprises also sometimes tried to build up larger stocks of raw materials than warranted by technical considerations in order to assure fulfillment or overfulfillment of targets. To the extent that this pressure of demand led to an expanded output of raw materials, new currency, not matched by additional receipts from the turnover tax, had to be created for financing the extra stocks. If the supply of raw materials did not rise, the scramble for them might make it impossible for certain groups of enterprises to reach their quotas. With the bias for capital over consumer goods embedded in Soviet planning, consumer goods industries were most likely to suffer, and thus, the supply of consumer goods would be smaller than planned.

A more important potential disturbance may result from the uncertainty of the harvest of food and commercial crops upon which the output of essential consumer goods depends. If the planned volume of consumer goods is not turned out at the planned time, or the quality remains below expectation, the discrepancy between the wage bill and the available supply of consumer goods may be considerable. Baykov[12] gives some examples indicating that, in various periods, the wage fund for certain branches was higher than expected due to low productivity of labor, ascribed to poor raw materials. This resulted in a large percentage of waste and spoilage and prolonged stoppage of machinery.

Another objection to Dobb's abstraction is that he takes a static view of the process of capital formation. In reality, owing to the multiplier effect, the amount of additional income created by a given investment is greater than the actual investment outlay. Not only do the rewards of the resources transferred to capital formation have to be taken into consideration, but also the effect of changes in demand in other sectors resulting from the reorganization of the production factors. If the equilibrium between the volume of income and consumable commodities is to be maintained, this implies that there must be a greater reduction in the purchasing power, unless the flow of consumer goods happens to increase as a result of the maturation of earlier investments. The determination of the prices of consumer goods is, therefore, certainly not as simple as Dobb claims it to be. Moreover, today in the U.S.S.R., the prices of capital goods are also established above cost, in order to eliminate the system of state subsidies in this sector and to provide an incentive for managers to increase the efficiency of their enterprises.[13]

Inflation probably has less opportunity to develop in a centrally planned economy, even if more purchasing power is created than corresponds to the supply of disposable consumer goods. The existing controls on prices, and the centralization of investment decisions, tend to prevent the pressure of this additional demand from being felt outside a small sector. A report of the Economic

Commission for Europe[14] demonstrates that the appearance of such an excessive demand for consumer goods is, however, a typical phenomenon in these economies. The aim seems always to be to surpass the planned production targets in the capital goods sector, while quotas in agriculture, which yields most of the raw materials for the consumption sector, are based on favorable weather conditions. Every disappointment results in a discrepancy between the quantum of available consumption goods and total effective demand, expressing itself in a rise in prices of output in the agrarian sector, after the compulsory state deliveries at a fixed price have been made. Such a process of development explains the introduction of rationing of scarce goods, differential pricing, and the revision of wage systems. Inflationary pressures have arisen in the centrally planned economies mainly because of discrepancies in growth between different sectors and the substantial transfer of manpower into nonagricultural employment, leading to an imbalance between the income stream and the supply of consumer goods. The measures that are available to the government in such countries make it possible, however, to keep the process under control, or to correct it from time to time, often drastically.[15]

Remedies Against Inflation in Chile

To illustrate the above argument, attention is drawn to a report by a United Nations mission, submitted to the Chilean government to help it combat inflation.[16] Starting from the premise that it was desirable to restore the equilibrium between demand, expressed in money, and the available quantity of consumer goods and services, and in addition, to break through the spell cast by continuing expectation of rising prices, it proposed to diminish the money flow by an ingenious system of saving and to increase the supply of consumer goods by suitable methods. A general price stop was recommended in order to eliminate the expectation of further price rises. It was hoped that this would reduce the volume of commodity stocks maintained for speculative purposes, thereby releasing such goods for consumption.

It was also suggested that the government import policy should aim at attracting more essential consumer goods, or such raw materials as could be processed in a relatively short time into commodities for the local market. Finally, special credits for the purchase of feed and fertilizer for the agricultural sector were proposed. Linked with an extension program, this was designed to increase agricultural production. The report recommended the introduction of efficiency teams and the temporary institution of two and three shift operations to increase the utilization of machinery and plant and thus to raise industrial production over the short run. The mission also judged that there was concealed unemployment, particularly in the government administration. It felt that this surplus labor should be weeded out and transferred in order to expand production elsewhere. The volume of investment was to remain at least at the present level, but it was hoped that the price freeze would, among other things, reduce the tendency toward the erection of apartments and dwellings for the well-to-do classes.

Since the government sector was responsible for a third of Chile's total investment in 1949, it was thought that the government possessed an instrument, in its expenditure and credit policy, for guiding investment into more desirable channels. Above all, it could thereby encourage the construction of housing for the lower income groups. Since profits would be reduced by the price ceilings, and the distribution of income would thereby be modified — probably leading to a higher rate of consumption — special measures had to be taken to increase the quantity of savings. The interest rate on ordinary savings deposits was to be increased to 6 per cent, and up to 10 per cent for deposits in blocked accounts. Measures were also recommended to improve the system of tax collection without changing the tax rates.

The most important means of warding off an increase of consumption expenditures was the proposal of a forced loan to the government. This would have involved deductions of 5 per cent from all wages and salaries and a surtax on income tax of 5 per cent rising to 10 per cent for the highest income groups. Compulsory saving deductions would continue for an 18-month period (July 1, 1950, to December 31, 1951). The amounts collected would be refunded during 1953 and 1954. It was estimated that the total contribution would be 4 billion pesos. This amount was considered higher than necessary to offset the expected increase in consumption expenditures. Since the extra income tax would also affect the volume of voluntary savings, it would provide an additional means by which the government might control the level of investment.[17]

These proposals, like so many others contained in reports made by experts to the governments of undeveloped countries, were not put into effect although during the stay of the experts in Chile, the government showed great interest, and the responsible officials manifested an understanding of the measures proposed and considered themselves capable of handling the administrative machinery required for the planned price stop and the forced loan. There is no single explanation for such inactivity. Governments in backward countries are often not strong enough to put through a bold and radical policy that is unpopular with certain groups and that may give weapons to the opposition. Also, officials probably tend to overestimate the efficiency of their administration, particularly in the presence of a mission of foreigners. There is also a fear that they will not receive energetic backing from the government if, for example, they adopt drastic measures against violators.

In this instance, the hand of the government was also weakened by the fact that, during the same period, Chile was visited by a mission of the International Monetary Fund investigating the monetary situation. Its report[18] criticized the compulsory savings proposal considering, (1) the timing inadequate, since in 1953 when repayments would begin, the supply and demand of consumer goods would probably still be out of balance and (2) the amount too low, since it would absorb only about 2 per cent of national income. More important, the plan itself was considered inadequate. Since the price stop did not provide for a wage freeze, workers could seek wage increases — the United Nations experts visualized such wage increases being paid out of profits which had been abnormally high in the past — and these might more than offset the forced savings. The I.M.F. mission recommended, instead, a ceiling on total outstanding credits, a granting of loans beyond this limit only in hardship cases, an increase in the rediscount rate of the central bank, a substantial increase in taxation, and the drawing up of a comprehensive investment plan to establish the socially most desirable projects.

It would seem fairly certain that the well-to-do group, from which many government leaders are usually recruited, includes a large number to whom continued price rises are not unwelcome. F. W. Fetter[19] found earlier that, in Chile, the inflation from 1879 to 1926 was favored by landowners who benefited from higher food prices without suffering any increase in their burden of interest on loans secured by land mortgages. Subsequent periods of inflation also reflected the dominant influence exerted on the government by groups that profited by price increases, and by advocates of industrialization who believed that capital formation could be increased only by inflation. The voice of labor, whose remuneration lagged behind during this process, was hardly heard. It does seem, in fact, that it might be mainly the increased power of wage earners that will lead, even in the undeveloped countries, to resistance against inflation as a means of capital formation, and to the insistence that increased investment shall lead to increased consumption for the masses with only a modest lag.

The question arises whether and how this awareness of the disadvantages of inflation, also partly linked to a strengthened social conscience, is reconcilable with statements by Keynes and Robertson.[20] They have already been cited to the effect that, in the past, a rising price level was the cause of increases in the marginal profit level and hence, through reinvestment of the profits so created, of increases in capital formation.

Inflation in the History of the Industrial Countries

As far as can be ascertained, no systematic study has yet been made of the significance of inflation in the development of the industrial countries. It would seem, however, that the views of Keynes and Robertson apply only to a certain phase in the evolution of the English economy and possess no general validity. During the period of commercial capitalism, the influx of precious metals led to a rising price level. As a result of the lag in wages, the distribution of income became increasingly unequal. Keynes[21] presents a table showing that, in England, the ratio between prices and production costs rose by 33 per cent between 1500–50 and 1614–50, and, in France, by 28 per cent during the same period. Wages were considered to represent 50 per cent of production costs, while the other half of costs were presumed to have followed the same course as the general price level. The disparity between the movement of price and wage levels should thus have been even greater than the ratio indicates.

The customary view is that the increasing incomes of the upper class formed a stimulus for foreign trade in luxury products, but that the rising incomes of entrepreneurs were directed primarily to additional investments, as the capitalists maintained a rather modest consumption level. J. E. Nef[22] believes that the price and wage series used by Keynes and others give a false impression of the decline in the real wages of the English worker. He gives various examples of prices that were important for the average workman's budget, but did not rise as much as the general price level did. He also points to technical changes — such as a substitution of coal for wood as a fuel as a result of the rising price of wood — that have not been taken into account in the price index. Thus, according to Nef, the price index used does not adequately reflect changes in the cost of living. In conclusion, he poses the pertinent question whether, if the material welfare of the masses did fall as much as is assumed by Keynes and others, the low level of wages, which is claimed to have encouraged investments, did not really serve just as much to frighten off new investments as a result of the contraction of the domestic market.

Nef's argument that the price and wage indices cited by Keynes and others are not representative of the trends seems indisputable. Assuming that the customary idea is correct, the increasing consumption level of the well-to-do classes, the higher productivity of factory industry as compared with cottage industry, and above all, the expansion of the export market were essential conditions for the rise of capitalism. According to E. J. Hamilton,[23] a continuous price rise resulting from profit inflation continued up to the beginning of the nineteenth century and led to an increasing inequality of income distribution. He explains the lag in wages by the 'natural' inertia of wage movements in the second half of the eighteenth century, and the over-supply of the labor factor as a result of rapid population growth and the influx of Irish immigrants.

The rise in profits enlarged the margin for capital formation and made possible investment in agriculture, road and canal construction, mining and housing. The low national wage level was not a perceptible obstacle to increasing sales, since the producers found themselves in a seller's market. Although the writer does not say so, this may have been a result of the expanding world market. Hamilton concludes that the fall in real wages naturally necessitated heavy sacrifices from the poorest inhabitants and that perhaps society as a whole would have benefited more if the rate of growth had been slower.

However, shortly after the period described by Hamilton, the situation changed entirely. A remarkable stabilization of the price level occurred in the United Kingdom, and this lasted until World War I.[24] May it be assumed that in this period the continuous rise in the productivity of factory industry, superimposed on the increasing purchasing power of the working classes,[25] plus the growth of population, provided adequate stimuli to entrepreneurs to invest?

An exhaustive study of the development of the Swedish economy[26] shows conclusively that a rising price level and an increasingly unequal distribution of income are not indispensable conditions for economic growth. Sweden began its industrialization late. In 1860 75 per cent of the population was still agricultural; this percentage had been reduced to 39 by 1930.[27] From a comparison of an index of the value added by industrial activity and an index of annual wages from 1860 to 1930, it will be seen that both curves took the same course. The conclusion follows that the share of labor did not lag behind during the process of development.[28] A table comparing an index of the annual nominal wage earned by male workers in industry with the cost of living over the period 1860–1913 also shows how real wages rose in the face of a more or less steady cost of living.[29]

This parallelism between two series does not prove that there was no increase in the inequality of income distribution. There could, for example, have been shifts in the relative number of independent and industrial workers. But, from the exhaustive material of the study — showing, among other things, a rise in the wage level in agriculture corresponding to that in industry[30] — it can only be concluded that all groups shared equally in the benefits of the increase in national income. Provided that the percentage of the increased national income saved and invested rises, so that the formation of capital increases, all factors of production can thus see their absolute share rise as a result of the expansion of the national income, although their relative shares may remain about equal.

There is probably an important hiatus in the above reasoning, since the cyclical movement — Schumpeter, in particular, has recognized it as having an important function in the process of investment — has been neglected. Without getting too involved in trade cycle theory, the following observations would seem in order. It seems logical that, during a cyclical upswing, there should be an initial surplus of unutilized or underutilized factors of production. When the factors of production are, for all practical purposes, fully occupied (within the technical and special limits appropriate to the period in question), expenditures for new investment, in the face of an inelastic factor supply, should tend to force up the price level.[31]

During this boom phase, the wage level, according to historical experience, lags behind.[32] Thus the expectation of profits rises. This, according to W. W. Rostow,[33] encourages entrepreneurs to expand and introduce technical improvements, particularly in branches of industry in which investments need a long period of gestation before their products and services appear upon the market. It is precisely this pattern of investment that brings the turning point in the cycle. In the period of depression that follows, profits and the price level fall, and entrepreneurs pass on the consequences to the workers by mass layoffs and wage cuts. Since the price level falls more than the wage level, however, those workers who remain employed see their real wages rise.[34]

If this summarized view gives a true picture of the real situation, and if the cyclical movement of the price level — with prices rising and wages lagging behind during the upswing (although the total wage bill increases), and prices falling during the downswing, while real wages rise and total wage payments diminish — has indeed been a catalytic agent in the process of economic development, it would be difficult to support the chain of thought developed by Keynes and Robertson from modest cyclical changes in the price level and their influence on profit expectations and wage level. Reiterating, we stress that an unequal income distribution and a rise in the price level are not necessary conditions for economic growth. Neither does the existence of these conditions assure economic development.

Many of the economically backward countries have a more unequal income distribution than the industrial countries, but because the economic climate of the former is still largely pre-industrial, this differential does not necessarily lead to increased savings or investments that will contribute to a rising level of living for the masses. The demonstration effect of the Western style of living has the tendency to increase the rate of consumption for those able to save. Part of the income of the upper income groups also leaks away in imports and in types of investment that do not add new resources to the economic system or bring about a more productive organization of the existing factors of production.

The undeveloped economies are also often characterized by an increasing price level. If this merely leads to an increase in the unequal income distribution, no expansion in productive investment may result. Capital formation may not increase because the groups, especially labor, already accustomed to the inflationary pattern, are able to recapture their former share of the national income. This, in turn, intensifies the upward pressure on the price level. In so far as productive capital formation is increased by public outlays, such investment need not offer inducement to complementary private investment. The nature of other government expenditure may nullify the effect of such investment or domestic entrepreneurs may not respond due to lack of managerial and technical qualities to start new ventures. For the moment, the effectiveness of inflation as a means for undeveloped countries to limit consumption by forcing up the price level and thus make available funds for enlarging capital stock, remains unproved. The apparent inability of the government to carry out those projects which economically and socially seem most desirable, to prevent the misallocation of private investment in an inflationary situation, and to control the pattern and volume of imports, may be partly responsible for the defects of an inflationary financing of economic development.

Although an exhaustive study would be required to determine the significance of inflation or a rising price level for economic growth, it may be stated in advance that such an economic-historical analysis would probably present no uniform picture.[35] Even in one country, economic development has probably been as marked in periods when the price level showed a strongly upward tendency as in periods with a relatively stable price level. The constellation of a large number of factors has to be favorable to accelerate the rate of growth. A better utilization of resources and the conquering of a foreign market for raw materials or manufactures depend largely upon the adoption of technical and organizational innovations. This in turn is related to the existence of a group with an eye for such possibilities. The present level of, or divergent movements in prices of production factors will, on occasion, have performed a catalytic function. They may also have led to stagnation in cases where the various sectors of the economy did not grow in the right relationship to each other and the resulting price modifications removed the inducement to additional investment.

PART THREE

INTERNATIONAL FINANCIAL RESOURCES

Chapter 13

INTRODUCTION

Underdeveloped countries usually base their appeal for international financial assistance on their low level of living. Mass poverty implies a low level of savings, which, in turn, hampers the capital accumulation that must take place if labor's productivity is to be increased and living standards ultimately raised. According to this line of reasoning, the temporary help of foreign capital is required to break this vicious circle, since any attempt to increase capital formation solely with domestic resources might have an adverse effect on the already low level of consumption of the general population. If foreign capital is effectively used, increasing productivity will lead, in time, to the development of the required domestic savings. It will then be possible to repay the loans and, at the same time, provide resources for new investments, thus assuring further economic growth.

The simplification implicit in this chain of thought is not entirely legitimate, since it disregards both the unequal income distribution in the backward countries and the possibility of modifying the existing pattern of private investment. It ignores, especially, the possibility of using public investment and other appropriate measures to encourage the channeling of capital formation into more productive activities. Furthermore, productive reserves exist in capital goods already available, so that by means of a reorganization of production, a larger output could be obtained from the production factors now being utilized. Japan affords a good example of what can be accomplished in building up capital stock in a country short of both domestic savings and natural resources, provided all energies are devoted to economic expansion and investments are carefully chosen.[1]

However, it can be argued that little can be done about the investment pattern followed by the small group able to save, and that the government, as a result of its inadequate administration, lacks the power to mobilize available resources for increasing capital formation. On social and humanitarian grounds, therefore, foreign aid is required, initially at least, if an attempt is to be made to improve living conditions in the undeveloped regions. At the same time, the hope may be cherished that the transfer of foreign capital will generate impulses modifying the domestic investment pattern and providing the government with additional resources for the production of such capital goods as will stimulate economic growth.

The acquisition of foreign capital means a transfer of purchasing power — the power of disposition over goods and services — from one country, the creditor, to the other country, the debtor. It depends on the use made of this command over extra resources whether the additional purchasing power so procured will contribute to the enlargement of domestic capital stock, and ultimately to an increase in future consumption. This implies that the subject of foreign assistance cannot be divorced from the economic climate prevailing in the debtor country. Nevertheless, we shall assume, in the following, that scarcity of capital is the main cause of underdevelopment, and acceleration of its formation the primary need of the underdeveloped world.

In order to determine what capital requirements can be satisfied by outside aid, it would seem useful to return to the previously used distinctions between social overhead capital, economic overhead capital, and directly productive capital. Each of these would seem to require a different form of financing. It may be recalled that the first category, social overhead capital, includes such items as canals, roads, hospitals, schools, and public buildings. The second category, economic overhead capital, consists of the installations needed for public utilities in the wider sense, including railroads and other means of transportation, electricity, gas, water, and the postal, telephone, and telegraph services. The third category, directly productive capital, includes all capital goods employed in agriculture, mining, and industry.

Projects within the first category (social overhead capital) can hardly be financed in such a way as to pay the capital charges directly out of future yield. Only the government can undertake their construction. It must meet their costs from state revenue, domestic loans, or the proceeds of foreign loans. Amortization and interest for such loans must be provided for out of income secured from a surplus in another sector. This form of capital obviously lends itself to foreign financing through grants-in-aid. UNRRA aid, and more recently the bilateral United States technical assistance programs are partly in this field. Many such projects can be carried out to a large degree with local materials and labor. Foreign loans or gifts can thus be used to import complementary capital goods — tractors, steam shovels, and the like. They can also be used to import those articles of mass consumption which, for the moment, cannot be supplied in sufficient quantity from domestic sources, but which must be provided to sustain the labor force employed in the production of such capital goods in the recipient country. [2]

The second category of capital goods (economic overhead capital) would seem to be suitable for private foreign financing, since they involve services the rates for which can be fixed at such a level that income will exceed expenditure. However, the central and local governments in undeveloped countries show an increasing tendency to take over such utilities. Even where this is not the case, rates are subject to government control. This capital is considered so important socially and strategically in the development process that setting the price for its services cannot be left to private initiative. Although in the past public utilities in the undeveloped countries were often constructed by private foreign capital, the possibility of such financing seems less likely now, in view of the increased concern of the state with these projects. From the standpoint of foreign financing, thus, there is no longer a sharp distinction to be made between the first and second form of capital goods.

The third category of capital goods (directly productive capital), remains, at least in principle, attractive for financing by private foreign capital. For sound and harmonious economic growth, a certain balance has to be maintained between the increases in the various forms of capital goods. Formation of capital of the third category, will tend to dry up unless at the same time transport, communications, and electric power facilities (capital goods of the second category) also increase. The whole process of investment is likely to stagnate ultimately if the necessary expenditures for education and health (investments of the first category) are not made. Although for a given country a certain quantitative relationship probably exists between the required rate of growth of the various forms of capital during successful economic development,[3] it does not necessarily follow that foreign capital should be attracted in some definite ratio to finance the various categories of capital goods. The government itself can undertake the necessary investments of the first category, and even of the second (possibly with the aid of private capital obtained by government loans placed in the capital market of a creditor country), and pay amortization and interest from increased state revenues resulting indirectly from the investment of private foreign capital in projects of the third category.

The need for foreign funds to stimulate capital formation has always existed, but the urgency of this need has never been the motivating force for the international movement of capital. Some countries, during certain stages of development, have actively sought foreign capital to supplement domestic investment, which was limited by the amount of domestic savings. In other countries, foreign capital flowed in almost exclusively as a result of foreign initiative, attracted by the lucrative potentialities of natural resources. The flow of international capital thus was induced by the expectation of future profits or by the fact that foreign governments in need of aid were prepared to pay higher interest rates.

Historically, public loans granted by governments formed only a small part of the capital flow, and political motives often overshadowed economic considerations in such transfers. Ohlin's statement that the "export of capital has fundamentally meant... the export of the industrial revolution from the industrialized countries to the 'undeveloped' countries" [4] is not incorrect, but it emphasizes only one factor out of the whole complex of phenomena that have brought about the linking of the various national economies into a world economy.

The international movement of capital has contributed substantially to economic development, particularly in the industrial countries, first in western Europe and later in the United States, Australia, and Canada, but this influence cannot be isolated from the internal factors encouraging growth. As we have also shown for international trade, what is of essential importance here is the extent to which a country is able to employ the additional resources made available by foreign funds for initiating or continuing the process of development. It would seem desirable to obtain a certain perspective from the history of capital movements, before considering in greater detail the significance of foreign private and public investment for the undeveloped countries today.

Chapter 14

A Brief History of
International Capital Movements

Keynes[1] has observed that the booty Drake brought back in 1580 in his ship the 'Golden Hind,' estimated at between £ 300,000 and £ 1.5 million and used to pay off the entire foreign debt of the state with the rest invested in the Levant Company, was the source and origin of English foreign investment. In that same year, an investment of £ 42,000 was made in the Levant Company, and subsequently the establishment of the East India Company was financed from the profits of the former.[2] At the end of the seventeenth century British foreign investment had risen to £ 2.5 million. It has been assumed[3] that the first phase of colonial expansion and the struggle for the trade in colonial products were connected with the excess capital, which could find no productive investment in the mother countries. In other words, profitability of shipping and foreign trade was generally greater than that of prevailing domestic activities whose expansion was checked by the limited size of the market. The example of the Levant Company suggests that profits were great enough to allow trade to expand in other areas as well, mainly by reinvestment.

The second phase of foreign investment, between 1815–75, found its stimulus in the industrial transformation of Europe. The governments of the countries that began their industrialization after Great Britain, borrowed on a large scale from abroad, especially for the construction of railroads. L. H. Jenks[4] accepts an estimate from another author that the government debt of certain European countries, mainly in central and eastern Europe, increased from £ 1.7 billion in 1848 to £ 4.6 billion in 1872, of which at least £ 2 billion came from abroad.

Among the developments that took place as a result of this flow of investment were the expansion of agricultural production in eastern Europe and the cultivation of cotton in Egypt. However, Jenks[5] notes that it was only around 1874 that British investment began to be directed toward the development of virgin regions in order to increase food output for the growing population and to produce the raw materials that were critical for the ever expanding and increasingly diversified needs of European industry.[6]

It is estimated that the foreign investments of Great Britain, France, and Germany rose from $ 6 billion to about $ 33 billion during the period from 1874 to 1914.[7] This growth was financed mainly from the yield of earlier investments, so that profits on foreign capital and new foreign investment, as a whole, more or less offset each other in the balance of payments of both creditor and debtor countries.[8] Contrary perhaps to what one would expect, during most of the nineteenth century, Great Britain recorded an import surplus, which, like the increasing volume of foreign investment, was financed by her income from shipping, trade, insurance, and banking, and by the savings of colonial officials and technicians serving overseas. It was only about 1870 that the volume of foreign investment had risen to the point that interest and dividends were the most important source of new investment.[9]

The table on page 262 gives an estimate, for the year 1914, of the value and geographic distribution of foreign holdings of creditor countries.

During the period of 1874–1914, British investments in Europe declined and increased elsewhere.[10] France and Germany took over the role of moneylender to the debtor countries of Europe. In 1914 about two-thirds of French and half of German foreign investments were in Europe. Half of these investments consisted of foreign government bonds.

After 1875 direct foreign investors[11] are generally assumed to have shown a distinct preference for the development of export activities in the countries where investment took place. However,

TABLE 10. VALUE AND GEOGRAPHIC DISTRIBUTION OF FOREIGN INVESTMENT, 1914

Creditor Countries	Millions of U.S. Dollars	Geographic Distribution	Millions of U.S. Dollars
United Kingdom	18,000	Europe	12,000
France	9,000	Latin America	8,500
Germany	5,800	United States	6,800
United States	3,500	Asia	6,000
Belgium, Netherlands, and Switzerland	5,500	Africa	4,700
Other Countries	2,200	Canada	3,700
		Oceania	2,300
Total	44,000		44,000

Source: United Nations, *International Capital Movements During the Inter-War Period* (New York: 1949), p. 2.

up to 1914 the volume of such investment was exceeded many times over by the volume of government borrowing financed by individuals in the creditor countries. In 1914, 30 per cent of total British foreign investment consisted of bonds of foreign governments and municipalities. Foreign railroad bonds made up 40 per cent of foreign investment, and other public utilities another 10 per cent. Thus a total of 80 per cent of Great Britain's foreign investment had been placed at the disposal of other countries chiefly to finance the construction of 'overhead' capital.[12] (Railway bonds were usually received by British industrialists in payment for the delivery of railroad material and for the services of British specialists in railroad construction.) The remaining 20 per cent consisted mainly of interests in mining and plantation enterprises, though the British capitalist was also investing in iron, steel, and textile industries in other countries. Both direct and portfolio investments exerted a strong influence on the structure of foreign trade of both debtor and creditor countries and thus on the trade of third countries as well.

During World War I, Great Britain and France liquidated investments equivalent to $ 4 billion, and $ 700 million, respectively, of their foreign investments. About two-thirds of the investments sold by Britain were United States securities, mostly railway bonds. These countries also suffered heavy losses on investments in Central America, eastern Europe, and in the

Middle East. British losses were estimated as the equivalent of $ 600 million while French losses exceeded $ 4 billion. Russian loans floated in France and later repudiated by the Soviet government amounted to the equivalent of $ 2.1 billion.[13] Germany suffered corresponding losses and was also compelled to liquidate the greater part of her foreign holdings after the war. Belgium, Switzerland, and Sweden also suffered great losses on their European investments.

E. H. Carr has made a few observations in this connection that merit consideration by the economist, although they fall short of doing justice to the whole complex of problems connected with international capital movements. "The international financial system which flourished until 1914 is often spoken of as if it had operated to the profit and advantage of everyone concerned. This system, in fact, involved a continuous flow of loans from Great Britain and certain other countries (especially France), the repayment of which was provided for when the time came by further loans; and when the cumulative process came to an end, default was the inevitable result. The advantages of the pre-1914 international financial system were paid for in the end by the British and French investors who lost their millions in South America or in Russia... It is not certain that the same confidence trick can be played again. If it cannot, it seems probable that those who occupy the most privileged position within any international financial system will be obliged from time to time to make deliberate sacrifices in order to make the system work; and these liabilities, like money spent on relief, must be regarded either as the discharge of a moral obligation or an insurance premium for the maintenance of civilization."[14]

During and after World War I, the United States substantially strengthened her financial position by repatriating securities formerly held by British and French investors, by purchasing an estimated $ 1.5 billion of British and French securities, and by investment in stocks and bonds of other countries. The United States also granted a total of about $ 10 billion in loans to Allied governments during the war and up to July, 1921. In spite of these important shifts in international financial relations and the resulting disequilibrium in the balance of payments of various countries, the flow of capital from creditor to debtor countries was resumed for a time in the old manner after World War I. It was the crisis of 1930–31 that brought home the fact that the disturbances were more serious than had been thought at first.

In 1929 a rough estimate showed British and United States foreign investments distributed as follows:[15]

	United Kingdom	United States
	(in millions of dollars)	
Portfolio investments	8,900	7,100
Direct investments	7,900	7,500
	16,800	14,600

Direct investments by the United States consisted of $ 1.3 billion in Europe, $ 2 billion in Canada and Newfoundland,[16] and $ 3.1 billion in Latin America. Direct investments by Great Britain in the British Commonwealth amounted to $ 3 billion, with $ 2.6 billion in Latin America, the second largest area of investment. About half the investments of both countries consisted of investments in underdeveloped countries, mainly in Latin America and Asia.[17]

Most of these direct investments were in public utilities and railways, distributive enterprises (to facilitate the sale of imported products), banking (to facilitate the export of primary products), plantations and mining enterprises (producing mainly for export), and plants processing primary products, such as smelting and meat freezing (again for export). Only a small percentage was invested in industries producing for the local market. It was estimated that about one-fifth of direct United States investment ($ 1.5 billion) was in manufacturing activities, but of this amount, 84 per cent was in the industrialized countries.

Relative profitability was, of course, the main reason why foreign investors preferred export-expanding to import-replacing industries. The imports and exports of many backward countries were extremely limited before they attracted foreign capital.

In such cases the transfer of dividends and profits from direct investment could be accomplished only by increasing exports or reducing imports. Since imports were already low, foreign investors usually showed a preference for investments that encouraged exports. Moreover, the domestic markets in undeveloped countries were too small to make the establishment of large-scale local industries attractive.

The lack of interest in domestic industries was also related to the deficiency in 'overhead' capital or 'external economies' in undeveloped countries. This consideration applied to export activities as well, but as the scale of operations was usually larger in this case, such facilities were often treated as part of the specific investment. Thus the construction of railroads was often linked with the production of export goods, a condition sometimes indispensable for increased exports.[18] Other public utilities — water supply, gas and electricity, telephone and telegraph systems — were also set up by foreign capital in a number of countries, especially when these were essential to the export industries and ancillary activities. If successful, such enterprises assured a regular flow of income, containing, in some instances, an element of monopoly profit.

As a result of the crisis of 1929, international capital movements took on a number of new aspects. It had always been assumed that the flow of capital from one country to another was actuated largely by differences in interest rates or yields. The difference in interest rates was a measure of the amount of compensation necessary to make foreign bonds or shares attractive to the average investor in order to overcome the problems and risks involved.[19] Now, however, the safety of the investment became the decisive factor; in some instances capital took flight from countries with a high interest rate.

The introduction of foreign exchange controls and similar measures also led to movements of capital that would not otherwise have occurred. The partial or complete default on payment of interest and amortization of foreign loans tended to depress the market value of the bonds of the debtor country. It became attractive for the country itself to purchase them and thereby effect an advantageous reduction of its foreign debt. When dividends and interest could not be transferred, the holder of shares or stocks often reinvested in industries producing for the local market. Since raw material prices had fallen more than those of manufactures, there was a relative rise in the yield of industrial activities. The drastic trade controls introduced by debtor countries to bring their balance of payments into equilibrium likewise opened up the possibility of domestic production of commodities that had formerly been imported. In this way, such controls sometimes encouraged the investment of free funds in industries processing local raw materials or assembling imported semi-manufactured goods and in distributive enterprises for the local market.

The depression of the 1930's had still another important consequence. British and other European direct investments in undeveloped countries had been based largely on a multilaterally oriented trade. The European countries themselves absorbed only part of the export production encouraged by their capital in backward countries. These products were thus sold on the international market, particularly in developed countries that were importers of raw materials. They financed these imports by an export surplus with other creditor countries.[20] The growth of direct American investments during the 1920's tended to upset this delicate structure, because such investments were usually based on bilateral trade between the United States and the particular undeveloped country. The fact that the United States offered a broader market than any single European creditor country,[21] eliminated all difficulties in the transfer of the proceeds — for example, from the copper mines in Chile, the sugar plantations in Cuba, the banana plantations in Central America, and the oil wells in Mexico and Venezuela.

The control of foreign exchange transactions by governments, the inconvertibility of many currencies, and the reduced volume of multilateral trade led to an increase in this form of direct investment, which was guided almost exclusively by the market requirements in the creditor country itself. But this method of investment strengthened the feeling in the undeveloped countries that the bilateral trade so developed was essentially of an exploitative nature. Therefore, some countries enacted special legislation prohibiting or restricting the establishment of foreign-controlled enterprises in certain branches of industry, or providing for the government to take over an increasing portion of the capital stock of such enterprises. The growth of nationalism during this period also led to the expropriation of various foreign enterprises. [22]

During the depression of the 1930's, international capital movements were placed under government control in most of the creditor countries as well. The object of these controls varied: to protect the foreign exchange position, to increase the supply of capital in the domestic market and hold down interest rates, to make foreign loans conditional on the use of the proceeds to purchase goods and services in the creditor country, to use loans as a method of arranging trade advantages, or to restrict loans to countries with which political or financial ties existed.

Until 1930 Great Britain had exercised no government supervision of any importance on foreign investments. But in that year some controls were instituted on loans to countries outside the Commonwealth. In 1933 these measures were supplemented by a prohibition on block purchases of securities from abroad. The controls were relaxed for members of the sterling bloc after its creation in 1934, but in 1939 a total embargo was placed on foreign loans. Following legislation in 1946 the granting of foreign credits was coordinated with the control of domestic investment activities.

In the United States, complete freedom to make foreign loans existed until March 1922, when preliminary consultation with the State Department became a requirement. The primary purpose of this action was to strengthen the position of the United States in the negotiations on Allied war debts. In the early 1930's these controls were abolished, but in 1934, when the Export-Import Bank was established, it was prescribed in the Bank's standard conditions for loans that only products of the United States could be purchased with the proceeds of the loans. The Johnson Act prohibited new loans to countries in default on their war debts. It was only in 1945 that this restriction was abolished by the ratification of the Bretton Woods Agreement, when the Johnson Act was amended making it inapplicable to countries that were members of the International Monetary Fund and the International Bank for Reconstruction and Development. In the same year, the National Advisory Council for International Monetary and Financial Problems was established to coordinate government policy on foreign lending. In other creditor countries, too, restrictions were placed on the granting of foreign credits during the postwar period.

During the depression, there was a larger percentage of defaults in the payment of amortization and interest on foreign loans placed in the United States than on those placed in other countries. In the years following World War I, 10 per cent of foreign bonds were in default on interest and amortization; these were mainly Mexican and Russian bonds. The default rate declined during the 1920's to between 4 and 5 per cent, but rose in the 1930's to 40 per cent, largely because of defaults by Germany and Latin American countries.

Although controversy still rages over the proportion of the foreign loans floated in the United States in the 1920's that were productive, [23] there is no doubt that the lenders did not investigate thoroughly the purposes for which the proceeds were to be used. The lenders — the banks or issuing houses — through which the loans were placed with the public were apparently not concerned with the possibility of the overextension of credit, thus beyond the capacity of the debtor country to mobilize domestic factors for execution of the underlying projects. In particular, during the latter part of the 1920's, little attention was paid to the capacity of the borrowing country to repay the loan, or even whether the floating of the loan would improve the balance-of-payments position of the recipient country and thus make it possible to transfer additional sums for interest and amortization.[24]

On account of the experiences of these years, the interest of the American investor in portfolio investments in underdeveloped countries declined appreciably. [25] As a result of modifications in the tax structure in the creditor countries, moreover, the individual investor who, in earlier years, might have been interested in foreign bonds was replaced to some extent by institutional investors — insurance companies, savings banks, etc. These institutional investors were often precluded, by their articles of incorporation, from purchasing bonds bearing fixed interest issued by foreign governments.

A rough estimate may be given for the year 1938 of the position of the principal creditor countries and the geographical distribution of their investment. [26]

TABLE 11. VALUE AND GEOGRAPHIC DISTRIBUTION OF FOREIGN INVESTMENT, 1938

Creditor Countries	In Millions of Dollars	Geographical Distribution	In Millions of Dollars
United Kingdom	23,000	Asia	11,000
United States	11,500	Latin America	10,700
The Netherlands	4,800	Europe	9,500
France	3,900	United States	7,000
Switzerland	1,600	Canada	6,500
Canada	1,600	Africa	4,000
Belgium	1,300	Oceania	3,600
Japan	1,200		
Germany	700		
Other Countries	2,700		
Total	52,300		52,300

Source C. Lewis, *The United States and Foreign Investment Problems* (Washington, D.C.: 1948), pp. 292–97.
Note: The figures have been grouped somewhat differently. Through exclusion of investment not attributable to any area, totals are lower than those given by Lewis.

In view of changes in the relative value of the currencies, it is difficult to compare this table with the table for 1914 shown previously. It does, however, confirm the rise of the United

States as an active foreign investor and the diminished importance of outside investments in its national economy. It also demonstrates the change in the position of France[27] and Germany as creditor countries and the decline of Europe as a debtor area. Investments in Africa seem to have declined, while those in Asia and Canada substantially increased. In Latin America and Oceania, investments probably remained about the same. Canada and Japan appear as newcomers among the creditor countries, while Great Britain, the Netherlands,[28] Switzerland, and Belgium appear to have maintained about the same positions.

During World War II, the Lend-Lease Act of March, 1941 prevented a repetition of the phenomenon of the uncollectable war debts, which had been the legacy of World War I. From 1940 to 1945, the United States government transferred, principally through the lend-lease program, a net amount of $ 41 billion in goods and services to friendly governments for the Allied war effort.

In the postwar period (1946–55), the United States government contributed a net amount of $ 51 billion in bilateral and international aid programs. The lend-lease transfers consisted almost entirely of grants-in-aid, while about three-fourths of the latter consisted of grants and one-fourth of loans. The total amount of $ 92 billion is almost twice as large as the total world foreign investment — mostly private — outstanding in 1938.[29] Even taking into account the decline in the value of money, this order of magnitude gives an idea of the changes brought about by World War II.

Over the period 1939–45, the book value of long-term foreign investments by private individuals in the United States rose from $ 11 billion to $ 13 billion, and for the first time, long-term government loans appeared – amounting to $ 1.1 billion. The increase in direct private investment from $ 7.3 billion to $ 8.1 billion was attributable mainly to reinvestment and to investments brought in by European refugees.[30] From 1939–45, portfolio investments increased from $ 4.1 billion to $ 5.6 billion, although the amount of amortization received exceeded that of new loans made. The increase was due to the purchase of foreign bonds, the price rise in foreign stocks and bonds, and the importation of such securities by refugees.

It is estimated that Great Britain liquidated £ 1.3 billion of its foreign investments for the war effort. [31] This was accomplished by the selective sale of shares and bonds, by offsetting wartime debts for deliveries to Great Britain against British-owned government bonds, and by making arrangements for private British concerns to be taken over by the country involved. [32] In spite of the fact that Great Britain had large short-term debts after the war (£ 3.3 billion) [33] and had received large long-term loans from the United States ($ 4.4 billion) and from Canada ($ 1.2 billion), it still granted substantial credits to various countries and undertook significant private investment abroad. Great Britain's foreign holdings in 1947 were estimated at $ 16 billion, and it seems safe to predict that it will remain an important capital-exporting country for many years.

Lewis estimates that the Netherlands lost about half of its foreign investments during the war chiefly by the reduction and depreciation of its holdings in Indonesia and Europe. [34] By 1947 France had become a debtor country through the debts incurred after the war ($ 2.6 billion) [35] and the losses resulting from the fall of the franc and the political changes in Europe.

Belgium, Sweden, Switzerland, and Portugal have probably maintained their prewar position without significant change; that is, their losses in Europe were probably compensated by the increase in value of their other holdings, above all in the United States. Italy and Japan lost their foreign holdings as a result of the war. Mainland China had its debt to Japan erased.

India has improved its position substantially with respect to its future balance of payments. [36] It may be pointed out that this decrease in foreign debt — and this also applies to mainland China and certain Middle Eastern countries — was not the result of an increase in the productive power of the country. Latin America had a long-term foreign debt of $ 11 billion in

1938, while by 1947 its total combined long and short-term debt had fallen to $ 5 billion. [37]

The question whether some of these countries would have been better off had they used their accumulated foreign exchange holdings to purchase new capital goods rather than to take over existing assets, is an academic one. However, merely posing this question reflects the fact that measures to improve the balance-of-payments position by replacing foreign capital, are not necessarily the most effective means of encouraging economic growth.

If we compare the postwar situation with that of 1938, we are struck by the decline in total foreign investment, above all by the decrease in holdings of European creditor countries — with the consequent reduction in foreign indebtedness of many undeveloped regions such as Latin America, India, and mainland China — and by the increased importance of the United States and Canada, both as a creditor area and as a source for investment. In the postwar period, the U.S.S.R. too has appeared as a creditor country by taking over German holdings in eastern Europe, and by loans granted to governments in this region and to mainland China, [38] but it is not possible to obtain an exact measure of these investments.

In the early postwar years it seemed improbable that the western European countries, because of the impoverishment brought on by the war and because of the more equal postwar income distribution, would again become large-scale exporters of private capital. However, as will be seen later, this conclusion was too hasty. Perhaps their concern with maintaining full employment, with its accompanying inflationary pressures and balance of payments difficulties, has impaired the capacity of these countries to export capital in the future. It is interesting to note [39] that in the United Kingdom the flow of capital abroad has been largely at the expense of home investment. Capital export was greatest in periods of relative depression in Britain and smallest when the demand for capital for home investment was brisk. On the other hand, a high level of employment in the industrial countries may also lead to a more even movement of foreign investment. Moreover, governments are bound to have greater control than in the past in such capital movements.

There is no doubt that foreign investments have substantially aided economic development, particularly in the industrial countries, first western Europe and later the United States, Australia, and Canada. Some countries, such as Australia and Japan,[40] consciously stimulated their economic growth by placing public loans abroad. In other countries, such as the United States, the Union of South Africa, and Argentina,[41] the influx of private foreign capital (portfolio and direct investment) did rather more to stimulate economic activity and internal capital formation required for continued expansion and the broadening of the economic structure.

In the less advanced countries, foreign investment also gave rise to new economic activities, but it did not result in the emergence of a dynamic economy in which all strata of the population partook of an ever increasing national income. However, the contention of H. W. Singer[42] that only the creditor countries profited from the capital flow to the underdeveloped countries, seems too extreme. Singer argues that the specialization in the export of food and raw materials absorbed such entrepreneurial initiative and domestic investment as there was in those countries and hampered the development of other points of growth in their economies. In many cases it can be proved that no indigenous talent or capital was involved in the new activities; these sprung up entirely because of foreign enterprise. Without the movement of foreign capital and managerial talent to those areas and the impact of modern techniques that it involved, those countries might still be unconscious of the relative stagnation of their economies, and the distinction between developed and underdeveloped countries might never have reached the prominence that it now occupies.

In the development of the industrial countries, capital provided from abroad was utilized to diversify the economy, since direct investments made additional resources available to governments and individuals. Meanwhile, the proceeds of public and private loans floated abroad were employed, directly or indirectly, for the construction of 'overhead' capital. In many instances this growth was supported by the substantial immigration of trained and enterprising people. In most of the undeveloped countries, however, similar opportunities were not grasped for various reasons, which were related to the institutional, as well as economic, structure. Thus, except insofar as the export of primary products was encouraged by direct investment, their economic life remained virtually unchanged. In the developed countries of today, direct foreign investment also turned, in a subsequent phase, to industrial production for the local market, while in some of the undeveloped countries further foreign private investment took place only insofar as these countries could provide additional or new raw materials to meet the requirements of the industrial countries. [43]

For the less advanced countries, the possibility of attracting portfolio investments seems, after the experiences of the 1930's, to have diminished considerably. [44] However, this is partially compensated for by the fact that today public loans from government to government, or semipublic loans, and even grants-in-aid have come to the forefront as substitutes for the portfolio form of investment. This change is not accidental. The development of the so-called 'regions of recent settlement' — Argentina, Australia, Canada, New Zealand, and the United States — could be left largely to private initiative.

In these countries, situated in the temperate zone, an appropriate climate for development existed which was strengthened by the immigration of Europeans with new ideas, so that in some respects these countries can be considered offshoots of western European civilization. Most of the underdeveloped countries lying in the tropical regions do not attract immigrants, while many of them lack natural resources that can be easily exploited as an inducement for such immigration. The relatively low cost of labor in the world's backward countries still offers an incentive for private foreign capital to move from the industrial countries to these areas, but only when there are locally exploitable resources suitable for the world market. The fact that the norms and mores of the undeveloped countries are not yet adjusted to modern technology, in addition, to the growing awareness of the disparity in welfare between different parts of the world and pressure to lessen this differential, make it likely that governmental transfers or gifts through bilateral and international channels from the developed to the underdeveloped regions will continue and may even increase in importance in the future. [45]

Chapter 15

PRIVATE FOREIGN INVESTMENT

Attitudes in the Creditor Countries

In the foregoing historical sketch we have referred to the changed international climate for foreign investment, particularly for private investment. We must go more deeply into this subject before we take up the present status of private capital movements.

We shall first appraise the sentiment in the creditor countries, the potential lenders, with respect to the participation of private capital in the development of the economically backward countries, and then consider the general outlook in the underdeveloped countries, the potential borrowers. We shall confine ourselves here mainly to opinions expressed by American spokesmen, since today the United States surpasses all other countries as a source of private capital. It may be assumed, moreover, that the views expressed in the United States are typical of those held by potential investors in other countries.

We have already mentioned that the United States is in an entirely different position from that of England and the other European countries at the time they emerged as providers of capital for the rest of the Western world. As indicated above, Europe gradually became a lender and was able to maintain this position as a result of changes in its economic structure that led to the importing of larger quantities of food and raw materials in exchange for the credits granted. The situation of the United States is totally different. In spite of the great expansion of production, it is not dependent upon increasing imports except for a few commodities. The Paley Report[1], cited above, predicts a growing dependence on imports, especially of metals.

However, even the impressive figures on the probable 1975 imports of those raw materials that are becoming scarce in the United States will remain insignificant in relation to the national product. As long as imports remain secondary or non-essential for the United States economy, the 'tendency to under-import' is likely to prevail, making the transfer of dividends and interest and the repayment of U.S. capital invested abroad, a serious problem for debtor countries.

United States imports, which in 1851–60 amounted to 9 per cent of the national product, had fallen to 5.1 per cent by 1926–30, and in the postwar period have averaged 3 per cent. Because of this characteristic of the United States economy — a function of its productive capacity and the variety of its resources — it is unlikely that financial aid from the United States will be a purely economic matter in the near future. In our opinion, the United States is likely, on political and humanitarian grounds, to feel compelled by its economic wealth and by the threat of an increase in the gap between its level of welfare and that of the rest of the world, to grant assistance to less-favored regions.

In part, this responsibility is related to the position of the United States as the principal creditor country. It is conceivable that, with suitable modifications of its trade policy,[2] the surplus in the balance of trade and payments might disappear. However, so many institutional obstacles stand in the way of 'trade-not-aid' that, for the time being, grants will probably remain an important means of maintaining the United States' economic and political leadership in the world. We shall not go further into the political side of the question.

The potential American investor seems to be convinced, on the basis of the history of his own country, that only private capital can bring about the desired acceleration in the rate of economic growth of the backward regions. Business spokesmen tend to look with a jaundiced eye at postwar developments in which such a large part of foreign assistance has been given through government channels.[3] A fairly typical example of the view of this group is contained in the following statement: "Public opinion in countries like the United States would not view with favor any permanent substitution of government loans for private investment." And further along in the same pamphlet: "It is, therefore, safe to assume that unless conditions favorable to the growth of private foreign investment are reestablished in capital-importing countries, capital exports by means of government loans will not permanently fill the gap caused by the disappearance of discouraged private foreign investors." [4]

There are various arguments adduced as reasonable grounds for believing in the superiority of private investment. For one thing, it is usually claimed that private investment never takes place without a detailed investigation of the project in mind. Furthermore, the talents of foreign managers and technicians are available to organize the new activity and give it the best possible chance for success. Such foreign skills also help to disseminate new techniques and organizational methods. In addition, direct private investments have the advantage of almost invariably involving an immediate net increase in capital stock, since they are guided by effective demand here and now. By contrast, public investments are not so closely geared to the present market situation, and they are more dependent on complementary investments, which must be made before such government outlays can become productive. From the point of view of the debtor, private foreign enterprises transfer dividends only when business is prosperous, while amortization and interest on foreign loans represent a constant burden on the balance of payments, whether times are good or bad.

The principal factors that now restrain private capital from foreign investment may be summarized as follows. The political situation in some underdeveloped countries is so unstable that the commitment of long-term capital is a risk that in most instances is too great for private individuals or enterprises to assume. (It is not surprising that the largest private United States investments in undeveloped areas in the postwar period have been made by the oil companies. [5] They are in a stronger bargaining position than most other investors by virtue of their

financial strength, the diversity of their interests in various countries, and the quasi-monopolistic character of the market for
petroleum products. An additional reason for the strong position
of the oil companies vis-à-vis governments in countries short of
fuel is the high elasticity of demand for petroleum products in a
developing economy.) Moreover, in some underdeveloped countries nationalist sentiment is so strong that it engenders an
unfriendly attitude toward foreign concerns, prompting governments to adopt discriminatory measures or even to expropriate
them without providing for prompt and adequate compensation. [6]

Foreign exchange controls, import quotas, and other restrictions
hampering international business activity, exist in many countries
today; their net effect is to make foreign investment less attractive.
Because of restrictions on the employment of foreign personnel,
many enterprises find it difficult to station the necessary number
of trained managerial and technical personnel in the undeveloped
country for an adequate period of time. In some undeveloped
countries, the cost of living for Americans and Europeans has
risen to such a level that the enlistment of the services of such
personnel to the extent required adds considerably to costs.

In a few undeveloped countries, direct or indirect taxes on
foreign enterprises have also been raised, or wages in export
industries through union action and government support have
been increased, to such a degree that the narrow margin between
the yield of foreign and domestic investment makes the former
less attractive. [7]

For these reasons, direct investment in undeveloped countries
in recent years, with the exception of that in petroleum and
mining activities, has been confined largely to the reinvestment
of profits — often from funds that could not be transferred
abroad — or to the expenditure required for the maintenance of
existing holdings.

Attitudes in Debtor Countries

The objections raised in the undeveloped countries to private foreign investment cannot be evaluated entirely on economic grounds. They lie partly in the socio-political and psychological sphere. Sometimes they are based on past experience, when, through political pressures, foreign capital obtained special privileges and, in some cases, maintained its position by corrupting the government administration. On the whole, though, present-day objections are of a more complex nature and are thus more difficult to analyze. For one thing, there is the fairly prevalent feeling that foreign capital makes exorbitant profits, but contributes comparatively little to the development of the economy.[8] On the average, these profits are sometimes relatively lower than those made by domestic entrepreneurs. Nevertheless, the foreigner who remains unassimilated and displays skills that no national possesses tends to arouse disfavor. Where a foreign enterprise occupies a key position in the national economy and remains an enclave in the country, it is likely to be even more vulnerable to nationalistic measures.[9]

A certain amount of resentment is also inspired by the fact that, because of the limited national market, foreign enterprises are generally directed toward export and exploit the country's natural resources or climate for the 'benefit' of external markets. People in the underdeveloped countries are apparently unwilling to recognize that the same circumstances have existed, or still exist, in the industrial countries, and that the additional income accruing to the country from foreign investment could serve to stimulate domestic enterprise and capital formation. They also overlook the fact that the government could use part of the yield of such exports to obtain capital goods, which would raise productivity in the domestic sector of the economy.

The resistance to direct investments also rests on an ignorance of contemporary conditions. Even some responsible leaders assume that, unless held in check by suitable legislation, foreign capitalists would be falling all over each other in the effort to invest in the underdeveloped world. The weakness of government in undeveloped countries, its lack of administrative and technical skills, and inability to stimulate the process of economic growth, despite the popular pressure for measures to raise the level of living, are also major factors in the antagonism that exists against the activities of foreigners and the influence of foreign capital.

On the other hand, complaints against private foreign capital alternate with assurances that, under certain conditions, direct investments would receive a warm welcome.[10] This ambivalent attitude is reflected in the various measures to encourage the influx of foreign capital that have been issued and subsequently rescinded or amended. For example, in February, 1946, a Brazilian decree provided for the registration of foreign capital with the Foreign Exchange Institute. Such capital, registered in the currency of the land of origin to eliminate the investor's fear of devaluation of the *cruzeiro*, could be withdrawn up to an amount of 20 per cent of total investment each year. Transfers of interest, dividends, or profits were allowed up to an amount of 8 per cent per annum on the original capital. Any transfer above this limit was regarded as a capital transfer. Thus, the foreign owner would be permitted to repatriate 28 per cent of his total investment every year.

The Foreign Exchange Institute had the authority to postpone transfers if the foreign exchange position was unfavorable, but until 1952, an 8 per cent transfer was always allowed, not only on the original capital invested, but also on reinvested profits. In January, 1952, however, the president of Brazil decreed that withdrawal of capital would be allowed only during the first five years, and that the limit of 8 per cent for interest or profit transfers would apply solely to the original capital. Previous transfers, to the extent that they had exceeded this percentage since 1945, were to be regarded as reductions of the invested capital, which would thus substantially reduce future interest transfers. After protests by those affected, the government adopted a law in February, 1953, that permitted the transfer of income on foreign capital "of special interest to the national economy" (note the vague wording of this restriction) at the official rate of exchange, and instituted a free market for other foreign transactions.

In many countries today there are impediments to the participation of foreign capital in certain branches of industry. A statement of industrial policy published on April 2, 1948, by the Pakistan government illustrates the difficulties.[11] After expressing a general welcome to foreign investors "seeking a purely industrial and economic objective and not claiming any special privileges," a series of restrictions were prescribed. Participation of Pakistan nationals in the administrative and technical functions of the foreign enterprise had to be assured, and the training of Pakistan citizens for leading positions guaranteed. Pakistan nationals were to be given the option to subscribe to at least 51 per cent of the capital in stocks or bonds of firms in any of thirteen branches of industry, including cement production, coal mining, cotton spinning and weaving, fish canning, the chemical and paint industries, mineral production, shipbuilding, sugar refining, and tanneries and at least 30 per cent of the share capital of other industries. If capital of Pakistan origin were not forthcoming, then foreign investors might take over these quotas, subject to approval by the government.

It is sometimes suggested that mixed enterprises, in which local capital and management participate, have a better chance of sparing the sensibilities of governments in underdeveloped countries. In some fields of activity, experience with this method seems to have been favorable, but it would still appear to be too early to formulate any general conclusions.[12]

On the whole, the loose wording of many of the declarations expressing a desire for foreign private investment has not offset the mistrust felt by foreign investors toward the ultimate objectives of the governments concerned. Foreign capital has been less hesitant in places where only the licensing of patents and technical assistance for the use of such patents are involved in the establishment of new activities with the aid of domestic capital. The foreign enterprise thus obtains a share of the capital in return for the transfer of its know-how, without assuming any special risk.

Such opportunities, however, are rather limited in under-developed countries, because of the lack of an industrial climate.[13]

In recent years, many underdeveloped countries have relaxed the restrictions imposed upon foreign investment.[14] In Egypt and Pakistan, for example, through legislation enacted in 1954, foreign investors were permitted to own all the share capital in approved projects. In several other countries, investment laws have been passed that give reasonable assurance for the remittance of profits and the repatriation of capital, and even offer tax concessions and exemption from import duties on required equipment. However, these privileges generally pertain only to new investments that have been officially approved. It is doubtful if they will lead to an increased flow of private capital as long as existing foreign enterprises continue to encounter difficulties with respect to the transfer of dividends, the withdrawal of capital, and the employment of foreign personnel.

American Views on and Interest in the Export of Private Capital

In recent years a good deal of attention has been paid in the United States to the question of international private investment. As we have noted, the International Chamber of Commerce has drafted an international investment code for the purpose of protecting the investor against arbitrary action by foreign governments.[15] The principal provisions of this code are: (1) that foreign investors shall not receive less favorable treatment than national investors, (2) that the country receiving capital shall adopt no discriminatory legislation placing restrictions on the nationality of the stockholders, the composition of the board of directors, or the selection of managerial and technical personnel deemed necessary for the efficient conduct of the business, (3) that only restrictions allowed by the International Monetary Fund shall be applied to the transfer of interest, dividends, and amortization on foreign capital, and (4) that, if foreign holdings are expropriated, the action should accord with proper legal procedures and with reasonable compensation fixed by international law.

The code has the merit of stating precisely the viewpoint of potential investors. It is difficult to appraise the objections of underdeveloped countries to this code. In general, they dislike any stipulations that may tie the hands of their governments in future economic policy. The actions of foreign enterprises are now subject to national laws practically everywhere. In several Latin American countries, however, the governments have tried to incorporate, into contracts relating to concessions, the specific provision that a foreign investor shall not call on the assistance of his own government in the event of a dispute concerning the interpretation of an agreement. This clause, called the Calvo clause after an Argentine jurist, is based on the doctrine that no government should interfere in another country, diplomatically or otherwise, to enforce the demands of its nationals. It is understandable that this clause is unacceptable to foreign investors in cases where they believe that their rights are being violated.

Underdeveloped countries would probably prefer to have item 2 of the code expressed in a more positive manner, to the effect that foreign investors have an obligation to train nationals for managerial functions and to facilitate the participation of national capital in their enterprises.[16] The postwar discussions on this subject have shown how far apart the viewpoints of capital-exporting and capital-importing countries are, and how difficult it is to negotiate on general principles. This explains why the individual investor tends to insist on specific provisions to protect his interests in his contract with the foreign government.

The aim of the International Chamber of Commerce code was to make clear, particularly to the United States government, the manner in which 'business' would like to see technical assistance provided to undeveloped countries, and on what conditions that aid should depend.[17] The United States government has taken up this suggestion in its treaties of "friendship, commerce and navigation." By May, 1956, eight such treaties were in force and eight others were still awaiting approval by the legislatures of the countries concerned.[18]

Even when such treaties have been concluded, there is still no guarantee that the foreign investor will remain secure against discrimination over the period of years envisaged in any long-term investment. This insecurity probably remains the most important obstacle to the flow of private investments.

For reasons already given, the foreign investor appears to be unwilling to risk capital in industries producing for the domestic market and in those industries comprising economic overhead facilities (public-service enterprises), which were often financed by private foreign capital in the nineteenth century. The latter industries naturally receive their income in local currency and are dependent upon the approval of the government to obtain foreign exchange for the transfer of interest and dividends and the repayment of the principal. If these services satisfy previously unfelt needs of private consumers, their influence in improving the country's balance-of-payments position may be almost nil and their chance of receiving foreign exchange very slight. If, on the other hand, they are linked with the establishment of export industries — for example, an electrical power plant using part of its output to reduce ores or a railroad transporting commodities for export — their prospects are more favorable. Public service enterprises have additional disadvantages for the foreign investor. Because they are of such great social significance, their rates are often either fixed or controlled by law, and in some cases these rates tend to lag behind the general change in prices.[19] Then there is always the danger of expropriation. It may be assumed, therefore, that investment being made by private foreign concerns in this type of undertaking is mainly reinvestment or new investment intended mainly to maintain the value of existing holdings.[20]

Despite the narrowing of the field of private foreign investment in the underdeveloped countries, business still clings to the idea of a greater role for private capital in the future economic development of those areas. This attitude persists even though there is little chance of a revival of portfolio investments in economic overhead facilities. The report, *Partners in Progress*,[21] though not unsympathetic toward public investment, makes the following recommendations for encouraging the flow of private capital abroad: (1) income from enterprises domiciled abroad to be tax-free in the U.S. to the extent that taxes have already been paid in the country of investment (to lessen the impact on the Treasury, it is proposed to extend this privilege only to new investments), (2) the conclusion of bilateral treaties against discriminatory levies on United States enterprises, (3) the negotiation of bilateral trade treaties obligating both parties to treat foreign investments reasonably, (4) the reservation of $ 100 million of the authorized loan capital of the Export-Import Bank to insure the risk of transferring interest and capital repayments on new foreign government loans purchased by private investors — upon payment of a prescribed premium and upon application of the interested parties — thereby making it attractive for institutional investors to invest in foreign bonds, and (5) the establishment of an International Finance Corporation, as a subsidiary of the International Bank, to make direct investments in foreign and local currencies in foreign private enterprises, without government guarantee or voting rights.

The last suggestion, implying a new form of direct investment, would make possible purely financial collaboration between investor and foreign enterprise. It would enable new foreign enterprises to avoid the fixed burden of interest, while the corporation would, to some extent, reduce the transfer risk, as it could reinvest local currency profits of successful undertakings. A $ 400 million capital was originally proposed for this subsidiary of the Bank, with the United States subscribing $ 150 million and the other countries subscribing on the basis of their present percentage contributions to the Bank's capital.

The Bank looked favorably on this proposal, and in its first report[22] on the subject to the Economic and Social Council of the United Nations, it suggested that operations could be started when one-third of the capital had been subscribed. Because the chief potential participants did not consider the time ripe for such an institution, the item remained on the agenda of the Economic and Social Council and on that of the General Assembly of the United Nations for several sessions. In November, 1954, the United States government reversed its attitude, and in 1955, the Bank drafted the 'Articles of Agreement' of the International Finance Corporation[23] with an initial capital of $ 100 million. The Corporation came into being in 1956, following ratification by the required number of countries.

Such an institution should give private entrepreneurs in under-developed countries access to a source of foreign capital, which now flows almost exclusively to the governments of such countries or for the development of exportable natural resources — the one form of investment in backward countries that still attracts private foreign capital.[24] Such investments tend to reflect the needs of the creditor country, or of the world as a whole. Estimates of future demand on these markets govern the use of foreign capital in the exploitation of the natural resources of the undeveloped countries.[25]

The following table gives some idea of the change that has occurred in U.S. imports of some critical raw materials.

Table 13. IMPORT OF CERTAIN METALS AND ORES INTO THE UNITED STATES (in thousands of metric tons)

Commodity	1937	1948	1953	1955
Copper (ores, concentrates, blister, refined, and scrap metal)	206.4	442.9	609.2	532.4
Lead (ores, lead bullion, pigs, bars, and scrap)	14.5	228.9	410.4	399.4
Zinc (ores, scrap, dross, blocks)	37.7	251.4	632.8	547.1
Aluminum (metal, scrap and alloys)	20.3	140.5	297.1	198.2
Iron ore & concentrates	2,481.2	6,200.9	11,174.3	23,823.4

Source: U.S. Department of Commerce, *Quarterly Summary of Foreign Commerce of the U.S.* (Imports of Merchandise for Consumption), Washington, D.C. Data obtained from the issues covering January–December of year stated, which are published in June or July of the following year.

Dependence on imports of these materials will probably be more marked in the future. This explains why new copper investments have been made in Chile, where production increased from 206,800 tons in 1928 to 444,000 tons in 1948, and where three United States-owned companies are responsible for 97 per cent of Chilean copper production. United States concerns have made important postwar investments in Brazil, Canada, Liberia, and Venezuela for iron ore exploitation, now that the principal high-grade ores in the United States, in the Mesabi range of the Lake Superior area, appear to be exhausted, and the working of lower-grade ores is increasing the cost of production.

Petroleum exploration and exploitation fall into a somewhat different category, since the interested companies are primarily concerned with meeting increasing world requirements and not with the consumption of any single country.

The advantages of such investments from the standpoint of United States investors — and in the case of oil, of Anglo-Dutch interests as well — are plain, but the governments of the undeveloped countries, naturally enough, are interested in seeing their own nationals participate in the financing and managing of such activities. Spiegel[26] has said that, from the viewpoint of the debtor country, direct investments lack one attraction of portfolio investments in that they are not self-liquidating. However, direct investors rarely intend the future liquidation of their holdings. In making his investment, the investor hopes for a continuing stream of dividends, and he adjusts his capital transfer to or from the country of investment according to expected yields. The proposal was recently made for India[27] that private foreign capital should participate to the extent of 70 per cent in a new industry, leaving 30 per cent to local capital, and after ten years should have reduced its share to only 30 per cent, with the share of local capital thus increasing to 70 per cent. This proposal seems to be based on a misinterpretation of the motives on which most foreign investment is based. Foreign investors are unlikely to sell their holdings to domestic investors unless the enterprise is less profitable than comparable undertakings elsewhere, or if difficulties are expected in the transfer of profits. Private capital is unlikely to be surrendered when the prospects of profits are favorable and no transfer difficulties are feared. Neither can private capitalists be expected to make an initial investment under the proposed procedure. [28]

Postwar Private United States Investment

In the light of the above discussion, it might be useful to take a look at some data on postwar United States private investments. A comparison between 1940–54 [29] figures shows a rise in portfolio investments from $ 3.6 to $ 6.7 billion. If we examine the detailed figures, we find that the increase was due almost entirely to the acquisition of Canadian securities and bonds (1940 = $ 1.7 billion; 1954 = $ 3.5 billion) and European securities and bonds (1940 = $ 636 million; 1954 = $ 1.5 billion). It has already been pointed out that Canada is not regarded as a foreign country by United States investors. Presumably the European securities were for the most part brought in by refugees, and to a small degree, investments in the stock of European enterprises recently listed on the New York Stock Exchange. Portfolio investments in Latin America, which had fallen to $ 1 billion by 1940, were valued at only $ 491 million in 1954, confirming our conclusion that portfolio investment in underdeveloped countries is of diminishing importance.

Direct investments showed a marked rise, as can be seen from the table on page 290, which shows the geographical and industrial distribution of direct investments in 1940 and 1954.

These figures show that Canada and Latin America are the most important outlets for United States private capital, accounting for more than two-thirds of total direct investment. Investments in Europe have increased, particularly in manufacturing, partly as a result of involuntary reinvested profits [30] reflecting the fact that the dollar shortage made it economical to expand certain production and assembly facilities in Europe to maintain markets for United States products. A publication of the Organization for European Economic Cooperation [31] notes that, according to

Table 14. VALUE OF DIRECT UNITED STATES INVESTMENT BY INDUSTRY AND AREA (In billions of dollars — end-of-year data)

Type of Investment	Total		Canada		Latin America		Western Europe		Other Areas	
	1940	1954	1940	1954	1940	1954	1940	1954	1940	1954
Manufacturing	1.6	5.7	0.6	2.6	0.2	1.2	0.6	1.4	0.1	0.4
Trade	0.5	1.1	0.1	0.4	0.1	0.4	0.2	0.2	0.1	0.2
Mining & Smelting	0.8	2.1	0.2	0.8	0.5	1.0	0.1	–	–	0.2
Petroleum	1.3	5.4	0.1	1.2	0.6	1.7	0.3	0.7	0.3	1.8
Public Utilities	1.5	1.5	0.4	0.3	1.0	1.1	0.1	–	0.1	0.1
Miscellaneous	1.2	2.0	0.6	0.8	0.4	0.8	0.1	0.2	0.1	0.2
Total	7.0	17.7	2.1	5.9	2.8	6.3	1.4	2.6	0.7	2.9

The blanks denote less than $ 50 million.

Source: R. L. Sammons and M. Abelson, "American Direct Investment in Foreign Countries – 1940", U.S. Department of Commerce *(Economic Series, No. 10)* Washington, D.C.: 1942; S. Pizer and F. Cutler, "International Investments and Earnings", *Survey of Current Business*, August, 1955.

balance of payments figures, during the period 1947–53 the total net outflow of private United States capital to member countries was about $ 688 million. However, in the same period the United States received $ 1.9 billion as profits on past investments in member countries, and, although $ 904 million had been reinvested, the part repatriated ($ 1 billion) exceeded the new capital export by over $ 300 million.

The increase of investments in 'Other Areas' can be attributed almost entirely to the rise in oil exploitation in the Middle East. In Canada, the increase in manufacturing industries is particularly striking, while in Latin America investments in mining and petroleum account for almost 50 per cent of the growth. Though local markets have broadened since the war, and high tariffs have made the establishment of certain industries attractive in Argentina, Brazil, and Mexico, it is probable that the increase of investment in the other branches of economic activity in Latin America represents, in part, profits reinvested involuntarily as a result of foreign exchange restrictions. It should also be noted that the value of investment in public utilities has remained unchanged despite the decline in the value of the dollar over this period.

If we disregard new investments in Canada and new petroleum investments, which together account for almost 70 per cent of the increase in United States direct investment between 1940 and 1954, and allow for involuntary reinvested profits elsewhere, it seems clear that during this period, new United States private investment for the economic development of the backward regions was of relatively minor significance. It would be premature to make any prediction, on the basis of events in this short period, about the function that private foreign capital will assume in the acceleration of economic development in the world. If we keep in mind the causes for the decreasing importance of investments, especially the changes in the investment climate in debtor countries, it is hard to see how private capital will ever again play a role in the expansion of the world economy comparable to the one it played in the nineteenth and early twentieth century. In this connection it might be pointed out, in anticipation of the next chapter, that United States government long-term foreign claims and credits (public investments) increased from $ 5.2 billion in 1946 to $ 15 billion in 1954, the latter figure being almost equal to United States direct private investments.

No comparable information is available on private foreign investment of the west European creditor countries. In the United Nations publication [32] mentioned above, it was estimated that the net outflow of private long-term capital from the industrialized countries during the period 1946–52 amounted to some $ 11 billion, of which the United States accounted for almost $ 8 billion. The United Kingdom, Switzerland, France, Belgium, and the Netherlands were considered responsible for the balance of $ 3 billion. Average private capital exports over the years 1949–52 have amounted to $ 2 billion which in real terms, as stated in the report, were only about half those in the 1920's. According to a more recent United Nations study [33] the same level of, and the same proportion between, investments from the U.S. and other capital-export countries seems to have prevailed in the period 1953–55. The relative decline of private capital exports is contrasted with the increase in the quantum of world trade of about 75 per cent and the rise in world industrial production of about 150 per cent over the last thirty years. The lag in private capital outflow reflects mainly the decrease in portfolio investment.

British direct investments over the period 1946–55 seem largely to have flowed to more developed countries of the Commonwealth (Canada, Australia, Union of South Africa) and to less developed areas for the exploitation of petroleum (the U.K. Economic Survey for 1949 mentions that during the period 1947–49 £ 240 million was invested abroad for this purpose) and other raw materials. Swiss capital exports have consisted largely of foreign bond issues for account of industrial countries and the International Bank. France has been a net importer of private capital from outside the franc area; private transactions between metropolitan France and its overseas territories are not published. However, it may be assumed that the decline in value of French foreign investment outside the franc area has been more than offset by private flows to territories within the French Union. Private capital from Belgium has been directed mainly to the Belgian Congo and to industrial countries.

On the basis of the scanty information available, it would seem that the investment pattern of western European nations in the backward countries does not differ much from that of United States direct investment, except that some of these countries have political ties with certain underdeveloped territories in which their investment structure is more diversified and reflects greater interest in public utilities. This also accounts for the floating of government loans of certain underdeveloped countries in the capital market of the mother countries. [34]

Chapter 16

PUBLIC FOREIGN INVESTMENT

Introduction

It has already been pointed out that the economic sectors, in which private foreign investment has taken place, have narrowed considerably in recent years. This is partly because the private investor is more aware of the risks that surround investments in the branches of industry which do not directly contribute to an improvement in the debtor country's balance of payments. It is also a consequence of the various restrictive measures that the undeveloped countries have introduced since the 1930's as part of their economic policies.

The governments of the underdeveloped regions prefer public loans because they are anxious to keep control of their natural resources in their own hands. They also want to reserve to themselves the right to fix priorities in their development programs, instead of leaving this to foreign private capitalists. The latter are primarily guided by the profit motive and cannot be expected to have in mind the achievement of the social and economic goals which the recipient country considers most desirable.

Governments of underdeveloped countries realize that the small size of domestic markets hold little attraction to foreign investors. Nevertheless, for the reasons given, they are reluctant to give complete freedom to investments that have the world market in view. They are anxious instead to borrow in order to obtain external economies that may help create a climate in which private investment by nationals would flow into activities directed toward the expansion of the domestic market.

In this chapter, public investment is generally considered from the underdeveloped countries' point of view. The term, as used, comprises all foreign funds, public or private, loans or gifts, made available to governments.

The Export-Import Bank of Washington

Among the institutions which have provided a certain amount of public capital for the economically retarded regions are the Export-Import Bank of Washington and the International Bank for Reconstruction and Development. The former is a United States government bank whose loans appear annually on the budget of the U.S. Treasury. It was established in 1934 to aid in the financing of exports and imports and in the exchange of goods between the United States and other countries.[1] Viewed from the creditor's standpoint, the loans are public ones but they have not always been given solely to governments or governmental institutions; they have also gone to private concerns, especially subsidiaries of United States enterprises. Credits to concerns controlled by foreign capital have only been granted with the approval of the government of the country involved, thereby assuring foreign exchange for the payment of interest and amortization. Even when the funds were not used for public investments, the government still had an opportunity of ensuring that the project for which the debt was contracted fitted into its own plans for economic development.

As a rule, this Bank grants loans and guarantees only for specific projects—to finance the purchase of raw materials and machinery produced in the United States and to obtain technical services from United States firms or from individual American citizens. These so-called 'tied' loans are granted only for purposes affording a reasonable assurance of repayment. Its charter contains a provision that the Bank shall not compete with private capital but rather shall attempt to supplement and encourage the flow of private capital to other countries. In practice, however, it has often granted credits of a type previously arranged through

private lending but now apparently considered too great a risk
for private individuals or corporations to assume. To put it more
precisely, because of the existence of the Bank, the private investor tends to pass the risk on to it, or at least obtain its support.

The primary objective of the Bank is the financing of United
States exports in the broadest sense. In 1940 it also received
permission to aid "in the development of the resources, the
stabilization of the economies and orderly marketing of the
products of the countries of the Western hemisphere." This
additional power was extended to other regions in 1950.[2]

As of June 30, 1955, the Bank's outstanding loans amounted to
$ 2.7 billion. Five billion dollars had been disbursed since 1934,
and $ 2.2 billion repaid. Credits amounting to $ 754 million
had been extended but not yet disbursed. Of the amount
outstanding, $ 1.4 billion was due from European countries
($ 0.9 billion from France alone); $ 0.9 billion from Latin American countries; $ 328 million from Asian countries (including
$ 122 million from Israel and $ 59 million from Japan;) $ 122
million from African countries (including $ 103 million from the
Union of South Africa); and $ 6 million from Australia. The
tables appended to the January-June, 1955 report[3] provide the
following breakdown of the purposes for which outstanding loans
had been given to Latin America, the most important underdeveloped region to receive Bank credit (p. 296).

The Bank's loans have, among other things, helped to establish
a state-controlled steel industry in Brazil and Chile; to expand
the steel industry in Mexico; to modernize electric power plants
(some owned by United States or other foreign capital) in Brazil,
Colombia, Cuba, Mexico, Nicaragua, Peru, Uruguay, and Venezuela; to aid in the rehabilitation of state-owned railroads in
Brazil, Chile, Ecuador, Mexico, and Uruguay; to procure machinery for road construction in Bolivia, Colombia, Ecuador,
Mexico, Nicaragua, Paraguay, Peru, and San Salvador;
to purchase ships for the establishment of national shipping
companies, and for the improvement of coastwise sea trade in
Argentina, Brazil and Colombia, and to purchase machinery

Table 15. EXPORT-IMPORT BANK OF WASHINGTON
Loans Outstanding to Latin American Countries, June 30, 1955

Purpose of Loans	Amount (In million dollars)
Transport & Communications	$ 159
Industry	146
Public Utilities	89
Mining	70
Agriculture	56
Miscellaneous	405*
Total	925

* Of this amount, $ 393 million comprised credits granted to Argentina and Brazil for temporary balance of payment difficulties.

Note: The distribution is somewhat arbitrary since the proposed uses of the machinery purchased with these credits is not stated in all cases.

for the working and processing of mineral deposits in Bolivia, Brazil, Mexico, and Peru. In the last case, credits from the Bank have also served partly to limit risks for private foreign investors.

In 1953, because of the United States government's retrenchment program, there was talk of curtailing the activity of the Export-Import Bank, confining it to the encouragement of United States international trade and leaving the public financing of industrial projects entirely to the International Bank for Reconstruction and Development. It was also suggested that the interest rate for long-term loans was to be raised to avoid competition with the International Bank, whose interest rates are related to the cost of borrowing on the open market, while the Export-Import Bank receives its funds from the U.S. Treasury at a lower rate of interest.[4] However, the reorganization of the Bank in 1954 was entirely administrative and did not put any of these proposals into effect.

The International Bank for Reconstruction and Development

The International Bank for Reconstruction and Development,[5] founded in June, 1946 in terms of the Bretton Woods Agreement, has broader objectives than the Export-Import Bank. According to its Articles of Agreement, it is to assist member countries by: facilitating the investment of capital for productive purposes, promoting private foreign investment through guarantees or participation in loans, and helping in the expansion of international trade and the maintenance of equilibrium in balance of payments by encouraging international investment for the development of the productive resources of member countries. Thus the International Bank also sees its task as a supplementary one and believes that private capital should have the principal role in economic development of underdeveloped countries.[6] Only when private capital is not available on reasonable terms is the Bank willing to grant a loan, and then only if the loan is for a sound and productive purpose of sufficient importance to warrant incurring a foreign exchange liability to finance it, and if there is a reasonable prospect of repayment.

As an international institution, the Bank naturally does not formally insist that its loans be expended for goods and services from the country whose currency is borrowed. However, its reports seem to indicate that, in practice, its lending policy is guided by criteria not very different from those of the Export-Import Bank. Although the International Bank is authorized to make loans for expenditures in local currencies in special circumstances where the borrowing country is unable to raise the required local funds on reasonable terms,[7] thus far it has granted its loans almost exclusively to pay for machinery and services imported for specific projects.

This policy has come in for some criticism. In defending it, the Bank has stated[8] that its charter prescribes that loans must be used for productive purposes, and that a loan must specify the goods and services for which it is to be expended and the uses to which these goods and services are to be put. Moreover, the Bank explained that, in considering a request for a loan, it first makes an intensive study of the applicant's economy, so that over-all economic needs can be assessed, and high-priority projects suitable for foreign financing selected.

The Bank would be prepared to finance local expenditures "(a) if the project to be financed is of such economic urgency that the country's ability to undertake foreign borrowing is better utilized in this way than in financing the direct foreign exchange costs of alternative projects; (b) if the local currency costs of the project cannot be met out of available domestic resources; and (c) if it is apparent that, unless foreign exchange is made available to the borrowing country to be employed for the import of consumer goods or raw materials, the local expenditures involved in this project will lead to inflationary pressures." The Bank did make an exception on these grounds in 1952, when $ 10 million was loaned to Italy for the development of the southern region by local or foreign expenditures. The 'specific projects' requirement was also abandoned to a certain extent in making loans to development banks or agencies (in Chile, Ethiopia, India, Mexico, and Turkey) which in turn were to lend the funds so obtained to a number of small enterprises in the debtor countries.

The principle of granting loans only for imports required for 'specific projects' is untenable from a theoretical viewpoint. In the first place, expenditures for various projects exert their effect as an indivisible whole. Secondly, it is the productivity of an investment policy as a whole, not that of a specific project — and hence even less that of the segment financed by foreign funds — which determines whether the future balance-of-payments position will assure repayment of loans. We have already mentioned the examples of Australia and Canada which raised foreign loans to purchase consumer goods, in order to make national resources available for the construction of capital goods with a higher productivity than the machinery or installations that might have been imported. But it is clearly far more difficult to maintain control over such expenditures. Therefore, it is understandable that the Bank should adhere, at least during the early years, to the criterion of 'specific project.'[9]

From 1947 to June, 1955, the Bank granted a total of $ 2,274 million in loans. Of this amount, $ 1.2 billion or about 50 per cent, is estimated to have been granted to industrial countries.

Disregarding the $ 497 million advanced for general postwar reconstruction to Denmark, France, Luxembourg, and the Netherlands, the distribution of the other loans can be seen in the table below. It is clear from this table that about 60 per cent of these loans have been granted to underdeveloped countries in Latin America, Africa, the Middle and Far East.

TABLE 16. INTERNATIONAL BANK FOR RECONSTRUCTION AND DEVELOPMENT, LOANS GRANTED 1947–55

Purpose of Loans	Total of Loans, 1947–55	Estimated Amount of Loans to Undeveloped Countries, 1947–55
	(In millions of dollars)	
Electric Power	617	420
Transportation	533	352
Communications	26	26
Agriculture & Forestry	225	121
Industry	236	99
General Development	140	46
Total	1,777	1,058

Source: International Bank for Reconstruction and Development, Tenth Annual Report, 1954–55 and Appendices (Washington, D.C.).

Since the International Bank belongs to its member countries, it applies commercial criteria in its lending policy[10] and tends to show considerable interest in the economies of potential borrowers. By sending out survey missions which have aided governments in fixing the priorities in their economic programs, it has not only directed the demand for loans, but has also advised its members on financial and technical problems during the execution of projects.[11] On the basis of experience gained through close contact with governments of underdeveloped countries, the Bank has observed on several occasions that speedy results cannot be expected.

"In focussing attention on this goal (a more rapid development of the natural resources of the undeveloped countries), it is easy to forget that development is necessarily a process measured in decades, not years... A fundamental obstacle to long-range development is the lack of capital to build the necessary productive facilities and buy equipment; to provide schools and shops to train workers in new skills; and to establish the housing, public utilities, transportation and other services needed for an efficiently functioning economy... Since foreign capital cannot be relied upon to do more than supplement local development efforts, it is important that the underdeveloped countries take all possible measures to encourage local savings and their investment for productive purposes... A second obstacle is the shortage of technical and managerial personnel, particularly those with advanced training and experience... Economic instability often imposes a third obstacle to healthy development... Again, there is lacking in many countries any well-formulated concept of the overall lines along which sound development is most likely to make progress... Another factor retarding development is the low educational level of the mass of the people of most under-developed countries... Finally, in a number of countries unsettled political conditions impair confidence in the future and thus impose an important restraint upon capital investment not only from abroad but also out of domestic savings." [12]

The factors which make economic development a difficult process both in the short and in the long run were enumerated by the Bank once again in order to prove that "sound economic development is best promoted, not by sporadic injections of large amounts of capital, but rather by a steady flow of capital in moderate amounts." [13]

The Bank is eager to see private foreign capital invest in the production and processing of agricultural and mineral raw materials, especially for export. The development of light industries, which ordinarily requires only a relatively small investment and yields a fairly early return should, in the Bank's view, be left to private domestic capital. [14] Irrigation and land reclamation projects, public utilities, and the like, which require a large initial investment and can be expected to yield a return only over a long period, could then be financed with the participation of the Bank or by direct foreign investment, or eventually by means of guarantees given to private capital. [15]

The Bank is prepared to make available the services of technicians to assess the needs and possibilities of member countries, and to indicate means by which development might best be undertaken — the projects, in the opinion of its experts, which should have priority, and the internal measures, financial and otherwise, which should be taken to carry out such projects. The Bank is also in a position to give the names of firms and individual technicians whose services can be enlisted for working out specific projects.

The Bank is convinced that "the major responsibility for promoting productive investments of local resources must be assumed by the local government itself, by following sound fiscal and monetary practices, by adopting tax policies designed both to encourage increased capital formation and to channel it into productive enterprise, and in appropriate cases by encouraging the creation of an active local capital market... Some part of the necessary foreign capital may be obtainable from public sources through intergovernmental and International Bank loans. In the long run, however, development on the scale that is within the range of practicability needs financial assistance in amounts which only the free flow of private capital can provide. Furthermore, it is desirable that a considerable part of the foreign capital employed for development purposes be in the form of equity investments in order to avoid an undue burden of fixed charges which might impair the credit of the borrowing country or intensify its balance-of-payments problems during a period of declining trade or falling prices." For this reason, the Bank considers that one of its principal objectives is "to help to create conditions which will encourage a steady and substantial stream of private investment, particularly equity investment, flowing into its underdeveloped member countries." [16]

These principles, on which the Bank's lending policy is based, are in agreement with the official United States pronouncements in this field. This is not surprising if we consider that as a result of its contribution to the Bank's capital, the United States holds almost one-third of the voting shares.

Most of the funds made available to undeveloped regions by

the Export-Import Bank and the International Bank for Reconstruction and Development have been used for the financing of those projects of economic overhead capital that formerly were financed by private foreign capital. In the past foreign capital had also provided the funds needed to pay for the local raw materials and labor, or the cost of such materials and labor was met from the proceeds of public loans placed on the capital market in the creditor countries.

The loans of the Export-Import and International Banks include credits for capital goods which, because they contribute directly to an improvement of the export position, might be attractive to private capital, even today, were it not that the changes in the investment climate in underdeveloped countries have made the risk seem too great to be borne by private individuals.

The criticisms voiced by governments of undeveloped countries of the policy of these Banks will be taken up at a later stage, but some of them should be mentioned at this point. These governments object to the emphasis which the Banks place on the future balance of payments. They are interested in the development of their own national economies, regardless of the effect on the international economy. In essence, the point at issue lies deeper than this. The Banks, in formulating their policies, hope for a return to 'normalcy' in economic relationships, while the underdeveloped countries have come to view as normal a situation that, especially in the United States, is still considered 'abnormal', — a situation in which a substantial part of foreign capital flow takes place in the form of gifts or public loans. As N. S. Buchanan rightly notes, [17] it is partly because the postwar foreign investment pattern is interwoven with political factors that it confronts economic theory with so many unsolved problems.

United States Aid Programs

Apart from the loans granted by the EXIM-Bank and International Bank, most of the other public investments, loans and grants, made in the postwar period came directly from governments. From March, 1944 to the beginning of 1947, the United Nations Relief and Rehabilitation Administration (UNRRA) gave material assistance, totalling $ 3.7 billion, to war-devastated regions in Europe and Asia. Of this amount, $ 2.7 billion was contributed by the United States and the equivalent of $ 1 billion by other member states.[18]

The United States government also granted credits to Great Britain in 1946 of $ 3.75 billion. In the same year, the Philippines received $ 75 million through the Reconstruction Finance Corporation and another $ 62 million in grants from the United States for the reconstruction of war-damaged roads, port facilities and public buildings and services. In July, 1947, a special law made available $ 1.403 billion of which $ 300 million went to Greece, $ 100 million to Turkey, $ 332 million to Germany and Japan, $ 600 million to Korea, and $ 71 million to the International Refugee Organization. To the end of 1947, the United States government had also provided $ 1 billion in credits for the purchase of surplus American war materials.

All this aid was intended mainly as a contribution to the reconstruction of a war-devastated world. It was thought that all further loans for reconstruction and development should be granted through the Export-Import Bank and the International Bank. This was indicated in a declaration by the United States National Advisory Council for International Financial and Monetary Problems in 1946. It was not until Secretary of State Marshall's speech at Harvard University on June 5, 1947, that the United States recognized publicly that further financial aid was necessary for the restoration of a disorganized world economy, particularly in western Europe. The Economic Cooperation Act of 1948 (April, 1948–June, 1949) appropriated $ 4 billion for this purpose. In addition, $ 400 million was made available for China, $ 1.3 billion for territories occupied by the United States, $ 225 million for Greece and Turkey, $ 35 million for the International Children's Fund, and another $ 71 million for the International Refugee Organization. This and similar aid was continued in succeeding years. The ECA Act of 1948 was amended and renamed the Mutual Assistance Act of 1949. Later it became the Mutual Security Act of 1951. The 1951 Mutual Security Program also included aid to underdeveloped countries on the basis of the 1950 Act for International Development (the so-called Point Four program) and the 1942 Institute for Inter-American Affairs Act.

From July, 1945 to June, 1955, the United States advanced a net total of $ 51.3 billion, of which $ 40.3 billion consisted of grants and $ 11 billion of credits. Most of the loans ($ 8.2 billion) were made before the adoption of the European Reconstruction program. The largest items in that category included credits to the United Kingdom, loans through the Export-Import Bank, and loans for the purchase of United States war surplus materials.[19] Of the total $ 51.3 billion in grants and credits, military grants accounted for $ 14.7 billion ($ 9.1 billion to western Europe and $ 5.3 billion to the Near East and other parts of Asia and the Pacific). The following table indicates the geographic distribution of the remaining $ 36.7 billion.

TABLE 17. U.S. GOVERNMENT FOREIGN AID, 1945–55

	Total Non-Military Aid 1945–June, 1955	Before June, 1950	After June, 1950
	(in billions of U.S. dollars)		
Net grants	25.7	15.6	10.1
Net credits	11.0	9.3	1.7
Total	36.7	24.9	11.8
Western Europe and Dependent Areas	26.0	18.8	7.2
Eastern Europe	1.1	1.1	–
Near East and Africa	0.8	–	0.8
Other Asia and Pacific	6.8	4.0	2.8
Latin America	1.0	0.3	0.7
International Organizations & Unspecified Areas	0.9	0.7	0.2

Thus, western Europe and its dependent areas had received 70 per cent of the United States grants and credits up to mid-1955. Prior to the Korean War, the percentage was actually closer to

75, but it tapered off to 60 per cent after the outbreak of this conflict. It is difficult to overestimate the importance of this aid to western Europe in the reconstruction of the industrial countries of that region. The same applies to Japan which received almost 40 per cent of the nonmilitary aid classified under 'Other Asia and Pacific'. The underdeveloped countries received relatively smaller amounts, and in certain countries a substantial part of these sums helped to bolster a precarious political situation rather than contribute to economic development. The recipients among the economically backward countries were in Europe: Greece ($ 1.3 billion), Spain ($ 91 million), Turkey ($ 312 million), Yugoslavia ($ 719 million); in the Near East: Iran ($ 196 million), Israel ($ 359 million); in Asia and the Pacific: China (Taiwan) ($ 1.2 billion), India ($ 328 million), Indo-China ($ 303 million), Indonesia ($ 241 million), Korea ($ 1.2 billion), Pakistan ($ 133 million), and the Philippines ($ 820 million).

In the fiscal year 1954–55, partly as a result of the carryover from prior authorizations, $ 4.5 billion in net grants and credits were extended (the new appropriation for 1954–55 was only $ 2.8 billion) of which $ 2.5 billion consisted of military grants. Of the $ 1.9 billion in other grants and credits, $ 888 million (46 per cent) went to European countries, $ 865 million (44 per cent) to Asian countries and the balance largely to Latin American countries. Even this nonmilitary aid included $ 422 million in net grants to France to help defray costs of military forces in Indo-China and $ 106 million in net grants to the United Kingdom for assistance in the production of military equipment. Part of the aid provided to the Indo-Chinese states of Viet-Nam, Cambodia and Laos in the amount of $ 216 million in 1954–55, fell into the same category.

The appropriation for 1955–56 of $ 2.7 billion (estimated expenditure $ 4.2 billion) consisted of $ 1 billion for military aid (estimated expenditure $ 2.5 billion), of which $ 800 million was to be received by Asian countries. Of the nonmilitary aid of $ 1.7 billion, about 50 per cent was to go to Korea and the Indo-

Chinese states, again largely to help sustain a delicate political position and aid rehabilitation in war-devastated regions. It might also be mentioned that in 1955–56 a sum of $ 100 million was included in the nonmilitary aid category to be used as a regional fund for Asian economic development in addition to the regular bilateral country programs. After July 1, 1955, all economic assistance was administered by the International Co-operation Administration, an agency of the U.S. State Department, while all foreign defense aid was to be supervised by the Defense Department.

Recently it has been suggested that there has been too much emphasis on military assistance in the United States programs of aid to underdeveloped countries. Such generalizations tend to over-simplify the matter. In certain areas, this military help has contributed to greater security and political stability, without which all economic progress would have been halted. The same could also be said of some of the loans and gifts of food made available to other countries. On the other hand, in some countries, providing military equipment might have done little to bolster government strength in view of the greater military power of neighboring states. Since it might have induced larger domestic outlays for defense purposes, such military aid might even have diverted resources from civilian ends. It seems unlikely that additional expenditure for military purposes in most undeveloped countries will stimulate a fuller and more efficient utilization of resources by providing the motivation for economic and social changes conducive to economic growth, as it has done in the history of some industrial countries. However, a stronger military apparatus may in the long run foster national discipline, remove surplus manpower, and given proper organization help to build up economic and social overhead capital, though these effects may be accompanied by short-run pressures on the balance of payments due to larger import requirements. These observations may suffice to show that it is difficult to make too precise a distinction between military and nonmilitary aid.

Western European Aid

The governments of western Europe have provided funds for the economic development of regions for which they have political responsibility or with which they have special political ties. In 1945, the United Kingdom enacted the Colonial Development and Welfare Act[20] and set aside an amount of £ 120 million for the economic and social development of its colonies over a ten-year period. This amount was increased by £ 20 million in 1950, in conjunction with the acceleration of various programs.[21]

The Act provides for contributions from the mother country to aid in the implementation of the ten-year plans formulated separately by the individual colonial regimes. In March, 1952, the costs of the approved ten-year plans totalled £ 456 million, of which £ 78.4 million were to be made available as grants from the Colonial Development and Welfare Act funds. The balance had to be raised by the colonies themselves or obtained through loans. Of the total £ 456 million, 43 per cent was to be spent for the development of social services (education, public health, housing, and water supply), 26 per cent for economic development (research, geological exploration, agriculture, fisheries, forestry, electric power, etc.), 21 per cent for transportation and communications (airfields, ports, railroads, roads, telephones, and telegraph), and 9 per cent for miscellaneous services (including administration, general surveys, and censuses). The law, which expired in March, 1956, was to be replaced by new legislation, and colonial governments have already been asked to supply information about their financial requirements for carrying forward development plans during the period 1956–60.[22]

There are two additional institutions for the British colonies, one of which is the Overseas Food Corporation with a capital of £ 55 million, which launched the Tanganyika ground-nuts plan[23] among other projects. There is also the Colonial Development Corporation which is capitalized at £ 110 million provided by the United Kingdom Treasury, and is authorized to undertake commercial activities. Both of these institutions were founded in 1948, pursuant to the Overseas Resources Development Act.

The function of the Overseas Food Corporation in such large-scale experiments as clearing land for mechanized agriculture in the tropics, has now been abandoned. Its goal is now a rather modest one, more that of an experimental station investigating how the yield of groundnuts, maize, sorghum and other crops can be improved by the application of modern agricultural practices. The Colonial Development Corporation is engaged in a great variety of projects, including pineapple and orange juice canning in the Bahamas, cultivation of tomatoes, vegetables, and potatoes on other islands in the Caribbean area for the United States market, gold mining and timber exploitation in British Guiana, livestock farming in Bechuanaland, a bag factory and a cotton spinning mill in Nigeria, and fisheries in the Seychelles.[24]

In 1946, France also announced a large-scale plan for the 'modernization and equipment' of its overseas territories.[25] The plan was to be financed through an Investment Fund for the Economic and Social Development of the Overseas Territories (FIDES). This Fund derives its capital from an annual appropriation from metropolitan France (fixed by the Finance Act), from contributions of the regions themselves (acquired through local taxation), and from long-term advances which the territories may request from the Central Fund of Overseas France. It is difficult to gain a comprehensive view of the plan's implementation, since information contained in different reports does not always seem consistent. According to a United Nations publication[26] based on official sources, a total expenditure of 154.8 billion francs ($ 442 million at the rate 350 frs. = $ 1) had been approved by FIDES for the period 1947–52. By 1949, only 46.3 billion francs ($ 132 million) of this amount had been allocated and 20.9 billion francs ($ 60 million) had actually been spent. Of the sum spent, 55 per cent came from grants, 40 per cent from loans and 5 per cent from territorial funds.

A 1954 report[27] on the plan for these territories indicated that over the period 1946–53 the sum of $ 332 billion francs ($ 949 million) had been committed from FIDES funds and 64.8 billion francs ($ 185 million) from the Central Fund for Overseas France. During the same period authorized expenditures from these two sources amounted to 303.6 billion and 46.8 billion francs, respectively. Of the 332 billion francs from FIDES funds, 282 billion ($ 806 million) were to be used directly on projects in the territories concerned, with the balance probably representing general research and administrative costs. Of those 282 billion francs, 60 per cent were intended for transport (railroads, roads, bridges, canals, and air transport), 15 per cent for production, 3 per cent for communications, 5 per cent for electric power, and 17 per cent for social services (public health, education, and housing).

The French North African territories (Algeria, Morocco, and Tunesia) were not included in this plan, since they were covered in the general program for the modernization and equipment of the French Union. For the years 1949–52, 148 billion francs ($ 423 million) in economic investments were planned for Morocco, and 44.2 billion francs ($ 126 million) for Tunisia. [28] In Morocco more than 80 per cent of the planned investments were for the expansion of the area under irrigation, the construction of power stations, the distribution of electric power, and the development of mining. Most of the expenditure was to be borne by the Moroccan budget, except for 46.2 billion francs ($ 132 million) to be raised by semipublic corporations, public bodies and private enterprises. In the development plan for Tunisia (44.2 billion francs) more than 50 per cent of the funds were to be spent on irrigation and water supplies. The 1954 report on the modernization and equipment of the French Union [29] stated that public investment actually realized over the period 1946–53 included 305.3 billion francs ($ 872 million) for Morocco, 102 billion francs ($ 291 million) for Algeria, and 258 billion francs ($ 737 million) for Tunisia — a total of 665.3 billion francs ($ 1,900 million) for French North Africa.

In 1953 alone, actual public investment in all three territories amounted to 152.6 billion francs ($ 436 million): 21 per cent for agriculture (including irrigation, drainage, and forestry); 11 per cent for mining (including petroleum); 16 per cent for electric power; 16 per cent for transport and communications; 29 per cent for social and cultural services (education, public health, housing, and sanitation) and the remainder for general administrative purposes. The year 1953 was apparently a year of transition, and at the beginning of 1954 all territories were again to submit four-year plans as they had done for the period 1949–52, subject to approval by the Council of Ministers.

Belgium has promulgated a ten-year plan, 1950–60, for the economic and social development of the Belgian Congo. [30] Its goals are to strengthen the local market, to raise productivity and the future level of production, with the ultimate objective of improving the level of living of the population. A sum of 25 billion Belgian francs ($ 500 million at the rate of 50 Belgian francs = $ 1) was to be expended for financing the establishment and expansion of public service enterprises and the improvement of the transportation system. The expansion of the industrial sector was to be left to private capital. [31] In addition, funds were to be made available from other sources for research, education, and social services.

The Netherlands has allocated the sum of 60 thousand guilders ($ 25,000) for a study of the possibility of expanding the economic base of the Netherlands Antilles, while the sum of 40 million guilders ($ 15 million) has been appropriated for a welfare fund for Surinam (Dutch Guiana), which is to receive 8 million guilders annually over a five-year period. An aerial survey of part of Surinam, a colonization plan for Dutch farmers in mechanized rice production, cocoa cultivation, and the improvement of fisheries, forestry, and livestock breeding are some of the projects to be carried out with the aid of these funds. [32]

The Colombo Plan [33] should also be mentioned here. It owes its name to a conference held at Colombo, Ceylon, in January, 1950, by the foreign ministers of the British Commonwealth. India, Pakistan, Ceylon, Malaya, Singapore, Sarawak, and Brunei were to be the original recipients, while Australia, Canada,

New Zealand, and the United Kingdom were to be the donor countries.[34] The countries in the area were to draw up six-year plans (1951–57) with July 1, 1951 as a starting date. The cost of the development programs worked out by the recipient countries was originally set at £ 1,868 ($ 5.2 billion), of which 34 per cent was allocated for transport and communications, 32 per cent for agriculture, including irrigation, 18 per cent for housing, public health, and education, 10 per cent for industry and mining, and 6 per cent for fuel and electric power.[35] Of this amount, it was expected that £ 1,084 would be made available from abroad, partly by the release of blocked sterling balances held in England by India, Pakistan, and Ceylon (totalling £ 246 million). It was hoped that the remainder would be forthcoming from private foreign investments, public loans floated on the London market, loans from the International Bank, and loans and grants from other countries.[36]

Through this plan, which stresses the development of agriculture transport, communications, and electric power, it was expected that an additional 13.5 million acres of land (an increase of 3.5 per cent) would be cultivated in the participating areas, 13 million more acres irrigated (an increase of 17 per cent), 6 million more tons of food produced (an increase of 10 per cent), and 1.1 million additional kilowatts of electric power capacity provided (an increase of 67 per cent).

At the same time, a fund of £ 8 million was set aside to provide technical aid for the various projects, both by dispatching experts to the recipient countries and by granting scholarships to enable citizens of those countries to study elsewhere, especially in the United Kingdom, Australia, New Zealand, and Canada.

Actually, the Colombo Plan is simply a collection of national plans, and the central organization only facilitates the conclusion of bilateral agreements between recipient and donor countries. This fact is reflected in the four reports published thus far by the Plan's Consultative Committee.[37] These reports consist largely of reviews of economic conditions in the individual countries, but give little information on overall performance.[38] From these reports it can also be seen that there is no simple economic yardstick by which to measure the degree of economic progress that is being made. Figures on national income per capita or, even better, on per capita consumption of certain goods and services, which might fulfill such a purpose, are not available on an up-to-date basis for most of the countries concerned.

For those countries for which such indices are given, they are often no more than 'guesstimates' and do not take into account the distribution of income or changes in the price level which have occurred. Reading the surveys for consecutive years, one gains the impression that, in some areas, considerable improvement has taken place in agriculture, industry, and electric power. Perhaps the most heartening aspect of these surveys is the fact that governments show a deep concern with economic development.

These reports also confirm the experience of the International Bank that a considerable period of time must elapse before projects suitable for foreign financing are ready for execution. For the Australian contribution of $ 70 million, it is mentioned that only $ 25 million was actually spent by the end of the fiscal year 1954–55, while an additional $ 37 million was committed. Of the external assistance offered to India for the period 1951–55, amounting to 2.7 billion rupees, only 1.4 billion rupees were utilized in the first four years of the plan. Only £ 3.5 million of the £ 8 million fund for technical assistance had been used by the end of June, 1955.

The impact of this plan, including the programs arranged through the United Nations and bilaterally with the United States government, may be gauged from the fact that in the period 1951–55, nearly 7,200 nationals of the recipient countries have studied abroad, and about 3,700 foreign experts have served countries in the area. Nevertheless, throughout the reports it is stressed that although progress has been made, the tasks ahead will be even harder. The question still remains whether this program, which has now been extended until 1961, will help to improve the living conditions of a population that numbered about 600 million in 1950 and is expected to rise to about 750 million by 1970.

This, and the other plans described, are based on a new social consciousness and an enlightened policy which recognizes that foreign help is needed in order to break through the vicious circle of technological backwardness, low level of living, low productivity, and the resulting scarcity of resources for development and social services. The idea of pump-priming forms the basis of this aid. Assistance from abroad is intended to stimulate the necessary investments, particularly in overhead capital, thus helping to create the conditions under which the countries in question will be able to stand on their own feet and enjoy a higher living standard in the future. It is still too early to express an opinion on the effectiveness of these plans. The funds made available by the industrial countries of western Europe are small by comparison, not only with the amounts involved in United States programs, but also with the capital requirements of the regions involved, and they may fail to exert a perceptible short-term influence on economic progress.

Estimates of Total Capital Needs

The independent underdeveloped countries are not satisfied with postwar aid, and above all they are dissatisfied with the volume of capital that has been made available to them through governments and international organizations. They consider the grants and loans extended to the industrial countries of western Europe, particularly by the United States, extravagantly large in view of the relatively high level of living that these countries already enjoy. At the same time, they feel that the criteria set up by the Export-Import Bank and the International Bank to guide their lending policies are too rigid and not adapted to the requirements of the backward regions. They do not contest the arguments that have been advanced, for instance by the International Bank, in defense of its lending policy. Rather, they base their

general dissatisfaction on the backwardness of their own economies as evidenced by the differences in real per capita income and
in capital stock. They are conscious of the political implications
of the western European aid programs; however, for the same
reasons they believe that the economies of their own countries
have a more valid claim to assistance.

The arguments of the backward countries have been reinforced
by economists who have tried to estimate the capital requirements
for the economic growth of the undeveloped countries and the
proportion of foreign capital needed for such projected capital
formation and development. At this point, some economists
abandon the firm ground of reality and enter the realm of
imagination by failing to consider the historical experience of the
underdeveloped regions' low absorptive capacity for capital imports as a consequence of the inelastic supply of complementary
production factors and the generally rigid social structures that
prevail.

These economists are motivated by the desire to mitigate the
inequality in the world distribution of income and to raise the
level of living in the backward regions through large-scale investment programs. Some authors[39] have gone so far as to say that
large-scale investment in undeveloped countries is required for
the creation of international economic equilibrium. On humanitarian grounds, one can accept the idea that per capita
income in the underdeveloped areas should rise faster than in the
industrial countries, but to identify this aspiration with international economic equilibrium is to make the concept of equilibrium meaningless.

E. Staley[40] was the first economist to develop an ingenious
method for measuring the anticipated capital growth in Asia.
Using the data available on capital investment in Japan over the
period 1900–36, he estimates the future investment in all Asia,
assuming that the capital growth over the next 40 years in other
countries of Asia will follow the same course it did in Japan. For
this purpose he divides Japanese net investment into investment
in industry, commerce, and public utilities, which he assumes

show a direct correlation with population, and investment in agriculture, which he assumes to be related to the land area. The figures for the former type of investment for each of the periods 1900–09, 1910–19, 1920–29 and 1930–36 are multiplied by the ratio between the population of Asia and the population of Japan in 1900. The figures for the second type of investment for the same periods are multiplied by the ratio between the land areas of Asia and that of Japan. Thus he obtains an estimate of the required capital investment in Asia for the next four decades: $ 26.6 billion for the first decade (based on the purchasing power of the 1936 dollar), $ 47.4 billion for the second decade; $ 91.5 billion for the third decade and $ 104.6 billion for the last decade.[41]

By assuming that the average annual capital investment in Asia would initially amount to $ 3 billion (of which $ 2 billion would be furnished from abroad), that $ 1.5 billion would be required in eastern and southeastern Europe[42] (of which half would be supplied from abroad), that in Latin America, $ 600 million would be invested annually in capital goods (of which $ 350 million would have to be made available from abroad), Staley arrives at a total figure of $ 3.1 billion (1936 dollar) in annual loans which the backward countries would require in the postwar period if their development, and in particular their programs of capital formation, were to follow the proposed course.[43]

Colin Clark[44] has used a different and far more involved method. Based on available and estimated data on real income per worker in the period 1935–38 for a great many countries and regions, he estimates their likely income in 1960, taking into account population growth, the expected increase in productivity per worker in agriculture, the resulting outflow into secondary and tertiary activities, and changes in the terms of trade. As he has found a close correlation between real income and available capital per worker, he is able to estimate the increase in capital requirements to obtain the postulated rise in incomes. He then estimates the amount of savings per worker in 1935–38 and in 1960 in the given countries and regions; by multiplying this by the probable working population he arrives at an estimate of the surpluses and deficiencies in savings which will occur, assuming that the rise in incomes and capital growth take place in the manner he has worked out. An estimate of the international flow of capital which will be needed to establish what he calls equilibrium in the world economy, follows logically from his preceding calculations. He reaches the conclusion that, during the period 1945–60, 215 billion International Units (dollars with the purchasing power of the period 1925–34) would have to flow abroad, mainly from the industrial countries (from the United States, 53 billion; from Great Britain, 71 billion;[45] from France, 22 billion). The principal beneficiaries of this flow of capital[46] would be Asian countries (among others, Japan, 17 billion; India, 51 billion; China, 59 billion, and the rest of Asia, 32 billion).

This amounts to an annual sum of 14.3 billion International Units in foreign investment, an amount four to five times as large as Staley's figure, but it must be borne in mind that Staley considered only backward countries. In a 1950 study, Clark[47] estimated, on the basis of expected savings, domestic capital formation resulting from increasing populations, and a postulated growth in the productivity of labor, that the annual foreign investing ability of the world would have to amount to 16.6 billion International Units net (each I.U. representing about $ 1.50 in 1949 prices). The United States alone would have to contribute 15.1 billion I.U.. He also calculates that in 1950 there was an accumulated world backlog in net capital formation of 495 billion I.U. He disregards this factor in the industrial countries (91.5 billion I.U. in the United States as a result of the lag in construction during the depression, 213.4 billion I.U. in Europe as a result of war-devastation) because, in his opinion, these lags are short-term phenomena. He therefore predicts that only a vast program of foreign investment largely in the backward regions will make it possible to maintain a high level of employment in the industrial countries over the long run.

Still another method was followed in a study of the postwar period made by the Food and Agriculture Organization of the United Nations.[48] This took, as its starting point, the development plans promulgated by 42 countries and 32 colonies after the war. After converting all the plans into a four-year basis, and estimating the data for the missing countries on the basis of population and land area (with the exception of the United States and Canada which, as capital-exporting countries, were left out of consideration) the report arrived at a total investment figure of $ 172.6 billion, $ 32.6 billion of which was to be financed from abroad. This figure of about $ 173 billion ($ 43 billion a year) was considered both reasonable and attainable, since total world income excluding North America was estimated at $ 300 billion. The total four-year investment in underdeveloped countries was estimated at $ 66.6 billion ($ 17 billion a year), compared with an aggregate national income of $ 150 billion. Foreign assistance was to provide $ 16 billion of this investment ($ 4 billion annually), leaving $ 50.6 billion, or $ 13 billion per year, to be contributed by the undeveloped areas themselves. The latter figure implies a domestic rate of investment of 8.5 per cent of national income, which is well above the savings ratio of some of the poorest countries. [49]

In another study by experts under the auspices of the United Nations, [50] an estimate was made on the basis of the following assumptions: (1) a total population of 1.5 billion for the underdeveloped countries in mid-1949; (2) a total national income in 1949 of these countries of $ 96.6 billion; (3) an annual transfer of one per cent of the active population (40 per cent of the total population) into nonagricultural employment; (4) an estimated amount of $ 2,500 capital required per worker in industrial activities, [51] and (5) an estimated 4 per cent of the national income needed for investment in agricultural extension services and farm equipment.

It was then calculated that an annual investment of $ 19 billion would be required for all undeveloped regions. Through such an amount of investment, national incomes might be expected to rise by 2 per cent per annum, assuming an average population increment of 1.25 per cent per annum. From domestic savings, only $ 5.2 billion (5.4 per cent of the estimated national income of $ 96.6 billion) would be available, so $ 13.9 billion would have to be raised in the capital-exporting countries. This estimate probably assumes too high a requirement of capital per industrial worker and too high a rate of agricultural investment for under-developed countries to reach a goal of a 3.25 per cent annual increase in their national incomes.

To add our own estimate of capital requirements, we would like to use an estimate, derived from the figures used in Chapter 2, of $ 127.1 billion as the national income for all underdeveloped countries (comprised of $ 26.4 billion for such countries in south and southeastern Europe, $ 58.7 billion for Asia excluding Japan, $ 28.8 billion for Central and South America, excluding Argentina, and $ 13.2 billion for Africa, excluding the Union of South Africa) for 1954. For a desired rate of increase in per capita income of 2 per cent per annum and an annual increment of population of 1.5 per cent, the national income would have to rise by 3.5 per cent per annum. If the productivity of new investment in terms of additions to income per unit of capital — the capital-income ratio — is assumed to be three, then the 'required' net investment corresponding to the target would amount to 10.5 per cent of the national income, or $ 13.3 billion. If the net savings capacity of the undeveloped world is only 5 per cent of national income ($ 6.3 billion), then $ 7 billion of foreign capital would have to be imported annually to make possible the postulated rate of growth. The latter figure is only half of the United Nations experts' estimate given above, but it is approximately twice as high as the foreign resources estimated to have been available for net investment in the countries in question during the period 1945–54 (see page 320).

It is difficult to argue against the logic of such estimates. They are theoretical, and on the basis of the assumptions, they are unassailable. They all indicate that capital requirements of the undeveloped countries are far in excess of what most of these countries are currently saving or investing. The authors of such figures may be reproached for not emphasizing sufficiently the inadequacy of the information they use on national income, capital stock, savings, and capital formation in the backward countries.[52] And they pass lightly over the economic difficulties connected with an assumed export of capital from the richer countries and also over the practical problems connected with the import of capital by the poorer countries.[53]

To lend these studies a sense of reality, they would have to be supplemented by specific analyses, country by country, sector by sector, showing how production increases are to be achieved, with the aid of what resources, and for what markets. Injections of capital in themselves constitute only a single factor in the process of development.

And yet, for all that, such visionary estimates will continue to dominate the minds of spokesmen for backward regions so long as the present differences in the levels of living exist. They will continually be held up before the industrial countries, in one form or another, to illustrate the relative backwardness of those parts of the world which, for whatever reasons, have failed to reap the fruits of two centuries of technological progress, and to prove the necessity of aid from the advanced countries to alter this situation.

Critics of these estimates may find it easy enough to belittle the intrinsic value of the foreign investments that are considered 'required', but they will probably find it difficult to set up a precise scheme for real investment as an alternative solution. The agencies that had to deal with the postwar economic problems of undeveloped countries are fully conscious of the social rigidities and political obstacles that impede investment programming in such regions. This, even apart from the general international climate which they have to take into account, makes them hesitant about formulating plans for foreign assistance during definite time periods.[54]

Postwar Discussions about New Public Investment Agencies

It is difficult to estimate the total amount of foreign capital, public and private, made available for reconstruction and development since World War II.[55] The following table is based on sources already mentioned. While the figures given do not claim completeness, they do indicate the subordinate importance of private investment in the present era.

TABLE 18. ROUGH ESTIMATE OF TOTAL FOREIGN PUBLIC AND PRIVATE INVESTMENT, INCLUDING GRANTS, 1945–54.

Type of Investment	Total	Undeveloped Regions
	(in billions of dollars)	
Public Funds from United States and Canada	51	10
Public Funds from western Europe	10	8
Private Investments from United States and Canada	13	7
Private Investments from western Europe	5	4
Estimated Total	79	29

It is clear, however, that in the case of undeveloped countries, private investments have been relatively important. It must also be taken into consideration that private investments have, for the most part, flowed to those undeveloped countries where raw materials, above all petroleum, could be produced for export. Public investments found their way chiefly to regions disorganized by the war or to colonies.

The time has certainly been too short to permit any judgment about the relative efficiency of recent public or private investment as a contribution to the development of backward countries. However, it would be difficult to escape the conclusion that the world economy has been modified — as a result of the war, new political factors, and a greater sense of social solidarity — in such a way that a return to the conditions envisaged by official American spokesmen and by the Export-Import Bank and the International Bank (including a revival of the prewar pattern of private investment) seems to be most unlikely. One has the feeling that institutional changes have been of such a nature that the idea of a return to an environment in which private foreign investment can again become the moving force in economic development is only a pipe dream.

In this connection, a British representative said in October,

1951, before the Economic Committee of the Sixth General Assembly of the United Nations: "There is a new conscience and a new philosophy in these matters, but as yet we have not succeeded in finding new and adequate machinery to take the place of the nineteenth century system, partly because we now cannot skim and do not wish to skim the cream from the milk."[56] There is a growing realization that underdeveloped countries may need grants and loans at a nominal rate of interest for projects promising no financial return, or at least no immediate return, before a great many projects which *could* be financed through existing public or private channels can even be started.

As early as 1943, Staley[57] favored the establishment of an international development agency to coordinate in a multi-national pattern the investment of available foreign capital in the countries requiring it. The advantages he cited are that it would spread the risk, make more efficient use of available capital, permit a broader view of the economic development of the whole world, and thereby help to prevent the implementation of un-economic or unbalanced plans. Furthermore, he reasoned that there would be less political conflict since there would be less danger of 'peaceful penetration' or political domination, and that it would make for better protection of investors against the unilateral abrogation of contracts, while giving better protection to borrowing countries against the exploitation of local labor.

Clark[58] also argued for an international organization. It will be recalled that, in his view, the development of Asia is essential for a sound growth of the world economy. Hence, his argument is based on the fact that the capital needs of Asia are primarily for funds to construct public utilities and, in general, for economic and social overhead capital. These are requirements which can be met only by government loans. Clark's article in *Fortune* (July, 1950) presented these ideas in greater detail. He proposed the establishment of a World Bank, receiving deposits from countries with a surplus of savings, on which the undeveloped countries could draw according to their requirements as determined by the Bank. The Central Banks in all countries would be assigned the function of regulating the flow of funds from the capital-exporting countries to the capital-importing countries. [59]

It cannot be denied that Clark has vision, but his proposals are not likely to be accepted. Like the plans already mentioned, he tends to ignore the fact that the volume of savings available in the industrial countries for foreign investment is not a predetermined amount and, indeed, is even less of a fixed figure than the capacity of the underdeveloped countries to absorb foreign capital. The relation between consumption and investment may be a calculable ratio in each country for any given period, but this does not imply that the component parts of these quantities can be precisely quantified or that they are not susceptible to change. Furthermore, no potential creditor country would be prepared, especially under the present political circumstances, to allow its foreign investments to be completely predetermined by a research agency of a World Bank.

The former chairman of the Sub-Commission for Economic Development of the United Nations proposed in 1948 that a new agency should be set up to finance projects "which are not financially productive in the banking sense" [60] and to assist underdeveloped countries in working out and executing projects for economic development. [61]

The report of the five experts on *National and International Measures for Full Employment*, [62] submitted in 1949 to the Secretary-General of the United Nations, recommended that the industrial countries follow a more deliberate foreign investment policy. The outflow of capital, the report says, should be adequate and stable. The International Bank is viewed as the appropriate agency for meeting the needs of borrowing countries, provided that the Bank has at its disposal adequate funds and is authorized to make loans "for the general purposes of overall development programs". The potential capital-exporting countries are advised to determine the sums that they are prepared to make available annually over a five-year period. These amounts would cover both private and public investment and would also take into account the amortization of earlier loans.

The sums intended for public loans would be placed at the disposal of the International Bank by the governments semi-annually, or the Bank could place loans up to this total on the national market of each country. The Bank's charter would, of course, be amended and the Bank reorganized to provide a separate department occupied exclusively with loans for general development and the procurement of funds for that purpose. The Bank would borrow from governments at the same rate of interest and on the same conditions as these governments themselves borrowed in their own national markets, and would repay the governments on the basis of repayments received, or use such amortization to reduce the capital export quota fixed for the countries in question. The criterion for loans by the Bank would be its conviction that the balance-of-payments position of the borrowing country would be so improved, as a result of the loan, as to assure, as far as possible, repayment of interest and principal.

Borrowing countries would be obliged to set up capital budgets for their development programs, in order to enable the Bank to survey the entire development program and to assure itself that its funds were not being used to finance current expenditures. The interest on these development loans would be based on the average interest paid by the Bank on its own loans plus a one per cent commission to cover administrative costs and to build up a reserve against defaults. The repayment schedule for such loans would be based on the Bank's obligation to amortize its own loans.

The report mentioned above, submitted in May, 1951, to the United Nations by another group of experts,[63] including three members from underdeveloped countries, is less favorably inclined toward the International Bank. The Bank is charged with an inadequate conception of its responsibility as a specialized agency of the United Nations for the encouragement of economic development. It is said to overemphasize the need for foreign currency in connection with individual projects instead of considering the impetus that a loan might give to the production of domestic goods and services in general.

The report also voices the opinion that the Bank has not sent out enough survey missions to help governments work out development programs. [64] The report recommended that the Bank set itself the goal of making at least $ 1 billion available annually within the following few years for undeveloped countries — at the time this flow is said to have been less than $ 300 million [65] — and if this target were not approached, the United Nations should reconsider the organization required for providing capital for the backward countries.

The report argues further that the successful utilization of loans, at the average 4 to 5 per cent rate of interest charged by the Bank, depends on simultaneous investment in social overhead capital (e.g. public health, education, and roads). Since domestic capital available for such investments is limited, and borrowing from abroad for such purposes is practically impossible, development tends to stagnate and the country concerned is also circumscribed in effectively attracting loan capital for other purposes. In order to meet the need for financing such overhead facilities, the establishment of an international development agency is recommended. It would be authorized to give grants-in-aid to the undeveloped world up to a total of $ 3 billion a year — one per cent of the combined estimated national incomes of western Europe, Oceania, the United States, and Canada.

Even if some countries wished to set up bilateral programs for the same purpose, the simultaneous establishment of an international agency is still recommended, because international control of the expenditures would be more readily acceptable to most of the recipient countries. [66] Such an agency would have to cooperate with the governments of the undeveloped countries in formulating and coordinating their development plans, and would make available the services of experts for this purpose. At the same time, it could assist in the execution of these plans, especially in the procurement of capital goods and the services of technicians.

The following types of projects are specifically cited as being suitable for grants: (1) research and education, (2) public health programs, particularly preventive medicine and nutrition rather than curative medical services, (3) subsidies for short-term and medium long-term agricultural credit, and (4) improvements in rural public works, such as roads, water supplies, reclamation, drainage, soil conservation, and reforestation.

During the Sixth General Assembly of the United Nations (1951), this proposal was discussed at length and the Economic and Social Council was requested to prepare a detailed plan for the establishment of a fund to give grants and low interest loans financing projects yielding no direct income, to accelerate the development of the backward regions.[67] The resolution was adopted, in spite of statements by the industrial countries, including the United States, that they were not prepared, under existing conditions, to make funds available for this purpose. The establishment of this Special United Nations Fund for Economic Development (SUNFED) occupied the attention of the General Assembly at subsequent sessions. In 1954 a resolution was adopted requesting the former president of the Economic and Social Council (Belgian Raymond Scheyven) to prepare a further report with recommendations on the form, functions, and responsibilities of such a fund and on the methods by which its operations might be integrated with the development plans of the countries likely to receive assistance from it.[68]

The problem of international capital movements lies on the political plane. These movements have usually been influenced by noneconomic considerations. This fact was partially hidden in the nineteenth century and the early part of the twentieth century by the existence of the 'pax Brittanica' and a delicate balance between the less important power centers. It is difficult to predict future developments, although if the present military tensions diminish it is not unlikely that public investments will flow in greater volume toward the underdeveloped countries.

In this connection, the statement of President Eisenhower in November, 1953 should be recalled. He pledged that if sufficient progress were made in internationally supervised world-wide disarmament, the United States would devote a portion of the resultant savings to assisting the development of economically backward countries, within the framework of the United Nations. This declaration was subsequently followed by a resolution, unanimously adopted at the Eighth General Assembly of the United Nations (1953), declaring that all member states will follow such a course if armament budgets can be reduced.

The attitude of the United States is naturally of decisive importance, and in spite of its preference for *private* foreign investment, there are indications of a growing awareness of the limitations of this form of investment under present conditions. The so-called Gray Report[69] notes that public funds are necessary for the construction of facilities providing basic services, and that only through such investments can the door be opened for an influx of private capital. Whether the United States should make loans rather than grants, the report says, depends on whether the necessity of repayment would so impair the development of the recipient country as to endanger the common interest of the free countries. The same criterion was applied to the western European nations under the Marshall Plan; however, it is realized that its application would be more difficult in the case of undeveloped countries.

The report proposed that the Export-Import Bank and the International Bank step up their operations to an annual level of $ 600 million in new loans, and that, in addition, the United States make available, for several years, about $ 500 million a year for grants and technical assistance, in comparison with the approximately $ 150 million provided annually for this purpose at the time. It was urged that loans and grants not be limited to the direct foreign exchange costs of the projects involved, but instead be calculated in terms of the overall economic position of the recipient country.

In the report of the International Development Advisory Board,[70] the proposals of the Gray Report were endorsed and the establishment of an International Development Authority recommended. The Authority would be set up with an initial capital of $ 500 million to help finance projects essential for economic development which could not be financed on the basis of loans. The United States would contribute $ 200 million of the initial capital of $ 500, and other countries would contribute according to their percentage shares of the capital of the International Bank. The Authority would have its own board of directors which would examine all applications, but a contract with the International Bank would make the latter's staff available for the investigation of proposed projects and for the supervision of the spending of the funds.

No matter how it is organized, acceleration of the process of development of backward countries will be a more complex undertaking than rehabilitation of western European industrial countries. It will also be a long-term task. One of the greatest difficulties will be to make sure that funds are used to raise the mass level of living in the undeveloped regions, and not to perpetuate the investment pattern and unequal income distribution that are now so prevalent. Supervision of the expenditure of foreign funds brought in to supplement domestic savings implies a certain limitation on the sovereignty of the governments. Because of strengthened nationalist sentiments, particularly in the undeveloped part of the world, this will be an obstacle of the first order.[71]

The distribution of the funds among the countries involved would probably be simpler than supposed, since only plans that have been thoroughly investigated could be financed. Such plans would be limited to those for which the local factors of production could be made available for use in conjunction with the raw materials, machinery, and technical services to be imported. Preparation of such plans takes time and the task of programming different plans in many countries would probably make the question of distributing funds a matter of subordinate importance during the first few years.

We have given a chronological description of the efforts that have been made to devise new agencies and channels to accelerate the rate of development of backward countries. Thus we have obtained an idea of the arguments pro and con accompanying the birth of new ideas and institutions, and of the political climate in which they are being developed. An evaluation of these paper plans is not feasible, but their existence is a sign of the times, in the sense that they consciously pose the challenge that the problem of development be attacked on an international scale, and that the request of underdeveloped countries for help in the struggle to better their position should not remain unheard.

CONCLUSION

Conclusion

The problem of the development of the economically retarded areas is one of the most important questions which confronts the world today. Recognition of its central importance is evident in the continually growing stream of literature. It is perhaps even more evident in the emotional overtones that mark the reactions of representatives of underdeveloped countries whenever the problem is discussed. There is no gainsaying the reality of the desire of the peoples of underdeveloped countries for a more ample supply of material goods and services, a desire aroused by their better acquaintance with the mode of living in western Europe and the United States; but this is only one aspect of the problem. The leaders of these countries are also conscious of the fact that economic backwardness often signifies political weakness. Therefore, their striving for economic betterment is also motivated by their wish to meet the industrial countries on an equal footing. A growing awareness of their social and political backwardness also strengthens the desire for economic growth felt by the majority of the population. [1] Our study has been generally confined to the economic side of the picture, but this aspect cannot be separated from the political and social factors which influence the aspiration for economic development.

In our study, we have noted the lack of a generally valid explanation of the phenomenon of growth. Th. W. Schultz [2] has rightly observed: "The economics of development, at this stage of our knowledge, is more akin to a collection of ideas and studies representing different approaches." We do not believe that this vacuum will soon be filled. The problem is so complicated, involving such a variety of interwoven political and social factors that no single economic theory could ever do justice to all the determinants. Even with thorough knowledge, from an economic point of view, of the way in which the development of industrialized countries has taken place, it would still not be possible to weigh precisely the significance of the political and social conditions which made this evolution possible. In any case, it is certain that, as a result of an entirely different historical constellation, the path which underdeveloped countries can follow will vary in many respects from that travelled by the industrial countries.

It is generally agreed that the leadership of western Europe, in economic development, was closely associated with the revolutions on the intellectual and political levels (the Renaissance and Reformation and the formation of larger political entities) and in geography (the discovery of the New World) which took place between the thirteenth and sixteenth centuries. Looking backward, it can be seen that the concepts of the individual and society, of the physical world and the extension of knowledge and organization which were developed during this period made those countries leaders even before they started on the road to industrialization.

These factors are also believed to be the principal reasons why many of these countries at present occupy the highest rungs on the ladder of economic development. It would take us too far astray to explain why Spain and Portugal, which in some respects led these revolutions, did not industrialize. Perhaps there is more than a kernel of truth in the comment of a cabinet minister of one of the less developed European countries to the effect that the plight of his country was caused by the fact that it had missed the Reformation. However, this is not to imply that a Protestant environment was the prime factor in the economic changes occurring in western Europe; the development of France and Belgium, for example, could not be explained on this basis.

In Western thought, the individualism emanating from the changes mentioned above was a *sine qua non* for the utilization of the technological innovations which characterized the industrial revolution. However, once a certain amount of technology was developed and available for adoption by everyone, it was proven, especially by Japan and the Soviet Union, that it could be grafted on to other cultural backgrounds. The latter countries had to make profound changes in their social organization as well to make such acculturation possible, but their experience shows that there is more than one road that leads to Rome. The under-developed countries are in a more favorable position, because they can borrow from an even greater array of technology and organization for developing growing points in their economies. But they, too, face the challenge of modifying such elements in their civilizations which, at the moment, present serious obstacles to the adoption of an industrial culture.

At the beginning of this book, we analyzed the great inequality among the levels of living in different parts of the world. It is generally thought that this inequality is of relatively recent origin, but there are indications that even before the period of rapid industrial growth the economically advanced nations enjoyed a higher per capita income than is the case today in most of the underdeveloped countries. Colin Clark,[3] of whose studies we have made ample use, has constructed a table of the real product per man-hour for a great many countries over a long period; from this table it can be deduced that in 1800 the difference in real product per man-hour between the highest and lowest country was five-fold, while in 1940 this difference was about forty-fold. This suggests that the discrepancy in levels of living existed at this early stage, though it has been enormously magni-fied since.

We have stressed the difficulties which the poorer countries encounter in their efforts to stimulate economic development. Only in a few countries does it seem possible to expand the amount of arable land without a capital outlay far beyond domestic resources. By contrast, the presently advanced countries had only small populations when they embarked on their indus-trialization. England and Wales, in 1770, had a population of not much more than 7 million, the Netherlands in 1829 had 2.9 million, and the United States in 1840 less than 20 million. Thus, these countries would seem to have possessed an important potential for extending cultivated land to meet the more varied food needs of their growing populations, though the factor of population density, especially in the case of the first mentioned countries, cannot be considered apart from the ensuing industrialization and the trade pattern which developed. With regard to the increase of agricultural production on the area cultivated we have emphasized the static institutional structure of the peasantry which makes the rapid introduction of better techniques in backward countries a difficult task. Also, as far as other natural resources are concerned, many underdeveloped countries seem to be unfavorably placed, though knowledge on this point is naturally deficient.

Capital formation is hampered by the general poverty and the small size of the domestic market. These conditions do not attract resources into activities directed to the provision of local manufactures. Increase in population does not itself augment investment. Indeed, as pointed out below, a certain amount of capital is usually absorbed in financing the increase. As a result of the high percentage of income spent on food, and the high income-elasticity of the demand for food, population growth tends to result in the consumption of surpluses if they arise.

The composition of production in every phase of development tends to correspond to the composition of demand which is determined in large measure by the expanding national income. In an underdeveloped country, if investment expenditure swells the money stream, prices tend to rise and an increased inequality of income distribution often results, in part because of the inelastic supply schedule of food and other essentials. Because of the high income elasticity of demand for food, the price of foodstuffs is likely to increase more than for other items in the average budget, so that the market for manufactured goods is, to that extent, smaller than it might otherwise be. In such a situation, there is no encouragement for the initiation of such complementary industrial activities as might follow investment if the food supply rose *pari passu* with the income stream.

The underdeveloped country often shows a resemblance to a Malthusian economy in which the power to expand production is matched by the power of population to multiply, so that when, under special circumstances, total income rises, income per head tends to remain constant. In this connection, it might also be pointed out that the rate of population growth in undeveloped countries at present is generally greater than it was in the advanced countries at the start of their industrial development. In western European countries, the rate of population increase at the beginning of the nineteenth century was about 1 per cent or less per year (an annual birth rate of about 30 per 1,000 and a death rate of 20 or more per 1,000). Growth was somewhat accelerated when economic expansion got under way. In comparison, growth rates of 2 or 3 per cent per annum (an annual birth rate of 40 per 1,000 and a death rate of 20 to 10 per 1,000) are not uncommon among the poorer countries at present. This large population increase means that substantial investments are required to maintain the present ratio between capital stock and population. To increase the level of living a higher rate of capital formation is necessary and this is very difficult to realize in countries with a low level of per capita income.

The occupational structures of many less developed countries also mirror the stationary character of their economies. Despite the industrial development which has taken place, and is in progress in such countries, the vast majority of the people remain bound to a meager subsistence type of living. In many cases, the percentage of workers in primary activities has been maintained at a high level over a long period, partly because of the higher birth rate in the rural areas compared with the urban centers. Low mobility of the rural worker (and the scant attraction seemingly exerted by higher remuneration in the cities) is probably more a result than a cause of this static situation.

The possibility of alternative employment is closely bound up with the 'high food drain' which characterizes the economic structure.[4] The transfer of labor from agriculture to industry, commerce and services, so characteristic of a progressive economy, reflects the fact that, given rising incomes, the demand for food products tends to approach a point of saturation.[5] This tendency is not found in the backward countries because, at their poor level of living, the demand for food remains predominant. Moreover, the safety valve of international migration, which the industrialized European countries possessed when they entered their phase of rapid population growth, is available to very few underdeveloped countries.

The aspiration to higher living standards, particularly marked among the urban populations of many underdeveloped countries, forms another obstacle to capital formation. This is most evident among the well-to-do classes who imitate Western consumption patterns and consume the part of their income that might be applied to additional investment.

Since international trade in processed goods, which might widen the market and provide the advantage of increasing returns from 'economies of scale', involves competition with the more efficient concerns of industrial countries, it offers little prospect of early success to most underdeveloped countries. Increased production of agricultural and mineral exports, stimulated by the ever-increasing need of the industrial countries for raw materials, continues to be one of the most important means of promoting economic growth. But this keeps the underdeveloped countries in a position which they consider inferior — 'hewers of wood' and 'drawers of water' — to that of their more fortunate neighbors.

Trying to break through this vicious circle, by raising tariff walls in order to stimulate the development of new industry, leads in the first instance to an increased burden upon local consumers. The technological and, even more, the organizational backwardness of the industrial sector results in such enterprises having, at least initially, high costs of production, by comparison with similar factories in industrialized countries. The argument that such protection is necessary in order to stimulate industrial entrepreneurship and train the required labor, has a certain validity. Protective tariffs, however, are not likely to give rise to progressive industrialization in undeveloped countries unless purchasing power in the internal market expands to the extent necessary for the development of the new activities on an economic basis. In practice, the result of high tariffs has often been the perpetuation of an inefficient industrial sector.

This brings us to the role of the state. In many industrial countries the government has taken an active role in constructing transport systems, establishing essential enterprises, creating conditions to attract immigrants, or facilitating the training of nationals abroad, and in general in helping to create an appropriate climate and environment for building up industrial leadership. Many underdeveloped countries are handicapped by the lack of a dynamic administrative class on which such a transformation greatly depends. Government machinery is often dominated by groups with a pre-industrial outlook and more or less feudalistic social traditions, who are afraid of the weakening of their own position which might result from changes in the economic system.

This confirms our previous observation that the struggle between the values of an industrial culture and those of a feudal one — which was, in Europe, settled to a large degree before the industrial revolution — is still at its height in some of the economically backward countries. It also helps to explain the political instability in those countries. Nevertheless, because of the absence of an indigenous managerial class and the paucity and inertia of local private investors, it is the state which has to lead the struggle for higher standards of living. Despite its weakness, the government is required to promote industrialization. Protective duties, cheap credits, tax exemptions, and a whole gamut of other measures to encourage private individuals to establish certain industries, as well as the erection of public service enterprises, can be used to create a dynamic economy. In many instances, however, the most important task of the state remains the creation of a new value system in which incentives and opportunities are given to those who, through technological and organizational knowledge, can contribute to a more dynamic economic structure. Since many of the sources of change have to come first from abroad, such stimulation depends, to a large extent, upon the willingness and ability of the local population to absorb innovations and learn from outsiders.

Granted that such pre-conditions for economic growth are accepted, it still seems likely that, because of their capital, enterprise, and skilled manpower, the advanced countries will continue to have a greater capacity for development than the backward countries. Thus, even if the latter make progress in their industrialization efforts, the disparity in scales of living is not likely soon to diminish. It has been demonstrated in a United Nations report[6] that, in 1936–38, the volume of production of the underdeveloped countries was only 4 per cent of world product in the case of footwear, 10 per cent for cement, 3 per cent for pig iron and 2 per cent for crude steel. In 1949–51 corresponding percentages were 4, 13, 4, and 3, respectively, showing that the relative position of the backward areas had scarcely changed. The index of manufacturing production of the undeveloped countries stood at 127 in 1953, compared with 64 in 1937 (taking as the base year 1948 = 100, while the index for the industrial countries was 140 in 1953, compared with 77 in 1937. If it is considered that the cost of manufactured products is often higher in underdeveloped countries than in industrial countries, these figures tend to confirm the conclusion reached in chapter 2 that the difference in income levels between industrial and undeveloped countries may have increased since prewar years.

The industrial nations, partly because of a growing sense of social justice, seem genuinely to want to share in the responsibility for bringing poorer countries up to a higher level. They are confronted, however, with a heavy, and in many cases, thankless task. Extreme nationalism in many underdeveloped countries, aggravated in some cases by consciousness of economic backwardness, makes it improbable that private foreign capital, which is primarily motivated by the pursuit of gain, can adequately assist in this function. Though nowadays, most foreign capitalists are aware of their social responsibility toward the countries in which they invest, the limited purchasing power of the local market tends to direct their resources into activities geared to demand on the world market.

The advantages which private investment possesses as an instrument of development — as a source of successful industrial experience and a means of providing opportunities for nationals to acquire new knowledge, for example, — make a code setting out the rights and obligations of foreign investors most desirable. Such a code — drawn up perhaps under the auspices of the United Nations, as several authors have recommended, would define as carefully as possibility the responsibilities and duties of both creditor and debtor. If an international court, backed by the authority of the United Nations, were established to adjudicate in case of dispute, there is a chance that the bad odor which now surrounds private foreign capital in many underdeveloped countries might disappear.

Because so much of the investment required to stimulate the growth process is not attractive to foreign private capital and will have to be initiated by governments, a more important role is reserved in our opinion for foreign public capital, under which we may also include foreign technical assistance. Recent experience indicates that most underdeveloped countries prefer such aid to be administered in an international framework, for they themselves wish to determine the purposes for which foreign capital and foreign technicians are required. On the other hand, it is necessary to the success of any economic development program that the growth investment should 'stick', and become self-generating. Therefore, a certain degree of supervision is needed to make certain that the political and social obstacles which hamper development are removed or at least reduced.

The fact that the machinery for such scrutiny does not exist, or exists only in embryo, in the international agencies, makes it understandable that much public aid is still given on a bilateral basis. It is worth recommending that in future such assistance be granted, to a larger degree, through the organs of the United Nations. Under this system, the United Nations would have to be empowered to screen applications for aid more rigorously than they now do and control the execution of plans. The conditions stipulated by an international agency, in connection with loans and grants, should be more readily acceptable than those of a foreign government. In that way, too, one of the mistakes so often associated with bilateral programs, namely the tendency to implant the economic and social structure of the donor country upon that of the underdeveloped country, may be avoided. An international approach may assist each country to work out its own unique economic destiny.

It is beyond dispute that to improve living conditions in the poorer countries much larger amounts are necessary than are now available. It serves no useful purpose, however, to try figuring out the precise amounts required to reach specific rates of growth. Favorable political and social conditions must be created if the process of economic development is to catch on in the underdeveloped countries, and there are bound to be disappointments along the road. In the course of time, studies might be made for each country, outlining what seems to be the most desirable investment program in the light of its resource pattern and the availability of foreign aid. Moreover, a continuous check on the nature and rate of development, on the problems which are arising, and the priorities for future expenditures will probably be required.

The underdeveloped countries appear to want the functions of the United Nations family to keep pace with the functions assumed by national governments. Since the national government is now concerned with the welfare of all its citizens, it seems to be expected that the international organizations should take the general welfare of the world to heart. Assuming that the world is moving in this direction, backward countries would have to grant power to the United Nations to exercise supervision not only over the manner in which foreign assistance is used, but over entire development programs. In many underdeveloped countries, the process of social adaptation required for the most productive investment of domestic and foreign capital will necessarily be slow and laborious. Whether the democratic world can and will make the required sacrifices and think through the implications of such a task, remains an open question.

A prominent factor in the development problem in its present world setting is the influence of the Soviet Union and other centrally planned countries whose recent growth is claimed by many to reveal the most efficient solution of the problem of developing backward countries. The results which the U.S.S.R. and some of the other countries have achieved in the industrial field prove that social reorganization can indeed increase the rate of capital formation and speed up the process of economic growth. That such a transformation demands major sacrifices and the use of drastic measures to smother ancient traditions which handicap economic development is usually granted, but the fact that the peasant class has generally been victimized in order to procure a food surplus to maintain increased numbers of industrial workers often goes unrecognized.

Nevertheless, to start with a clean slate — to do away with the conspicuous consumption and out-of-date customs and relationships of the feudal leadership that impede economic growth — has a strong appeal among certain groups in the underdeveloped countries where democratic influences have only begun to take root. Improvement of the scale of living, it is true, may perhaps have to be deferred to some distant future, but expansion of those sectors of production which represent economic might, such as iron, steel, and similar industries, seems to promise them the satisfaction of challenging the supremacy of the industrial countries.

It is perhaps no coincidence that only the western European countries, and those countries which can be considered offshoots of their civilization, have been industrialized democratically. Japan and the Soviet Union, by contrast, chose a dictatorial form of government at the start of their industrialization. It is probable that democracy as known in the West is, in part, the fruit of a higher living standard. But if this is so, it implies that, in order to help sustain democratic forms of organization, everything should be done to raise the level of living of the poorer nations. Foreign help is, in a sense, an alternative to ruthless planning and austerity, making possible gradual removal of the political and social obstacles hampering economic growth, while maintaining humanitarian values and individual freedom. That much more than financial aid is needed is obvious.

It is also necessary for the industrial countries to continuously adapt their economic structures to give the underdeveloped countries a chance to continue their economic expansion once it has started. Certain countries may require the opportunity to export manufactured goods in order to develop industrially in view of their unfavorable population-resource ratio. This would require an improvement in the skill of their workers and the efficiency of the industrial sectors. Even if this readiness on the part of the industrial countries does exist, it may be that the nationalistic élan which seems to be an indispensable element of economic growth, may cause the underdeveloped countries to turn toward totalitarian forms of government.

There are several conflicting tendencies. On the one hand, the speed with which the backward countries want to develop is likely to impose great social stresses. These, with the cohesion and discipline required for the transition, may bring autocratic leadership to the fore. On the other hand, the social expectations and immediate demands already existing in many undeveloped countries may prevent the emergence of political power to the neglect of welfare objectives. In any event, the challenge of world economic development is bound up with the struggle for the minds and attitudes of mankind. And in this struggle, economic matters, while important, are often secondary.

The magnitude of the differences in levels of living between the industrial countries and the underdeveloped countries indicates the possibilities for the latter to make better use of their resources. This process can be assisted by the knowledge and wealth of the advanced countries. Only when differences have been reduced to an acceptable minimum can one expect any modification in the political and social feelings that now influence the attitude of underdeveloped countries toward the West. Only the future will tell whether this is possible.

NOTES

1 E. F. Heckscher, *Mercantilism* (London: 1931), pp. 25–26. This implied that a certain country could only enrich itself at the cost of other countries, a fundamental disharmony that was the cause of the continual trade wars.

2 Adam Smith, *An Inquiry Into the Nature and Causes of the Wealth of Nations* (London, Everyman's Library: 1933), I, p. 10.

3 W. J. Baumol, *Economic Dynamics* (New York: 1951), for a concise description of the different and more recent dynamic theories. See also B. S. Keirstead, *The Theory of Economic Change* (Toronto: 1948), who makes an effort to put the growth problem into sharper focus through the construction of various models and then seeks to determine which changes occur as a result of innovations, population increase, etc. As a general survey of the problem, especially of the lacunae in our knowledge, the article of M. Abramovitz, "Economics of Growth", *A Survey of Contemporary Economics*, B. F. Haley (ed.) (Homewood, Ill.: 1952), II, pp. 132–82, should be mentioned.

4 We have in mind the main opus of J. M. Keynes, *The General Theory of Employment, Interest and Money* (London: 1936), which is often considered as having been inspired by the belief that in the industrial countries, especially England, the stimulus for private investment had been so weakened, that public investments were required to continue the process of economic growth, and more particularly the article by A. H. Hansen, "Economic Progress and Declining Population Growth", *The American Economic Review*, XXIX, No. 1 (March, 1939), pp. 1–15, which asserts that due to human factors and the limitation of area, the economies of the highly developed countries show a tendency towards stagnation.

5 See *Problems in the Study of Economic Growth*, Universities-National Bureau Committee on Economic Research (New York: 1949), in which S. Kuznets, J. M. Clark, J. J. Spengler, and others attempt to determine which factors are interrelated in economic growth. See also W. W. Rostow, *The Process of Economic Growth* (New York: 1952), who introduces six propensities of a psychological nature which he believes should be incorporated into economic analysis in order to understand the problem of growth.

6 *A Report to the President by the President's Materials Policy Commission* (Washington D.C.: 1952).

7 J. G. Chapman in her article, "Real Wages in the Soviet Union, 1928–52", *The Review of Economics and Statistics*, XXXVI, No. 2, (May, 1954), pp. 135–56,

has estimated, on the basis of available Soviet data and using 1928 weights, that real wage in 1952 was only 68 per cent of the 1928 level, or using 1937 weights, 95 per cent of the 1928 level. These weights represent the percentage composition of expenditure for different commodity groups in the budget of the average urban family. The study thus shows particularly the sharp decline in the consumption of urban workers between 1928–37.

8 We shall thus not consider the models developed by Harrod and Domar. See R. F. Harrod, *Towards A Dynamic Economics* (London: 1939); E. D. Domar, "Expansion and Employment", *The American Economic Review*, XXXVII, No. 1 (March, 1947), pp. 34–55 and "The Problem of Capital Accumulation", *The American Economic Review*, XXXVIII, No. 5 (December, 1948), pp. 777–94. In these studies a continuous growth ratio is postulated. These writers then attempt to establish the rate of capital formation and savings needed for a hypothetical income increase.

9 For an interesting model of economic growth for a poor country, see H. W. Singer, "The Mechanics of Economic Development", *Indian Economic Review*, I, No. 2 (August, 1952), pp. 1–18. Singer shows the total annual investment necessary to attain certain development objectives, given certain assumptions as to the occupational distribution, the levels of income, the rate of population growth and the capital-income ratio. The logic of his scheme may be unassailable, but it does not explain why things do not happen the way Singer describes in underdeveloped countries.

10 In the otherwise admirable study of I. Svennillson, *Growth and Stagnation in the European Economy*, United Nations, Economic Commission for Europe (Geneva: 1954), almost no explanation is given for the stagnation of the European economy between World War I and World War II. In several places, he implies that the decline in the growth rate of the population has been a cause for the decrease in capital formation and the inertia in transformation. It might be argued, on better grounds perhaps, that the decline in population growth was due to the stagnation of the economy.

11 This idea is contrary to the thought expressed by C. Clark: "It is worth while to absorb oneself in a future economic equilibrium for the reason that long-period world economic equilibria develop themselves in their peculiar manner, entirely independently of political and social changes." See *The Economics of 1960* (London: 1942), p. X.

12 J. M. Keynes, *Essays in Persuasion* (New York: 1932), pp. 366–67.

13 A. Toynbee, *Civilization on Trial* (New York: 1948), p. 203.

CHAPTER 2. QUANTITATIVE ANALYSIS OF THE
INEQUALITY OF INTERNATIONAL INCOME DISTRIBUTION

1 C. Clark, *The Conditions of Economic Progress* (1st ed.; London: 1940), pp. 2–3.

2 *Ibid.*, pp. 40–41.

3 S. H. Frankel, "Some Conceptual Aspects of International Economic Development", *Essays in International Finance*, No. 14 (Princeton, N.J.: May, 1952).

4 S. Kuznets, "National Income and Industrial Structure", reprinted in *Economic Change* (New York: 1953), pp. 145–91. The fact that in general the underdeveloped countries have a smaller percentage of active workers and a heavier dependency burden than the industrial countries also depresses their average income per capita.

5 The United Nations has estimated that of the 70 countries for which national income figures were available in 1949, 40, or 57 per cent, had annual per capita incomes of less than $ 200. These 40 countries accounted for 66 per cent of the combined population, but only 15 per cent of total income. Also, it was estimated that one-third of the total population of these 70 countries — with an average annual per capita income of $ 50 — received only 4 per cent of total income. See United Nations, *National and Per Capita Income for Seventy Countries, 1949*, Series E, No. 1 (New York: October, 1952).

6 E. H. Carr, in *The Twenty Years' Crisis* (Edinburgh: 1939), and *Conditions of Peace* (New York: 1944), has emphasized the lack of harmony between the 'haves' and 'have-nots', and that only a reorientation in the economic thinking of the governments of the richer countries will reconcile the poorer countries with a peaceful and gradual change in the *status quo*. This means, as he says, that the supremacy of the 'haves' can be defended only if they are prepared to make sacrifices on behalf of the underdeveloped world. See *The Twenty Years' Crisis*, p. 168.

7 The effort by M. K. Bennett to measure the consumption level of thirty-one countries for the period 1934–38 by using nonmonetary indicators gives results that differ little from those obtained when figures on the national income per capita or real income per man-hour are used. Although some of the differences found lead Bennett to conclusions which seem unwarranted without further research, his article does show that factors other than national or real income should be taken into account for a full appreciation of the differences in material wellbeing. M. K. Bennett, "Disparities in Consumption Level", *The American Economic Review*, XLI, No. 4 (September, 1951), pp. 632–49.

8 In the Statistical Yearbooks of the United Nations, the Food and Agriculture Organization and the International Labor Organization, one finds a treasure of material regarding the differences between countries in devel-

opment, nutritional and health levels. W. S. Woytinski and E. S. Woytinski, *World Population and Production* (New York: 1953), give an extensive description and analysis of the differences in production levels in relation to population numbers and allied phenomena.

9 United States Department of Labor, Bureau of Labor Statistics, "Work Time Required to Buy Food, 1937–50", *Monthly Labor Review*, 72, No. 2 (February, 1951), pp. 143–51. A comparison such as this reveals the great difficulties due to differences in the extent and detail of available wage information, in the weighting of the various food items in the average diet, and especially of the conversion into dollars in view of the sometimes artificial foreign exchange rates. The article explains how some of these difficulties have been surmounted.

10 With the aid of C. Clark's terminology, an attempt has also been made to measure the level of living for various countries in real national product per man-hour on the basis of the purchasing power of the dollar in the United States for the period 1925–34. It is estimated that the real national product per man-hour in 1945 was 99 units in the United States, 94 in New Zealand, 87 in Canada, 62 in England and in Australia, 42 in Argentina, 38 in Switzerland, 31 in Denmark, 20 in France, 14 in the Soviet Union (1947) and 9 in India. Queensland Bureau of Industry, *Review of Economic Progress*, I, No. 4 (April, 1949), p. 49.

CHAPTER 3. LAND

1 The population density of the inhabited area in Egypt was 659 persons per square kilometer in 1955. The grain output per capita of the population engaged in agriculture (4.4 millions) was less than 935 kg in 1947.

2 W. E. Moore, *Economic Demography of Eastern and Southern Europe* (League of Nations, Geneva: 1945), p. 43. In *Industrialization and Foreign Trade* (League of Nations: 1945), p. 37, it is stated that the wheat yield in northwestern Europe usually averages between 23 and 30 quintals per hectare, while the yield for eastern Europe varies between 9 and 12 quintals. C. Clark estimated that for the period 1925–34 the net agricultural productivity per farmer was 2,444 international units in New Zealand, 1,524 in Australia, 661 in North America, 579 in the Netherlands, 120 in Japan, 88 in the U.S.S.R., and only 46 in China. See *The Conditions of Economic Progress* (1st ed.; London: 1940), p. 242.

3 G. F. Winfield, *China: The Land and the People* (New York: 1948), pp. 34 and 58. The standard work on China's agriculture remains J. Lossing Buck, *Land Utilization in China* (Chicago: 1937).

4 P. Gourou, *Les Pays Tropicaux* (Paris: 1948).

5 C. H. Edelman, *Sociale en Economische Bodemkunde* (Amsterdam: 1949).

6 W. E. Moore, *op. cit.*, p. 81.

7 United Nations, *Land Reform: Defects in Agrarian Structures as Obstacles to Economic Development*, Series ST/ECA/10 (New York: 1951), pp. 8–9; 15–17.

8 *Land Utilization in China* (Chicago: 1937), p. 196.

9 According to the India census of 1931, only 28 per cent of the agricultural population were owners and 68 per cent were laborers and tenants. Of those classified as owners, more than one-half owned less than 2 hectares of land and were thus compelled to supplement their income by working on the land of others more privileged. Of the 68 per cent classified as nonowners, about half were tenants and the other half were laborers, both of which were practically landless and in certain parts of India had positions resembling those of slaves. The situation has probably deteriorated since 1931, but the 1951 census does not give comparable information on this point. For the significance of the form of land tenure on methods of cultivation in the Middle East, see D. Warriner, *Land and Poverty in the Middle East* (London: 1948).

10 United Nations, *op. cit.*, chap. ii. See also, Supreme Commander Allied Powers, "Japanese Land Reform Program", *Natural Resources 127* (Tokyo: 1950), p. 86, which shows that before the land reform the proportion of farms with less than 0.5 hectare cultivated area was 34 per cent, as compared with 41 per cent after the redistribution. This indicates that the new legislation even increased the percentage of small farmers and thus offers no relief to the Japanese countryside.

11 The census of 1936 in Chile showed that 18.9 million hectares or 68 per cent of the cultivable area was held by one-quarter of one per cent of the farmers who, on the average, held more than 1,000 hectares. Quoted by P. T. Ellsworth, *Chile: An Economy in Transition* (New York: 1945), p. 156. Similar information is also available for other Latin American countries. In Egypt, 11,000 landowners hold 37 per cent of the cultivated area while 2.5 million small farmers own only 34 per cent; in Iran about half of the privately owned cultivated land belongs to large landowners and only 5 per cent to small holders. Syria and Iraq showed similar conditions. See United Nations, *Review of Economic Conditions in the Middle East* (New York: March, 1952), p. 35.

12 United Nations, *op. cit.*, pp. 59–62. For a more extensive description see N. L. Whetten, *Rural Mexico* (Chicago: 1948).

13 Owing to lack of capital the small farmer cannot undertake on his own the improvement of his land through irrigation, drainage, or otherwise. Moore records that following the division of the large estates in southeast Europe after World War I, yields declined and crop rotation practices were sometimes discontinued. See W. E. Moore, *op. cit.*, p. 103.

14 United Nations, Economic Commission for Europe, *Economic Survey of Europe in 1953, Including a Study of Economic Development in Southern Europe* (Geneva: 1954), chap. xii, pp. 156–62.

15 W. E. Moore also mentions the possibility that better land utilization in southern and east Europe may be achieved by the consolidation of scattered holdings. He stresses, however, that a strong government policy is required to induce the peasant to relinquish certain holdings.

16 Tarlok Singh estimated, on the basis of 2.5 hectares per farm family, that the surplus of farmers in India amounted to 15.5 millions. Quoted by D. Ghosh, *Pressure of Population and Economic Efficiency in India* (New Delhi: 1946), p. 87.

17 S. H. Frankel, *Capital Investment in Africa* (London–New York: 1939). See, also, United Nations, Economic Commission for Latin America, *Report of the Joint ECLA–FAO Working Party*. Document E/CN.12/83 (New York: May 15, 1949).

18 *Land and Labour in China* (2nd ed.; London: 1937), p. 18.

19 According to the above mentioned ECLA–FAO study, food production in Latin America increased 20 per cent between 1934–38 and 1947–48, while the population increased 24 per cent. During this same period food exports declined 2 per cent, but food imports increased 45 per cent.

20 G. F. Winfield, *op. cit.*, pp. 286ff.

21 Natural fertilizer is often used as fuel in east and south Europe, Africa, China, and India, and this again is a sign of poverty. Poverty causes, also, the overcutting of forest area so important for the protection of the cultivated area. Even grass upon which cattle might be grazed is often used as fuel.

22 In the underdeveloped countries artificial fertilizer is principally used in the cultivation of export products, which cultivation is often in the hands of foreigners. The use of artificial fertilizer by the small farmer requires working capital which he does not possess. If he obtains credit for purchasing such fertilizer the possible result may be that the increase in output will lead to additional family consumption, under which conditions the loan might be irrecoverable. A strict control system is required to assure the repayment of loans given for this purpose.

23 G. W. Gray, "Blueprint for Hungry Nations", *The New York Times Magazine* (January 1, 1950), for a description of the project initiated jointly in 1943 by the Mexican Department of Agriculture and the Rockefeller Foundation for the successful introduction of hybrid corn and new wheat and bean varieties, with considerable increases in yield.

24 In 1947 Latin America imported pesticides amounting in value to four times that of the prewar years. Incidentally, many of these pesticides were manufactured from raw materials exported by the area. The need for pesticides is indicated by the estimates of the Food and Agriculture Organization that about 10 per cent of the total world grain production is lost due to pests and plagues, and especially to fungi diseases.

25 G. F. Winfield, *op. cit.*, p. 294. A new iron plow originally imported from Japan, but later also manufactured in Indonesia, making possible deeper

plowing, led to considerably higher yield on certain types of soils. Also, Moore, *op. cit.*, p. 90, mentions that plowing in eastern and south Europe is too shallow, although this depends, as he remarks, on the type and use of the soil. Warriner, *op. cit.*, pp. 121–23, states that deeper plowing and the use of natural fertilizer does not give necessarily higher yields in the Middle East. Where there is scanty rainfall moisture is longer retained by shallow plowing. Also possibly due to the much quicker oxidation and the composition of the soil the use of animal manure does not improve yields under dry-farming conditions.

26 In Shanghai and even in Tientsin, which is located in a wheat region, the flour mills have usually purchased large quantities of wheat from Canada and the U.S. in order to be assured of a standard quality and a regular supply. The alternative would be to buy thousands of small quantities in the interior and to transport them by rail. The difficulties involved in such an assembly, the lack of storage facilities near the stations, the need for guards on the trains to avoid thefts, and the need to clean the wheat upon arrival, made this method more expensive than the import of foreign wheat despite the ocean freight. See Winfield, *op. cit.*, p. 308.

27 Better tools can be given free of charge or the government can establish machinery parks from which the farmer can rent machinery with an operator for certain periods. In an agrarian society any lending for these purposes remains precarious, as one cannot really expect from a farmer living a marginal existence that he can or will make provisions for the repayment of a loan.

28 The above-quoted ECLA–FAO report estimates that in Latin America, due to lack of efficient storehouses, 15 per cent of the crop is lost in the temperate zones and as much as 50 per cent in the tropical areas.

29 United Nations, *Progress in Land Reform* (New York: 1954), p. 43.

30 K. G. Sivaswamy, "Indian Agriculture — Problems and Programmes", *Pacific Affairs*, XXIII, No. 4 (December, 1950), pp. 356–70. Sivaswamy may have been unduly pessimistic. In a reply to a United Nations questionnaire on land reform the Government of India indicated that intermediary tenure, which prevailed in 43 per cent of the area before the reform, existed in only 8.5 per cent of the area in 1954. However, in the same reply it was stated that in 1954, 93 per cent of the agricultural borrowings were still given through moneylenders, 3 per cent each through government-sponsored credit agencies and cooperatives and 1 per cent through commercial banks.

31 K. Davis, *The Population of India and Pakistan* (Princeton, N. J.: 1951), p. 207. In 1953–54 the food situation in India considerably improved largely due to favorable weather conditions. It has been estimated that the especially good monsoons were responsible for two-thirds or more of the rise in agricultural output also in 1954–55. The prospects remain poor in view of the annual population increase of between 4 and 5 millions. See R. A. Gopalaswami,

Report on the Census of India, 1951, 1, Part I–A (New Delhi: 1953), chap. iv.

32 M. Dobb, *Soviet Economic Development Since 1917* (London: 1948), p. 2.

33 The information on Soviet agriculture is drawn from N. Jasny, *The Socialized Agriculture of the U.S.S.R.* (Stanford, Cal.: 1949). The page numbers of Jasny's book where particular references can be found are noted in parenthesis.

34 According to Dobb, *op cit.,* p. 208, the percentage of owner-farmers rose from 70 to 96. Since the number of peasant families increased by one-third between 1914–28, there was practically no change in the average size of the farm.

35 The Sovkhozes or state farms contributed only about one-tenth (Jasny, *op. cit.,* p. 40) of the total agricultural output in 1937 and are thus of less importance in this respect. It should be mentioned that as a result of concentration the number of kolkhozes has since been reduced to an estimated 80,000.

36 According to a 1935 publication of the Ministry of Agriculture (Jasny, *op. cit.,* p. 116) only 230 million hectares of the Soviet Union's total land area of 2,213.6 million hectares consisted of arable land. Only 135 million hectares were in actual use, and this cultivated area had one of the lowest yields per hectare in the world. Jasny is of the opinion that, despite all propaganda to the contrary, the possibilities for expansion of the cultivable area in Russia are rather limited because of unfavorable climate and poverty of the soil. For a criticism of the recent claims about the potential increase of the arable area see also C. D. Harris, "Growing Food by Decree in Soviet Russia", *Foreign Affairs,* 33, No. 2 (January, 1955).

37 I. M. Finegood, "A Critical Analysis of Some Prevailing Concepts Concerning Soviet Agriculture", *Soviet Studies,* IV, No. 1 (July, 1952). See also *the New York Times* (December 5, 1954), which refers to a recent Soviet publication showing that the average annual cash income of an average family on a kolkhoz is less than 3,000 rubles.

38 The editor of *The Economist* (December 31, 1949) believes that the estimates given by Jasny must be too low. He asks, if cereal production had not increased, how it could be explained that (a) 30 million more urban workers were being fed, (b) food could be provided for the peasants producing industrial crops, as it is admitted that the production of sugar beets, oil seeds, cotton, and flax has been considerably expanded, and (c) as shown by the war experience, substantial stocks were accumulated. In our opinion, Jasny may have referred to the decline in quantities available for consumption and the decrease in exports (only 1 million tons in 1938 compared with 10.5 million tons in the period 1909–14). See also R. Schlesinger, "Some Prospects of Present Kolkhoz Organization", *Soviet Studies,* II, No. 4 (April, 1951), and A. Baykov, "Industry and Agriculture in the U.S.S.R.", *The Political Quarterly,* XXIII, No. 1 (January–March, 1952).

39 H. Schwartz (*New York Times*, February 13, 1955) for an account of what happened between Malenkov's announcement in November, 1952 that the foodgrain problem had been solved once and for all, and his resignation acknowledging his "guilt and responsibility for the unsatisfactory state of affairs which has arisen in agriculture." Jasny's later publications, e.g., "Kolkhozy—The Achilles heel of the Soviet Regime", *Soviet Studies*, III, No. 2 (October, 1951), and "Prospects for Soviet Farm Output and Labor", *The Review of Economics and Statistics*, XXXVI, No. 4 (November, 1954), show that he has not changed his mind. For an optimistic review of the prospects for dairy farming, see R. Schlesinger, "The Decisions on Agriculture", *Soviet Studies*, V, No. 3 (January, 1954).

40 I. T. Sanders, "Changing Status of the Peasant in Eastern Europe", *The Annals of the American Academy of Political and Social Science*, September, 1950, pp. 78–93.

41 *Economic Survey of Europe in 1953* (Geneva: 1954), pp. 68–73.

42 Research Staff of Free Europe Press, *Satellite Agriculture in Crisis*, A Study of Land Policy in the Soviet Sphere (New York: 1954).

43 W. W. Rostow and others, *The Prospects for Communist China* (Cambridge, London: 1954), p. 151.

44 *Ibid.*, p. 152. In November, 1955 it was officially announced that the number of producer cooperatives had increased to 1,240,000, showing that the target had been revised. In January, 1956 it was reported that 40 per cent of the peasantry was organized in cooperatives.

45 A. Baykov, *The Development of the Soviet Economic System* (New York: 1948), pp. 324–26.

46 Sivaswamy (*op. cit.*, p. 365) states that the Indian peasant is prejudiced against keeping of poultry and pigs. He estimates that in his country 90 million head of cattle roam the land and only consume without being productive in any sense.

47 W. H. Pawley and others, *Possibilities of Increasing the Supply of Food and Agricultural Products by Exploitation of New Areas and Increasing Yields*, Proceedings of the World Population Conference, Rome: 1954 (United Nations, New York: 1955), Vol. V, pp. 429–78.

48 G. J. Bottemanne, *"Het Zeevisserij Vraagstuk van Indonesië"*, Bulletin No. 3, Department of Economic Affairs of Indonesia, December, 1946.

49 It is estimated that 54 per cent of the world production of timber is still used for fuel, 23 per cent for construction purposes, 5 per cent for paper production, 2 per cent for railway ties, 1.6 per cent in mining, 0.4 per cent for rayon production, and the remainder for other purposes. E. Glesinger, *The Coming Age of Wood* (New York: 1949), pp. 13–4.

50 This, and the information which follows, can be found in a publication of the Food and Agriculture Organization, *Forest Resources and their Utilization*, Document E/CN.1/Sub.3/28.15 (New York: March, 1950).

51 E. C. Olson, "Factors Affecting International Differences in Production", *The American Economic Review*, XXXVIII, No. 2 (May, 1948), pp. 502–22.

52 E. Wagemann, *Struktur und Rhytmus der Weltwirtschaft* (Berlin, 1931), p. 361.

53 F. Tabah, "La Population du Monde et les Besoins en Matières Premières", *Population*, No. 4 (October–December, 1953), pp. 631–48.

CHAPTER 4. CAPITAL

1 C. Clark, *The Conditions of Economic Progress* (London: 1940), pp. 270–71. He shows that agricultural production in particular can be increased without capital investments by pointing to the example of how the amount of agricultural production per farmer increased in the United States between 1920–30, while the amount of capital per unit of labor declined.

2 C. Clark, *The Economics of 1960* (London: 1942), pp. 72–73.

3 United Nations, *Measures for the Economic Development of Underdeveloped Countries*, Series ST/ECA/10 (New York: 1951), p. 52.

4 N. S. Buchanan, *International Investment and Domestic Welfare* (New York: 1945), p. 13. This composition of capital in the industrial countries goes far to explain the relative speed of postwar rehabilitation in western Europe. Since buildings, housing, and means of transport were still largely intact, the provision of machinery, inventories and food for "a population trained in the atmosphere of industrial pursuits" (J. S. Mill) made possible the rather quick restoration and renewal of capital stock.

5 C. Clark, *The Conditions of Economic Progress* (2nd. ed.; London: 1951), chap. xi.

6 Queensland Bureau of Industry, "Capital Resources and their Accumulation", *Review of Economic Progress*, II, No. 1 (Brisbane, Australia: January, 1950), pp. 1–4.

7 United Nations, Economic Commission for Latin America, *Analyses and Projections of Economic Development* (New York: 1955), p. 4.

8 J. Schumpeter, *The Theory of Economic Development* (Cambridge, Mass.: 1934), pp. 67–68.

9 It has been calculated that the cultivation of one hectare of rice required per annum 285 hours of male labor, 674 hours of female labor, 5 hours of child labor, and 59 hours for a team of oxen. See J. J. Boeke, *The Structure of the Netherlands Indies Economy* (New York: 1942), pp. 48–52.

10 M. Dobb, *Soviet Economic Development since 1917* (London: 1948, p. 26) shows that the first five-year plan of the Soviet Union envisaged an increase of consumption of 6 per cent in the first two years and as much as 75 per cent over the entire five-year period, though the share of consumption in the national income was to decline from 81 to 66 per cent. This goal was not

achieved, partly for internal reasons, but according to Dobb, mainly as a result of the external threats to the Soviet state.

11 A. R. Prest, *War Economics of Primary Producing Countries* (Cambridge: 1948), p. 298.

12 R. Nurkse, *Some Aspects of Capital Accumulation in Underdeveloped Countries* (Cairo: 1952), pp. 27–35.

13 See table, League of Nations, *Industrialization and Foreign Trade* (Geneva: 1945), p. 44.

14 It would be interesting to investigate how the now industrial countries financed the construction of their economic 'overhead' capital. For the Netherlands it is known that as late as the 1860's the profits flowing from the the so-called Culture System (instituted in the 1830's, under which the Indonesian had to cultivate one-fifth of his plot with products designated by the government or, alternatively, work for sixty days per annum for the government) in Indonesia were used for the construction in the metropolitan country of railways, canals, and harborworks, which prepared the ground for the spurt in industrial development which was to come afterwards. J. and A. Romein, *De Lage Landen bij de Zee* (Utrecht: 1934), p. 564.

15 P. Mantoux, *The Industrial Revolution in the Eighteenth Century* (London: 1928), chap. iii, pp. 140–90. England was also in a privileged position, as we shall show later, due to the capital accumulation previously contributed by shipping and foreign trade.

16 *Ibid.*, p. 105. It has been estimated that in the middle of the eighteenth century, exports amounted to between only 7 to 10 per cent of the national product of England.

17 J. H. Clapham, *An Economic History of Modern Britain, The Early Railway Age 1820–1850* (Cambridge: 1950), chap. iv, pp. 98–142; xi, pp. 450–75. *An Economic History of Modern Britain, Free Trade 1850–1885* (Cambridge: 1952), chap. vii, pp. 252–96.

18 B. F. Johnston, "Agricultural Productivity and Economic Development in Japan", *The Journal of Political Economy*, LIX, No. 6 (December, 1951), pp. 498–513.

19 G. E. Hubbard, *Eastern Industrialization and its Effect on the West* (London: 1938), pp. 31–182. See also S. Tsuru, "Economic Fluctuations in Japan, 1868–1893", *The Review of Economic Statistics*, XXIII, No. 4 (November, 1941), pp. 176–89.

20 W. Hoffman, *Wachstum und Wachstumsformen der englischen Industriewirtschaft* (Jena: 1940), pp. 79–80.

21 J. B. D. Derksen and J. Tinbergen, "Berekeningen over de economische betekenis van Nederlands-Indië voor Nederland", *Monthly Bulletin of the Central Bureau of Statistics*, Nos. 10–12 (1945).

22 A. Smith, *Wealth of Nations, op. cit.*, I, p. 340.

23 "The Growth of the Stock of Certain Capital Goods in Six Countries from

about 1870", *Monthly Bulletin of the Central Bureau of Statistics*, Nos. 2–3(1942), as quoted by J. Tinbergen in *Economische Bewegingsleer* (Amsterdam: 1946), p. 37.

24 J. J. Spengler, *Capital Requirements and Population Growth in Underdeveloped Countries*, Proceedings of the World Population Conference, 1954 (United Nations, New York: 1955), V, pp. 765–77.

25 V. Nath, *Urbanization in India with special reference to the Growth of Cities*, Proceedings of the World Population Conference, 1954 (United Nations, New York: 1955), II, pp. 843–54.

26 W. Hoffmann, *op. cit.*, pp. 29–31.

27 *Ibid.*, pp. 180–82.

28 J. Schumpeter, *op. cit.*, p. 223. Schumpeter builds on this line of thought his explanation for the economic cyclus, to which some reference will be made later. See also his *Business Cycles: A Theoretical, Historical and Statistical Analysis of the Capitalist Process* (New York–London: 1939).

29 W. Hoffmann, *Studien und Typen der Industrialisierung, Ein Beitrag zur Quantitativen Analyse historischer Wirtschaftsprozesse*, Probleme der Weltwirtschaft 54 (Jena: 1931), p. 124. Hoffmann's figures only pertain to factory production and do not include handicrafts and cottage industry.

30 *Ibid.*, pp. 113 and 119. The percentages of consumer goods and capital goods production do not add up to 100. Some industries, such as gas and electric power services and the building industry, have been left out of the computation, because, without further investigation, their production cannot be accurately distributed between the two sectors. *Ibid.*, pp. 103–105.

31 *Ibid.*, pp. 102 and 119. Elsewhere, Hoffmann has indicated that the production of the consumer goods industries was 84 per cent of total net industrial production in 1740, but only 47 per cent in 1924. During the same period, the capital goods industries showed a rise from 16 to 53 per cent. W. Hoffmann, *Wachstum und Wachstumsformen der englischen Industriewirtschaft von 1700 bis zur Gegenwart*, Probleme der Weltwirtschaft 63 (Jena: 1940), p. 35.

32 A. Yugor, *Russia's Economic Front for War and Peace: An Appraisal of the Three Five-Year Plans* (New York: 1942), Table I, p. 14.

33 The ratio between consumer goods and capital goods production was 6.2:1 in Brazil in 1919, 5.2:1 in Chile in 1912, and 4.2:1 in India in 1925. See Hoffmann, *Studien und Typen der Industrialisierung*, pp. 178–79.

34 In Japan, the share which the textile industry contributed to total industrial production fell from 45.5 to 28.6 per cent between 1923 and 1936, while the share which the metal ware and implement industries contributed increased from 6.5 and 6.9 per cent to 18.0 and 13.6 per cent, respectively.

35 Hoffmann, *Wachstum und Wachstumsformen der englischen Industriewirtschaft von 1700 bis zur Gegenwart*, p. 83.

36 M. Dobb, "Note sur le degré d'intensité capitaliste des investissements dans les pays sous-développés", *Economie appliquée*, VII, No. 3 (July–September, 1954), pp. 299–318.

37 United Nations, Economic Commission for Europe, *European Steel Trends in the Setting of the World Market* (Geneva: 1949), p. 99.

38 N. S. Buchanan and H. S. Ellis, *Approaches to Economic Development* (New York: 1955), p. 202. They quote that in 1926 two-thirds of the males in Russia of nine years and over were able to read or write.

39 *Ibid.*, p. 199. In 1913 Russia possessed approximately 70,000 kilometers of railroad. In 1940 the railroad network amounted to 106,102 kilometers, of which 15 per cent was acquired from territories annexed in 1939-40, so that in comparison with 1913 only an estimated 18 per cent was newly built.

40 Hoffmann, *Wachstum und Wachstumsformen der englischen Industriewirtschaft von 1700 bis zur Gegenwart*, p. 68.

41 *Ibid.*, pp. 84; 90.

42 A. E. Kahn, "Investment Criteria in Development Programs", *Quarterly Journal of Economics*, LXV, No. 1 (February, 1951), pp. 38–61.

43 The report of the International Bank on Turkey gives the following general rules for determining priorities in the investment program: (1) the need for the product or service in the present stage of economic development; (2) the quantity and quality of the domestically available raw materials; (3) the required quantity and quality of manpower in relation to supply; (4) the contribution which the proposed investment would make to the national income; (5) the amount of capital required in relation to manpower and value of product, and the relative proportion of domestic and foreign capital; (6) the contribution of the proposed investment to an improvement of the balance of payments; (7) the types of skills and managerial ability required; (8) auxiliary services required and by-products to be produced, i.e., the interrelationship of the activity in question with other types of economic activity; (9) the minimum size of an economic production unit in relation to the Turkish market. International Bank for Reconstruction and Development, *The Economy of Turkey* (Washington, D.C.: 1951), pp. 41–42.

44 H. B. Chenery, "The Application of Investment Criteria", *The Quarterly Journal of Economics*, LXVII, No. 1 (February, 1953), pp. 76–96.

45 K. A. Bohr, "Investment Criteria for Manufacturing Industries in Underdeveloped Countries", *The Review of Economics and Statistics*, XXXVI, No. 2 (May, 1954), pp. 157–66.

46 H. B. Chenery, "The Role of Industrialization in Development Programs", *American Economic Review*, XLV, No. 2 (May, 1955), pp. 40–57.

47 J. Romein, *Het Onvoltooid Verleden* (Amsterdam: 1937), p. 29.

48 I. Svennillson, *Growth and Stagnation in the European Economy* (Geneva: 1954), p. 13. He states, for example: "The less developed countries may jump several of the intermediate stages in economic development through which the more developed countries have had to pass and, in this way, avoid the competition between old and new capital, which is responsible for the inertia in the development of pioneering countries."

49 J. Romein, *op. cit.*, pp. 36–37.

50 United Nations, *Labour Productivity of the Cotton Textile Industry in Five Latin American Countries* (New York: 1951), p. 11.

51 J. Romein, *Tussen Vrees en Vrijheid* (Amsterdam: 1950), p. 310.

52 C. Clark, *The Conditions of Economic Progress* (1st ed.; London: 1940), pp. 253–54. A breakdown of the cost of tractor plowing shows that 5.18 dollars would have been required for kerosene and lubricants, 0.5 dollar for labor, and 4.75 dollars for depreciation and repairs.

53 F. R. Jervis, "The Handicap of Britain's Early Start", *The Manchester School of Economic and Social Studies*, XV, No. 1 (January, 1947), pp. 112–22. "No complaint of our pioneering costs could be justified when as fast as other countries copied our inventions and methods, we made better inventions which put their copies out of date. There would be legitimate ground of complaint if the pace of our progress fell behind that of other countries. But the handicap would then be the lack of progress, not the long start." (p. 115)

54 T. Veblen, *Imperial Germany and the Industrial Revolution* (2nd ed.; New York: 1939), pp. 130; 194.

55 G. C. Allen "Economic Progress, Retrospect and Prospect", *The Economic Journal*, LX, No. 239 (September, 1950), pp. 463–80. He has pointed out a certain lack of resilience in the British entrepreneurial class after World War I. He asserts that this group no longer shows the same power of leadership in introducing innovations and creating new demands, because of its pre-occupation with the defense of gained positions — resulting in restrictive business practices — and of the change in social environment, which is no longer congenial to the exercise of individual responsibility in making decisions regarding new combinations of resources.

56 H. W. Spiegel, *The Brazilian Economy: Chronic Inflation and Sporadic Industrialization* (Philadelphia: 1949), p. 231.

57 According to the census, 26 per cent of the machinery was estimated to be less than ten years old, 34 per cent more than ten years old, and 46 per cent of unknown age. Spiegel says that it can be assumed that the latter group was completely obsolete, and that even the first group included second-hand machinery that was considered as relatively new machinery because of the date of its acquisition.

58 *The Theory of Economic Development* (Cambridge, Mass.: 1934), p. 274.

59 T. Uyeda, *The Small Industries of Japan* (New York: 1938), p. 8.

60 The Indian census of 1931 shows that 6,5 million workers were employed in small-scale industries and 1.5 million in large factories. According to a publication of the International Labour Office (*The Economic Background of Social Policy Including Problems of Industrialisation.* [New Delhi: 1947], p. 47), a 1936 census in Indo-China showed that there were about 1.4 million workers in small industries and only 120,000 in large ones. In Indonesia during the 1930's there were 2.5 million and 300,000 workers, respectively,

in these categories, and in the Philippines, in 1939, at least 60 per cent of 610,000 industrial workers were occupied in small or cottage industries. From census data, H. W. Spiegel (*The Brazilian Economy* [Toronto: 1949], pp. 225–27) indicates that in the state of São Paulo, where 40 per cent of Brazil's industrial production is concentrated, in 1939 there were no employees (only the owner) in 55 per cent of all industrial firms, and 38.8 per cent of all workers were in enterprises employing 1–20 workers. Of all enterprises 59 per cent had a capital of less than $ 500 in 1943, but 41.4 per cent of all industrial capital was concentrated in enterprises with over $ 500,000 capital.

61 In India the percentage of workers in mining and industry fell from 38.4 to 12.4 between 1881 and 1911. C. Clark (*op. cit.* [2nd ed.], p. 423), relates this decline to the competition of imported manufactures with the products of cottage industry. Comparison of the 1911 and 1931 census data shows a further decline in the number of workers in the textile, metal, pottery, food, and building industries. This reflected the downtrend of handicraft as a result of the lower cost of factory-made products.

62 P. S. Lokanathan, "Cottage Industries and the Plan", *Eastern Economist* (New Delhi: July 23, 1943).

63 Government of India, Ministry of Finance, *First Report of the National Income Committee* (New Delhi: April, 1951), p. 30.

64 H. Belshaw, "Observations on Industrialization", *The Economic Journal*, LVII, No. 22 (September, 1947), pp. 379–87.

65 P. H. W. Sitsen, *Industrial Development of the Netherlands Indies* (New York: 1944).

66 Sitsen, *op. cit.*, pp. 18–19.

67 Uyeda, *op. cit.*, p. 9.

68 *Ibid.*, pp. 180–81. This author points out also (pp. 11 and 150) that the Japanese are extremely individualistic in their demands. Thus, small-scale industry is said to have its own market, which cannot be captured by large-scale industry with its standardized product.

69 *Ibid.*, p. 8.

70 E. Reubens, "Small-Scale Industry in Japan", *The Quarterly Journal of Economics*, LXI, No. 4 (August, 1947), pp. 577–604. The factory statistics used by Uyeda did not include workshops with one to four workers, so that he made an estimate for the extent of cottage industry on the basis of the 1930 population census. In 1939, the workshops employing less than five workers were for the first time included in the factory census so that the 1939 figures used by Reubens reflect the true position. Reubens shows, too, that all observations indicate that a decline in the significance of the smallest shops, as a comparison between the 1930 estimate by Uyeda and the 1939 factory statistics would show, is inconceivable. He concludes, therefore, that the 1930 method led to an exaggeration of the prevalence of cottage industry.

71 United Nations, Economic Commission for Asia and the Far East, "Report of the Study Group of Small-Scale Industry Experts on their Visit to Japan", New York: February, 1955, E/CN.11/I & T/108, p. 21.

72 In factory industry, the proportion of output in establishments with 5–29 and 30–99 employees fell from 20.4 and 18.7 per cent respectively in 1928 to 18.2 and 15.6 per cent respectively in 1951. Meanwhile, the share of large-scale industries (more than 100 employees) rose from 60.6 to 66.1 per cent over the same period. Industries with from five to less than thirty workers continued to account for around 86 per cent of all establishments over the period 1909–51. See above-mentioned report, pp. 20–21.

73 Ministry of Finance and Revenue, *Economic Survey of Burma* (Rangoon: 1951), and Government of India, *The First Five Year Plan* (New Delhi: 1951), chap. xii.

74 United Nations, *Processes and Problems of Industrialization in Under-Developed Countries* (New York: 1955), pp. 47–51.

75 P. C. Mahalanobis, *Draft Recommendations for the Formulation of the Second Five Year Plan 1956–1961* (New Delhi: March, 1955), and Planning Commission, The Second Five-Year Plan, *A Memorandum prepared by the Panel of Economists* (New Delhi: April, 1955).

CHAPTER 5. LABOR

1 In the Netherlands between 1846–50 and 1896–1900, population increased by 64 per cent, while in the rest of northwest Europe the increase was only 39 per cent. From the latter period until 1946–50 the Netherlands population rose by 95 per cent, whereas in the rest of northwest Europe the increment was 27 per cent.

2 D. Ghosh, *Pressure of Population and Economic Efficiency in India* (New Delhi: 1946), p. 22.

3 C. Clark, "World Resources and World Population", in *Proceedings of the United Nations Scientific Conference on the Conservation and Utilization of Resources*, I, Plenary Meetings (Lake Success: February, 1950), pp. 15 ff.

4 On the basis of the latest count of China's population, the estimated annual rate of increase of the world population has been raised from 1–1.3 to around 1.5 per cent. It is estimated that the annual rate of increase in the near future in North America, Europe, and Oceania will be only 1 per cent, in Africa and the U.S.S.R. 1.5 per cent, in Asia between 1.5 and 2, and in Latin America between 2 and 3 per cent. For the methods used in arriving at these estimates, see United Nations Population Division, *Framework for Future Population Estimates, 1950–80 by World Regions*, World Population Conference, 1954 (United Nations, New York: 1955), III, pp. 283–328.

5 In another article, Clark has estimated that the earth could feed a

population of twelve billion people, on the basis of the population density of Denmark per square kilometer of cultivated land and the agricultural output per farmer in that country. He selects Danish agriculture as representative, because according to him, the quality of the soil there is about average. Clark fails, however, to take into account the fact that agricultural productivity in Denmark is connected with the country's location in the midst of a number of industrial countries that take its surplus dairy production, in exchange for which it imports cereals from overseas. Clark could hardly claim that such a process could be imitated throughout the whole world. Colin Clark, "Population Growth and Living Standards", *International Labour Review*, LXVIII, No. 2 (August, 1953), pp. 99–117.

6 See literature mentioned in United Nations, *The Determinants and Consequences of Population Trends* (New York: 1953), especially chap. xv, pp. 262–87.

7 League of Nations, *Industrialization and Foreign Trade* (Geneva: 1945), p. 63.

8 N. S. Buchanan and H. S. Ellis, *Approaches to Economic Development* (New York: 1955), p. 105.

9 G. F. Winfield, *China: The Land and the People* (New York: 1948), p. 339.

10 Winfield, *op. cit.*, p. 314. Chang Chih-yi, in "China's Population Problem: A Chinese View", *Pacific Affairs*, XXII, No. 4 (December, 1949), presents a somewhat different view of the Chinese population problem from the usual one. He blames the negligent administration of the Manchus for the decreasing productivity of the soil. Higher lands were cleared and worked, which resulted in their deforestation and erosion. The peasant, in turn, attempted to check the process by using more labor. This demand for more labor led, according to Chang, to the fatal growth of population, which in turn caused a rise in land rents and produced the vicious circle that has remained unbroken ever since, partly because the Manchus systematically resisted industrial development. His argument is not convincing, for he fails to explain how the policies of the Manchus affected fertility. It would seem more logical to assume that the fall in mortality was, in part, caused by the period of peace under the Manchus. His assertion that total or partial abolition of exorbitant land rents would eliminate the need for using extra labor suggests that this measure might lead to a fall in agricultural yield, accompanied perhaps by increased consumption on the part of the peasants themselves.

11 *Far Eastern Economic Review*, "China's Population Problem" (Hongkong: November 18, 1954).

12 As reported by *The New York Times*, November 10, 1954.

13 Ghosh, *op. cit.*, pp. 106–109.

14 Government of India, *The First Five-Year Plan* (New Delhi: 1951), pp. 206–207.

15 K. Davis, *The Population of India and Pakistan* (Princeton, N. J.: 1951), p. 82.

16 Radhakamal Mukerjee, *Races, Lands and Food* (New York: 1946).

17 The forecast given by C. Clark, in *The Economics of 1960* (London: 1942), p. 17, for expected emigration during the period 1940–60 from Italy, the Balkans, Poland, and the U.S.S.R. (the countries he views as having the greatest number of potential emigrants) and for the immigration into the United States, Canada, Argentina, Uruguay, and the rest of America, has found no support in postwar reality.

18 See also L. H. Bean, "International Industrialization and Per Capita Income", in *Studies in Income and Wealth*, Conference on Research in Income and Wealth, 8 (National Bureau of Economic Research, New York: 1946), Part V.

19 Colin Clark, *Conditions of Economic Progress* (2nd ed.; London: 1951), p. 366.

20 *Cf.* the table by M. Ezekiel, reproduced by C. Clark, in *Conditions of Economic Progress* (1st ed.; London: 1940), p. 446.

21 V. K. R. V. Rao, *The National Income of India, 1931–32* (London: 1940), p. 187. In 1950 the daily wage of a casual laborer in agriculture in India was given as 1.35 rupees per day (405 rupees annually on the basis of 300 working days) and 81.0 rupees per month (972 rupees per annum) in the textile industry. International Labour Office, *Year Book of Labour Statistics* (Geneva: 1953).

22 It is reported that in Colombia the productivity of the worker in agriculture is about one-sixth of a worker in other activities. See United Nations, Economic Commission for Latin America, *Economic Survey of Latin America 1948* (Lake Success: 1949), p. 86.

23 *Cf.* in connection with this phenomenon, *inter alia*, the empirical study carried out in Mexico by W. E. Moore as described in *Industrialization and Labor: Social Aspects of Economic Development* (Ithaca, N.Y.: 1951). The report of the International Bank on Turkey also describes how Turkish peasants and their families show a reluctance to enter permanent employment off the land. See International Bank for Reconstruction and Development, *The Economy of Turkey* (Washington, D. C.: 1951), p. 118 ff. Similarly in the Bank report on Ceylon it is pointed out that difficulties are encountered in obtaining local replacement for Indian immigrants on estates and in other enterprises. The result has been a reduction in output and in some cases has even led to the prospect of closing down of the establishments involved. See The International Bank for Reconstruction and Development, *The Economy of Ceylon* (Baltimore: 1953), p. 522.

24 "Economic Progress and Occupational Distribution", *Economic Journal*, LXI, No. 244, December, 1951, pp. 741–55, and by the same authors, "Further Notes on Economic Progress and Occupational Distribution", *Economic Journal*, LXIV, No. 253, March, 1954, pp. 98–106.

25 We have calculated for a certain number of countries the percentage of economically active workers in commerce, presuming that this category is

probably more easily definable and rather homogeneous in most countries. According to the respective censuses this percentage of the total active population was 3.5 in Colombia (1938), 4.6 in the Philippines (1948), 5.3 in India (1931), 5.3 in Brazil (1950), 7.9 in Thailand (1947), 8.1 in Venezuela (1941), 9.2 in Egypt (1937), 9.3 in Chile (1940), 9.4 in Mexico (1940), 9.8 in Cuba (1943), 10.0 in Italy (1951), 11.6 in Japan (1950), 14.0 in Denmark (1952), 14.1 in the Netherlands (1947), 14.1 in the United Kingdom (1951), and 18.5 in the United States (1950). These figures would seem to indicate that this ratio has a certain usefulness in evaluating the status of development of a country.

26 Colin Clark, *The Conditions of Economic Progress* (2nd. ed.; London: 1951), p. 366.

27 *The Wealth of Nations*, I, Everyman's Library (London: 1933), Book II, chap. iii, p. 294 ff.

28 R. H. Tawney, *Religion and the Rise of Capitalism* (London: 1938), p. 241.

29 A. Bonné, *State and Economics in the Middle East* (London: 1948). An interesting illustration for Antigua is reported by S. Rottenberg in "Income and Leisure", *Journal of Political Economy*, LX, No. 2, April, 1952, 95–102. There the view still prevails that the worker nurtures only slight aspirations toward a higher level of living, and has a strong desire to do nothing at all. Rottenberg shows that it is primarily the social stigma of the work on the sugar plantations and, more generally, the absence of any alternative employment opportunities and the persistence of traditional values, that keeps the worker from exerting himself.

30 J. L. Keenan, *A Steelman in India* (New York: 1943).

31 A. R. Prest, *War Economics of Primary Producing Countries* (Cambridge: 1948), p. 285, remarks that the low educational level in the Middle East and India made it impossible to augment the supply of trained workers during the war, by giving short, intensive courses as was possible in the case of Great Britain.

32 Winfield, *op. cit.*, pp. 360 ff. likewise assumes that the program outlined by him for China must be accompanied by education toward literacy — "the basic tool of knowledge", a substantial expansion of "secondary education", and the training of higher-level technical personnel in order to increase the supply of leaders.

33 Of persons marrying in France in 1855, 32 per cent of the men and 48 per cent of the women were illiterate. Similarly, of those marrying between 1841–45 in Great Britain, 33 per cent of the men and 49 per cent of the women were illiterate.

34 N. S. Buchanan and H. S. Ellis, *Approaches to Economic Development* (New York; 1955), pp. 163 and 186.

35 International Labour Office, *Labour Conditions in the Oil Industry in Iran* (Geneva: 1950).

36 See Government of India, *Monthly Abstract of Statistics* (New Delhi), and Labour Bureau, *The Indian Labour Year Book* (New Delhi).

37 *U.S. Monthly Labor Review*, May, 1944, pp. 921–22, quoted in N. S. Buchanan, *International Investment and Domestic Welfare* (New York: 1945), p. 149.

38 See the pronouncements made in pamphlets of the confederation of Bolivian trade unions. United Nations, *Report of the United Nations Mission of Technical Assistance to Bolivia* (New York: 1951), pp. 95–96.

39 At the annual meeting of the Steel Company of Bengal it was reported that average annual wages had risen from 1,200 to 1,740 rupees between 1942–48, while production per employed worker had fallen from 51 to 31 tons over the same period. The equipment of the enterprise had remained virtually unchanged, so that overstaffing in the factory was given as the explanation of the decreased productivity of labor. The management claimed that it had been compelled to engage 60 per cent more labor than was technically required, while the workers practised 'go-slow' methods. Moreover the management reported it was unable to make any change or take disciplinary measures against the offending workers without risking a strike. See Netherlands Department of Economic Affairs, *Economische Voorlichting*, February 3, 1950, p. 24. The report reflects the employer's point of view, but it does indicate the fact that management in many underdeveloped countries faces a self-conscious working class.

40 United Nations, *Labour Productivity of the Cotton Textile Industry in Five Latin-American Countries* (New York: 1950), p. 84.

41 International Bank for Reconstruction and Development, *Report on Cuba* (Baltimore: 1952), pp. 142–52. For an explanation of the motivations behind these exaggerated demands of the labor movement, see pp. 356–402 of this report.

42 This point will be further discussed in chap. 15, Private Foreign Investment.

CHAPTER 6. LEADERSHIP AND ORGANIZATION

1 G. C. Allen, "Economic Progress: Retrospect and Prospect", *The Economic Journal*, LX, 239 (September, 1950), p. 469. He argues that the initial disadvantage of a labor deficit has been turned into an advantage by the American entrepreneur. Operating cumulatively, in the course of time the labor shortage has led to the introduction of more capital-intensive production methods than is the case in other countries, where relatively more skilled labor is available.

2 J. Schumpeter, *The Theory of Economic Development* (Cambridge, Mass.: 1934), p. 74.

3 A. Marshall, *Principles of Economics* (London: 1898), pp. 10–51, which devotes two chapters to "The growth of free industry and enterprise".

4 J. A. Schumpeter, *Business Cycles* (New York: 1939), I.

5 *Ibid.*, p. 274.

6 E. B. Schumpeter, et al., *The Industrialization of Japan and Manchukuo, 1930–40* (New York: 1940).

7 I. Asahi, *The Economic Strength of Japan* (Tokyo: 1939), p. 15;17, states that in 1905 and 1906 the revenue of the state and local administrations amounted to 38 and 33 per cent, respectively, of the national income. This share fell to 18 per cent in 1920 and to 14 per cent in 1936. He assumes that the relative importance of government revenues in the national income was even greater before 1905–06 and suggests that the retraction of government illustrates that the government's responsibility for economic affairs was gradually turned over to private initiative.

8 T. Uyeda, *The Small Industries of Japan* (New York: 1938).

9 E. B. Schumpeter, *op. cit.*, pp. 627–29.

10 More recently the superior selling methods of Japanese machinery suppliers in an underdeveloped country have been described in a letter to the *Manchester Guardian*, December 6, 1951, p. 6, by P. Talco, Adviser for Light Industries to the Government of the United Provinces (India). In a country such as India, many inquiries for price quotations are vague, and the English manufacturers often tend to answer them by giving prices for several machines, without further details. The Japanese, in contrast, provide information on how to set up a factory, information on the machinery and implements to be employed, and the stocks of the necessary raw materials that should be maintained. Furthermore, they provide technicians to establish the factory and to train local workers. In other words, they submit a plan for delivering a factory in complete running order. This sales technique is apparently helping the Japanese to make headway in the postwar Indian market, even though the Indian buyer might prefer to buy British machinery, even at higher prices and with longer delivery dates, if the British would give more technical aid to the new and still 'ignorant' industrialist.

11 L. C. A. Knowles, *Economic Development in the Nineteenth Century* (Reprint: London: 1932; 1948), pp. 178–87.

12 M. Dobb, *Soviet Economic Development Since 1917* (London: 1948), p. 34.

13 W. Wilhelm, "Soviet Central Asia: Development of a Backward Area", *Foreign Policy Reports*, XXV (February 1, 1950), p. 220.

14 M. Holdsworth, "Soviet Central Asia, 1917–40", *Soviet Studies*, III, 3 (January, 1952), p. 276.

15 A. Bonné, *State and Economics in the Middle East* (London: 1948), p. 217. "Capitalism in the West owed its existence, *inter alia*, to the influence of a class of citizens endowed with specific virtues as organizers and entrepreneurs, a class which did not exist in the East. The rational-scientific techniques which formed the starting point for the profusion of industrial discoveries in

the seventeenth, eighteenth, and nineteenth centuries, remained unknown to Oriental civilizations."

16 See chap. 8 on the pattern of consumption in the underdeveloped countries.

17 K. Davis, "Demographic Fact and Policy in India", Milbank Memorial Fund, *Demographic Studies of Selected Areas of Rapid Growth* (New York: 1944), p. 52.

18 A. Marshall, *op. cit.*, p. 38.

19 R. H. Tawney, *Land and Labor in China* (2nd. ed.; London: 1937), pp. 173–74.

20 A. Marshall, *op. cit.*, p. 348.

21 L. C. A. Knowles, *op. cit.*, p. 111.

22 *Ibid.*, pp. 183–84. A. Baykov, *The Development of the Soviet Economic System* (New York: 1948), p. 31, gives a few figures showing that in 1914 a substantial part of the capital of Russian heavy industry was in foreign hands, including 90 per cent of all mining shares, 42 per cent of the shares in the iron, steel and tool industry, 50 per cent in the lumber industry, and 28 per cent in the textile industry. Of the total shares of capital stock in foreign ownership, 32.6 per cent was owned by French, 22.6 by British, 14.3 per cent by Belgians, and 17 per cent by Germans. In that same year foreigners owned 40 per cent of the shares in the eighteen large banks closely connected with heavy industry.

23 United Nations, *Report of the United Nations Mission of Technical Assistance to Bolivia, op. cit.*, pp. 2–3.

24 *Ibid.*, p. 3.

25 A. J. Toynbee in *Civilization on Trial* (New York: 1948), p. 188ff., distinguishes between the Zealots, who take refuge from the unknown by fleeing into tradition, and the Herodians, who strive to make the secret of the unknown their own in order to protect themselves. We can observe such a clash between those opposed ideologies in almost every backward country. There are the conservatives, who want their lives undisturbed and, in their fear of the consequences of Western technology, attempt to reinforce the old values. On the other hand, there are those who believe that the only path to economic development is through adoption of the methods of the West. Toynbee sees in Japan and Turkey extreme examples of the victory of the Herodians and he might have added the U.S.S.R.

26 L. C. A. Knowles, *op. cit.*, p. 343. This does not imply that England did not foster industrialization by protective duties. Even in 1824–25, when the tariff was reduced, imported manufactures still encountered a duty of about 20 per cent *ad valorem* which was "enough to keep most of them out". Parnell could rightly say of this revision: "If free trade ...is the right policy, the work of introducing it still remains to be done." Quoted by J. H. Clapham, *An Economic History of Modern Britain*, "The Early Railway Age 1820–1850" (Cambridge: 1950), p. 326.

27 L. C. A. Knowles, *op. cit.*, p. 25. The author does not examine the more moderate tariff support which the United States introduced directly after the War of Independence to allow native producers to meet British competition in manufactured goods, particularly textiles and iron goods. It was this protection that was gradually extended, under the pressure of the northern industrial interests, in spite of opposition from the southern agricultural states.

28 A. Marshall, *Industry and Trade* (London: 1927), p. 161.

29 From an article by O. Alvarez Andrews in *El Mercurio*, Valparaiso, Chile (May 14, 1942). Quoted by P. T. Ellsworth, *Chile: An Economy in Transition* (New York: 1945), p. 132. The article recommended a gigantic program of industrial expansion for Chile, but contained only the call for Chile to become great, without giving any concrete measures for attaining that object.

30 "Every Chinese with any sensitivity of mind who is not bound to vested interests realizes there is no future for China unless it is speedily renovated by the economic and social uplift of the entire people. The true and noble administration of today is inseparably linked with the determination to effect that general uplift." This is how Chien Tuan-sheng puts it in *The Government and Politics in China* (Cambridge, Mass.: 1950), p. 394, as quoted by S. B. Thomas, "Government and Administration in China Today", *Pacific Affairs*, XXIII, 3 (September, 1950), p. 249.

31 L. H. Hughes, *The Mexican Cultural Mission Programme* (UNESCO, Paris: 1950).

32 A. Bonné, *op. cit.*, p. 275. The report of the International Bank for Reconstruction and Development, *The Economy of Turkey* (Washington, D.C.: 1951), p. 7, also quotes the following pronouncement by former President Inönü of Turkey: "The policy of economic étatism above all, by being a means of defense, appears to be a necessity in itself."

33 The following statement, illustrating this point of view, is to be found in the report of the first session of the United Nations Economic and Employment Commission, Document E/255, May 25, 1946 (Lake Success, N.Y.): "The greatest and most lasting improvements of the standard of living of the less developed countries or areas are likely to flow from projects which are integral parts of long-term and balanced programs of development. Such programs should embrace not only the economic aspects of development but should include the social, scientific, health, educational, and cultural aspects of community life, and every member country should ensure, so far as possible, that all of these aspects are comprised in an harmonious programme of development."

34 "Approach to Planning", *The First Five Year Plan*, Planning Commission of India (New Delhi: July, 1951), chapter 1, already mentioned, contains a number of candid views on the difficulties connected with planning in India.

35 J. and A. Romein et al., *De Lage Landen bij de Zee* (3rd ed.; Utrecht: 1949), p. 286, relates how extensive corruption in municipal and state administration

went hand in hand with the flourishing of Holland in the seventeenth century. Knowles, *op. cit.*, p. 346, footnote says in the same vein: "It is only recently that we have ourselves adopted the principle of a salary, devotion to the State interests only and services rendered freely when such services are deemed necessary for the general welfare of the community. Honesty in administration is very modern."

36 R. Nurkse, "Some International Aspects of the Problem of Economic Development", *The American Economic Review*, XLII, 2 (May, 1952), pp. 578–79.

37 The United Nations has a particular interest in this aspect of economic development. See, *inter alia*, United Nations, *Standards and Techniques of Public Administration* (New York: 1951). In the United States one meets many intellectuals from underdeveloped countries who have received their education in the United States and after disappointing experiences with their attempts to introduce new ideas and methods into their mother countries, have given up and returned to their country of study.

PART TWO: DOMESTIC FINANCIAL RESOURCES

CHAPTER 7. INTRODUCTION

1 In the illustration presented, consumption accounts for 87.5 per cent of the national product, private and public investment for 7.5 per cent, and the export surplus for 5.0 per cent. In Cuba, in 1950, these proportions were, respectively, 85.5, 10.2, and 4.3 per cent.

2 That savings would be used for investment purposes was self-evident to Adam Smith. Hence, he regarded savings as the primary factor in the process of capital formation. "Parsimony, and not industry, is the immediate cause of the increase of capital. Industry, indeed, provides the subject which parsimony accumulates. But what ever industry might acquire, if parsimony did not save and store up, the capital would never be the greater." See *An Inquiry Into the Nature and Causes of the Wealth of Nations* (London, Everyman's Library: 1933), I, p. 301.

3 The problem is actually more complex than here described. The precise connection between economic growth and the various components of the national income, and their relative changes is still a matter for debate, especially in the more advanced countries. We shall, however, assume that our simplified analysis applies to the backward countries. J. S. Duesenberry, *Income, Saving and the Theory of Consumer Behavior* (Cambridge, Mass.: 1949), *passim.*

4 Rao points out that investment expenditures in underdeveloped countries — in spite of their high theoretical multiplier effect, due to the high rate of

consumption — often fail to lead to an increase in real wages or an expansion in employment opportunities, because of the lack of elasticity in the factor supply. This inelasticity — corresponding to an economy in which all production factors are fully occupied — is characteristic of the agricultural sector. As this is primarily a subsistence economy in most of the backward countries, an increase in demand of food is likely to result in higher food consumption in the countryside because of higher incomes. Even if the peasant released the same marketable food surpluses as before and used his increased income to purchase more manufactured consumer goods, there are many factors which may inhibit the expansion of industrial production. Among such factors Rao mentions the absence of idle capacity in agriculture, making it impossible to increase the output of industrial crops, the difficulties of procuring additional raw materials of other types, the inadequate supply of skilled labor, etc. Thus production may not expand as a result of income increases; instead there tends to be a rise in prices, an increase in imports or a retention of larger cash reserves. V.K.R.V. Rao, "Investment, Income and the Multiplier", *Indian Economic Review*, II, No. 1 (February, 1952), pp. 55–67.

5 D. H. Robertson, *Money* (2nd ed.; Cambridge: 1948), p. 139.

CHAPTER 8. THE CONSUMPTION PATTERN

1 The League of Nations study, *Industrialization and Foreign Trade* (Geneva: 1945), p. 25, states that, in Peking in 1931, the lowest-income groups (60–120 and 180–240 Chinese dollars a year) spent 65 and 64 per cent, respectively, of their income for food. See also the data for other Asian countries in International Labour Office, *The Economic Background of Social Policy Including Problems of Industrialization* (New Delhi: 1947), p. 7.

2 United Nations, *Report of the United Nations Mission of Technical Assistance to Bolivia* (New York: 1951), pp. 91–2.

3 Memoria de la Secretaria de Economia presentada al H. Congreso de la Union por el Secretario Lic. Gilberto Loyo (Mexico, D.F.: 1954), pp. 50–3.

4 *Land Utilization in China* (Chicago: 1937), p. 468.

5 "Economic Growth and Income Equality", *The American Economic Review*, XLV, No. 1 (March, 1955), p. 21.

6 *The Conditions of Economic Progress* (2nd ed.; London: 1951), pp. 533–37. The Pareto coefficient is found from an empirical law formulated by Pareto, according to which, at every income level x, the following formula holds:

$$\log n = \log A - a \log x$$

where n is the number of incomes at or above the level x, and A and a are constants. If a cumulative frequency curve of the number of persons in different income groups is plotted logarithmically, it turns out to be a straight line. A depends on the size of the population, while a represents the measure of equality or inequality of the income distribution, a low value indicating an unequal distribution and a high value a relatively equal one. This co-efficient was 1.27 for Brazil in 1942; 1.24 for Venezuela in 1945; 1.20-1.30 for Argentina in 1942; 1.79 for India in 1945-46; while for the United States it was 1.95 in 1945; for Canada, 2.28 in 1946; the Netherlands, 1.83 in 1935; the Soviet Union, 1.96 in 1924; Australia, 2.12 in 1943-44; and New Zealand, 2.35 in 1938-39.

7 *The Brazilian Economy* (Toronto: 1949), pp. 28-29. The Gini index runs from 0 to 1, where 0 represents a perfectly equal distribution of income, and 1 a distribution in which all income accrues to a single person. The index is equal to the ratio of the area of the segment enclosed by the Lorenz curve and a diagonal of the square, to the area of half the square.

8 De levenswijze van de arbeiders in de cultures en van de tanis op Java in 1939-40. *Eindrapport van de Koelie Budget Commissie* (Batavia: December 30, 1941).

9 *Op. cit.*, p. 381 ff.

10 "Economic Development with Unlimited Supplies of Labour", *The Manchester School of Economic and Social Studies*, XXII, No. 2 (May, 1954), pp. 139-91.

11 *Ibid.*, p. 160.

12 United Nations, *World Economic Report 1950-51* (New York: April, 1952), pp. 96-100.

13 *A Treatise on Money* (New York: 1930), II, pp. 152-63.

14 *Ibid.*, pp. 162-63.

15 *The Rise of the Spanish American Empire* (New York: 1947), chap. xviii.

16 *Ibid.*, p. 294.

17 *Ibid.*, p. 297.

CHAPTER 9. PRIVATE INVESTMENT

1 A. H. Hansen gives examples of the growth of new industries and private fortunes in the United States due almost exclusively to reinvestment of profits. *Fiscal Policy and Business Cycles* (New York: 1941), chap. xviii.

2 Adam Smith, *An Inquiry Into The Nature and Causes of the Wealth of Nations* (London: Everyman's Library, 1933), I, p. 302. According to the census of 1851 of Great Britain, the number of men and women employed in domestic service was more than 1 million out of a total population of 15.9 million of ten years old and over. After agriculture (providing work to 1.8 million persons), domestic service ranked second as an occupation. J. H. Clapham, *An Economic History of Modern Britain, Free Trade and Steel 1850-1886* (Cambridge: 1952), pp. 23-4. According to a 1900 estimate, 200,000 horses were being kept in Great Britain exclusively for fox hunting, a striking indication of the persistence

of this style of living, and perhaps also of its attraction for the *nouveaux riches*.

3 Reserve Bank of India, *Report on Currency and Finance for the Year 1950–51* (Bombay: 1951). J. M. Keynes says of the gold influx into India: "The history of India at all times has provided an example of a country impoverished by a preference for liquidity amounting to so strong a passion that even an enormous and chronic influx of precious metals has been insufficient to bring down the rate of interest to a level which was compatible with the growth of real wealth." *The General Theory of Employment, Interest and Money* (London: 1936), p. 337. However, the fact that interest rates have not fallen does not explain why there has been no stimulus in Indian society for the type of dynamic investment conducive to economic growth.

4 *The Economics of Industrialization* (Calcutta: 1952), p. 241.

5 International Bank for Reconstruction and Development, *Report on Cuba* (Baltimore: 1952), p. 73.

6 A. Marshall, *Principles of Economics* (London: 1898), p. 317.

7 D. Spring tells how, in England, part of the landed aristocracy were burdened by debt. Here, however, as a result of the rise in land prices — especially in the suburban areas, the procurement of mining rights and exploitation of coal mines, and their involvement in industrial activities, this group identified itself with the new economic development, and thus bettered its position. "The English Landed Estate in the Age of Coal and Iron: 1830–1880", *The Journal of Economic History*, XI, No. 1 (Winter, 1951), pp. 3–24.

8 *Op. cit.*, pp. 337–38.

9 In Rio de Janeiro and São Paulo combined, the average profit in wholesale trade amounted to 33.8 per cent of capital and reserves in 1946, and to 22.7 per cent in 1947. Corresponding percentages in retail trade were 28.0 and 23.6, respectively. On the other hand, the average profit in industry in the same years was only 16.9 and 14.3 per cent of capital and reserves. See table following page 7 in United States Department of State, *Report Joint Brazilian-United States Technical Commission* (Rio de Janeiro: 1949).

10 International Bank for Reconstruction and Development, *The Economy of Turkey* (Washington, D.C.: 1951), p. 160.

11 According to an unpublished report by an expert of the International Bank, industrial profits in Guatemala are four to five times higher than in similar industries in the United States. The Bank's report on Guatemala, International Bank for Reconstruction and Development, *The Economic Development of Guatemala* (Washington, D.C.: 1951), pp. 97–98, mentions that on account of the political instability in the country, investors often want to amortize plants in as few as three years to assure recovery of their capital. P. S. Lokanathan states that dividends declared by the mills operated by five leading managing agencies in India ranged from 24 to 100 per cent of share capital annually in the period 1914 to 1928 and from 8.5 to 83 per cent

in the period 1928 to 1932. *Industrial Organization in India* (London: 1935), p. 291 ff.

12 In Brazil, for example, in 1947 the total value of all corporate bonds and shares listed on the stock exchange amounted to 18.6 billion cruzeiros, but for the preceding ten years the total amount of securities traded never exceeded 850 million cruzeiros per year. U.S. Department of State, *op. cit.*, p. 123.

13 *Ibid.*, pp. 108–09.

14 International Monetary Fund, *A Report on the Process of Inflation in Chile Together With Recommendations* (Washington, D. C.: November, 1950), p. 19.

15 International Bank for Reconstruction and Development, *Report on Cuba*, *op. cit.*, p. 629.

16 *Report to the President of the United States by the Economic Survey Mission to the Philippines* (Washington, D.C.: October, 1950), pp. 11–13.

17 International Bank for Reconstruction and Development, *The Economic Development of Ceylon* (Baltimore: 1953), p. 515.

18 S. May et al., *Costa Rica: A Study in Economic Development* (New York: 1951), p. 252. Automobiles and other consumers' durable goods accounted for about 12 per cent of total imports in 1948. *Ibid.*, p. 241.

19 M. W. Thornburg, *Turkey: An Economic Appraisal* (New York: 1949), p. 200.

20 *Industry in Latin America* (2nd ed.; New York: 1949), p. 51.

21 The quantitative information on the composition of investment given above for certain countries only applies to *one* year that might have been an exceptional choice. From a compilation we made of the percentual breakdown of investment over several years in construction and equipment, see United Nations, *Monthly Bulletin of Statistics* (October, 1955), Special Table: D, pp. XVII–XX, no significant difference between developed and underdeveloped countries could be deduced. It must be admitted, that the breakdown of these figures is rather broad and that there may be a large margin of error in the figures supplied by governments of the more backward countries.

CHAPTER 10. FOREIGN TRADE

1 L. M. Dominguez in *International Trade, Industrialization, and Economic Growth*, Pan American Union, Working paper (Washington, D.C.: 1953), pp. 61–2, presents a table showing that, with 1880 taken as the base year, the volume of international trade increased from 6 in 1820 to 397 in 1952.

2 B. Ohlin, *Interregional and International Trade*, Harvard Economic Studies, no. 39 (Cambridge, Mass.: 1933).

3 K. E. Hansson, "A General Theory of the System of Multilateral Trade",

The American Economic Review, XLII, No. 1 (March, 1952), pp. 59–68. Chiefly, for statistical reasons, the foreign trade of the Middle East, China, Japan, the Soviet Union, and North Africa was not included. However, since ninetenths of world trade in 1928 was embraced by the study, it may be assumed that the true relationship is adequately represented.

4 League of Nations, *The Network of World Trade* (Geneva: 1942).

5 "The Theory of International Trade Reconsidered", *The Economic Journal*, XXXIX (June, 1929), pp. 195–209, reprinted in *Readings in the Theory of International Trade*, Selected by a Committee of the American Economic Association (Philadelphia and Toronto: 1950), p. 255.

6 United Nations, *Instability in Export Markets of Under-Developed Countries* (New York: 1952). This report shows that the average annual value of exports of eighteen products that make up a substantial part of the exports of the underdeveloped countries fluctuated by 22 per cent between 1901 and 1950, with the cyclical fluctuation amounting to about 22 per cent in the rising and falling periods and the secular fluctuation to about 6 per cent.

7 T. de Scitovsky, "A Reconsideration of the Theory of Tariffs", *Review of Economic Studies*, IX (Summer, 1942), pp. 89–110, and reprinted in *Readings in the Theory of International Trade, op. cit.*, pp. 358–89. De Scitovsky, among other things, has the following to say: "In an agricultural economy the difficulties of beginning may make an industrial firm's marginal productivity significantly lower than its social marginal productivity and to make up for the difference, protection or the payment of subsidies is economically justified." *Ibid.*, p. 387.

8 J. Viner, *International Trade and Economic Development* (Glencoe, Ill.: 1952), p. 58.

9 *Economic Development in Latin America* (Washington, D.C.: 1951), p. 168.

10 *Industry in Latin America* (2nd ed.; New York: 1949), p. 65.

11 G. Wythe et al., *Brazil: An Expanding Economy* (New York: 1949), p. 178.

12 United Nations, *An Inquiry into the Iron and Steel Industry of Mexico of a United Nations Team of Technical Experts* (New York: 1951).

13 United Nations, *Processes and Problems of Industrialization in Under-Developed Countries* (New York: 1955), pp. 66–7. In Egypt the most important textile industry, however, still is a high cost producer, as are the sugar and dairy industries, because of the price support provided by the government for the producers of the raw materials for those industries. It is reported that in 1947 the production cost for sugar and milk was between two and three times greater than the price of the imported commodity.

14 P. T. Ellsworth, *Chile: An Economy in Transition* (New York: 1945), p. 131.

15 Expressed in economic jargon, the multiplier effect, i.e., the ratio between an initial income increase, arising from an increase in export income, to the total income increase, resulting from the initial income increase, is slight. Rightly in our opinion, H. W. Singer says: "I would suggest that if the

proper economic test of investment is the multiplier effect in the form of cumulative additions to income, employment, capital, technical knowledge, and growth of external economies, then a good deal of the investment in underdeveloped countries which we used to consider as 'foreign' should in fact be considered as domestic investment on the part of the industrialized countries." (p. 475). H. W. Singer, "The Distribution of Gains Between Investing and Borrowing Countries", *The American Economic Review*, XL, No. 2 (May, 1950), pp. 473–85.

16 S. E. Harris et al., *Economic Problems of Latin America* (New York: 1944), 'Introduction'. H. C. Wallich, *Monetary Problems of an Export Economy: The Cuban Experience, 1914–1947*, "Harvard Economic Studies", No. 88 (Cambridge, Mass.: 1950), p. 209, writes: "The power of exports to induce additional investment and government expenditures is greater than that of these variables themselves."

17 F. Perroux, "The Domination Effect and Modern Economic Theory", *Social Research*, XVII, No. 2 (June, 1950), pp. 188–207.

18 H. W. Spiegel, *The Brazilian Economy* (Toronto: 1949), pp. 179; 182.

19 The average price of the export products of most nonindustrial countries at the end of 1930 was about 20 to 25 per cent lower than in 1929. The fall in the export price of the manufactures of industrial countries was only 5 to 10 per cent lower. League of Nations, *Review of World Trade, 1930* (Geneva: 1931), p. 13.

20 This argument has been strikingly developed by W. A. Lewis, "The Industrialization of the British West Indies", *Caribbean Economic Review*, II, No. 1 (May, 1950), pp. 1–61.

21 United Nations, Economic Commission for Latin America, *International Cooperation in a Latin American Development Policy* (New York: 1954), pp. 62–7.

22 League of Nations, *Industrialization and Foreign Trade* (Geneva: 1945), pp. 13–4. World industrial production rose again from 100 in 1937 to 182 in 1954, but the United Nations Statistical Office assumes that the share of the industrial countries remained approximately the same, and that, as yet no former undeveloped country has made a dent in the relative position of the industrial countries.

23 *Ibid.*, p. 19.

24 *Ibid.*, p. 20.

25 *Ibid.*, p. 120.

26 A. Loveday, *Britain and World Trade* (London: 1931), p. 177, says: "The future lies with the countries whose whole economic organization is the most mobile, with those which have the imagination to foresee future needs, the courage to scrap obsolete plant, and the skill to adopt and adapt new inventions."

27 S. H. Frankel, "Industrialization of Agricultural Countries and the Possibilities of a New International Division of Labour", *The Economic Journal*, LIII, Nos. 210, 211 (June–September, 1943), pp. 188–201.

28 It may also be deduced from his figures that after 1911–13 world trade grew but slowly. From 1880 to 1911–13, the annual rate of increase was 5.8 per cent, but after that, and down through 1952, it was only 2.8 per cent. See Dominguez, *op. cit.*, p. 62.

29 Dominguez shows that for the United Kingdom the average annual value of its exports (converted to constant prices) to an important group of industrial countries was $ 811 million between 1881–87, but only $ 682 million in 1950. This would confirm the inflexible nature of trade between the industrial countries. *Ibid.*, pp. 68–9.

30 The reciprocal exports among the less industrialized countries have gone up between 1900 and 1950 by 692 per cent. Dominguez, *op. cit.*, p. 74.

31 Dominguez shows that the results of their efforts may already have become apparent, as is shown by the fact that the reciprocal exports of the industrial countries rose from 32 per cent of their total exports in 1948 to 37 per cent in 1950. *Ibid.*, pp. 66–7. This seems also to be confirmed by the table contained in *International Trade 1954*, The Contracting Parties to the General Agreement on Tariffs and Trade (Geneva: July, 1955), p. 5. This shows that the value of exports within and among industrial areas (here defined as North America, European sterling area, Continental Western Europe, and Japan) increased between 1950 and 1954 from 34.8 to 38.5 per cent in total world exports.

32 *Ibid.*, p. 8. It should be mentioned that Canada and certain under-developed European countries (Greece, Portugal, and Turkey) have been grouped in this study with the industrial areas (North America, the European sterling area, Continental Western Europe, and Japan).

33 *Ibid.*, pp. 20–1.

34 *Ibid.*, pp. 21–2.

35 The share of trade within the industrial areas, which are distinguished, in the total trade within the industrialized world has risen from 52.2 per cent in 1951 to 57.0 per cent in 1954. Of the total trade of the industrial areas with nonindustrial areas the share with associated areas has increased from 36.1 per cent in 1951 to 40.4 per cent in 1954. *Ibid.*, p. 10.

36 *Ibid.*, p. 19. For the United States it has been estimated that between 1939 and 1947 the total consumption of metal ores increased by 61 per cent, but the physical volume of fabricated metal products rose by 98 per cent. The tendency toward more elaborate fabrication, the increased efficiency of the use of raw materials, the introduction of synthetic substitutes, and the rising availability and use of scrap are being held responsible for this development. U.S. Department of Commerce, Bureau of the Census, Raw Materials in the U.S. Economy, 1900–1952, Working paper No. 1, 1954, p. 13. Quoted by S. May, *The Outlook for Industrial Raw Materials Demand in 1980 and Its Relation to Economic Development*, Proceedings of the World Population Conference, Rome, 1954 (United Nations, New York: 1955, V), pp. 107–47.

37 *Ibid.*, p. 24.

38 *Ibid.*, pp. 27–8.

39 *Ibid.*, p. 12.

40 *Ibid.*, pp. 28–9.

41 R. F. Harrod, *Towards a Dynamic Economics* (London: 1948), p. 109: "If the rate of growth of output per head in the products in which a country has comparative advantages exceeds the rate of growth of her national income, then the rate of growth of her exports will tend to exceed her total rate of growth and the balance of trade will tend to increase. This was no doubt the governing factor in the course of British trade in the time following the industrial revolution."

42 J. M. Keynes, *The General Theory of Employment, Interest and Money* (London: 1936), p. 336 ff.

43 The example of Japan is a good case in point. Raw materials accounted for only 4 per cent of total imports in the period 1868–72, but they had reached the formidable percentage of more than 61 per cent in the period 1933–36.

44 It should be noted that these are long-run tendencies. May shows that in 1952 two-thirds of the industrial materials (minerals and agricultural products) used by the world were produced in industrialized areas. Industrial raw materials accounted in 1952 for about 38 per cent of total imports of industrialized nations and were drawn in substantially equal amounts from intertrade with industrial countries and underdeveloped countries. Food and beverage crops accounted for 25 per cent of total imports in industrial countries, of which 52 per cent originated from industrial countries and 48 per cent from underdeveloped countries. S. May, *op. cit.*, pp. 5–8.

45 *Ibid.*, chap. V.

46 *Processes and Problems of Industrialization in Under-Developed Countries*, *op. cit.*, pp. 107–18.

47 The need for imported primary commodities is also related to the structure of the secondary industries which are established. In Australia, in the years before World War II, the imported raw material intake amounted to from 14 to 16 per cent of the total raw material intake, but in the years 1948–52 had increased to 19 to 28 per cent. In the Union of South Africa, however, a decrease from 45 to 50 per cent in the 1930's to 37 to 46 per cent in the years 1945–50 was noted. *Ibid.*, p. 47.

48 "World Population, Prices and Trade 1870–1960", *The Manchester School of Economic and Social Studies*, XX, No. 2 (May, 1952), pp. 105–38.

49 W. R. Allen, "The International Trade Philosophy of Cordell Hull, 1907–1933", *The American Economic Review*, XLIII, No. 1 (March, 1953), pp. 101–16.

50 In Australia, exports of manufactures amounted to 3.2 per cent of total exports in the period 1914–15 to 1916–17 and to 3.6 per cent in the period

1948–49 to 1950–51. For Brazil, corresponding percentages were 0.2 in 1929 and 1.5 in 1949–51. It might be noted that Australia is considered as a high-cost producer of manufactures and faces, moreover, in the markets of neighboring Asian countries, the competition of Japan.

51 In Mexico, manufactures amounted to only 0.4 per cent of total exports in 1928–29, but had increased to 10.3 per cent in 1949–50. In the Union of South Africa the respective percentages were 4.8 in 1914–18 and 28.3 in 1946–49. Some of South Africa's manufactures seem competitive in price, and there is no other industrial country in the region, so that other industrial countries have therefore to reckon with higher transport cost.

52 In the case of Mexico, the increase in exported manufactures consists to a large extent of raw materials that have undergone a limited amount of processing. Mexican manufactures exported in 1950 were 2.3 per cent of the total value of industrial production compared with 1.7 per cent in 1939. International Bank for Reconstruction and Development, *The Economic Development of Mexico* (Baltimore: 1953), pp. 115; 276.

53 *Op. cit.*, p. 39.

54 In 1945 Brazil exported more than 24,000 tons of cotton piece goods, but this export declined to 5,600 tons in 1948. It was practically nil in 1953 and 1954. Mexico exported 232.4 million pesos worth of cotton fabrics in 1946, but only 82.3 million pesos worth in 1948 and 32.6 million and 40.6 million pesos respectively in 1953 and 1954.

55 India exported 47.8 million rupees of cotton goods in 1938, 1,145.7 million rupees in 1950, 517.2 million rupees in 1951, and 630.1 million rupees in 1953. Measured in million meters, the volume of 1951–53 exports of cotton piece goods seems to have been roughly about 3.5 times as high as in 1938.

56 T. Tyszynski, "World Trade in Manufactured Commodities, 1899–1950", *The Manchester School of Economic and Social Studies*, XIX (1951), pp. 272—304. On the basis of the exports of the eleven principal industrial countries, Tyszynski shows that the exports of manufactured goods increased from £ 667 million in 1899 to £ 7,399 million in 1950. If deflated by a suitable price index, this represents an increase in volume from 100 to 269. He also shows that the United States exported 11.2 per cent of the world's exports of manufactured goods in 1899, but 29.1 per cent in 1950. The rise of the United States as an exporter of manufactures he attributes to the fact that her exports fall largely in the groups in which world trade is expanding.

57 This decline is most noticeable in the field of cotton goods. A recent publication estimated that export of cotton goods of western European countries, especially of the United Kingdom, declined from 9 billion yards in 1913 to 2,150 million in 1953. Cotton goods imports in India decreased from 3,200 million yards in 1913 to 3 million in 1953, and in South and Central America they declined from 1,100 million yards to 300 million over the same

period. Organization for European Economic Cooperation, *The Textile Industry in Europe* (Paris: 1955), p. 105.

58 A number of countries in the Middle East (Saudi Arabia, Kuwait, Iraq, Quatar, and Bahrein) are in this favorable position. But up to now there has been no sign that the extra income, provided by increasing petroleum exports, has contributed to economic development improving the level of living of the population. The unequal income distribution results in a large share of the increased income being used for luxury consumption or for investments that benefit only a small upper class. The backwardness, especially in the land tenure system and the absence of complementary factors of production — particularly leaders with the technical capability for converting this new source of income into capital goods to strengthen the economic structure — makes development difficult and a necessarily long-term process. International Bank for Reconstruction and Development and the Government of Iraq, *The Economic Development of Iraq* (Baltimore: 1952).

59 "Some International Aspects of the Problem of Economic Development", *The American Economic Review*, XLII, No. 2 (May, 1952), p. 575.

60 United Nations, *World Iron Resources and Their Utilization* (Lake Success: 1950).

61 Ohlin, *op. cit.*, p. 187.

62 R. Prebisch, *The Economic Development of Latin America and its Principal Problems*, United Nations Document E/CN.12/89 (Lake Success: May, 1949), p. 3.

63 *Ibid.*, p. 13.

64 *Ibid.*, pp. 18-9.

65 *Ibid.*, p. 22.

66 W. Schlote, *Entwicklung und Strukturwandlungen des englischen Aussenhandels von 1700 bis zur Gegenwart*, Probleme der Weltwirtschaft 62 (Jena: 1938), pp. 121-23. A. H. Imlah, "The Terms of Trade of the United Kingdom 1798-1913", *The Journal of Economic History*, X, No. 2 (November, 1950), pp. 170-94. He criticizes on technical grounds the indices used by Schlote. It is interesting to note that the indices developed by Imlah yield substantially the same results. However, he does show that if, in addition to the unfavorable terms of trade, other factors are taken into consideration, such as the increase in the volume of exports and imports and the more rapid decline in the production cost of export articles, as compared with their selling prices (which resulted from increasing productivity), the terms-of-trade movement gains another dimension.

67 Schlote, *op. cit.*, pp. 158-59.

68 A similar picture is shown for Japan from the following:

	1921	*1928*	*1931*
Index of Export Prices (1913 = 100)	184	160	87
Index of Import Prices (1913 = 100)	163	159	87

These indices compiled by the *Oriental Economist* were obtained by dividing the indices of the value of total foreign trade by the indices for the volume of trade. Quoted by E. B. Schumpeter et al., *The Industrialization of Japan and Manchukuo* (New York: 1940), p. 901.

69 League of Nations, *The Network of World Trade, op. cit.*, p. 85.

70 United Nations, *Relative Prices of Exports and Imports of Under-Developed Countries* (Lake Success: December, 1949), p. 7.

71 In contrast to the general tendency during the depression, Japan as an industrial country experienced a deterioration in the terms of trade. The terms of trade (i.e., the ratio between the index of export prices and that of import prices with 1928 = 100) in Japan fell from 88 in 1932 to 64 in 1938. G. C. Allen, *Japanese Industry: Recent Development and Present Condition* (New York: 1940), p. 96.

72 R. E. Baldwin, "Secular Movements in the Terms of Trade", *The American Economic Review*, XLV, No. 2 (May, 1955), pp. 259–69.

73 Wright gives several examples showing that during recessions in industrial countries idle shipping was usually diverted to haul goods from primary producing areas to Europe. In the case of bulky raw materials, the decline in freight rates was greater than the decrease in c.i.f. prices in Europe, hence prices of such materials in the primary producing countries actually rose expressed in local currency. The resulting rise in purchasing power in the raw material producing countries in its turn initiated often the revival in the industrial countries. C. M. Wright in "Convertibility and Triangular Trade as Safeguards against Economic Depression", *The Economic Journal*, LXV, No. 259 (September, 1955), pp. 422–35.

74 "The Gains from International Trade and the Backward Countries", *The Review of Economic Studies 1954–55*, XXII 2, No. 58, pp. 129–42.

75 A report issued by the Secretariat of the General Agreement on Tariffs and Trade entitled *International Trade 1952* (Geneva: 1953), p. 110, presents a table that shows a rise in the ratio between the prices of primary products and manufactures for the whole world from 103 in 1925 (1929 = 100) to 154 in 1951.

76 C. Clark, *Conditions of Economic Progress* (1st ed.; London: 1940), p. 453.

77 C. Clark, *The Economics of 1960* (London: 1942), p. 90. Clark (*Ibid.*, p. 52) has estimated that the world price for primary products would be 90 per cent higher in 1960, in terms of the prices for manufactures and services, than in the base period 1925–35. Lewis, on the basis of estimated rates of growth of world industrial production and agricultural and other raw material production, and on the basis of a certain ratio between industrial production and world trade in raw materials, arrives at much lower price increases for raw materials and foodstuffs between 1950 and 1960, with the price level in the period 1921–38 taken as the base. His arguments appear to be more realistic, but much speculation is possible in this field. Lewis, "World Production, Prices and Trade 1870–1960", *op. cit.*, p. 131.

78 *International Trade 1952, op. cit.*, pp. 5–7.

79 H. G. Aubrey, "The Long-Term Future of United States Imports and its Implications for Primary-Producing Countries", *The American Economic Review*, XLV, No. 2 (May, 1955), pp. 270–87.

80 In the study of the U.S. Department of Commerce already mentioned, it has been calculated that over the period 1902–50 the U.S. per capita consumption of raw materials in constant dollars has shown an average annual growth of 1.43 per cent. This rate of growth was only 1.21 per cent for foodstuffs, 1.50 per cent for industrial raw materials and 1.96 per cent for fuels. This tendency may well be representative of other industrial countries and indicative of their future requirements for growth. However, for under-developed economies the increase in food consumption will probably initially be more elastic than the demand for other raw materials and, therefore, lead to an entirely different trade pattern.

81 For the United Kingdom it can be calculated that between 1861–80 the real wage level increased by 32 per cent, but from 1880 to 1900 by 49 per cent. During the period 1900–30, however, it only rose by 18 per cent. See tables, A. L. Bowley, *Wages and Income in the United Kingdom Since 1860* (Cambridge: 1937), p. 30.

82 It can be argued, as H. W. Singer (*op. cit.*) has done, that the concentration on export of primary commodities of the backward countries has given them less opportunities for developing growing points in their economies than if they had tried to encourage manufacturing industries. The question seems rather academic, since an underdeveloped country has always to export in order to earn foreign exchange for the import of capital goods and foreign skills. In the light of the governmental efforts in undeveloped countries to modify by public investment some of the less desirable effects of the private investment pattern, and the relative ease with which parts of the proceeds of well-organized export industries can be tapped by the government in comparison with domestic activities, the export of raw materials would seem to offer one of the most promising channels to increase the resources at the disposal of the state.

83 W. A. Lewis, *Aspects of Industrialization* (Cairo: 1953), pp. 6–14. Japan is an example of a country whose growth would have been impossible without the export of finished articles. Its export of manufactures increased from 2 per cent of its total exports in 1868–72 to almost 59 per cent in 1933 and to 60.6 per cent in 1937.

84 *Op. cit.*, pp. 30–4.

85 H. S. Perloff, *Puerto Rico's Economic Future* (Chicago: 1950). The national per capita income in Puerto Rico rose from $ 122 in 1940 to $ 430 in 1954 in current prices and to $ 227 in 1940 prices.

86 See Agenda Item 25, Seventh Session, General Assembly, United Nations, 1952–53, pp. 12–3.

87 Secretariat of the General Agreement on Tariffs and Trade, *op. cit.*, p. 3. A table in League of Nations' study, *Industrialization and Foreign Trade, op. cit.*, p. 14, indicates that the lag of world trade in both raw materials and manufactures behind world industrial production has been in evidence since 1870.

88 "The Future of World Trade", *The Economic Journal*, XLVIII (March, 1938), pp. 1–14.

89 "The Prospect for Foreign Trade in the Post-War World", Transactions of the Manchester Statistical Society; Address given at Annual Meeting, June 19, 1946. Reprinted in *Readings in the Theory of International Trade*, Selected by a committee of the American Economic Association (Philadelphia – Toronto: 1949), pp. 514–29.

90 This is especially noticeable for the United Kingdom in the case of engineering and electrical export goods. These exports comprised 25 per cent of total exports in 1913, 33 per cent in 1938, and as much as 50 per cent in 1953.

91 *Industrialization and Foreign Trade, op. cit.*, p. 106.

92 See U.S. Department of State, *Havana Charter for an International Trade Organization*, Publication 3206, (Washington, D.C.: 1948).

CHAPTER II. THE GOVERNMENT SECTOR

1 B. F. Johnston, "Agricultural Productivity and Economic Development in Japan", *The Journal of Political Economy*, LIX (1951), pp. 498–512. The revenue from the land tax constituted only 22 per cent of the total state revenue in 1906–07. The decline in the relative importance of revenue from the land tax was due to the relatively greater increase of other revenue, mainly that derived from the taxation of industrial profits.

2 United Nations, Economic Commission for Asia and the Far East, *Economic Survey of Asia and the Far East 1949* (New York: 1950), pp. 159–61.

3 A. Smith, *An Inquiry Into the Nature and Causes of the Wealth of Nations* (London: Everyman's Library, 1931), II, pp. 210–11.

4 *Report on Cuba* (Washington, D.C.: 1951), p. 683. It has been estimated that about 90 per cent of state revenue in Ceylon, India, and the Philippines is used for current expenditure.

5 It is reported that in Mexico, 45 per cent of the total expenditures for irrigation works consisted of wages and 10 per cent for supervisory and administrative cost, while 35 per cent went for local raw materials and 10 per cent for imported machinery and implements. United Nations, *Domestic Financing of Economic Development* (New York: 1950), p. 148.

6 *State and Economics in the Middle East* (London: 1948), p. 51.

7 V. Anstey, *The Economic Development of India* (3rd ed.; London – Toronto: 1936), p. 388. The proportion of land taxes diminished further from 13 per cent in 1938–39 to 5 per cent of total revenue in 1949–50.

8 H. C. Wallich, "Fiscal Policy and the Budget" (pp. 117–40) in S. E. Harris et al., *Economic Problems of Latin America* (New York: 1944), pp. 122–23.

9 United Nations, *Economic Bulletin for Asia and the Far East*, "Taxation and Economic Development in Asian Countries", IV, No. 3 (Bangkok: November, 1953).

10 In Burma, in 1950, a married man with wife and three children paid no income tax unless the ratio of earned income to average national per capita income was 21:1 or more. Similarly, such a man was exempt from income tax if the ratio was below 15:1 in Ceylon (1952), and below 15:1 in the Philippines (1950). However, the ratios below which there was exemption from income tax were only 4:1 in Egypt (1951) and 1.5:1 in Mexico (1950), *ibid.*, p. 8.

11 United Nations, Economic Commission for Asia and the Far East, *op. cit.*, p. 155.

12 *Public Finance* (London – Cambridge: 1947), p. 143.

13 *Fiscal Policy and Business Cycles* (New York: 1941), pp. 125 and 129.

14 M. Dobb, *Soviet Economic Development Since 1917* (London: 1948), p. 360.

15 In Brazil, excise taxes represented 25 per cent of the total federal revenue in 1929 and 41 per cent in 1944. Excise taxes on tobacco and beverages accounted for 21 per cent of the total excise revenue in 1944, while textiles and matches yielded 10 and 7 per cent, respectively. See H. W. Spiegel, *The Brazilian Economy* (Toronto: 1949), pp. 72–3.

16 Planning Commission, *The Second Five Year Plan*, A memorandum prepared by the panel of economists (New Delhi: April, 1955).

17 In Ghana and various British colonies (Sierra Leone, Tanganyika, North Borneo, Sarawak, and others) such export duties have also been used to establish price stabilization funds as a cushion against a future price decline, though part of the revenue is used for public investment.

18 *Multiple Exchange Rates and Economic Development*, "Studies in International Finance", No. 2. (Princeton, N. J.: 1952), p. 20.

19 *Ibid.*, pp. 50–3.

20 E. Reiche, *Aussenhandelsverflechtung und Industrialisierung Argentiniens*, "Kieler Studien", Nr. 25 (Kiel, 1953), p. 133.

21 H. S. Bloch, "La Politique Fiscale des Pays Sous-dévelopés", *Revue de Science et de Législation Financiéres* (January-March, 1953).

22 International Bank for Reconstruction and Development, *The Economy of Turkey* (Washington, D.C.: 1951), p. 224.

23 *Ibid.*, p. 225.

24 J. Schumpeter notes that, as late as 1891, the Prussian minister of finance declared that a 5 per cent income tax would be so high as to give rise to anxiety. This should set in historical perspective the objections raised by the higher income groups in undeveloped countries against this form of taxation. J. Schumpeter, *Business Cycles: A Theoretical, Historical*

and Statistical Analysis of the Capitalist Process (New York – London: 1939), I, p. 224.

25 In Argentina, the finance minister declared as late as 1942 that 80 per cent of the recipients of dividends did not pay the tax imposed on them.

26 C. H. Max states that, in Chile, fiscal revenue rose from 1.6 billion pesos in 1938 to 7.8 billion pesos in 1947. In the former year, import and export duties accounted for 46 per cent of the total revenue and internal taxes for 40 per cent, while in 1947 the percentages for these two groups had changed to 13 and 61, respectively. See his *Informe sobre la Inflacion chilena* (Santiago: 1948). In Colombia, customs duties provided one-half, and direct taxes one-fourth, of total revenue in 1937, but in 1948 these proportions had been reversed.

27 This report has not been published. A similar situation has recently been reported in Bolivia. In 1947, 291 out of 330 taxes were earmarked, wholly or partly, for subordinate authorities or marginal entities and only 39 taxes were left to the national government for general use. United Nations, *Taxes and Fiscal Policy in Under-Developed Countries* (New York: 1954), p. 44.

28 In Brazil, in 1948 and 1949, federal bonds were sold 10 to 40 per cent under par, so that the average effective interest rate on these obligations rose from almost 6 per cent in the first half of 1944 to 7.6 per cent in the first half of 1948. U.S. Department of State, *Report Joint Brazilian-United States Technical Commission* (Rio de Janeiro: March, 1949), p. 119.

29 Spiegel, *op. cit.*, p. 113. In Argentina, Brazil, and Chile social security receipts in 1948 amounted to 7.5, 3.5 and 6.2 per cent respectively of national income as compared with 2.9 per cent in the United states.

30 In Bolivia, in 1949, the central bank held 99.5 per cent of the internal public debt. United Nations, *Report of the United Nations Mission of Technical Assistance to Bolivia* (New York: 1951), pp. 22; 42.

31 A similar role — mobilizing equity finance for new industrial ventures — is to be filled by the Industrial Credit and Investment Corporation of India Ltd., established in 1955 with a nominal capital of 250 million rupees. Of the initial paid up capital of 50 million rupees, private Indian investors subscribed 35 million and British and American financial institutions 10 and 5 million rupees, respectively. The International Bank for Reconstruction and Development lent $ 10 million to provide foreign exchange for use in the corporation's operations. In addition, the government of India made an interest-free advance of 80 million rupees.

32 International Bank for Reconstruction and Development, *The Economic Development of Ceylon* (Baltimore: 1953), p. 90. In the meantime, the Development Finance Corporation of Ceylon has been established with an initial capital of 24 million rupees. Of this amount, 8 million are to be subscribed by banking institutions and private investors in London and Colombo and 16 million by the government in the form of an interest-free loan.

33 Government of India, Ministry of Finance, *First Report of the National Income Committee* (New Delhi: April, 1951), p. 34.

34 International Bank for Reconstruction and Development, *The Economy of Turkey, op. cit.*, p. 50. Government expenditures for investment represented about half of total gross capital formation in 1949.

35 United Nations, Economic Commission for Asia and the Far East, *op. cit.*, pp. 162–63.

36 The Third Annual Report of the Consultative Committee on Economic Development in South and Southeast Asia, *The Colombo Plan* (London: October, 1954), p. 113.

37 It has been stated, for example, that capital formation for India, in the private sector, cannot be estimated with the data currently available and that efforts must be made to obtain some idea of the total domestic capital formation as a basis for making policy decisions. See Government of India, *op. cit.*, p. 33.

38 *Op. cit.*, p. 155.

39 *Ibid.*, p. 46.

40 M. W. Thornburg, *Turkey: An Economic Appraisal* (New York: 1949), pp. 107–12.

41 G. Wythe et al., *Brazil: An Expanding Economy* (New York: 1949), p. 352.

42 International Bank for Reconstruction and Development, *The Economic Development of Mexico* (Baltimore: 1953). Over the period from 1939 to 1950, Mexico's national product grew from 5.8 to 38.1 billion pesos, *ibid.*, p. 171. After deflation by a wholesale price index, this leaves an increase in the real national product from 100 to 214.4. If, also, the population increase is taken into account (1939 = 100, 1950 = 132.3), then per capita real net domestic product rose only by 62 per cent over the period 1939–50, *ibid.*, p. 178.

43 *Ibid.*, p. 188.

44 *Ibid.*, p. 195.

45 The length of the road system increased from 8,463 kilometers in 1938 to 28,864 kilometers in 1950, *ibid.*, p. 299, and in 1951 the railroads transported a 62 per cent greater tonnage than in 1939, *ibid.*, p. 315. From 1939 to 1950 the cultivated land area increased by 40 per cent, or 2.8 million hectares, *ibid.*, p. 224, and the volume of agricultural production increased by 90 per cent, *ibid.*, p. 228. Electric power generated rose almost 80 per cent, and the consumption of electricity almost 91 per cent over this period, *ibid.*, pp. 262–63, while the production of petroleum increased 77 per cent, *ibid.*, p. 258.

46 *Ibid.*, p. 206.

47 Compared with 1939 (as equal to 100), the production index for the textile industry rose to 166 in 1950, *ibid.*, p. 278, for the iron and steel industry to 279, *ibid.*, p. 280, for the cement industry to 291, *ibid.*, p. 282, the pulp and

paper industry to 366, *ibid.*, p. 282, and the chemical industry to 818, *ibid.*, p. 286. Excess capacity in manufacturing allowed the initial spurt in industrial production. Gross investment in industrial equipment amounted to 171 million in 1939 and to 208 million pesos in 1940. It increased, however, in 1948 and 1950 to 1,279 and 1,205 million pesos respectively, *ibid.*, p. 186. In evaluating this it should be kept in mind that the money supply rose almost sixfold, and the index of wholesale prices and of the cost of living rose fourfold over the same period, 1939–50. Figures on investment in manufacturing industry in the Bank's report have been obtained as the difference between estimated total private investment and private investment in other fields (agriculture, transport, construction, power, mining), for which apparently more precise information is available.

48 Over the period 1939–50, the estimated increase in total per capita consumption was 55.2 per cent, *ibid.*, p. 202, and in per capita food consumption 30 per cent, *ibid.*, p. 234.

49 *Ibid.*, p. 11.

50 H. Flores de la Peña, *Crecimiento Denografico, Desarollo Agricola y Desarollo Economico*, Proceedings of the World Population Conference, Rome, 1954, Vol. V (United Nations, New York: 1955), pp. 301–20.

51 A. H. Hansen states that, in 1843, 70 per cent of the securities traded on the stock exchange in England were bonds of the British government, and another 10 per cent were bonds of foreign governments, *op. cit.*, p. 112.

52 R. W. Tufts, in a supplement to E. Staley's book, *World Economic Development* (Montreal: 1944), gives a number of tables on average annual investment in Japan. From these tables we have calculated that public investment constituted 44 per cent of total investment in the period 1900–9, only 19 per cent over the period 1910–19 (probably as a result of the rise in defense expenditures), 26 per cent for the period 1920–29, and 36 per cent during the depression period 1930–36.

CHAPTER 12. INFLATION

1 United Nations, *Inflationary and Deflationary Tendencies, 1946–1948* (Lake Success: 1949) and E. M. Bernstein, *Inflation in Relation to Economic Development*, International Monetary Fund, Staff Papers, II, No. 3 (Washington, D.C.: November, 1952).

2 J. Schumpeter, *Business Cycles: A Theoretical, Historical and Statistical Analysis of the Capitalist Process* (New York – London: 1939), I, p. 348. He shows how in England, the accumulated trade profits and other factors which caused a relative abundance of savings so that entrepreneurs as a rule only invested their own or borrowed savings, have obscured, for British banking theory and practice, the role of credit creation in the financing of industrialization.

However, in France, Germany, and, above all, in the United States, credit creation by the banking system or the state have been influential in guiding production factors into new channels. Whether an increase in money supply induces a rise in prices depends upon whether the flow of consumer goods rises to the same extent. The process is never synchronous, since some investments may take years to mature. However, if when new investments are made, commodities become available as a result of earlier investments, the development process may proceed without unduly large shocks.

3 For a detailed analysis of the factors responsible for the inflation in Chile, for example, see United Nations, *World Economic Report 1953–54* (New York: 1955), pp. 78–88, "Inflation in Chile 1940 to 1953".

4 H. C. Max says that, in his country, economic development has gone hand-in-hand with inflation since 1870. C. H. Max, *Informe sobre la Inflación Chilena* (Santiago: 1948). From approximate parity with the U.S. dollar in 1870, the Chilean peso fell gradually to about 12 cents in the late 1920's, and to the official parity of about 0.9 cents (free rate, 0.4 cents) in 1954. For Brazil, Spiegel indicated that the price level rose 13-fold between 1840 and 1940, and 28-fold from 1840 to 1945. Over the latter period, the value of the English pound, expressed in Brazilian currency, increased 8 to 10-fold, depending on whether the official or free exchange rate is used for the conversion. H. W. Spiegel, *The Brazilian Economy* (Toronto: 1949), pp. 43–4.

5 R. H. Tawney, *Religion and the Rise of Capitalism* (London: 1938), p. 130.

6 *Op. cit.*, p. 97. For Chile it has been shown that over the period 1940–52 the real earnings of workers in industry and mining and of salaried employees rose, but those in agriculture and domestic service declined. United Nations, *World Economic Report 1953–54, op. cit.*, p. 82.

7 United Nations, *World Economic Report 1951–52* (New York: 1953), pp. 55–62.

8 *Ibid.*, p. 396.

9 M. Dobb, *Soviet Economic Development Since 1917* (London: 1948), pp. 361–62.

10 Dobb's scheme is somewhat oversimplified. Besides the turnover tax, the state revenue also consists of a profits tax, state loans for which subscription is more or less compulsory, a few special levies on services, and, in recent years, income tax, and social insurance contributions have also been added. See A. Baykov, *The Development of the Soviet Economic System* (New York: 1948), pp. 373; 397, for some specific examples of the composition of the state income.

11 It is estimated that the cost of living index in the U.S.S.R., using 1928 weights, increased to 701 in 1937 (1928 = 100), and that the food price index, based on Moscow official prices and also using 1928 weights, increased to 892. J. G. Chapman, "Real wages in the Soviet Union, 1928–1952", *The Review of Economics and Statistics*, XXXVI, No. 2 (May, 1954), p. 147.

12 *Op. cit.*, pp. 279–80.

13 A. Zauberman, "Gold in Soviet Economic Theory and Policies", *The American Economic Review*, XLI, No. 5 (December, 1951), p. 886. Zauberman's remarks on the attempts being made in the U.S.S.R. to maintain the illusion of money, particularly to give an authentic character to the profits earned by enterprises, are also of interest.

14 United Nations, Economic Commission for Europe, *Economic Survey of Europe Since the War* (Geneva: 1953), pp. 31–2. The report concluded that "none of the governments concerned has been able to avoid some open and some suppressed inflation."

15 The most drastic example of the results of inflationary tensions that accompany rapid industrialization in a planned economy, is the monetary reform carried out in Czechoslovakia in May, 1953. One new crown was paid for fifty old crowns, while a rate of five old crowns to one new crown was fixed for the savings of workers, with the maximum set at 5,000 crowns. All future wage and pensions payments were to be made at the rate of one to five. At the same time, it was announced that all bank deposits made before 1945, and all state bonds issued after 1945, were annulled. This measure primarily affected the workers, who had been forced to invest part of their wages in state bonds. Poland, Bulgaria, and Rumania had already gone through similar monetary reforms, but in none of these countries was the level of living of industrial workers as adversely affected as in Czechoslovakia.

16 United Nations, *Report of the United Nations Economic Mission to Chile 1949–1950* (New York: 1951). The mission consisted of C. Iversen, University of Copenhagen (Denmark), S. Leland, Northwestern University (Evanston, Illinois), and E. Lindahl, University of Upsala (Sweden).

17 The report of the Mission also included a number of longer term proposals, such as the introduction of a national budget, and establishment of an economic council. All ministers responsible for the various sectors of the economy would be represented on the council, which would be serviced by a special research agency and an advisory credit council. A foreign exchange equalization fund was also proposed to build up reserves in the boom years to carry out an anticyclical policy whenever the prices of export goods slumped. A number of these proposals were incorporated in legislation, which was rejected by the Chilean parliament, whereupon the responsible finance minister resigned. The cost of living (1937=100) in the capital, Santiago, which by 1945 had risen to 244, had reached 446 in 1948, 609 in 1950, and 1,285 in 1954, showing that inflation had continued unabated.

18 International Monetary Fund, *A Report on the Process of Inflation in Chile Together with Recommendations* (Washington, D.C.: November, 1950). This report contains a more thorough analysis of the causes and effects of the inflation in Chile than does the United Nations report.

19 F. W. Fetter, *Monetary Inflation in Chile* (Princeton, N.J.: 1931), as quoted in P. T. Ellsworth, *Chile: An Economy in Transition* (New York: 1945), p. 114.

For Brazil, Spiegel, *op. cit.*, p. 46, found: "…the dominant interests, including the commercial interests, are so much attached to the system of permanent depreciation of money in internal and external terms that they do nothing to stop it."

20 J. M. Keynes, *A Treatise on Money* (New York: 1930), II, pp. 162–63; and D. H. Robertson, *Money* (2nd ed.; Cambridge: 1948), p. 139. Robertson, *ibid.*, p. 140, has in addition said the following: "As long as the control of production is in the hands of a minority rewarded by means of a fluctuating profit, it is not impossible that a gently rising price level will in fact produce the best attainable results, not only for them but for the community as a whole."

21 J. M. Keynes, *op. cit.*, pp. 159–60. S. B. Clough and C. W. Cole state that the commodity price level in England rose from 100 in the first decade of the sixteenth century to 256 in the last decade, while wages increased only from 100 to 130, and that this divergence lasted until about 1650. S. B. Clough and C. W. Cole, *Economic History of Europe* (Boston: 1941), pp. 128–29. A note of caution should, perhaps, be sounded in the interpretation of price indices covering such a long period as the composition of production and consumption tend to be subject to continuous change.

22 J. E. Nef, "Prices and Industrial Capitalism in France and England, 1540–1640", *The Economic History Review*, VII (1937), pp. 155–85, and reprinted in F. C. Lane and J. C. Riemersma, ed., *Enterprise and Secular Change* (Homewood, Ill.: 1953), pp. 292–321.

23 E. J. Hamilton, "Profit Inflation and the Industrial Revolution 1751–1800", *The Quarterly Journal of Economics*, LVI (1942), pp. 256–73.

24 J. M. Keynes, *Essays in Persuasion* (New York: 1932), pp. 88–9. Keynes points out that if the 1914 price level is taken as 100, the fluctuations in both directions over the whole period from 1826 to 1914 did not exceed 30.

25 See the table presented by Ashton that shows the movement of wages for British factory workers during the period 1806–50. T. S. Ashton, "Some Statistics of the Industrial Revolution in Britain", *The Manchester School of Economic and Social Studies*, XVI, No. 2 (May, 1948), p. 232. He shows that, in the beginning, the nominal weekly wage rose gradually, and after 1820 declined (1806, 121 pence; 1820, 124 pence; 1830, 115 pence, and 1850, 110 pence). However, because the cost of living fell more rapidly (1829, 100; 1806, 140; 1820, 125; 1830, 102; 1850, 79), there was an almost uninterrupted rise in real wages during this period from 74 in 1806 to 86 in 1820, 99 in 1830, and 120 in 1850 (1829 = 100).

26 The Institute for Social Sciences of Stockholm University, *Wages, Cost of Living and National Income in Sweden, 1860–1930*, I: *The Cost of Living in Sweden 1830–1930* (Stockholm: 1933); II: *Wages in Sweden 1860–1930*, in two parts (Stockholm: 1937); and III: *The National Income of Sweden 1861–1930* (Stockholm: 1937).

27 *Ibid.*, III, p. 242.

28 *Ibid.*, II, Part 2, p. 245. Here it is pointed out that, as a result of the continued labor shortage in the industrial sector, which was intensified by the emigration of potential workers, a relatively high wage had to be paid in order to attract the necessary labor.

29 *Ibid.*, II, Part 1, pp. 60–4.

30 *Ibid.*, II, Part 2, p. 302 ff.

31 Rostow gives an example of this trend by showing how, in Great Britain, in the first phase of the boom from 1868 to 1871, the index of total production rose from 52 to 60 (1900 = 100), unemployment fell from 7.9 to 1.6 per cent, and the price level increased only from 132 to 133. In contrast, as the turning point approached, production continued to increase between 1871 and 1873 from 60 to 64, unemployment further declined from 1.6 to 1.2 per cent, but the price level rose from 133 to 148. See W. W. Rostow, *British Economy of the Nineteenth Century* (Oxford: 1948), p. 79.

32 See A. L. Bowley, *Wages and Income in the United Kingdom Since 1860* (Cambridge: 1937), for an illustration of this proposition.

33 *Op. cit.*, p. 55.

34 In the Swedish study already mentioned, we find a remark on the course of wage movements during the cyclical upswing and downswing that confirms this thought: "The increase in real wages has thus for the most part taken place during periods when prices have had a falling tendency. At such times the wages have been either constant or else slowly rising. In periods of general economic progress, both the cost of living and wages go up, and the increase in real wages is generally of minor significance." The Institute for Social Sciences of Stockholm University, *op. cit.*, II, Part 1, p. 65.

35 A League of Nations publication describes how the capital stock was restored by a moderate inflation in several regions affected by World War I. This success is ascribed to the lag in wages while commodity prices rose, and to the willingness of the population to continue saving. That the population regarded the depreciation of the monetary unit as a temporary phenomenon can be attributed to its ignorance of the course of an inflation, a matter easily understood when it is recalled that inflation had been unknown in Europe for a century. See League of Nations, *The Course and Control of Inflation: A Review of Monetary Experience in Europe after World War I* (Geneva: 1946).

PART THREE: INTERNATIONAL FINANCIAL RESOURCES

CHAPTER 13. INTRODUCTION

1 E. P. Reubens, "Foreign Capital in Economic Development: A Case Study of Japan", *The Milbank Memorial Fund Quarterly*, XXVIII, No. 2

(April, 1950), pp. 173–90. Between 1868 and 1895, Japan received two foreign loans amounting to a total of £ 3.4 million, and a few direct investments were also made there by foreigners. By 1896, Japan had almost repaid these obligations to foreign countries. From 1896 until 1914, bonds were placed abroad almost every year. These were issued mainly by the state, but also, in small amounts, by municipalities and corporations. However, the total amount of foreign capital remained small in comparison with domestic capital formation, even though over this period, the average annual import surplus of goods and services amounted to 17 per cent of total imports. During World War I, Japan accumulated a substantial amount of foreign exchange by its export surpluses, and part of this was used to liquidate foreign obligations and to provide an import surplus during the 1920's. It was during this period that direct foreign investment became more important than government loans and that Japan began to export capital to Asia and other regions. Except for the 1923 earthquake, Japan was aided by favorable historical factors. However, Reubens believes that other factors were also decisive for Japan's success in development. In the scheme of industrialization, projects which were most productive were emphasized. In the beginning, capital-intensive industries were not established but, rather, those industries which would more readily begin to yield a surplus. In selecting new industries, Japan stressed those which would produce for export, and a deliberate policy was developed for controlling the level of domestic consumption. For an analysis of the care with which Japan enlisted Western capital and technical aid, by contrast with China where there was resistance to all external influences, see G. C. Allen and A. G. Donnithorne, *Western Enterprise in Far Eastern Economic Development: China and Japan* (London: 1954).

2 C. Iversen in *Aspects of the Theory of International Capital Movements* (London: 1935), p. 51, shows that the foreign loans obtained by Australia and Canada at the beginning of the twentieth century were used mainly to purchase consumer goods. For the development of new regions and the construction of capital goods that could only be built in the country itself, imports of consumer goods from the creditor country constituted the supplement that made these activities possible.

3 A report of the Organization for European Economic Cooperation, *Investment in Overseas Territories in Africa South of the Sahara* (Paris: 1951), gives an idea of the order of magnitude of the estimated capital needs for the investment program of an undeveloped region embracing all of the colonies south of the Sahara in Africa. Many of these territories had development plans formulated for the ten-year period 1946–55. The total amount of capital needed for this period was estimated at $ 8 billion, of which $ 5 billion was to come from public funds and $ 3 billion from private funds. For about $ 4.4 billion of the public investment (87 per cent of the total), it is estimated that 30 per cent would be expenditures yielding no direct income (for education,

public health, and administration, our first category of capital); 60 per cent would consist of 'basic equipment' expenditures (for transportation, communications, and electric power, our second category); and 10 per cent would represent directly productive expenditures, those of our third category, for which, in view of the risks involved, no private funds were available. The pamphlet describes how, as far as is known, the various expenditures were running according to plan. For other undeveloped countries the relative division between public and private investment and the composition of public investment will probably be different, as such a distribution is dependent on the stage of development and the resource endowment of each individual country.

4 B. Ohlin, *Inter-regional and International Trade*, "Harvard Economic Studies", XXXIX (Cambridge, Mass.: 1933), p. 350.

CHAPTER 14. A BRIEF HISTORY OF INTERNATIONAL CAPITAL MOVEMENTS

1 J. M. Keynes, *A Treatise on Money* (New York: 1930), pp. 156–57.

2 Probably these investments were at first mainly in inventories, ships, and local settlements for the collection and shipment of valuable high-quality products intended largely for the luxury consumption of well-to-do groups.

3 G. U. Papi, *The Colonial Problem: An Economic Analysis* (London: 1938).

4 L. H. Jenks, *The Migration of British Capital to 1875* (New York: 1927), p. 281.

5 Jenks states that as late as 1868 Great Britain produced four-fifths (as measured in value) of the cereals, meat, dairy products, and wool consumed by its population, but by 1875 this proportion had fallen to less than one-half. *Ibid.*, p. 325.

6. The following quotation from J. S. Mill, *Principles of Political Economy* (7th ed., London–New York: 1871), p. 490, will serve to illustrate an economist's view of the significance of these investments for England: "It is to the emigration of English capital that we have chiefly to look for keeping up a supply of cheap food and cheap materials of clothing, proportional to the increase of our population: thus enabling an increasing capital to find employment in the country, without reduction of profit, in producing manufactured articles, with which to pay for this supply of raw produce. Thus, the exportation of capital is an agent of great efficacy in extending the field of employment for that which remains." Iversen also notes that capital import in Denmark made butter and bacon cheap in the creditor countries of western Europe, while British loans to Sweden, Norway, and Finland caused the prices of wood pulp and paper in Great Britain to fall. See C. Iversen, *Aspects of the Theory of International Capital Movements* (Copenhagen – London: 1935), p. 230.

7 United Nations, *International Capital Movements During the Inter-War Period* (New York: 1949), p. 1. In the balance of this chapter we have made liberal use of data in this document.

8 Some authors go so far as to assert that real transfers have practically never taken place between creditor and debtor countries, but that new or increasing foreign investments were always reinvested profits. Quoted in Iversen, *op. cit.*, p. 56.

9 A. H. Imlah, "British Balance of Payments and Exports of Capital, 1816–1913", *The Economic History Review*, 2nd Series, V, 2 (1952), pp. 208–40.

10 The following figures are from Jenks, *op. cit.*, p. 335, and Sir George Paish, "The Export of Capital and the Cost of Living", *The Statist*, Supplement 14, (February, 1914), pp. v–vi:

British Foreign Investments	1875	1913
	(in millions of pounds sterling)	
Total	1,200	3,715
In Europe and Egypt	500	240

11 Direct investments are holdings in foreign corporations which give the person or group owning them control over the management of the companies in question. Portfolio investments are stocks and bonds of foreign governments or enterprises held by individuals, which do not entail any important voice in the management of the enterprises concerned.

12 Imlah, *op. cit.*, p. 228, gives a 1907 estimate by Sir George Paish, showing that direct foreign investment amounted to only 18.5 per cent of the amount held by individuals in foreign government bonds. Imlah believes that this ratio had been approximately the same in 1845. A general word of caution is in order to indicate that value estimates of direct foreign investments contain a considerable margin of error. Figures on foreign assets often only reflect their book value, not their market value or replacement cost and thus do not take into account changes in the price level or accounting practices tending to understate the book value. Information on reinvestment of undistributed profits is particularly scanty.

13 C. Lewis, *The United States and Foreign Investment Problems* (Washington, D.C.: 1948), p. 46.

14. E. H. Carr, *Conditions of Peace* (New York: 1944), pp. 268–69.

15 United Nations, *op. cit.*, p. 29.

16 The investments in Canada and Newfoundland reflect the geographical position of these areas with respect to the United States. The close ties between the economies of these countries reduced the risk normally involved in foreign investment. Canada's attractiveness to United States investors is also related to the relatively high purchasing power of the Canadian population and to the fact that, by its membership in the British Commonwealth, Canada has had a preference over the United States in the British market.

Furthermore, Canada's proximity to the United States makes the control of the operations of subsidiaries a relatively simple matter.

17 The Royal Institute of International Affairs in *The Problem of International Investment* (London: 1937), p. 19, estimates that 70 per cent of the British investments in underdeveloped countries consisted of government loans and stocks and bonds placed on the British market by public utilities.

18 Frankel has pointed out that it was the discovery of diamonds in 1867 and of gold in 1886 that brought about industrial development in South Africa, and that it was the anticipated profits from mining activities that led to the construction of the principal railroads. Taxation of these mineral industries subsequently furnished the state with the funds for a good deal of public investment, including the financing of scientific institutes to improve agriculture. See S. H. Frankel, *Capital Investment in Africa* (London – New York: 1936), p. 375.

19 Iversen (*op. cit.*, p. 156) has said that the underlying course of international capital movements "is to be found in the varying relative scarcity of capital in different countries... Capital sets out in search of the other immobile factors, so to speak, in order to get combined with them in the most advantageous proportions. Its movements tend to neutralize the disadvantages of the uneven productive equipment of different countries." This economic explanation, while not inaccurate, does not explain the phenomenon fully. Jenks (*op. cit.*, p. 49; pp. 79–80) gives examples showing that in the nineteenth century it was not high interest rates in the debtor countries that caused the emigration of British capital so much as the profits made by financial middlemen in the floating of foreign stocks and bonds.

20 League of Nations, *The Network of World Trade* (Geneva: 1942), illustrates this multilateral structure of prewar foreign trade.

21 In the 1920's, the United States was responsible for more than 40 per cent of the world's industrial production.

22 At various times, the Mexican government has expropriated foreign capital invested in railroads (1914), land (1915–30), and oil wells (1938). It was only in 1946 that a settlement was finally reached on the payment of the outstanding railroad bonds, for which practically no interest or amortization had been paid since 1914. (Lewis, *op. cit.*, p. 151). In 1941 the Mexican government compensated the foreign landowners by acknowledging a debt of $ 40 million. The oil industry, 95 per cent of which was in foreign hands, was taken over by the government in 1938, when foreign companies refused to observe Mexican wage and labor legislation; settlements were reached with the United States and Anglo-Dutch interests in 1943 and 1946, respectively. (*Ibid.*, p. 151; p. 154).

Various public enterprises were taken over by other Latin American governments: Uruguay (1934), Argentina (1943–44), Brazil (1942), Chile (1939), and Colombia (1943). While nationalist motives were no doubt involved, the governments claimed in some cases that the companies were inefficient and, in particular, that they did not maintain their installations adequately. This complaint is also heard in other underdeveloped countries. The reason for this condition is in part the reluctance of foreign capital to expand its investment where there is the possibility of nationalization. Also, in the case of public utilities, it is the opinion of foreign management that the governments do not grant the rate increases necessary to make operations profitable. In 1937, the holdings of the oil companies in Bolivia and Chile were also taken over by the local governments. As far as is known, compensation was paid in almost all these cases, partly through the pressure of the United States government, *in casu* the Export-Import Bank, which makes no loans to countries refusing just compensation on expropriation of foreign holdings. However, spokesmen for the foreign investors involved claim that practically none of the settlements adequately covered the value of their interests. (*Ibid.*, pp. 154–56). In more recent years such expropriations have taken place in a number of other countries.

23. United Nations, *op. cit.*, pp. 67–8. The traditional reasoning followed here, is that 'unproductive' utilization of a foreign loan might nevertheless have allowed the release of domestic capital for 'productive' investment. It was found in some cases, however, that foreign loans were used to construct unnecessary roads or churches, uses which could hardly have increased productivity, even taking into consideration the claim that local capital was thereby released for productive investment.

24 It may be argued, on the other hand, that the bank or the potential investor in this period did not foresee the future collapse in the prices of primary products. This was one of the main reasons leading governments of the undeveloped countries to impose stringent controls on foreign payments during the 1930's. For an analysis of the quality of these portfolio investments, see Ilse Mintz, *Deterioration in the Quality of Foreign Bonds Issued in the United States 1920–1930* (New York: 1953).

25 S. Pizer in "The International Investment Position of the United States", *Foreign Commerce Weekly*, April 2, 1951, shows that United States investors held $ 5.3 billion in foreign bonds and shares (i.e., portfolio investments) in 1946 and $ 5.2 billion in 1949. More than half of these investments were Canadian and a quarter were European.

26 According to Lewis (*op. cit.*, pp. 37–8) only 10 of 65 politically independent countries were in the creditor group in 1938. Of these ten, six European countries (Belgium, France, the Netherlands, Sweden, Switzerland, and Great Britain) accounted for more than 63 per cent of all foreign investment. Of the debtor countries, eleven (Canada, Mexico, Brazil, Argentina, Chile, Germany, South Africa, India, China, Indonesia, and Australia) had long-term obligations amounting in each instance to more than $ 1 billion.

27 The figure of $ 3.9 billion for France is overestimated, since it includes

\$ 900 million for investments in European countries in default in interest and amortization. Lewis (*op. cit.*, p. 46) remarks: "On the whole, the French have long made their lending power an adjunct of their foreign policy – with unhappy results."

28 Lewis, *op. cit.*, pp. 44–5, estimates that by 1938 the Netherlands had invested the equivalent of \$ 2 billion in Indonesia, \$ 1 billion in the United States, and \$ 1.6 billion in European countries.

29 For further details see U.S. Department of Commerce, *Foreign Aid by the U.S. Government 1940–1951* (Washington, D.C.: 1952).

30 Lewis, *op. cit.*, p. 34; p. 199.

31 *Ibid.*, pp. 60–3; p. 346. Up to 1947, liquidations in India (£ 332 million), Argentina (£ 247 million), Canada (£ 225 million), and the United States (£ 203 million) accounted for £ 1,132 million.

32 According to another calculation by the Bank of England, the nominal value of British foreign holdings fell from £ 3,545 million in 1938 to £ 1,960 million in 1948 or by 45 per cent. The yield of these holdings fell from £ 155,4 million in 1938 to £ 116,4 million in 1948, or by only 25 per cent, indicating perhaps what we have designated selective liquidation. Bank of England, *U.K. Overseas Investment 1938 to 1948* (London: 1950).

33 Lewis, *op. cit.*, p. 61; p. 345.

34 *Ibid.*, pp. 65–6.

35 *Ibid.*, p. 69. The franc fell from a value of U.S. \$ .04 in 1937 to \$ .008 in 1947, a depreciation of 80 per cent, which also affected the French bonds held by foreign countries.

36 British long-term investments in India amounted to £ 545 million in 1938 but had fallen to £ 223 million in 1947. Against this India had a claim of £ 1,200 million on Great Britain. *Ibid.*, p. 76; p. 345.

37 *Ibid.*, p. 81.

38 In January, 1948, the U.S.S.R. granted a five-year loan of the equivalent of \$ 450 million to Poland. In February, 1950, it granted a loan of \$ 300 million to mainland China for a period of five years. In 1953, the latter was incorporated into a new ten-year loan estimated at the equivalent of \$ 1 billion.

39 A. K. Cairncross, *Home and Foreign Investment, 1870–1913*, "Studies in Capital Accumulation" (Cambridge: 1953), p. 187ff.

40 E. R. Reubens in "Foreign Capital in Economic Development: A Case Study of Japan", *The Milbank Memorial Fund Quarterly* (April, 1950), p. 182, states that in 1930 three-fourths of the foreign capital invested in Japan consisted of government loans, while Frankel (*op. cit.*, p. 14) states that a like proportion of the foreign debt of Australia in 1930 consisted of government bonds.

41 Of the foreign investments in Argentina in 1940, which amounted to a total of nine billion pesos, it has been estimated that over seven billion were in direct private investments and almost two billion in portfolio investments.

U.S. Department of Commerce, *Factors Limiting U.S. Investing Abroad* (Washington, D.C.: 1953), I, "Survey of Factors in Foreign Countries". See also E. Reiche, *Aussenhandelsverflechtung und Industrialisierung Argentiniens*, "Kieler Studien" (Kiel: 1953), p. 9; p. 61. Reiche states that in Argentina from 1872 on, railroad construction, financed by British private capital, went hand in hand with the expansion of the cultivated land area. Also, since 1883, investments in meat-freezing plants, again mainly financed by British private capital, yielded the increasing export surplus for financing the country's industrialization. Another important factor in Argentina's economic development was the influx of immigrants, mainly Italian and Spanish, but also French, Polish, Russian and German, who were attracted to the country because of the opportunity to exploit its undeveloped resources.

42. H. W. Singer, "The Distribution of Gains Between Investing and Borrowing Countries", *The American Economic Review*, XL, 2 (May, 1950), pp. 473–85. We quote a relevant passage, which illustrates the stimulus to growth: "The capital-exporting countries have received their repayment many times over in the following five forms: (a) possibility of building up exports of manufactures and thus transferring their population from low-productivity occupations to high-productivity occupations; (b) enjoyment of the internal economies of expanded manufacturing industries; (c) enjoyment of the general dynamic impulse radiating from industries in a progressive society; (d) enjoyment of the fruits of technical progress in primary production as main consumers of primary commodities; (e) enjoyment of a contribution from foreign consumers of manufactured articles, representing as it were their contribution to the rising incomes of the producers of manufactured articles." (p. 480).

43 The following table, which is based on information contained in a U.S. Department of Commerce publication, *Survey of Current Business*, International Investments and Earnings (August, 1955), pp. 10–20, corroborates our argument mentioned above.

TABLE 12.   U.S. DIRECT INVESTMENT 1954 (end of year data)

Branch	Developed Areas (a) (millions of dollars)	In %	Undeveloped Areas (b)	In %
Manufacturing & Distribution	4,926	54	1,877	22
Mining & Petroleum	2,782	31	4,642	53
Public Utilities	331	4	1,214	14
Miscellaneous	1,004	11	972	11
Total	9,043	100	8,705	100

(a) Canada, Western Europe, Union of South Africa, Australia, New Zealand, and Japan.

(b) Latin America, Western European dependencies, and Other Countries, mainly in Africa and Asia.

44 Nurkse believes that there is a definite possibility that this form of investment will be revived, mainly because it fills the need for public investment required by the governments of the undeveloped countries in fields in which, direct investors are not interested because of the initially unrenumerative character. Furthermore, he believes this will be necessary since, in his opinion, the United States will not continue indefinitely to make public loans and grants to these undeveloped countries. R. Nurkse, *Some Problems of Capital Accumulation in Underdeveloped Countries* (Oxford: 1953), p. 19; p. 139.

45 R. Nurkse, "International Investment Today in the Light of Nineteenth-Century Experience", *The Economic Journal*, LXIV, 256 (December, 1954), pp. 744–58.

CHAPTER 15. PRIVATE FOREIGN INVESTMENT

1 *Report to the President of the United States of the President's Material Policy Commission* (Washington, D.C.: 1952).

2 *Cf.*, *inter alia*, Public Advisory Board for Mutual Security, *A Trade and Tariff Policy in the National Interest* (Washington, D.C.: February, 1953). This report recommends the gradual introduction of a number of measures aimed both at increasing imports and at maintaining exports at a high level. Among the measures recommended are lower tariffs, especially on manufactured goods, improved tariff legislation, the abolition of provisions favoring American shipping and manufactures, etc.

3 What is objected to is not aid in the form of grants but rather the loans made through the government by the Export-Import Bank and through the participation in the International Bank for Reconstruction and Development, which up to 1954 amounted to about 25 per cent of the total bilateral foreign aid.

4 International Chamber of Commerce, *Draft International Code of Fair Treatment for Foreign Investment* (Paris: 1949), p. 7. Cleona Lewis also remarks: "The large loans that many countries have obtained in the postwar period have been mainly intergovernmental, a fact that reflects the risks inherent in the unsettled political and economic conditions of the present. But as fas as the United States is concerned, intergovernmental lending is a wartime phenomenon that may be presumed to come to an end eventually, leaving to private capital the risks and gains involved in the development of world resources." See C. Lewis, *The United States and Foreign Investment Problems* (Washington, D.C.: 1948), p. 118.

5 Most oil companies now have arrangements with the countries in which they exploit oil resources whereby the governments receive 50 per cent or some similar share of net profits. In those countries where little oil is produced, they are in a strong bargaining position, partly because of the high capital cost and particular skills required in operating oil refineries. An agreement

made by the government of India with an American oil company in November, 1951 may serve as an example. The company agreed to build a refinery valued at $ 35 million. Of the required capital, 75 per cent was to be supplied by the oil company and the remaining 25 per cent through the issue of preferred stock which could be purchased by Indians. The oil company was guaranteed foreign exchange to transfer profits and it was given the right to import crude oil duty-free and construction materials and machinery at a low tariff. The agreement made no provision for the participation of Indians in management, but the company undertook to train Indians in refining methods. Similar agreements involving other oil companies contained the additional provision that the plants would not be nationalized during the first twenty-five years of the contract term.

6 *The Economist*, "Commonwealth Development. V. The Question of Capital" (June 28, 1952), p. 568, has put it sharply but to the point: "It is not polite in international discussions to suggest that very few of the undeveloped countries that are crying out for capital can be trusted, over the next thirty to fifty years, to treat it fairly."

7 Double taxation of income from foreign investment is still a deterrent to international capital movements in some cases. The prevailing viewpoint is that the debtor country should tax foreign enterprises on the same basis as native undertakings and the creditor country should permit the investor to deduct foreign taxes on income earned abroad from his liability to his own government.

8 National income, as it has been defined up to now, does not include the income paid abroad, mainly the compensation for the services of foreign capital. There are often exaggerated ideas of the share accruing to foreign capital out of the national product of the undeveloped countries. A study by the United Nations indicates that out of the 46 countries examined in 1949, there were only 4 countries from which more than 5 per cent of the net national product flowed abroad as yield on foreign investment: Northern Rhodesia, 27 per cent; Venezuela, 17 per cent; Iran, 13 per cent in 1947; and the Dominican Republic 6 per cent in 1948. See United Nations, *National Income and Its Distribution in Under-Developed Countries* (New York: 1951).

9 *Cf.* the I.L.O. report on the Anglo-Iranian Oil Company in Iran which indicates that this company was exemplary with respect to working conditions and otherwise, by comparison with the state enterprises and private companies managed by Iranians. International Labour Organization, *Labor Conditions in the Oil Industry in Iran* (Geneva: 1950). In the above-mentioned article from *The Economist*, *op. cit.*, p. 868, we find another passage that is relevant here: "It is difficult for a community to be fully capital-minded unless it produces some savings of its own and has shown that it knows how to use them. If the capitalist is also exclusively a foreigner, the temptation to rob him, once he has made his investment, will be well-nigh irresistible."

10 A law adopted in Argentina in August, 1953 for the encouragement of foreign investment is a recent example in point. In the preamble, it was stated that only investments in mining and industry which would operate to increase exports or replace imports in the framework of the government's development plans were to be included. The law allowed such enterprises to transfer abroad, two years after the registration of the investment, an 8 per cent annual dividend; profits in excess of 8 per cent could be registered as new foreign capital for which similar transfer facilities were allowed after two years. Ten years after registration, the invested capital could itself be withdrawn in annual installments of 10 to 20 per cent of the total. Transfer of dividends and capital withdrawal had to be made at the official exchange rate. No provision was made for foreign capital already in Argentina, or for the limited margin of profit that could be remitted, and United States and British investors expressed their lack of confidence that these guarantees would not be invalidated by some future law or become worthless on account of a special exchange rate.

11 A similar declaration was made in India in April, 1949 stating: (1) that there would be no discrimination between foreign and national enterprises in general industrial policy, (2) that reasonable facilities would be extended, taking into consideration the foreign exchange position, for the transfer of profits and the repatriation of capital, and (3) that a 'fair and equitable' compensation would be paid in the event of nationalization.

12 At a conference of representatives of India and the United States, held at New Delhi from December 12–22, 1949, one of the U.S. delegates stated that American capital insisted on having a majority control in direct foreign investments. He gave specific examples of how Americans had refused to collaborate on a minority basis in Latin-American enterprises. See *Far Eastern Survey*, XIX, No. 2 (January, 1950), p. 13.

13 Postwar investments in Japan are a good example of this procedure. Up to 1952, about $ 75 million had been invested directly in Japan, of which 40 per cent was in the oil industry. Up to 1954, 430 contracts for technical aid had been concluded, of which 70 per cent were with United States firms and the balance with western European firms. From data on the guaranteed transfers of profit during the postwar years, it can be gathered that the amount of investment involved in these contracts was about 10 times greater than the amount of direct private investment.

14 For further particulars, see United Nations, *Financing of Economic Development: Recent Governmental Measures Affecting the International Flow of Private Capital* (New York: June 2, 1955).

15 International Chamber of Commerce, *op. cit.*, p. 114.

16 Articles 11 and 12 of the Charter for an International Trade Organization deal with the same subject. See U.S. Department of State, *Havana Charter for an International Trade Organization* (Publication 3206) (Washington,

D.C.: September, 1948), pp. 34-6. Articles 22-27 of the (April, 1948) Economic Agreement of Bogota among the American states are also related to this subject. Neither the Charter nor the Agreement has a legal status, since they were not adopted by the required number of governments.

17 The President of the United States Council of the International Chamber of Commerce, for example, accused the United States government of failure to make it clear to the recipient governments that help can be given only "to those countries whose governments are determined to respect contractual agreements and grant fair treatment to possible private investors." *New York Times*, January 19, 1952.

18 See W. J. Brown, Jr., "Treaty, Guaranty and Tax Inducements for Foreign Investments", *The American Economic Review*, XL, No. 2 (May, 1950), pp. 486-94. In India, negotiations for such an agreement were broken off because, although the government was inclined to offer attractive conditions to foreign capital, it would not give "unequivocal guarantees that might be interpreted as impairing the sovereign freedom of action." *New York Times*, November 13, 1951.

19 In United Nations, *The International Flow of Private Capital, 1946-1952* (New York: 1954), p. 44, it is stated that foreign electric power companies have found it increasingly difficult, despite prevailing inflationary tendencies, to obtain authorization to raise their rates, in order to compensate for higher cost of operation and replace worn-out equipment. Earnings on U.S. investment in public utilities in 1954 were $ 75 million, or 4.8 per cent of the $ 1,545 million invested in that branch of activity. In contrast, earnings on all direct U.S. investments were $ 2,306 million or 13 per cent of total private investment of $ 17,748 million (Survey of Current Business, International Investments and Earnings, August: 1955). This comparison, albeit crude, illustrates the relative low yield on foreign-controlled public utilities compared to that in other activities and also explains the decreased attraction of this form of investment.

20 One of the vice-presidents of the American and Foreign Power Company, which owns many electric plants in Latin America, has pointed out that no local capital is interested in this branch of industry since the profits to be made in commerce and by purchase of real estate are higher. See *New York Times*, November 18, 1949. H. W. Spiegel in *The Brazilian Economy* (Toronto: 1949), p. 148, also states that public service enterprises are typical foreign investments in Brazil since, in general, Brazilian capitalists are not in a position to raise the capital required for the high initial investments; even if they could, given present pricing policies they would still not be interested because of the relatively low income from this form of investment. The same argument applies also to some extent to many developed countries where the government has for economic and social reasons undertaken the responsibility of providing eletric power. However, the latter countries because of their larger

wealth and diversified industrial structure have far less to depend on capital imports for the expansion of such services.

21 *A Report to President Truman by the International Development Advisory Board* (New York: March 1951), pp. 78–86.

22 International Bank for Reconstruction and Development, *Report on the Proposal for an International Finance Corporation* (New York: April, 1952).

23 Articles of Agreement of the International Finance Corporation and Explanatory Memorandum, As approved for submission to Governments by the Executive Directors of the International Bank for Reconstruction and Development, April 11, 1955.

24 Though all or most foreign exchange resulting from export transactions must be delivered to the Central Bank in many underdeveloped countries, an export business is still in a favorable negotiating position to obtain part of its proceeds for capital service. An export enterprise can also increase its share in the yield of foreign exchange by undervaluing its exports and by other methods well-known to foreign businessmen. This is especially the case in countries in which the administrative machinery is inadequate.

25 According to one estimate, 25 per cent of U.S. imports during the period 1946–50 originated from enterprises abroad that were controlled by American investors. See S. Pizer and F. Cutler, "Foreign Investment and Income", *Survey of Current Business*, November, 1954.

26 *Op. cit.*, pp. 151–52.

27 Proposed in a speech delivered by the Indian Ambassador in New York. *New York Times*, January 30, 1952.

28 In the industrial countries, as local leadership and capital became available for industrial activity, foreign-owned or controlled enterprises were taken over by domestic interests. However, it must be remembered that this change of ownership and control was not arranged in advance by legislation.

29 For the 1940 figures, see H. B. Lary and P. Dickens, "*The Balance of International Payments of the United States in 1940*" (U.S. Department of Commerce, Economic Series, No. 19) (Washington, D.C.: 1941). For the 1954 figures, see S. Pizer and F. Cutler, "International Investments and Earnings", *Survey of Current Business*, August, 1955. The figures are not strictly comparable; the 1954 figures are based on a census of the book value in 1950 which probably undervalues these holdings. According to this census, total direct investments amounted to $ 11.8 billion, *Cf.* J. A. Zettler and F. Cutler, "United States Direct Investment in Foreign Countries", *Survey of Current Business*, December, 1952. An earlier estimate for 1949 arrives at a figure of $ 12.4 billion (S. Pizer and F. Cutler, "Private United States Direct Investments Abroad", *Survey of Current Business*, January, 1951). However, the differences between the two sets of figures do not affect the general conclusions drawn in the text.

30 Under the Economic Cooperation Act of 1948 the Export-Import Bank

of Washington was authorized to issue transfer guarantees and guarantees against loss from expropriation or confiscation for new industrial investments abroad. The fact that up to June 30, 1955, only $ 71.2 million had been invested under this guarantee indicates the relatively small interest of new U.S. private capital in European investment. See Export-Import Bank of Washington, *Twentieth Semi-annual Report to Congress for the Period January–June 1955* (Washington, D.C.: 1955), pp. 99–103.

31 *Private United States Investment in Europe and the Overseas Territories* (Paris: 1954).

32 *The International Flow of Private Capital, 1946–1952, op. cit.*

33 United Nations, *The International Flow of Private Capital, 1953–1955* (New York: June, 1956), Document E/2901.

34 From 1945 to mid-1955, public loans amounting to £ 157 million were placed on the London market by Commonwealth governments, mostly colonies. In 1954, the U.K. government agreed that Commonwealth governments might borrow on the London market not only for specific projects but for general development programs as well. Following this agreement, the government of Ceylon successfully floated a loan of £ 5 million.

CHAPTER 16. PUBLIC FOREIGN INVESTMENT

1 See Export-Import Bank of Washington, *General Policy Statement* (Washington, D.C.: September, 1945). The Bank's capital amounts to $ 1 billion. In addition, it is authorized to offer for purchase by the Secretary of the Treasury bonds or other obligations up to an amount of $ 4 billion. The Bank's total lending capacity is therefore $ 5 billion.

2 Under the Defense Production Act of 1950, the Bank was also authorized to make loans to private enterprises "for the expansion of capacity... the production of essential materials... including strategic and critical metals and minerals... in foreign countries", wherever these materials were of importance for the defense of the United States. The Bank has also acted as agent, arranging and administering the loans made under the Economic Cooperation Act of 1948 and the Mutual Security Acts of subsequent years. Also, since 1948 the Bank has been authorized to guarantee, for a fixed premium, the transfer of dollars from abroad for American investors and to insure them against loss from expropriation or confiscation of new investments approved by the Foreign Operations Administration.

3 Export-Import Bank of Washington, *Twentieth Semi-annual Report to Congress for the Period January-June 1955* (Washington, D.C.: 1955).

4 In 1954 the Export-Import Bank paid the United States Treasury interest on its capital at the rate of 2.25 per cent. On the loans received from the Treasury, the Bank pays the Treasury the same rate of interest as the Treasury

pays on its short-term debt. In 1953 this interest rate was 2 per cent per annum up to February 28 and 2.125 per cent from March to June 30. On the other hand, the International Bank borrowed on the United States market at 3 per cent per annum. According to its charter, the International Bank must build up a reserve against possible losses; therefore, it charges a 1 per cent commission over and above the rate at which it borrows. Thus it must charge its member states at least 4 per cent for long-term loans.

5 As of June 30, 1955, the International Bank had a capital of $ 9,078 million (authorized capital, $ 10 billion). This was the capital subscribed by its 56 members. However, only an initial 2 per cent had to be made available in gold or U.S. dollars, and 18 per cent in currency of member states, or non-interest-bearing short-term paper. In 1948 the sum of $ 992.5 million available for lending consisted of 20 per cent of the total United States subscription, 2 per cent in gold or dollars from the other members, the proceeds of two dollar loans placed on the open market in the United States, and certain other revenue. A number of other member-states have since made the remaining 18 per cent of their initial subscription available for loan purposes, and bonds have been placed on other markets; thus, in June, 1955 the available loan capital amounted to $ 2,262 million.

6 See, for example, International Bank for Reconstruction and Development, *Fourth Annual Report, 1948–1949* (September, 1949), p. 13: "In the long run, it is only the sustained flow of private capital that can provide external financial assistance in amounts sufficient to make a sufficient inroad on the world's development needs. In particular, it is plainly desirable that private investments, on mutually fair terms, be the major source of foreign capital for development, in order to avoid an undue burden of fixed charges, and more important, to take advantage of the essential technical and managerial skills, which are normally associated with such investments and often are not obtainable in any other way."

7 International Bank for Reconstruction and Development, *First Annual Meeting of the Board of Governors. Proceedings and Related Documents* (Washington, D.C.: October 29, 1946).

8 *Fifth Annual Report, 1949–1950* (September, 1950), pp. 7–11.

9 *Cf.,* A. E. Kahn, "Investment Criteria in Development Programs", *The Quarterly Journal of Economics*, XLV, No. 1, February 1951, p. 53: "The indirect requirements of foreign exchange to meet expanded demands for foreign consumption goods resulting from the shift of factors into domestic capital formation is less obvious, less certain, less readily measurable. To finance such needs gives the foreign lender less assurance of an efficient utilization of the funds and raises the danger of a direct dissipation of foreign exchange in enhanced consumption."

10 The Bank like the EXIM-Bank has also extended loans to Brazil and Mexico, for example, for the expansion of electric power plants owned by

foreign capital. This more or less confirms the fact that private capital was not interested in further investment in public utilities, but was attempting to strengthen the position of its existing holdings by bringing the International Bank into the picture. In connection with our previous remark as to the lag of public utilities rates behind the general price level, it is of interest that the loan to Mexico was made on the condition, *inter alia*, that the government approve higher rates and guarantee a minimum annual profit of 8 per cent on the appraised value of the foreign investment.

11 A good example is the help given by the Bank in placing a local bond issue in San Salvador, the first in the history of that country. The purpose of the bond issue was to obtain local currency for financing the internal costs of an electric power plant, for which the Bank had made a loan of $ 12.5 million to San Salvador to be used for importing the necessary machinery. See, also, *Ninth Annual Report, 1953–1954*, chap. i.

12 International Bank, *Third Annual Report, 1947–1948*, pp. 15–6. In the *Fourth Annual Report, 1948–1949* (September, 1949), pp. 8–9, we also find the following remarks which are characteristic of the Bank's way of thinking: "Perhaps the most striking single lesson which the Bank had learned in the course of its operations is how limited is the capacity of the under-developed countries to absorb capital quickly for really productive purposes... The principal limitation upon Bank financing in the development field has not been lack of money but lack of well-prepared and well-planned projects ready for immediate execution. The explanation lies in the gap which exists between the concept of development potentialities, on the one hand, and the formulation of practical propositions designed for the realization of those potentialities, on the other."

13 *Third Annual Report, 1947–1948*, p. 16.

14 *Ibid.*, p. 18.

15 *Ibid.*, p. 18. It should be mentioned that the International Bank, by placing its bonds on the capital markets of creditor countries ($ 825 million by June 30, 1955) and by selling part of debtor's obligations to institutional investors ($ 194 million by June 30, 1955) in such countries has, to some extent, revived portfolio investment. There is a definite possibility that, through the existence of an international supervisory agency such as the Bank, in due time a greater amount of private capital could thus be channeled to governments of underdeveloped countries.

16 *Ibid.*, p. 20.

17 "International Finance". In *A Survey of Contemporary Economics*, B. F. Haley, ed. (Homewood, Ill.: 1952), II, pp. 346–50.

18 In an article by J. N. Behrman, "Political Factors in U.S. International Financial Cooperation, 1945–1950", *The American Political Science Review*, XLVII, No. 2 (June, 1953), pp. 431–60, a good argument is presented to the effect that the United States was induced by its experience with the UNRRA

Aid program to place its future assistance on a bilateral basis, as a component of its foreign policy.

19 This, and the following data, are from E. S. Kerber, "Foreign Grants and Credits, U. S. Government, Fiscal Year 1955", *Survey of Current Business*, October, 1955.

20 A predecessor to this law was the Colonial Development Act of 1929, the purpose of which was to finance economic development, particularly in agriculture and industry, and "thereby promote commerce with or industry in the United Kingdom". The narrower formulation of the purpose of this earlier law is characteristic of the philosophy prevailing at that time with regard to the economic development of the backward countries. Under this law, £ 8.8 million was made available over a period of 11 years. In 1940, under a new law, the Colonial Development and Welfare Act, £ 10.4 million was allocated over a period of five years, and this was increased by another £ 19.6 million before the law of 1945 went into effect.

21 Of the total of £ 140 million, £ 34.7 was designated for general planning and research, £ 92.7 directly for the colonial regions, and £ 12.6 million was held as a reserve. In March, 1955, £ 101 million had been disbursed under the plan, of which £ 14 million and £ 16 million were disbursed in 1953–54 and 1954–55, respectively. For further details see "British Development and Welfare Act", British Information Services I.D. (Revised) February, 1952; and "Colonial Development and Welfare Acts: Return of Schemes made under the Acts by the Secretary of State for the Colonies with the concurrence of the Treasury, 1954–1955" (London: June, 1955).

22 It has been announced that, for the period 1956–60, under the Colonial Development and Welfare Acts the sum of £ 120 million is to be made available, or roughly double the previous amount on an annual basis.

23 This plan originally intended the exploitation of three million acres but later was revised to include only 40,000 acres. Apart from expenditures in Tanganyika a sum of £ 6 million was set aside for a period of seven years to 1957, and of this amount, £ 2.8 million had been spent by March 31, 1953. In 1951, responsibility for the Corporation passed from the Minister of Food to the Secretary of State for the Colonies. See, *inter alia*, Overseas Food Corporation, *Reports and Accounts for 1952–53* (London: December, 1953).

24 See, *inter alia*, Colonial Development Corporation, *Reports and Accounts for 1952 and 1953* (London: April, 1953, and April, 1954). The Colonial Development Corporation is charged with "the duty of securing the investigation, formulation and carrying out of projects for developing resources of colonial territories with a view to the expansion therein of foodstuffs and raw materials, or for other agricultural, industrial or trade development therein." It has undertaken a number of projects which have failed, among them the Gambia egg scheme (loss of £ 1 million) and the Atlantic fishery schemes (loss of more than £ 500,000). In mid-1955, the corporation had in operation

some fifty projects with a total cost of £ 57 million but in the case of only a few of these is it possible to evaluate the results as yet. The financing of the corporation through bonds has been criticized in a number of quarters, since the interest burden constitutes an overhead which is excessive for the type of commercial activities undertaken. See H. Wilson, *The War on World Poverty* (London: 1953), pp. 107–12.

25 These include French West Africa, French Equatorial Africa, Cameroon, Madagascar, French Somaliland and certain other smaller territories.

26 United Nations, *Non-Self Governing Territories: Summaries and analyses of information transmitted to the Secretary-General during 1950* (New York: 1951), II, p. 358ff. The following figures have been converted at the 1955 exchange rate of the franc. This conversion rate undervalues the sums allocated and spent prior to 1950 when the franc-dollar rate was lower. See also footnote 29.

27 Commissariat général au Plan de Modernization et d'Equipement, *Rapport annuel sur la réalisation du plan de modernization et d'équipement de l'Union française* (Paris: 1954), pp. 366–70.

28 Investments for social purposes were carried on the budgets of these regions and were not covered out of the Fund. See United Nations, *Non-Self Governing Territories*, *op. cit.*, pp. 380–87. Algeria, as a part of metropolitan France, is not included in this report.

29 Commissariat général au Plan de Modernization et d'Equipement, *op. cit.*, pp. 342–43. It is also stated that the realized investment in North Africa of 665.3 billion francs amounted to 807.9 billion francs ($ 2,308 million) at 1953 prices or about 21 per cent higher than when expressed in current prices. A table on page 23 of this report shows that 52 per cent of the investment in North Africa in 1953 was financed out of the territories' own resources.

30 Belgian Ministry of Colonies, *Plan décennal pour le développement économique et social du Congo belge* (Brussels: 1949), I, chap. xiii.

31 *The Sixth Annual Report, 1950–1951*, of the International Bank states (p. 17) that $ 500 million are to be expended in public investments and a similar amount in private investments. About one-half of the public investment in the form of loans is to be allotted for the improvement of transportation and communications, about one-tenth for electric power and the balance for improvements in agriculture, housing, public health, and education. A United Nations report has estimated that the capital of Belgian enterprises operating in the Congo increased by $ 235 million between 1947 and 1952. See United Nations, *The International Flow of Private Capital 1946–1952* (New York: 1954), pp. 44–5.

32 In 1955 a Ten Year Development Plan for Surinam was launched, with a total projected capital expenditure equivalent to $ 136 million. Of this amount, one-third will be contributed by Surinam itself and the remainder by the Netherlands government in the form of equal amounts in grants and loans.

33 Commonwealth Consultative Committee, *The Colombo Plan for Cooperative Economic Development in South and South East Asia* (London: 1950). See, also, J. R. E. Carr-Gregg, *The Colombo Plan: A Commonwealth Program for South-East Asia* (Carnegie Endowment for International Peace, *International Conciliation*, No. 467) (New York: January 1951).

34 The Colombo Plan organization has tended to blur the distinction between donors and recipients. Some of the less developed countries, e.g. India and Ceylon, have extended aid, especially by way of fellowships, to other members of the group. Since 1951, Burma, Cambodia, Laos, Viet-Nam, Nepal, Indonesia, the Philippines, Thailand, and Japan have also become members of the organization. The United States government joined the Consultative Committee of the Organization but has stipulated that it will provide economic assistance only in bilateral agreement with each country.

35 The share of India in the program was £ 1,379 million, that of Pakistan £ 280 million, that of Ceylon £ 102 million, while the joint plans for Malaya, Singapore, Sarawak, and North Borneo involved £ 107 million.

36 Australia pledged $ 70 million as its contribution over the six year period; New Zealand and Canada were to contribute annually about $ 2.8 million and $ 25 million, respectively, so that their contributions for the duration of the plan will probably amount to $ 16.8 and $ 150 million, respectively. Great Britain, in addition to its releases from sterling accounts, made available $ 168 million, mainly for the programs of Malaya, Singapore, Sarawak, and North Borneo. Under its bilateral aid program, the United States gave about $ 841 million in grants over the period 1950–55, while up to June 1955, the International Bank had loaned $ 260 million to countries in the area. It was estimated in 1954 that total external assistance for the period of the plan would amount to $ 1.5 billion, as compared with an estimated $ 8 billion which would be spent by the governments concerned in the execution of their programs. The latter figure is substantially higher than the $ 5.2 billion mentioned earlier, since it takes into account the upward revision of the cost of some of the projects and includes estimates for the new countries admitted to the Plan.

37 The Colombo Plan for Cooperative Economic Development in south and southeast Asia, *First Annual Report of the Consultative Committee* (H.M.S.O., Cmd. 8529) (London: 1952), *Second Annual Report of the Consultative Committee*, (H.M.S.O., Cmd. 9016) (London: 1953), *Third Annual Report of the Consultative Committee*(H.M.S.O., Cmd. 9336) (London: 1954) and *Fourth Annual Report of the Consultative Committee* (Singapore: 1955).

38 In the Fourth Annual Report (*op. cit.*, p. 3) a table is shown from which it can be calculated that the total development expenditures for the period 1953–55 in eight of the more important countries and territories in the region was £ 2,001 million ($ 5.6 billion). Of this amount, 41 per cent was spent for agriculture (including irrigation and power projects), 27 per cent for transport

and communications, 8 per cent for industry and mining, and 24 per cent for social welfare. If those percentages are compared with the planned breakdown of expenditure in the original program as mentioned before, it will be seen that actual outlays for transport and communications, industry and mining were apparently below, and the share of social welfare above the initial targets.

39 See, for example, T. Balogh, "International Equilibrium and U.S. Private Investment", *Bulletin of Statistics*, Oxford University, August, 1951, pp. 247-55.

40 *World Economic Development: Effects on Advanced Industrial Countries* (Montreal: 1944), pp. 69-72. The calculations were made by R. W. Tufts and are described in detail in an appendix to the book.

41 This amounts (in 1936 dollars) to $ 2.7 billion, $ 4.7 billion, $ 9.1 billion and $ 10,5 billion a year, respectively, for each decade. For the first ten years following 1910, it has been calculated that 40 per cent of the capital investment in Japan consisted of imported capital goods, but that this percentage had fallen to 34 per cent in 1930-34. Staley believes that these percentages give some indication of the amount of capital goods Asian countries would be purchasing from the industrial countries if Asia develops in the same manner as Japan.

42 This calculation is based on an article by P. N. Rosenstein-Rodan, "Problems of Industrialization of Eastern and South-Eastern Europe", *Economic Journal*, LIII, No. 210 (June-September, 1943), pp. 202-11. This writer assumes that to transfer the agricultural excess population (estimated at 20-25 per cent of the total population of 100-110 million) in this area and provide nonagricultural employment for part of the increase in working population over a ten-year period (1946-56) additional jobs in industry, etc., would have to be created for 12 million active workers. On the basis of Rosenstein-Rodan's estimate of £ 300 to £ 350 investment per capita required to transfer workers to industrial activities, Staley calculated that a sum of £. 3.6 billion, or $ 14.5 billion, of investment would be necessary for such a transformation. Of this amount, an estimated $ 7.3 billion would have to be contributed from external sources or roughly $ 750 million per annum. K. Mandelbaum, using a far more intricate method of calculation, has drawn up an imaginary five-year plan for the same area. He estimates that £ 1.5 billion in new capital, exclusive of land, would be required over this period for industry to absorb the assumed surplus of 10 to 12 million active workers and the estimated average increase of 400,000 additional workers in the labor force during this period. Of this amount, £ 750 million would have to be financed by foreign loans, or an average of £ 150 million per annum ($ 645 million at the 1947 rate of exchange). See K. Mandelbaum, *The Industrialization of Backward Areas* (Oxford: 1947), p. 86.

43 E. Staley, *op. cit.*, pp. 78-9. He deduces from this that such an import

demand, although not that alone, would be a substantial stimulus for the maintenance of a high employment level in the industrial countries. He also compares (*Ibid.*, p. 80) his own estimates of the capital needs of under-developed countries with the prewar annual capital outflow from industrial countries (United Kingdom, $ 900 million; France, $ 240–350 million; Germany, $ 125 million, and the United States, $ 125–150 million), and reaches the conclusion that his estimates are realistic if it is granted that the postwar productive capacity will be greater than that of the prewar period. He realizes that primary attention will be given to the reconstruction of the war-devastated industrial countries, through grants and loans, and also that new industrial countries like Australia and Canada will initially be better prepared to absorb foreign capital for economic expansion than the backward countries will be. These facts, however, coincide with his assumptions that foreign investment for the underdeveloped regions will assume larger proportions at a later phase. The Middle East, including Turkey and Egypt, have not been included in Staley's calculations, but A. Bonné has estimated, on the basis of a capital requirement of £ 225 per new worker, that an investment of £ 2.5 billion (at 1939 prices) would be necessary for a development program between 1943–62 in this region. See his book, *The Economic Development of the Middle East* (New York: 1945), pp. 110–11. Total domestic savings over this period are assumed to be £ 1.6 billion (6.5 per cent of the estimated national income) or £ 78 million a year, so that £ 916 million, or £ 45 million a year, would have to be provided from abroad.

44 C. Clark, *The Economics of 1960* (London: 1944), chap. vi, "The Availability of Capital", pp. 72–83.

45 The high potential capital export of Great Britain and of France, Clark says, (*op. cit.*, p. 76) is connected with the fact that there are few opportunities for investment within those countries themselves, so that a large part of their savings must seek investment abroad.

46 *Ibid.*, p. 83. Clark assumes in his postulates a reasonable measure of political stability during this 'capital-hungry' phase. Later (*Ibid.*, p. 113) he reiterates that this reasoning is dependent on the condition that there will be economic development in Asia and that this part of the world will become an importer of food as well as capital.

47 C. Clark, "The World Will Save Money in the 1950's ", *Fortune*, XLII, No. 1 (July, 1950), pp. 88–91; 117–28.

48 *International Investment and Financial Facilities* (Washington, D.C.: 1949), reprinted in United Nations, *Methods of Financing Economic Development in Under-Developed Countries* (Lake Success: 1949), pp. 43–88.

49 An increased debt burden of $ 40 billion over a ten-year period was considered reasonable; it would mean an additional annual burden of $ 3 billion in service charges on the total balance of payment. *Ibid.*, p. 53. Although not explicitly stated in the report, this calculation probably as-

sumed repayment over a twenty-year period at an interest rate of 2.5 per cent.

50 *Measures for the Economic Development of Underdeveloped Countries* (New York: 1951), pp. 75–80.

51 The figure of $ 2,500 should be taken as an average, since light industries require a lower investment per capita and heavy industries and public utilities a higher one. It also allows for the necessary research and training. This figure is about twice as high as Rosenstein-Rodan's estimate (*op. cit.*, p. 210) but the difference can probably be attributed primarily to price changes.

52 The potential capital export of a country depends on the volume of its private and public savings, the willingness to invest abroad, the practical opportunities for investing abroad, and the feasibility of creating and maintaining a surplus in its balance of trade and services. One of the anomalies in the investment situation is that, although the United States should play the role of a creditor country, conditions for investment are, in many cases, more favorable in the United States than in other countries not only for U.S. citizens but for nationals of other countries as well.

53 "Development is not something which can be sketched on a drawing board, and then be brought to life through the magic wand of dollar aid. If proof of this is needed, it is supplied by the numerous reports which have been compiled during recent years suggesting comprehensive development schemes for various areas of the world, most of which are now gathering dust on library shelves. If money were all that were required to translate these projects into reality, the Bank's primary task would have been the relatively simple one of allocating its resources among various claimant schemes. In point of fact, however, the principal limitation upon Bank financing in the development field has not been lack of money but lack of well-prepared and well-planned projects ready for immediate execution." J. J. McCloy, "The Lesson of the World Bank", *Foreign Affairs*, 27, No. 4 (July, 1949), p. 554.

54 The International Bank would probably be in the best position to carry out such a study, but its president, in his addresses to the annual meetings of the Bank, has generally criticized mass investment plans in undeveloped countries because the lack of leadership, trained labor, and facilities for transportation and electric power hamper the absorption of foreign capital. See: International Bank for Reconstruction and Development, *Summary Proceedings*, Fifth, Sixth, Seventh, and Eighth Annual Meetings of the Board of Directors (1949–50, 1950–51, 1951–52 and 1952–53).

55 This is partly due to the scanty data available on the international capital flow out of and into Europe, including the repayment of debts and the settlements, arranged for foreign holdings taken over by local interests out of accumulated balances (especially in Latin America and India).

56 Lord Ogmore, quoted in British Information Services, Reference Division (New York: October, 1951), ID 1032.

57 E. Staley, *op. cit.*, chap. II, pp. 83–91. In 1943 Staley thought that the International Bank, whose establishment the United States government had just proposed, would perform this function.

58 C. Clark, *The Economics of 1960, op. cit.*, pp. 111–15.

59 For twenty years or longer, debtor-creditor relations would remain fixed as established by the World Bank, since any attempt to demand repayment prematurely might have catastrophic consequences. Clark and other authors have failed to give the attention it deserves to the problem of how the world economy would be affected by the pressure upon the balance of payments on current account of underdeveloped countries, by the requirements of debt service (interest and amortization) which grow proportionally with the accumulation of foreign debt.

60 V.K.R.V. Rao, "Suggestions for the Creation of a New International Agency for Financing Basic Economic Development", printed as an annex in United Nations, *Methods of Financing Economic Development in Under-Developed Countries* (Lake Success: 1949), pp. 129–32.

61 The International Bank (*Fourth Annual Report 1948–1949, op. cit.*, p. 14) had this plan in mind when it said: "The desire of the underdeveloped countries to set the speed of their development faster than their own resources will permit has sometimes led to the suggestion that loans should be made, either by the Bank or by some new agency created for the purpose, at nominal interest rates and repayable over a very long period of time. Such loans, it should be noted, would probably involve a substantial international subsidy, and to that extent, a disguised grant to the borrower. If the governments of those few countries in a position to provide international subsidies should consider it desirable in certain instances to provide supplementary grants in order to expedite the processes of economic development, it would be the Bank's judgment that such assistance should be rendered as outright grants rather than in some form of 'fuzzy' loans which would tend to cast discredit upon the integrity of normal international investments."

62 These experts were: J. M. Clark, (United States), A. Smithies, (United States), N. Kaldor (Great Britain), P. Uri (France), and E. R. Walker (Australia). The proposals here discussed will be found on pages 90–4 of this report.

63 United Nations, *Measures for the Economic Development of Under-Developed Countries, op. cit.*, especially pp. 82–7. The members of this group were: A. Baltra Cortiz (Chile), D. R. Gadgil (India), G. Hakim (Lebanon), W. A. Lewis (Great Britain), and Th. W. Schultz (United States).

64 Up to the end of 1955, the Bank had dispatched survey missions to British Guiana, Ceylon, Colombia, Cuba, Guatemala, Iraq, Jamaica, Jordan, Malaya, Mexico, Nicaragua, Nigeria, Surinam, Syria, and Turkey. In addition, its experts had undertaken studies in connection with loan applications in almost all member countries.

65 United Nations, *Measures for the Economic Development of Under-Developed Countries, op. cit.*, p. 82.

66 In this connection, the remarks of McCloy, *op. cit.*, p. 558, on the establishment of such an agency, may be quoted: "Finally, I feel strongly that any expanded program of financial assistance for development should, to the fullest extent practicable, be under international rather than national auspices. I recognize that the United States Government, which would undoubtedly be the heaviest contributor to any such program, might well wish control over the funds it supplied in order to secure immediate bargaining advantages. But the longer-term disadvantages of such control, in my judgment, far outweigh the immediate advantages. Nothing would be more productive of ill-will toward the United States than to have the other nations of the world over a long period of time regard the United States as the principal source of foreign capital. Under such circumstances, those receiving financial aid would not regard it as a favor but as a matter of right, while those who received nothing, or less than they thought they were entitled to, would consider the United States guilty of unfriendly discrimination. There would be no end to the calls made upon the United States and, should the United States itself decide to halt the program, it would be confronted by outcries from every side. To the extent that an international rather than a national agency is the instrument of investment, these consequences can be mitigated if not wholly avoided."

67 Resolution A/32 of January 14, 1952. Discussion of the Second Committee of the General Assembly of the United Nations, 162nd to 168th session, December 7–18, 1951.

68 See his subsequent report, United Nations, Economic Development of Under-Developed Countries, *Special United Nations Fund for Economic Development* (New York: 1955), discussed at the 1955 session. For the latest position on the United Nations Special Fund for Economic Development, in particular the views of governments of developed and underdeveloped countries on the establishment, role, structure, and operations of such a Fund, see United Nations, *Interim Report of the Ad Hoc Committee on the Question of the Establishment of a Special United Nations Fund for Economic Development prepared in accordance with General Assembly Resolution 923 (X)*, Document E/2896 (New York: June 8, 1956). As regards the first point the industrial countries Czechoslovakia, Denmark, France, Poland, and the Netherlands were in favor of setting up the Fund without awaiting agreement on disarmament, while the United Kingdom wanted the Fund's establishment deferred until a program of internationally supervised worldwide disarmament under the auspices of the United Nations had been embarked upon. Canada opposed the immediate establishment of the Fund, while New Zealand stated that it would be unable, in view of its existing commitments to contribute to the Fund should it be established. The U.S. and the U.S.S.R. did not submit a reply on any of the

above mentioned topics. All undeveloped countries were as might be expected in favor of setting up the Fund without delay.

69 *Report to the President on Foreign Economic Policies* (Washington, D.C.: November 10, 1950), pp. 61–73.

70 Partners in Progress (New York: March, 1951), p. 71 ff.

71 See, for example, *The Economist*, "Self Help for Developing Nations", January 31, 1953, in which a plea is made for more discriminating assistance under the international and bilateral aid programs, namely, that aid be granted only to those countries showing a desire for development and that it not be given to countries characterized by maladministration, corruption, and political instability. In our opinion, the formulation of the question in this article is oversimplified, since there is not a single undeveloped country that could give guarantees on all these points. It is, moreover, possible, that if such conditions were insisted on, aid might be withheld from countries which, because of their poverty, are precisely those most in need of foreign assistance.

Conclusion

1 E. Staley, *The Future of Under-developed Countries; Political Implications of Economic Development* (New York: 1954), and B. F. Hoselitz *et. al.*, *The Progress of Under-developed Areas* (Chicago: 1952).

2 *The Economic Organization of Agriculture* (New York: 1953), p. 4.

3 Queensland Bureau of Industry, "Levels of Real National Product Per Man Hour", *Review of Economic Progress* (Brisbane, Australia: April, 1949), I, No. 4.

4 Schultz, *op. cit.*, p. 32. By a 'high food drain' is meant a situation in which 75 per cent or more of income is spent on food.

5 In a highly developed country like the United States, the weight of food consumed per person per annum was 1,576 pounds in 1909 and 1,573 pounds in 1949. Schultz, *op. cit.*, p. 46.

6 *Processes and Problems of Industrialization in Under-developed Countries* (New York: 1955), Appendix B, The Present Status of Secondary Industry in Under-Developed Countries (pp. 141–52). The comparison is even more unfavorable for the least developed countries since, in all compilations, Argentina and the Union of South Africa are counted among the backward areas and in some cases Australia and New Zealand are in the latter group.

BIBLIOGRAPHY

Bibliography

Abramovitz, M. "Economics of Growth" (*A Survey of Contemporary Economics.* Ed. B. F. Haley, Vol. II). Homewood, Illinois: 1952, pp. 132–82.

Allen, G. C. *Japanese Industry: Recent Development and Present Condition.* New York: 1940.

Allen, G. C. "Economic Progress, Retrospect and Prospect", *The Economic Journal*, LX, No. 239 (September, 1950), pp. 463–80.

Allen, G. C. and Donnithorne, A. G. *Western Enterprise in Far Eastern Economic Development: China and Japan.* London: 1954.

Allen, W. R. "The International Trade Philosophy of Cordell Hull (1907–1933)", *The American Economic Review*, XLIII, No. 1 (March 1953), pp. 101–16.

Anstey, V. *The Economic Development of India* (3rd ed.). London–Toronto: 1936.

Asahi, I. *The Economic Strength of Japan.* Tokyo: 1939.

Ashton, T. S. "Some Statistics of the Industrial Revolution in Britain", *The Manchester School of Economic and Social Studies*, XVI, No. 2 (May, 1948), pp. 214–34.

Aubrey, H. G. "The Long-Term Picture of United States Imports and its Implications for Primary Producing Countries", *The American Economic Review*, XLV, No. 2 (May, 1955), pp. 270–87.

Baldwin, R. E. "Secular Movements in the Terms of Trade", *The American Economic Review*, XLV, No. 2 (May, 1955), pp. 259–69.

Balogh, T. "International Equilibrium and U.S. Private Investments", *Bulletin of Statistics* (Oxford University) (August, 1951), pp. 247–55.

Bank of England. *U.K. Overseas Investments 1938 to 1948.* London: 1950.

Bauer, P. T. and Yamey, B. S. "Economic Progress and Occupational Distribution", *The Economic Journal*, LXI, No. 244 (December, 1951), pp. 741–55.

———. "Further Notes on Economic Progress and Occupational Distribution", *The Economic Journal*, LXIV, No. 253 (March, 1954), pp. 98–106.

Baumol, W. J. *Economic Dynamics.* New York: 1951.

Baykov, A. *The Development of the Soviet Economic System.* New York: 1948.

———. "Industry and Agriculture in the U.S.S.R.", *The Political Quarterly*, XXIII, No. 1 (January–March, 1952).

Bean, L. H. *International Industrialization and Per Capita Income* (Studies in Income and Wealth). New York: National Bureau of Economic Research, Inc., 1946.

Behrman, J. N. "Political Factors in U.S. International Financial Cooperation (1945–1950)", *The American Political Science Review*, XLVII, No. 2
(June, 1953), pp. 431–60.

Belshaw, H. "Observations on Industrialization for Higher Incomes", *The
Economic Journal*, LVII, No. 22 (September 1947), 379–87.

Bennett, M. K. "Disparities in Consumption Levels", *The American Economic
Review*, XLI, No. 4 (September, 1951), pp. 632–49.

Bernstein, E. M. *Inflation in Relation to Economic Development* ("International
Monetary Fund Staff Papers", Vol. II, [No. 3]). Washington, D.C.:
November, 1952.

Boeke, J. J. *The Structure of the Netherlands Indian Economy*. New York: 1942.

Bloch, H. S. "La Politique Fiscale des Pays Sous-dévelopés", *Revue de Science
et de Législation Financières* (January–March, 1953).

Bohr, K. A. "Investment Criteria for Manufacturing Industries in Under-
Developed Countries", *The Review of Economics and Statistics*, XXXVI,
No. 2 (May, 1954), pp. 157–66.

Bonné, A. *The Economic Development of the Middle East*. New York: 1945.

———. *State and Economics in the Middle East*. London: 1948.

Bottemanne, G. J. *Het Zeevisserij Vraagstuk van Indonesië*. Department of
Economic Affairs in Indonesia, December, 1946.

Bowley, A. L. *Wages and Income in the United Kingdom Since 1860*. Cambridge:
1937.

Brown, W. A. Jr. "Treaty, Guaranty, and Tax Inducements for Foreign
Investments", *The American Economic Review*, XL, No. 2 (May, 1950),
pp. 486–94.

Buchanan, N. S. *International Investment and Domestic Welfare*. New York: 1945.

———. "Deliberate Industrialization for Higher Incomes", *The Economic
Journal* (December, 1946), pp. 533–53.

———. "International Investment" (*A Survey of Contemporary Economics*, ed.
B. F. Haley, Vol. II). Homewood, Illinois: 1952, pp. 307–54.

———. and Ellis, H. S. *Approaches to Economic Development*. New York:
1955.

Cairncross, A. K. *Home and Foreign Investment, 1870–1913* ("Studies in Capital
Accumulation"). Cambridge: 1953.

Carr, E. H. *The Twenty Years' Crisis, 1919–1939*. Edinburgh: 1939.

———. *Conditions of Peace*. New York: 1944.

Carr-Gregg, J. R. E. *The Colombo Plan, A Commonwealth Program for Southeast
Asia* ("Carnegie Endowment for International Peace, International
Conciliation", No. 467, January, 1951).

Chang Chih-yi. "China's Population Problem: A Chinese View", *Pacific
Affairs*, XXII, No. 4 (December, 1949), pp. 339–56.

Chapman, J. G. "Real Wages in the Soviet Union (1928–1952)", *The Review
of Economics And Statistics*, XXXVI, No. 2 (May, 1954), pp. 134–56.

Chenery, H. B. "The Application of Investment Criteria", *The Quarterly Journal of Economics*, LXVII, No. 1 (February, 1953), pp. 76–96.

——. "The Role of Industrialization in Development Programs", *The American Economic Review*, XLV, No. 2 (May, 1955), pp. 40–57.

Clapham, J. H. *An Economic History of Modern Britain, The Early Railway Age 1820–1850*. Cambridge: 1950.

——. *An Economic History of Modern Britain, Free Trade 1880–1885*. Cambridge: 1952.

Clark, C. *Conditions of Economic Progress*. London: 1940.

——. *Conditions of Economic Progress* (2nd ed.). London: 1951.

——. *The Economics of 1960*. London: 1944.

——. *World Resources and Population* ("Proceedings of the United Nations Scientific Conference on the Conservation and Utilization of Resources") United Nations, February, 1949.

——. "The World will Save Money in the 1950's", *Fortune* (July, 1950).

——. Capital Resources and their Accumulation", *Review of Economic Progress*, II (1950).

——. "Population Growth and Living Standards", *International Labour Review*, LXVIII, No. 2 (August, 1953), pp. 99–117.

Clough, S. B. and Cole, C. W. *Economic History of Europe*. Boston: 1941.

Colombo Plan for Co-operative Economic Development in South and South-East Asia. ("First Annual Report of the Consultative Committee", H.M.S.O., Cmd. 8529. London: 1952.), ("Second Annual Report of the Consultative Committee", H.M.S.O., Cmd. 9016. London: 1953.), ("Third Annual Report of the Consultative Committee", H.M.S.O., Cmd. 9336. London: 1954.), ("Fourth Annual Report of the Consultative Committee". Singapore: 1955.).

Commonwealth Consultative Committee. *The Colombo Plan for Co-operative Economic Development in South and South-East Asia*. London: 1950.

Datta, B. *The Economics of Industrialization*. Calcutta: 1952.

Davis, K. *Demographic Fact and Policy in India* ("Demographic Studies of Selected Areas of Rapid Growth", Milbank Memorial Fund). New York: 1944, pp. 35–57.

——. *The Population of India and Pakistan*. Princeton, N. J.: 1951.

Derksen, J. B. D. and Tinbergen, J. "Berekeningen over de economische betekenis van Nederlands-Indië voor Nederland", *Monthly of the Central Bureau of Statistics*, No. 10/12 (1945).

Dobb, M. *Soviet Economic Development since 1917*. London: 1948.

——. "Note sur le degré d'intensité capitaliste des investissements dans les pays sous-développés", *Economie Appliquée*, VII, No. 3 (July–September, 1954), pp. 299–318.

Domar, E. D. "Expansion and Employment", *The American Economic Review*, XXXVII, No. 1 (March, 1947), pp. 34–55.

Domar, E. D. "The Problem of Capital Accumulation", *The American Economic Review*, XXXVIII, No. 5 (December, 1948), pp. 777–94.

Dominguez, L. M. "International Trade, Industrialization and Economic Growth". Pan American Union, working paper. Washington, D.C.: 1953.

Duesenberry, J. S. *Income, Saving and the Theory of Consumer Behavior*. Cambridge, Mass.: 1949.

Economist, The. "Commonwealth Development", Articles I–VI (May 31, June 7, June 14, June 28, July 5, July 12, 1952).

———. "Self-Help for Developing Nations" (January 31, 1953).

———. "The Economy of Development" (August 22, 1953).

Edelman, C. H. *Sociale en Economische Bodemkunde*. Amsterdam: 1949.

Ellsworth, P. T. *Chile: An Economy in Transition*. New York: 1945.

Export-Import Bank of Washington. *Semi-Annual Reports*.

Finegood, I. M. "A Critical Analysis of Some Prevailing Concepts Concerning Soviet Agriculture", *Soviet Studies*, IV, No. 11 (July, 1952).

Flores de la Peña, H. *Crecimiento Demografico, Desarollo Agricola y Desarollo Economico* ("Proceedings of the World Population Conference", Rome, 1954, Vol II). United Nations, New York : 1955, pp. 301-20.

Food and Agriculture Organization of the United Nations. *Forest Resources and their Utilization*. Document E/CN.1/Sub. 3/28, 15 March, 1950.

Frankel, S. H. *Capital Investment in Africa, Its Course and Effects*. London–New York: 1938.

———. "Industrialization of Agricultural Countries and the Possibilities of a New International Division of Labour", *Economic Journal*, LIII, Nos. 210–211 (June–September, 1943), pp. 188–201.

———. *Some Conceptual Aspects of International Economic Development of Underdeveloped Territories* ("Essays in International Finance", No. 14 [May, 1952]). Princeton, N. J.

———. *The Economic Impact of Underdeveloped Societies*. Oxford: 1953.

Ghosh, D. *Pressure of Population and Economic Efficiency in India*. New Delhi: 1946.

Glesinger, E. *The Coming Age of Wood*. New York: 1949.

Gopalaswami, R. A. *Report of the Census of India, 1951* (Vol. I). New Delhi: 1953.

Gourou, P. *Les Pays Tropicaux*. Paris: 1948.

Government of India. *The First Five Year Plan*. New Delhi: 1951.

———. Ministry of Finance. *First Report of the National Income Committee*. New Delhi: 1951.

Gray, G. W. "Blueprint for Hungry Nations", *The N.Y. Times Magazine* (January 1, 1950).

Hamilton, E. J. "Profit Inflation and the Industrial Revolution, 1751–1800", *The Quarterly Journal of Economics*, LVI (1942), pp. 256–73.

Hansen, A. H. Economic Progress and Declining Population Growth, *The American Economic Review*, XXIX, No. 1 (March, 1939), pp. 1–15.

Hansen. A. H. *Fiscal Policy and Business Cycles*. New York: 1941.

——. *Monetary Theory and Fiscal Policy*. New York: 1949.

Hanson, S. G. *Economic Development in Latin America*. Washington, D.C.: 1951.

Hansson, K. E. "A General Theory of the System of Multilateral Trade", *The American Economic Review*, XLII, No. 1 (March, 1952), pp. 59–68.

Harris, C. D. "Growing Food by Decree in Soviet Russia", *Foreign Affairs*, 33, No. 2 (January, 1955).

Harris, S. E. *et al. Economic Problems of Latin America*. New York: 1944.

Harrod, R. F. *Towards a Dynamic Economics*. London: 1948.

Heckscher, E. F. *Mercantilism*. London: 1931.

Hicks, U. K. *Public Finance*. London – Cambridge: 1947.

Hoffmann, W. *Studien und Typen der Industrialisierung, Ein Beitrag zur Quantitativen Analyse historischer Wirtschaftsprozesse*. Jena: 1931.

——. *Wachstum und Wachstumsformen der englischen Industriewirtschaft*. Jena: 1940.

Holdsworth, M. "Soviet Central Asia, 1917–1940", *Soviet Studies*, III, No. 3 (January, 1952).

Hoselitz, B. F. *et al. The Progress of Underdeveloped Areas*. Chicago: 1952.

Hubbard, G. E. and Gregory, T. E. *Eastern Industrialization and its Effect on the West*. London: 1935.

Hughes, L. H. *The Mexican Cultural Mission Programme*. UNESCO, Paris: 1951.

Hunter, J. M. "Foreign Investment and Under-developed Countries", *The Journal of Political Economy*, LXI, No. 1 (February, 1953), pp. 15–24.

Imlah, A. H. "The Terms of Trade of the United Kingdom 1798–1913", *The Journal of Economic History*, X, No. 2 (November, 1949), pp. 170–94.

——. "British Balance of Payments and Exports of Capital, 1816–1913, *The Economic History Review, Second Series*, V, No. 2 (1952), pp. 208–40.

Institute for Social Sciences, University of Stockholm. *Wages, Cost of Living and National Income in Sweden, 1860–1930. The Cost of Living in Sweden*, Vol. I, 1933. *Wages in Sweden, 1860–1930*, Vol. II, 2 parts, 1933. *National Income of Sweden, 1861–1930*, Vol. III, 1937. Stockholm.

International Bank for Reconstruction and Development, Annual Reports, Summary of Proceedings.

——. *The Basis of a Development Program for Colombia*. Washington, D.C.: 1950.

——. *Report on Cuba*. Washington, D.C.: 1951.

——. *The Economic Development of Guatemala*. Washington, D.C.: 1951.

——. *The Economy of Turkey*. Washington, D.C.: 1951.

——. *Report on the Proposal for an International Finance Corporation*. New York: April, 1952.

——. *The Economic Development of Iraq*. Baltimore: 1952.

——. *The Economy of Ceylon*. Baltimore: 1953.

International Bank for Reconstruction and Development, *The Economic Development of Mexico*. Baltimore: 1953.

International Chamber of Commerce. *Draft International Code of Fair Treatment for Foreign Investors*. Paris: August, 1949.

International Development Advisory Board. *Partners in Progress*. New York: March, 1951.

International Labour Office. *The Economic Background of Social Policy Including Problems of Industrialization*. New Delhi: 1947.

——. *Labour Conditions in the Oil Industry in Iran*. Geneva: 1950.

International Monetary Fund. *A Report on the Process of Inflation in Chile Together with Recommendations*. Washington, D.C.: November, 1950.

Iversen, C. *Aspects of the Theory of International Capital Movements*. Copenhagen/London: 1935.

Jasny, N. *The Socialized Agriculture of the U.S.S.R., Plans and Performance*. Stamford, Cal.: July, 1949.

——. "Kolkhozy — The Achilles Heel of the Soviet Regime", *Soviet Studies*, III, No. 2 (October, 1951).

——. "Prospects for Soviet Farm Output and Labor", *The Review of Economics and Statistics*, XXXVI, No. 4 (November, 1954).

Jenks, L. H. *The Migration of British Capital to 1875*. New York: 1927.

Jervis, F. R. J. "The Handicap of Britain's Early Start", *The Manchester School of Economic and Social Studies*, XV, No. 1 (January, 1947), pp. 112–22.

Johnston, B. F. "Agricultural Productivity and Economic Development in Japan", *The Journal of Political Economy*, LIX, No. 6 (1951), pp. 498–513.

Kahn, A. E. "Investment Criteria in Development Programs", *The Quarterly Journal of Economics*, LXV, No. 1 (February, 1951), pp. 38–61.

Keen, B. A. *Agricultural Development of the Middle East*. 1946.

Keenan, J. L. *A Steel Man in India*. New York: 1943.

Keirstead, B. S. *The Theory of Economic Change*. Toronto: 1948.

Kerber, E. S. "Foreign Grants and Credits, U.S. Government, Fiscal Year 1955", *Survey of Current Business* (October, 1955).

Keynes, J. M. *A Treatise on Money*. New York: 1930.

——. *Essays in Persuasion*. New York: 1932.

——. *The General Theory of Employment, Interest and Money*. London: 1936.

Knowles, L. C. A. *Economic Development in the Nineteenth Century*. London: 1932. Reprint, 1948.

Koelie Budget Commissie. Eindrapport van de, *De levenswijze van de arbeiders in de Cultures en de Tanis op Java in 1939–1940*. Batavia: 1941.

Kuznets, S. *Patterns of Industrialization*. United Nations: mimeographed, 1949.

——. *Economic Change, Selected Essays in Business Cycles, National Income and Economic Growth*. New York: 1953.

——. "Economic Growth and Income Equality", *The American Economic Review*, XLV, No. 1 (March, 1955), pp. 1–28.

Lary, H. B. and Dickens, P. P. *The Balance of International Payments of the United States* ("Economic Series", No. 19). U.S. Department of Commerce, Washington: 1941.

League of Nations. *The Network of World Trade*. Geneva: 1942.

———. *Industrialization and Foreign Trade*. New York: 1945.

———. *The Course and Control of Inflation, A Review of Monetary Experience in Europe After World War I*. New York: 1946.

Lewis, C. *The United States and Foreign Investment Problems*. Washington, D.C.: 1948.

Lewis, W. A. "The Industrialization of the British West Indies", *Caribbean Economic Review*, II, No. 1 (May, 1950), pp. 1–61.

———. "World Production, Prices and Trade 1870–1960", *The Manchester School of Economic and Social Studies*, XX, No. 2 (May 1952), pp. 105–38.

———. *Report on Industrialization and the Gold Coast*. Accra, G. P.: 1953.

———. *Aspects of Industrialization*. Cairo: National Bank of Egypt, 1953.

———. "Economic Development with Unlimited Supplies of Labour", *The Manchester School of Economic and Social Studies*, XXII, No. 2 (May, 1954), pp. 139–91.

Lokanathan, P. S. *Industrial Organization in India*. London: 1935.

———. "Cottage Industries and the Plan", *Eastern Economist*. New Delhi (July 23, 1943).

Lossing Buck, J. *Land Utilization in China*. Chicago, Ill.: 1937.

Loveday, A. *Britain and World Trade*. London: 1931.

Madariaga, S. de,. *The Rise of the Spanish American Empire*. New York: 1947.

Mahalanobis, P. C. *Draft Recommendations for the Formulation of the Second Five-Year Plan, 1956–1961*. New Delhi: March, 1955.

Mandelbaum, K. *The Industrialization of Backward Areas*. Oxford: 1945.

Mantoux, P. *The Industrial Revolution in the Eighteenth Century*. London: 1928.

Marshall, A. *Principles of Economics*. London: 1898.

———. *Industry and Trade*. London: 1927.

Max, C. H. *Informe sobre la Inflacion chilena*. Santiago: 1948.

May, S., et al. *Costa Rica: A Study in Economic Development*. New York: 1951.

May, S. *The Outlook for Industrial Raw Materials Demand in 1980 and its Relation to Economic Development* ("Proceedings of the World Population Conference", Rome, 1954, Vol. V). United Nations, New York: 1955, pp. 107–47.

McCloy, J. J. "The Lesson of the World Bank", *Foreign Affairs*, 27, No. 4 (July 1949).

Mill, J. S. *Principles of Political Economy* (7th ed.). London–New York: 1871.

Ministry of Finance and Revenue. *Economic Survey of Burma 1951*. Rangoon: 1951.

Mintz, Ilse. *Deterioration in the Quality of Foreign Bonds Issued in the United States 1920–1930*. New York: 1953.

Moore, W. E. *Economic Demography of Eastern and Southern Europe*. League of Nations, Geneva: 1945.

Moore, W. E. *Industrialization and Labor: Social Aspects of Economic Development.* Ithaca: 1951.

Mukerjee Radhakamal. *Races, Land and Food.* New York: 1946.

Myint, H. "The Gains from International Trade and the Backward Countries", *The Review of Economic Studies, 1954–55,* XXII (2), No. 52, pp. 129–42.

Nath, V. *Urbanization in India with Special Reference to the Growth of Cities* ("Proceedings of the World Population Conference", Rome, 1954, Vol. II). United Nations, New York: 1955, pp. 843–54.

Nef, J. E. "Prices and Industrial Capitalism in France and England, 1540–1640", *Economic History Review* (1937). Reprinted in *Enterprise and Secular Change.* F. C. Lane and J. C. Riemerma (ed.). Homewood, Ill.: 1953, pp. 292–321.

Nurkse, R. *Some Aspects of Capital Accumulation in Underdeveloped Countries.* Cairo: 1952.

———. "Some International Aspects of the Problem of Economic Development", *The American Economic Review,* XLII, No. 2 (May, 1952), pp. 571–83.

———. *Problems of Capital Formation in Underdeveloped Countries.* Oxford: 1953.

———. "International Investment Today in the Light of Nineteenth-Century Experience", *The Economic Journal,* LXIV, No. 256 (December 1954), pp. 744–58.

Ohlin, B. *"Interregional and International Trade"* ("Harvard Economic Studies", Vol. 39). Cambridge, Mass.: 1933.

Olson, E. C. "Factors Affecting International Differences in Production", *The American Economic Review,* XXXVIII, No. 2 (May, 1948), pp. 502–22.

Organisation for European Economic Cooperation. *Report on International Investment.* Paris: 1950.

———. *Investments in Overseas Territories in Africa, South of the Sahara.* Paris: 1951.

———. *The Textile Industry in Europe.* Paris: 1955.

Overseas Food Corporation. *Reports and Accounts for 1952–53.* London: December, 1953.

Papi, G. U. *The Colonial Problem: An Economic Analysis.* London: 1938.

Patterson, G. and Behrman, J. N. *Survey of United States International Finance.* Princeton, N. J.: 1953.

Pawley, W. H. *et al. Possibilities of Increasing the Supply of Food and Agricultural Products by Exploitation of New Areas and Increasing Yields* ("Proceeding of the World Population Conference", Rome, 1954, Vol. V). United Nations, New York: 1955, pp. 429–82.

Perroux, F., "The Domination Effect and Modern Economic Theory", *Social Research,* 17, No. 2 (June 1950), pp. 188–207.

Pizer, S. and Cutler, F. "Private U.S. Direct Investments Abroad", *Survey of Current Business* (January, 1951).

Pizer, S. and Cutler, F. "Foreign Investment and Income", *Survey of Current Business* (November, 1954).

―――. "International Investments and Earnings", *Survey of Current Business* (August, 1955).

Pizer, S. "The International Investment Position of the United States", *Foreign Commerce Weekly* (April 2, 1951).

Planning Commission. *The Second Five-Year Plan* (A memorandum prepared by the Panel of Economists). New Delhi: April, 1955.

Prebisch, R. *The Economic Development of Latin America and its Principal Problems.* United Nations, Lake Success: 1949.

Prest, A. R. *War Economics of Primary Producing Countries.* Cambridge, England: 1948.

Public Advisory Board for Mutual Security. *A Trade and Tariff Policy in the National Interest.* Washington, D.C.: February, 1953.

Queensland Bureau of Industry. *Review of Economic Progress*, I, No. 4 (April, 1949).

Rao, V. K. R. V. *The National Income of British India 1931–1932.* London: 1940.

―――. "Investment, Income and the Multiplier in an Under-Developed Country", *Indian Economic Review*, 2, No. 1 (February, 1952), pp. 55–67.

Reiche, E. *Aussenhandelsverflechtung und Industrialisierung Argentiniens* ("Kieler Studien", No. 25). Kiel: 1953.

Report and Recommendations. Joint Philippine-American Finance Commission. Manila: 1947.

Report to the President of the United States by the Economic Survey Mission to the Philippines. Washington, D.C.: 1950.

Report to the President of the United States on Foreign Economic Policies. Washington, D.C.: 1950.

Report to the President of the United States of the President's Material Policy Commission. Washington, D.C.: 1952.

Research Staff of Free Europe Press. *Satellite Agriculture in Crisis, A Study of Land Policy in the Soviet Sphere.* New York: 1954.

Reserve Bank of India. *Report on Currency for the year 1950–1951.* Bombay: 1951.

Reubens, E. R. "Small-Scale Industry in Japan", *Quarterly Journal of Economics*, 61, No. 4 (August, 1947), pp. 577–604.

―――. "Foreign Capital in Economic Development: A Case Study of Japan", *Milbank Memorial Fund Quarterly* (April, 1950), pp. 173–90.

Robertson, D.H. "The Future of World Trade", *The Economic Journal*, XLVIII, (March, 1938), pp. 1–14.

―――. *Money* (2nd ed.). Cambridge: 1948.

Romein, J. *Het Onvoltooid Verleden.* Amsterdam: 1937.

Romein, J. and A. *et al. De Lage Landen bij de Zee* (3rd ed.). Utrecht: 1939.

Romein, J. *Tussen Vrees en Vrijheid.* Amsterdam: 1950.

Rosenstein-Rodan, P. N. "Industrialization of Eastern and South-Eastern

Europe", *The Economic Journal*, 53, No. 210; 211 (June–September, 1943), pp. 201–11.

Rostow, W. W. *British Economy of the Nineteenth Century*. Oxford: 1948.

———. *The Process of Economic Growth*. New York: 1952.

Rostow, W. W. *et al*. *The Prospects for Communist China*. Cambridge–London: 1954.

Rottenberg, S. "Income and Leisure in an Underdeveloped Economy", *The Journal of Political Economy*, LX, No. 2 (April, 1952), pp. 95–102.

Royal Institute of International Affairs. *The Problem of International Investment*. London: 1937.

Sammons, R. L. and Abelson, M. *American Direct Investment in Foreign Countries 1940* ("Economic Series", No. 10). U.S. Department of Commerce, Washington, D.C.: 1942.

Sanders, I. T. "Changing Status of the Peasant in Eastern Europe", *The Annals of the American Academy of Political and Social Sciences* (September, 1950), pp. 78–93.

Sauvy, A. *Théorie Générale de la Population*. Paris: 1954.

Schlesinger, E. R. *Multiple Exchange Rates and Economic Development* ("Princeton Studies in International Finance", No. 2). Princeton, N. J.: 1952.

Schlesinger, R. "Some Prospects of Present Kolkhoz Organization", *Soviet Studies*, II, No. 4 (April, 1951).

———. "The Decisions on Agriculture", *Soviet Studies*, V, No. 3 (January, 1954).

Schlote, W. *Entwicklung und Strukturwandlungen des englischen Aussenhandels von 1700 bis zur Gegenwart, Probleme der Weltwirtschaft 62*. Jena: 1938.

Schultz, Th. W. *The Economic Organization of Agriculture*. New York: 1953.

Schumpeter, E. B. *et al*. *The Industrialization of Japan and Manchukuo 1930–1940*. New York: 1940.

Schumpeter, J. *The Theory of Economic Development*. Cambridge, Mass.: 1934.

———. *Business Cycles, A Theoretical, Historical and Statistical Analysis of the Capitalist Process*, 2 vols. New York–London: 1939.

———. *Capitalism, Socialism and Democracy* (2nd ed.). New York–London: 1947.

Scitovsky, T. de,. "A Reconsideration of the Theory of Tariffs", *The Review of Economic Studies*, IX (1942), pp. 89–110, reprinted in *Readings in the Theory of International Trade* (Selected by a Committee of the American Economic Association). Philadelphia–Toronto: 1949, pp. 358–389.

Secretariat of the General Agreement on Tariffs and Trade. *International Trade 1952*. Geneva: 1953.

———. *International Trade 1954*. Geneva: 1955.

Singer, H. W. "The Distribution of Gains between Investing and Borrowing Countries", *The American Economic Review*, XL, No. 2 (May, 1950), pp. 473–85.

Singer, H. W. "The Mechanics of Economic Development", *Indian Economic Review*, I, No. 2 (August, 1952), pp. 1–18.

Sivaswamy, K. G. "Indian Agriculture — Problems and Programmes", *Pacific Affairs*, XXII, No. 4 (December, 1950), pp. 356–70.

Sitsen, P. H. W. *Industrial Development of the Netherlands-Indies*. New York: 1944.

Smith, A. *An Inquiry into the Nature and Causes of the Wealth of Nations*, 2 vols. London: Everyman's Library, 1931.

Spengler, J. J. *Capital Requirements and Population Growth in Under-Developed Countries* ("Proceedings of the World Population Conference", Rome, 1954, Vol. V). United Nations, New York: 1955, pp. 765–77.

Spiegel, H. W. *The Brazilian Economy: Chronic Inflation and Sporadic Industrialization*. Philadelphia–Toronto: 1949.

Spring, D. "The English Landed Estate in the Age of Coal and Iron: 1830–1880", *The Journal of Economic History*, XI, No. 1 (Winter, 1951), pp. 3–24.

Staley, E. *World Economic Development*. Montreal: 1944.

——. *The Future of Underdeveloped Countries: Political Implications of Economic Development*. New York: 1954.

Supreme Command Allied Powers. *Japanese Land Reform Program* ("Natural Resources" 127). Tokyo: 1950.

Svennilsson, I. *Growth and Stagnation in the European Economy*. United Nations, Economic Commission for Europe, Geneva: 1954.

Tabah, F. "La Population du Monde et les Besoins en Matières Premières", *Population*, No. 4 (October–December, 1953), pp. 631–48.

Tawney, R. H. *Land and Labour in China* (2nd ed.). London: 1937.

——. *Religion and the Rise of Capitalism*. London: 1938.

Thomas, S. B. "Government and Administration in China Today", *Pacific Affairs*, XXIII, No. 3 (September, 1950), pp. 248–70.

Thornburg, M. W. *Turkey: An Economic Appraisal*. New York: 1949.

Tinbergen, J. *Economische Bewegingsleer*. Amsterdam: 1946.

Toynbee, A. J. *Civilization on Trial*. New York: 1948.

Tsuru, S. "Economic Fluctuations in Japan 1868–1893", *The Review of Economic Statistics* (November, 1941), pp. 176–89.

Tyszynski, H. "World Trade in Manufactured Commodities 1899–1950", *The Manchester School of Economics and Social Studies*, XIX (1951), pp. 272–304.

United Nations. *Economic Development in Selected Countries, Plans, Programmes and Agencies*. Vol. I; II. Lake Success: 1947; 1950.

——. *Inflationary and Deflationary Tendencies 1946–1948*. Lake Success: 1949.

——. *International Capital Movements in the Inter-War Period*. 1949.

——. *World Economic Report 1948* (Part III, 4. Availability of Foreign Funds for Economic Development). Lake Success: June, 1949.

——. *Report of the Joint ECLA/FAO Working Party, Economic Commission for Latin America*. May 15, 1949.

United Nations. Economic Commission for Europe. *European Steel Trends in the Setting of the World Market.* Geneva: 1949.

————. *Postwar Price Relations in Trade between Under-developed and Industrialized Countries.* Lake Success: 1949.

————. *Relative Prices of Exports and Imports of Under-Developed Countries.* Lake Success: December, 1949.

————. *Methods of Financing Economic Development in Underdeveloped Countries.* Lake Success: 1949.

————. *World Iron Ore Resources and their Utilization.* Lake Success: 1950.

————. *National and Per Capita Income for Seventy Countries 1949.* New York: 1950.

————. *Domestic Financing of Economic Development.* New York: 1950.

————. *An Inquiry into the Iron and Steel Industry of Mexico of a United Nations Team of Technical Experts.* New York: 1951.

————. *Labour Productivity of the Cotton Textile Industry in Five Latin-American Countries.* New York: 1951.

————. *Land Reform, Defects in Agrarian Structure as Obstacles to Economic Development.* New York: 1951.

————. *Report of the United Nations Economic Commission to Chile 1949–1950.* New York: 1951.

————. *Measures for the Economic Development of Underdeveloped Countries.* New York: 1951.

————. *National Income and its Distribution in Underdeveloped Countries.* New York: 1951.

————. *Report of the United Nations Mission of Technical Assistance to Bolivia.* New York: 1951.

————. *Non-Self-Governing Territories, Summaries and Analyses of Information Transmitted to the Secretary-General during 1950.* Part 2. New York: 1951.

————. *Standards and Techniques of Public Administration.* New York: 1951.

————. *Special Study on Economic Conditions and Development in Non-Self-Governing Territories.* New York: 1952.

————. *World Economic Report 1950–1951.* New York: 1952.

————. *Review of Economic Conditions in the Middle East.* New York: March, 1952.

————. *Instability in Export Markets of Under-Developed Countries.* New York: 1952.

————. *World Economic Report, 1951–1952.* New York: 1953.

————. Economic Commission for Europe, *Economic Survey of Europe Since the War.* Geneva: 1953.

————. *Commodity Trade and Economic Development.* New York: 1953.

————. "Taxation and Economic Development in Asian Countries, *Economic*" *Bulletin for Asia and the Far East,* IV, No. 3 (November, 1953), Bangkok.

————. *The Determinants and Consequences of Population Trends.* New York: 1953.

United Nations. *The International Flow of Private Capital 1946–1952.* New York: 1954.

———. Economic Commission for Europe. *Economic Survey of Europe in 1953 Including a Study of Economic Development in Southern Europe.* Geneva: 1954.

———. *Taxes and Fiscal Policy in Under-Developed Countries.* New York: 1954.

———. Economic Commission for Latin America. *International Cooperation in a Latin American Development Policy.* New York: 1954.

———. *Processes and Problems of Industrialization in Under-Developed Countries.* New York: 1955.

———. Economic Commission for Asia and the Far East. *Report of the Study Group of Small-Scale Industry Experts on their visit to Japan.* New York: February, 1955.

———. *Financing of Economic Development: Recent Governmental Measures Affecting the International Flow of Private Capital.* New York: June, 1955.

———. Economic Commission for Latin America. *Analyses and Projections of Economic Development.* New York: 1955.

———. *Economic Development of Under-Developed Countries, Special United Nations Fund for Economic Development.* New York: 1955.

———. Proceedings of the International Conference on the Peaceful Uses of Atomic Energy, Geneva, 1955, Vol. I. New York: 1956, pp. 96–101.

———. *The International Flow of Private Capital, 1953–1955* (Document E/2901). New York: June, 1956.

U.S. Department of Labor, Bureau of Labor Statistics. "Work Required to Buy Food, 1937–50", *Monthly Labor Review*, 72, No. 2 (February, 1951), pp. 143–51.

U.S. Department of Commerce. *Foreign Aid by the U.S. Government 1940–1951.* Washington, D.C.: 1952.

———. *Factors Limiting U.S. Investing Abroad* (Part I, Survey of Factors in Foreign Countries). Washington, D.C.: 1953.

U.S. Department of State. *Havana Charter for an International Trade Organization* (Publ. 3206). Washington, D.C.: September, 1948.

———. *Report Joint Brazilian-United States Technical Commission.* Rio de Janeiro: March, 1949.

———. *Point Four, Cooperative Program for Aid in the Development of the Economically Undeveloped Areas.* Washington, D.C.: January, 1950.

Uyeda, T. *The Small Industries of Japan.* New York: 1938.

Veblen, T. *Imperial Germany and the Industrial Revolution* (2nd ed.). New York: 1939.

Viner, J. *The Prospects for Foreign Trade in the Post-War World, 1940.* Reprinted in *Readings in the Theory of International Trade* (Selected by a Committee of the American Economic Association). Philadelphia–Toronto: 1949, pp. 514–29.

———. *International Trade and Economic Development.* Glencoe, Ill.: 1952.

Wagemann, E. *Struktur und Rhytmus der Weltwirtschaft*. Berlin: 1930.

Wallich, H. C. *Monetary Problems of an Export Economy: The Cuban Experience, 1914–1947* ("Harvard Economic Studies", No. 88). Cambridge, Mass.: 1950.

Warriner, D. *Land and Poverty in the Middle East*. London: 1949.

Whetten, N. L. *Rural Mexico*. Chicago: 1948.

Wilhelm, W. "Soviet Central Asia: Development of a Backward Area", *Foreign Policy Reports*, XXV (February 1, 1950).

Williams, J. H. *The Theory of International Trade Reconsidered*. Reprinted in *Readings in the Theory of International Trade* (Selected by a Committee of the American Economic Association). Philadelphia–Toronto: 1950, pp. 253–72.

Wilson, H. *The War on World Poverty*. London: 1953.

Winfield, G. F. *China: The Land and the People*. New York: 1948.

Woytinski, W. S. and Woytinski, E. S. *World Population and Production*. New York: 1953.

Wright, C. M. "Convertibility and Triangular Trade as Safeguards Against Economic Depression", *The Economic Journal*, LXV, No. 11 (September, 1955), pp. 422–35.

Wythe, G. *et al. Brazil: An Expanding Economy*. New York: 1949.

——. *Industry in Latin America* (2nd ed.). New York: 1949.

Yugor, A. *Russia's Economic Front for War and Peace, An Appraisal of the Three Five-Year Plans*. New York: 1942.

Zauberman, A. "Gold in Soviet Economic Theory and Policies", *The American Economic Review*, XLI, No. 5 (December, 1951), pp. 879–90.

Zettler, J. A. and Cutler, F. "U.S. Direct Investment in Foreign Countries", *Survey of Current Business* (December, 1952).

INDEX

INDEX